If It Ain't Broke, Break It

If It Ain't Broke, Break It

How Corporate Journalism Killed the *Arkansas Gazette*

Donna Lampkin Stephens

The University of Arkansas Press
FAYETTEVILLE
2015

Manufactured in the United States of America
ISBN: 978-1-55728-814-1
e-ISBN: 978-1-61075-561-0
19 18 17 16 15 5 4 3 2 1
Designed by Ellen Beeler

∞The paper used in this publication meets the minimum requirements of the American National Standard for Permanence of Paper for Printed Library Materials Z39.48–1984.

Library of Congress Control Number: 2014955739

To the men and women who worked for the Arkansas Gazette from November 20, 1819, to October 18, 1991—and to everyone else who loved the Old Gray Lady

Contents

Preface

I was barely twenty-one in the spring of 1984 when Bob Carey, one of my journalism professors at the University of Arkansas, approached me in the hallway to tell me that the *Arkansas Gazette* needed a sports intern, and I was to be it. Thanks to the influence of Bob Douglas, managing editor of the *Gazette* before becoming chair of the UA journalism department, a recommendation from the faculty there was good enough for those in charge at the newspaper. I happened to live in a coed dorm where the Arkansas Razorback track team also lived, and for an assignment for Mr. Carey's class early in the semester, I had written a feature story on Bill Jasinski, a high jumper. Mr. Carey told me after that assignment that the *Arkansas Traveler*, the student newspaper, needed sportswriters, so that's how my sportswriting career began.

Although by April I had already arranged for a summer job with my hometown *Camden News*—ironically, as it would turn out, a Hussman paper—I quickly told Mr. Carey, "Yes sir," and made plans to spend my summer in Little Rock.

My family in south Arkansas were *Gazette* people. I remembered watching as a child while my late grandfather, Jim Douthit, scoured the sports pages, particularly for news about the Razorbacks. I am sad that he died in March 1984, shortly before that life-changing conversation with Mr. Carey in the basement of Kimpel Hall, and never knew that I made it to the *Gazette*. But I think he would be pleased with how my story has turned out.

I was to report to my internship at 9 on a Monday morning in late May. Whoever made those arrangements obviously hadn't figured out that at that time of day, every sports department in the country is nearly vacant. Kim Brazzel was the only soul there that morning when I walked in. Those who knew him can imagine how a naïve young woman might fare with him as my introduction to the *Arkansas Gazette*, but despite some adventures that are stories for another day, we became good friends. Indeed, I was welcomed by all of my new colleagues in Little Rock—James Thompson, Wadie Moore, Nancy Clark, Jake Sandlin, Joe Mosby, James Gilzow, Aris Jackson, David Smith, David Goodloe, Bob Buchanan, and the incomparable Jim Bailey. With an intern's salary of $4 per hour, working 3 P.M. until midnight Thursday through Monday, I learned sportswriting and journalism that summer, but the most important thing I learned was that I had to come back. I couldn't get enough. I had found my place.

But twenty-one-year-olds weren't hired at the *Arkansas Gazette*, by then nearly thirty years past its zenith—its Pulitzer Prize–winning coverage and stand in the Central High crisis—but still one of the country's most respected newspapers. Surely I would have to toil for several years at smaller, less prestigious newspapers before I could make it back to the big time. But a combination of hard work and more good luck enabled me to freelance for the *Gazette* after I returned to Fayetteville for my senior year, when I worked under Nate Allen and the legendary Orville Henry, who then staffed the Razorback bureau. After I graduated in May 1985, I returned to the *Gazette* even though there was no permanent position. Instead, I was invited to return as an intern for a second summer—again for $4 an hour—with the promise that I would have the next available position.

I didn't tell them, but I would have paid for the privilege.

From May 1985 until October 18, 1991, I was a proud *Gazette* employee. I started as the agate clerk, taking phone calls as people reported scores in the evenings. Eventually I would cover high school sports, golf, the Arkansas Intercollegiate Conference, and the Rollin' Razorback national champion wheelchair basketball team, among other assignments, and ultimately I got to return to Fayetteville as part of the bureau covering the Razorbacks. But I was so enthralled with living my dream that I didn't pay close enough attention to the business aspects of Arkansas's newspaper war. I naïvely thought the Gannett Corporation would be our savior and that our superior product would be enough for us to win. Alas, I was so young and so dumb.

Periodically, I would wonder—"Why me? Why am I lucky enough to have never had to work anywhere else?" It was only with the passage of time and the wisdom it provided that I found my answer.

When the *Arkansas Gazette* died on October 18, 1991, I was twenty-eight. The closing was like the death of a loved one, easily the worst thing to happen to me aside from losing family members. Like most of my colleagues, I grieved for a long time. As Deborah Mathis told me fifteen years after the closing, "I will never get over it." Today, I still feel the same way. For those of us who loved it, the *Arkansas Gazette* was much more than a job. It was an institution, the oldest business in the state, one that took brave stands and offered leadership in crises and, most importantly, showed us what journalism should be. Nearly twenty-five years later, I am still idealistic enough to miss it every day.

And then, many years after the *Gazette* died, it hit me—*that* was the answer to my question of why I was the lucky one. While I was one of the youngest *Gazette* employees when the Old Gray Lady breathed her last, I had been there long enough to *get it*—to understand that spirit of the *Gazette* that Deborah Mathis spoke so eloquently of in the futile late rallies to save her life in the fall of 1991. I also had the contacts, the energy, and—most important—the drive and the passion to tell her story. They say the winners get to write the history, but this time, the losing side also has its say.

I am honored to be her voice.

Acknowledgments

This book would not have been possible without the dedication and support of a number of people, starting with Kevin Clark, a documentary filmmaker who came to the University of Central Arkansas in 2005 to seek out the story of the *Arkansas Gazette*. Knowing my background as a sportswriter at the *Gazette* from 1984 until October 18, 1991, my department chair, Dr. Joseph Anderson, got me involved with the project. Eighteen months, much research, and nearly twenty in-depth interviews later, the result was the 2006 film, *The Old Gray Lady: Arkansas's First Newspaper*. At the premiere at the Clinton Presidential Center on the fifteenth anniversary of the death of the newspaper, my *Gazette* colleague, Dr. David R. Davies, by then on the journalism faculty and dean of the Honors College at the University of Southern Mississippi, encouraged me to apply for the Ph.D. program there. His final sales pitch was, "And we want your dissertation to be on the history of the *Gazette*." With all the work that had already been done, it seemed meant to be.

Graciously agreeing to interviews—some on more than one occasion as my project moved from film to written word—were old *Gazette* hands and friends Charles Allbright, Jim Bailey, Paul Borden, Max Brantley, Jerry Dhonau, Ernest Dumas (without whom I never would have been at UCA to start with), Susie Ellwood, Gene Foreman, Wayne Jordan, Harry King, Bob Lancaster, Bill Lewis, Deborah Mathis, Jerry McConnell, Robert McCord, Wadie Moore, Carrick Patterson, James O. Powell, Gene Prescott, John Reed, and my dear mentor, Roy Reed. Others interviewed were Meredith Oakley and Walter Hussman of the *Arkansas Democrat*, Arkansas politicians Senator Dale Bumpers, Senator David Pryor, and Justice Jim Johnson, and historian Dr. Michael Dougan. Sadly, several of these have since died, thereby making their contributions even more valuable.

The *Arkansas Gazette* Project of the David and Barbara Pryor Center for Arkansas Oral and Visual History at the University of Arkansas was absolutely invaluable, both for preparation for the above interviews and for interviews with and about many others whose input was necessary for the film and book to be complete, namely the late Hugh B. Patterson, Orville Henry, Margaret Ross, Bill Shelton, and my other dear mentor, Bob Douglas.

My former dean, Dr. Rollin Potter, and my current dean, Terry Wright, and the staff of the UCA College of Fine Arts and Communication, as well as John Gale, chair, and my colleagues in the UCA Department of Mass

Communication and Theatre, have been endlessly supportive and good friends as well.

My Southern Miss advisers, Dr. David R. Davies, Dr. Christopher Campbell, Dr. Kim LeDuff, Dr. Gene Wiggins, and Dr. Fei Xue, gave sage advice, guidance, and support. Dr. Bruce Plopper and Dr. Christina Drale of the University of Arkansas at Little Rock and Dr. Sondra Gordy of UCA also helped in the completion of this journey.

Mike Bieker and Larry Malley of the University of Arkansas Press were professional and a pleasure to work with.

My parents, Don and Noris Lampkin, as well as my siblings, Jerry Lampkin, Sherry Lampkin Young, and Becky Lampkin Harris, were always eager to talk about this project and lend moral support. My late grandmother, Oleta Lampkin, would take great pride in this accomplishment. She always believed I could do anything.

And finally, thanks to my husband, Ken, whom I met on the football field at Arkansas Tech University when I was a sportswriter for the *Gazette* and he was the head football coach. He held down the home front while I embarked on this long project and has always had a willing ear for me to bounce off ideas and frustrations. He has been my biggest supporter and my best friend.

CHAPTER ONE

Introduction

THE DEATH OF the almost 172-year-old *Arkansas Gazette*, one of the country's most respected newspapers, on October 18, 1991, is a story with far more than just local ramifications. As a newspaper facing decline because of competition, ruthless business practices, and inept corporate tactics, the *Gazette* is reflective of an industry that has found itself unable to cope with the most substantial changes since the invention of the printing press. The newspaper industry today is facing the biggest challenge of its history—a panoply of constantly evolving facets of the world of the Internet. The industry has faced the twin demons of change and competition since its existence, but changing economic realities have put the onus on another C—the corporations that have become the vast majority of American newspaper owners. In the case of the *Arkansas Gazette*, the Gannett Corporation proved to be no better at facing competition than the family owners had been. A look back at the industry's previous experiences, although different from the current ones in specifics, can only give perspective as the business faces today's minefields. The newspaper industry must recognize that much of the past is mirrored in the present and future, and even if its responses to previous challenges were wrong, the knowledge of those responses and the ensuing results can help inform the tactics used in the battles of today and tomorrow.

From the Heiskell family's 1902 purchase, the *Arkansas Gazette* grew in quality, stature, and reputation. Its glory days came following World War II, including its suffering and ultimate triumph during and after the Central High crisis; its 1991 demise was the result of its newspaper war with the *Arkansas Democrat*. But the experience of the *Gazette* is not just a story of one newspaper. The *Arkansas Gazette* is an example of what has happened to newspapers under long-distance corporate ownership, and its story offers lessons from that experience for the industry today.

Arkansas's newspaper war featured three ownership models—the Heiskell/Patterson family's enlightened, engaged local ownership of the *Gazette* (until

1986); Walter Hussman's local family privately held chain ownership of the *Democrat* (1974–1991); and Gannett's distant publicly held corporate ownership of the *Gazette* (1986–1991). The inability of the *Gazette*'s key players to cope with the challenges of Arkansas's newspaper war has lessons for today's tumultuous climate that has only intensified in the nearly twenty-four years since the *Gazette* died. Independently owned properties have strengths and potential weaknesses, but they are almost always better off than newspapers whose corporate masters have a bottom-line emphasis on profit at all cost.

The challenges to the industry are many. Weekday readership of newspapers has declined significantly since 1970. In that year, 77.6 percent of the total United States adult population classified themselves as weekday readers. Except for four years of slight increases, that percentage has declined every year since 1970, with the 1999 figure at 56.9 percent—a decline of 1.9 percent from 1998.[1] Sunday and weekend readership has also declined, although not as significantly, from 72.3 percent in 1970 to 66.9 percent in 1999.[2] Readership has not been the only decline. The number of daily newspapers has fallen fairly steadily since 1950, from 1,772 (combined morning and evening) in that year to 1,397 in 2009.[3]

These troubles are nothing new. Since the industry's heyday in the years following World War II, there has been a steady litany of hurdles to jump. The world seemed to become more complex in the years after the war, and newspapers found it more difficult to explain those changes to their readers. Their cost of doing business increased, with reader demands for print photographs forcing newspapers to make heavy investments in new presses. Newsprint became more expensive; labor unions pushed for higher wages for newspaper employees. Television came into its own, resulting in the first serious competitor for the industry and forcing newspapers to reevaluate their way of doing business.[4] In the second half of the twentieth century, many long-term family-owned newspapers were unable to withstand the difficult economic realities of the time and turned to chains for their salvation. Chain ownership of American newspapers was nothing new. In 1910, 62 dailies were chain owned; by 1930, that number had increased to 311 (15 percent of all dailies). The trend continued; by 1960, chains owned 560 American dailies (32 percent of all dailies).[5] While the family owners profited from the sales, many times the newspapers and their readers did not. Too often, the corporations, often large, diversified—and more importantly, with headquarters far removed from the local property—turned the newspaper into a byproduct of their other business activities. Entertainment and fluff came to the forefront, and as news became less relevant, the newspaper industry found itself damaged.

William E. Woodruff, at age twenty-eight, c. 1823. Courtesy of UALR Center for Arkansas History and Culture.

The *Arkansas Gazette* was an example of a newspaper that, under enlightened family ownership, provided leadership to its community and the nation during a time of crisis, and its suffering in a fierce newspaper war against the *Arkansas Democrat* that led to the family's sale to the Gannett Corporation and its eventual death under corporate ownership are now an example of what has happened to the industry into the twenty-first century. The newspaper, founded by William E. Woodruff in 1819, seventeen years before Arkansas became a state, passed through a succession of eight different owners throughout the first eighty-three years of its life before the Heiskell family of Tennessee bought it, taking control on July 1, 1902. Judge Carrick White Heiskell and his sons, John Netherland (Ned) and Fred, partnered with Frederick W. Allsopp, the *Gazette*'s business manager, to buy controlling interest in the paper. J. N. Heiskell served as editor for seventy years until his death at age one hundred in 1972; his son-in-law, Hugh B. Patterson, ultimately consolidated ownership under that branch of the Heiskell family. Fourteen years after Mr. Heiskell's death, wounded by the fiercest newspaper war in the United States against

Walter E. Hussman Jr. and his reinvigorated *Arkansas Democrat*, Heiskell's heirs sold the *Gazette* to the Gannett Corporation, the country's largest newspaper chain, then based in Arlington, Virginia. Patterson, the *Gazette*'s longtime publisher, had been acquainted with Al Neuharth, CEO and chair of the Gannett Corporation, for years. That company, which counted a number of lightly regarded newspapers among its holdings, wanted to establish sort of a "separate division of quality newspapers," remembered Carrick Patterson, Hugh's son and J. N. Heiskell's grandson.[6] Neuharth assured the Patterson family that Gannett would maintain the *Gazette*'s personality and dignity.[7] The sale, with a purchase price of $51 million and assumption of $9 million in debt, was announced on October 30, 1986.

After the change in ownership, the newspaper war with Hussman escalated. Gannett owned the *Gazette* for just five years but lost $108 million before it sold the paper and its assets to Hussman on October 18, 1991. Hussman's newspaper then took the *Gazette*'s name and began publishing the next day as the *Arkansas Democrat-Gazette*. Today it makes its claim as the descendant of Woodruff and Heiskell's newspaper.

But make no mistake. The *Arkansas Gazette* died on October 18, 1991.

The final fifty years of the *Arkansas Gazette* provide a microcosm of the decline of the American newspaper industry in the pre-Internet era. The *Arkansas Gazette*'s story is typical of the long-distance corporatization of the industry as more and more cities became one-newspaper towns in the half-century following World War II.

While the *Arkansas Gazette* flourished under the principal ownership of the J. N. Heiskell family, which coincided with the newspaper industry's glory days following World War II, the old man's death left a void in leadership that would eventually lead to the death of his beloved Old Lady. Remote corporate journalism ultimately delivered the deathblow. It was primarily J. N. Heiskell's ownership that had enabled the *Gazette* to reach the very apex of American journalism, and it did not take long after his death for the paper to begin to struggle for its very life. Thanks to Walter Hussman's *Arkansas Democrat* and the Gannett Corporation, the struggle ended on October 18, 1991, as, nineteen years after Heiskell's death, the Old Gray Lady followed her grand old man to the grave. Gannett took its paycheck and left town.

Like the *Gazette* before Gannett, the surviving *Arkansas Democrat* was also a family business. Although the Hussman family had other interests, including five small Arkansas daily newspapers and cable television investments, mostly in Arkansas and all within the South, theirs was not a mega corporate entity. Nor is it so today. Hussman himself said in 2005 that that fact had made a difference in his winning Arkansas's newspaper war:

> Generally speaking, there's a lot more pride [with family ownership]. Newspapers are a business, just like others, but with a great obligation to the public. If a family owns it, they normally live in the community and have a real stake in the community. People want to come up and talk about the newspaper. There's a bit more of a responsive type of ownership structure.[8]

Although Hussman in effect has it both ways—his is both family and chain ownership—indeed, that type of ownership would prove to be one of the biggest factors in his triumph over Gannett.

Gannett's corporate model, based on its shareholders worldwide, stressed profits above all and featured an absentee ownership that had no stake in the community or state. Outsiders were brought in as experts at every level of the newspaper operation; their changes did not sit well with longtime *Gazette* readers or employees who resented "what was happening to their beloved *Arkansas Gazette*," as one former *Gazette* employee remembered.[9] The death of the *Arkansas Gazette* is one example of what has happened to many well-respected publications during the trend of absentee corporate ownership of American newspapers, which became more and more prevalent in the years following World War II. For several years, economic factors and a dwindling number of heirs interested in taking over family newspapers had led to many of them being sold by their longtime family owners to outside corporations. While this situation bears some similarities to others, Gannett had never before been in such a competitive market. Little Rock was the site of the country's fiercest newspaper war in the late 1980s; economic forces had led to a trend of fewer and fewer cities with competing newspapers. As media monopolies have expanded, a dwindling number of independent voices is now responsible for distributing the news. This trend is an alarming one for journalism and, ultimately, for democracy itself.

The story of the *Arkansas Gazette* is more relevant today than it was nearly twenty-four years ago; whereas in 1991 the tale was an Arkansas tragedy, with the perspective of time and history, it becomes much more. Its story shows a typical transformation of an American newspaper from independent, local ownership to remote corporate control that illustrates what happened to American newspapers in the generation following World War II. As the newspaper industry and journalism itself have evolved over the last twenty-three years, what happened to the *Gazette* is a lesson it would behoove the industry to heed. While no one yet knows what this evolution will ultimately mean for newspapers and journalism itself, the story of the *Arkansas Gazette* offers lessons that could, perhaps, save them.

While Gannett made some improvements in the *Gazette*, in many ways, the quality of the newspaper declined under corporate ownership. One former *Gazette* reporter, who worked there under the family and later under Gannett, said ownership made a fundamental difference. "The heart had gone out of it, and I think it was because when corporations started buying newspapers and consolidating newspapers, it just became a different thing, and the institution itself no longer mattered," Bob Lancaster said.[10] The lessons of the *Arkansas Gazette* provide a primer on how the industry can fight back against the challenges it continues to face into the twenty-first century, regardless of the ownership—if that ownership is willing to learn.

From 1945 to 1965, David R. Davies writes in *The Postwar Decline of American Newspapers*, the industry's biggest sin was its slowness in responding to the changing postwar world. A few years later, Heiskell's heirs were guilty of not realizing quickly enough the changing Arkansas newspaper market after the addition of Walter Hussman at the *Democrat*. Publishers increasingly saw their properties as businesses first—at the expense of journalism. Publishers were generally too concerned about diminishing profits to invest money in editorial improvements.[11] In many ways, these lessons can be illustrated by what happened to the *Arkansas Gazette* during its days as a corporate property.

Sadly, this trend of the profit line dictating the journalistic product has continued into the twenty-first century, as detailed in the third volume of the History of American Journalism series, *Journalism at the End of the American Century, 1965–Present*, by James Brian McPherson. Newspapers were forced to look for new ways of doing their job as Americans turned more and more to television for their news while news magazines, news radio, and alternative newspapers became more pervasive. Gannett's *Today* in Florida in 1966 was the early model for its *USA Today* in 1982, with its trademark large color photos, short stories, few jumps, and increased emphasis on graphics. *USA Today* had a great effect on journalism in the second half of the twentieth century, as the Gannetization of the stately old *Arkansas Gazette* showed. After the 1964 *New York Times v. Sullivan* case defined American freedom of the press, the industry stressed better training and investigative reporting, as evidenced by Woodward and Bernstein's Watergate coverage in the 1970s, but public criticism of the press began to increase. McPherson contends that generally the industry did a poor job of explaining its function and justifying its First Amendment protections.[12] These trends, too, can be localized to the story of the *Arkansas Gazette*.

Since 1965, the trend toward entertainment as news has increased. There has been greater focus on scandal and the trivial. In the second half of the 1980s, there was less investigation. Mergers marked media. McPherson recalled Ben Bagdikian's warning of potential conflicts of interest and diminishing voices from increasing corporate consolidation. Bagdikian reported that large, diversified corporations were turning journalism into a byproduct of their other business activities. By 1986, chains controlled 75 percent of newspapers' circulation, and independent publications fell to less than one-third of the total. Business began to control the newsroom, and appeasing readers and advertisers became more important than news values. Profits became more important; editorial staffs were cut; the number of bureaus decreased, and there was less competition and international news. Focus groups stressed readers' desires more than their needs. In summary, McPherson writes that probably nothing changed and defined American journalism more after 1965 than business. Journalism shifted from an honorable calling to just another business, resulting in the trend of businessmen and women—rather than journalists—becoming publishers, often to the detriment of journalism. Consolidation and corporatization helped from a short-term, profit-oriented perspective, but often the ownership went too far. Chains did improve quality in some ways, such as in overall appearance, but journalistic quality often took a big hit as news staffs shrank and investigative journalism almost disappeared.[13] The story of the *Arkansas Gazette* is marked by many of these movements.

Gene Roberts reiterates these trends in his two volumes on the corporatization of American journalism, *Leaving Readers Behind: The Age of Corporate Newspapering,* and *Breach of Faith: A Crisis of Coverage in the Age of Corporate Newspapering.* In *Leaving Readers Behind,* he refers to corporatization as the most momentous change in the American newspaper industry in its three-hundred-year history, "one that is diminishing the amount of real news available to the consumer and undermining the traditional nature and role of the press."[14] The symptoms are increasingly common: investors demand increasing profit, and if economic conditions are not conducive to growth, companies squeeze their products to meet the often-unrealistic profit expectations. Too often, cost-cutting leads to diminished journalism; the trend is toward less "real news," such as government and international news, which is more expensive to produce than feature copy. Chains increasingly press their managers and editors to focus more on corporate goals and less on the news. While profit margins of American newspapers have remained almost obscenely high (up to 35 percent in the Thomson chain), salaries for the working journalists are often barely above poverty level. Roberts cites Gannett's Neuharth as a prime example of focus on profit at the expense of quality. The loss of local ownership also hurts, as Roberts points out in comments that anticipated those of Hussman and Lancaster on the same topic:

> Nobody can have the commitment that a longtime family owner can have to the communities they serve. . . . The idea of these papers in the ultimate authority of someone who doesn't live in the community in which they are published, and who has hundreds of other products to cultivate and look after and prod for more products, stabs at me. Because even if these papers look the same as they were before the sale, they are no longer the same, and they never will be.[15]

The experience of the *Arkansas Gazette* is a dead-on example of these chain demands, as it is this one: A growing disconnect between working journalists and their corporate bosses, with many considering those bosses as "greedy, unethical and traitorous to the cause of good journalism."[16] This was certainly the case in Little Rock. Editors, most of whom were Gannett imports, were paid better than ever, but their bonuses were linked to profit and circulation goals, leading to this Roberts quote: "The challenge of the American newspaper is not to stay in business, it is to stay in journalism."[17] In its siege against the *Arkansas Democrat*, the Gannett *Gazette*, with its newsroom staff still primarily made up of Heiskell/Patterson hires, won the battle of quality journalism, but it lost the war—of business.

In *Breach of Faith*, Roberts explores one of the byproducts of the corporate trend: More and more, newspapers are giving readers what they think they want rather than what they need to know to be engaged citizens. The greater emphasis on the bottom line has led many newspapers to decrease or eliminate public affairs reporting, which is essential to the functioning of democracy. Often this is the result of downsizing and layoffs in newsrooms in which the more experienced reporters and editors—with their greater salaries—are cut in favor of younger, more inexperienced journalists who have little or no institutional knowledge.[18]

In *The New Media Monopoly*, Bagdikian goes into great detail about Gannett, by far the nation's leading chain with ninety-seven dailies and a circulation of seven million. He traces the history of the company back to founder Frank Gannett and how it evolved over the years from his cardinal principle of local autonomy to Neuharth and his guidance that turned the company into a modern empire—still singing the "local autonomy" song that had by then become a myth. Under Neuharth, Gannett had an unbelievable record of constantly increasing quarterly earnings that would eventually become more and more difficult to sustain. Money became the mantra as he courted Wall Street, and monopoly situations were the only way to continue the growth. Competition, as the company learned in Little Rock, costs, and the cost there became too great; after five years, Gannett gave up the battle in 1991. Bagdikian writes that the company had manufactured its own myth.[19] Indeed, the *Arkansas Gazette* today merits few words in Gannett's company history. In building that myth, the company does not like to admit its mistakes.

It is clear that the transition of the *Arkansas Gazette* from family to corporate ownership and, as a result, its ultimate death, offers lessons for an industry that has been shaken to its very foundations by the arrival of the Internet. Newspapers and those who love them should take heed of the experience, ultimately remembering the wise words of Deborah Mathis, who, along with hundreds of others, lost her job at the *Arkansas Gazette* on October 18, 1991: "I always said that I thought Gannett's motto was, 'If it ain't broke, break it.'"[20]

CHAPTER TWO

1902–1946: Early Heiskell Family Ownership

J. N. HEISKELL, whose family would own the *Arkansas Gazette* for nearly half of its 172-year history, epitomized much of what can make local family ownership of a newspaper preferable to distant corporate ownership. He and his family believed that a newspaper was an institution first and only incidentally a business, and the Heiskell ownership ran the *Arkansas Gazette* from that philosophical bent, even when they paid the price for those beliefs. "Newspapers are not sawmills," he once said.[1] Although previous owners of the newspaper preceded the trend of pervasive growth of chain ownership in American journalism, the Heiskell family was the first to take seriously this philosophy—commitment to quality, fairness—and consequently, the newspaper thrived under their control. Indeed, independent ownership gives quality owners the leeway to pursue quality in their properties, and under Heiskell family ownership, the *Arkansas Gazette* became a quality newspaper that embraced a conservative philosophy of journalism. The Heiskell family, which had journalistic roots reaching back to well before the Civil War, was not afraid to take a chance with the purchase and ultimately allowed the *Gazette* to become a courageous newspaper, not hesitating to take on powerful figures such as governors of Arkansas and to champion worthy causes—no matter their popularity among the citizens of the state. The Heiskell family believed that a good newspaper's value to a democracy could not be overstated, and under their ownership, the *Gazette* became just that. Such enlightened family ownership allowed the Heiskells through their newspaper to become a leading force for the ideals of Progressivism and marked a clear distinction between their philosophy and that of chain ownership, which would stress profits above everything else. Over the years, with the deaths of family members and business partners, J. N. Heiskell was left to steward the paper and become its face as he continued to work as editor until shortly before his death at age one hundred in 1972.

This reprint produced by the Arkansas Gazette.

THE ARKANSAS GAZETTE.

BY WM. E. WOODRUFF.] *ARKANSAS, (ARKANSAS TER.) SATURDAY, NOVEMBER* 20, 1819. *[Vol. 1—No. 1.*

TERMS OF THE GAZETTE.

This paper is published weekly, (on Saturdays), at THREE DOLLARS *per annum, if paid in advance, or* FOUR DOLLARS, *payable at the end of the year. No paper will be discontinued until arrearages are discharged, unless the editor declines extending the credit.*

ADVERTISEMENTS, *not exceeding fifteen lines, will be published one week for one* dollar, *and continued at* fifty cents *for each subsequent insertion. Orders for advertising from a distance must be accompanied with the cash.*

Letters to the Editor, inclosing Communications or Advertisements, must have the postage paid.

From the St. Louis Enquirer.

MOUTH OF THE COLUMBIA.

Most of our readers, it is presumed, are already apprised of the fact that government has sent the Macedonian frigate and a sloop of war to take possession of the mouth of the Columbia river, and to cruise on the shores of the Pacific ocean. This measure, it is conceived, evinces great extension of views in the administration, and probably, in the lapse of a few years will be considered of more importance than is at present attached to it.

The views of the British government, or more properly speaking, of the fur companies of that nation, have been long turned to this point. They have sent several travellers to explore the Columbia river, and examine into the practicability of carrying on a trade with the East Indies by this channel, and in case of its being feasible, their intention was to exchange the valuable furs of the North American forests for the elegant luxuries of the east. They were only prevented from acting upon this suggestion from the want of proper means.

With a view to this object, a compa- ... value. Hence this transportation will be attended with much less difficulty."

If this route is taken, no adequate idea can easily be formed of the future importance of a town at the mouth of this river. Mr. Brackenridge observes that the soil in the vicinity of the Columbia "is represented as rich and highly susceptible of cultivation; the climate is more temperate than in the same latitude in the United States. "The natives on the Columbia river are very numerous; Gen. Clark informed me that their number might be safely estimated at 80,000 souls."

This seems to indicate a capacity of supporting a dense population, practicably exemplified by the number of its inhabitants who live upon its spontaneous productions. Probably there are as many Indian inhabitants on this river and its branches as in any other parts of North America, of the same extent.

Among other objections against the expediency of taking this route, it has been urged that the distance of the Columbia river from any white settlement, and the consequent difficulty of making it the channel of active commerce, will present insufferable obstacles to the successful prosecution of this plan. To this objection we answer, that until the country becomes inhabited, posts might be established at proper distances, as is frequently done in other countries thus situated, which will subserve every necessary purpose. In process of time, these posts will become the residence of families, and assume the appearance of towns. The fertility of the soil will invite farmers to settle around them, and by this means the country contiguous to the route will acquire a population sufficiently dense to answer the demands incident to such a trade.

If it be asked where can be obtained the requisite means of carrying on this intercourse, we answer, that independent of the supply derived from the fur of this country, the mines of Mexico can be very easily diverted to this channel, and that in such quantities as to obviate the

FOREIGN NEWS.

London, July 3.

It was stated in London that Attigas has formed a connection with Buenos Ayres, and that they had declared war against the Portuguese.

Petitions from all parts of the country was pouring into parliament, praying for reform. The marquis of Tavistock had presented one signed by 1800 of the most respectable inhabitants and manufacturers, praying that they might be permitted to have a voice in the councils of their country—Sir Francis Burdett was also making exertions for the same object.

The volunteers under Gen. Devereux had sailed from Ireland for South America—the General was shortly to follow.

There was a rumor in Stockholm of disturbances expected between the Russians and the Danes.

July 12.

The rumors respecting a misunderstanding between Sweden, Denmark and Russia, are corroborated by the movements of troops on both sides. The King of Sweden has a camp at Scania, where he himself resides: and the Emperor Alexander has ordered the formation of three camps in Finland, towards which the troops are marching, and the Emperor is expected to review them there.—The fort of Scania was supposed to be chosen for the purpose of overawing the Danes, who were disputing a short time back about the Norwegian debt; but as the payment of that debt was (according to official announcements in the Swedish journals) arranged by negociations in London, the keeping up the force and the presence of its royal general look very like some apprehension of attack from Russia, though it might not be thought politic to show any fear or suspicion by moving nearer to the Russian frontier.

It is stated in letters from Italy, that the recent visit of the Austrian Emperor to Italy, was for the purpose of sounding the dispositions of the holy college, respecting the views his Majesty has on the

ed, and two more will meet the same fate on the 19th inst. The Grand Jury has brought in a bill against the invincible Sir G. M'Gregor, who stands charged with aiding and abetting piracy, by issuing commissions in the Bahamas to subjects of powers in amity with Spain. But I suppose this will be chase after a wild-goose."

Washington City, Aug. 24.

We have learnt from the newspapers that some misunderstanding had taken place amongst our Naval Officers on the Mediterranean station. We are sorry to say that private letters received in this city, confirm these accounts. It is said to have arisen upon the occasion of the disapprobation of Com. Stewart, of the proceedings of a Court Martial, held whilst the squadron lay off Naples. About that time the squadron sailed for Gibraltar, and the officers who had composed the court met off that port, and addressed a remonstrance to the commanding officer against the terms of his disapprobation of the proceedings of the court.—Whereupon, he arrested those officers, being four captains and one lieutenant. Among the former are said to be captains Macdonough and Ballard. We are so much in hopes that this matter will be amicably adjusted, that we should not have noticed it but that statements respecting it are already in general circulation. The captains being arrested, the first lieutenants are now in command of the ships respectively which, previous to this occurrence, were commanded by the officers now under arrest. *[Nat. Intel.*

New-York, Aug. 19.

It gives us great pleasure to have it in our power to give the following pleasing result of the late disturbances at Gibraltar between the American and British officers. We have seen a letter from an officer of the American squadron at Gibraltar, stating that a court of inquiry was held on board of the Guerriere, on the 1st of July, by request of Gov. Don, who had brought charges against the Ameri-

Commemorative edition of the inaugural Arkansas Gazette, *November 20, 1819.*

After its founding by William E. Woodruff on November 20, 1819, the *Arkansas Gazette* endured a succession of eight different owners until it came into its own beginning with the purchase in 1902 by the Heiskell family of Memphis. Judge Carrick White Heiskell and his sons, John Netherland (Ned) and Fred, partnered with Frederick W. Allsopp, the *Gazette*'s business manager, to buy controlling interest in the property from a group of prominent Arkansans, led by the banker W. B. Worthen.[2] At that time, the newspaper was housed in the Fulk Building on West Markham Street in Little Rock; its press was "one of the most obsolete in the nation," and it had six thousand subscribers, "a number of whom were in arrears," according to the *Arkansas Gazette*'s coverage of the fiftieth anniversary of the Heiskells' ownership.[3] The purchase came about with the help of Maxwell Coffin, a relative of the Heiskells from Little Rock who worked in real estate. During Coffin's visit to the Heiskell home in Memphis, Eliza Netherland Heiskell, Judge Heiskell's wife and his sons' mother, asked his investment advice, and Coffin recommended the purchase of the *Arkansas Gazette*. Eliza Heiskell later recalled: "Ned had told me that his ambition was to own a newspaper so I wrote to him that night. He answered at once, saying it would be exactly what he would want if it could be accomplished, and that he believed it could be."[4]

The family took on a debt of $80,000,[5] and the deal was official on June 17, 1902,[6] with the new owners taking control of the *Gazette* on July 1.[7] In later years, the group gathered all the stock to become sole owners; the Heiskell family eventually bought out Allsopp's heirs, and ultimately, the J. N. Heiskell branch consolidated the extended family's ownership.[8] J. N. Heiskell, who had been working with the Associated Press in Louisville, moved to Little Rock and began his duties as editor of the paper and president of the company. At the time of the purchase, his younger brother, Fred, who had begun his journalism career with the *Memphis Scimitar* in 1893, was working in the Philippines as secretary to Luke E. Wright of Memphis, a lawyer who was a member of the first Philippine Commission, appointed by President William Howard Taft.[9] Fred Heiskell joined his brother at the *Gazette* and started work as managing editor upon his return from abroad at the end of the year. Allsopp continued his duties as business manager and served as secretary of the *Gazette* Publishing Company. The Heiskells' father was a circuit judge in Memphis who, while an interested partner, did not take part in the day-to-day management of the paper. He did, however, serve as vice president of the company.[10] The Heiskell brothers' previous journalistic experience helped ensure the quality of their family ownership.

"We did not get much for our money except opportunity and a going concern with a name that had been familiar in Arkansas for generations," J. N. Heiskell wrote later, recalling the risk his parents had taken with the investment and the hard work that followed it. "My life has had no greater satisfaction than seeing father and mother well rewarded for their courage in making this investment and their confidence in the ability of their sons to measure up to the opportunity."[11]

J. N. Heiskell published his first *Arkansas Gazette* editorial, which turned out to be prophetic, on July 1, 1902:

> A Democratic newspaper. That is what the *Arkansas Gazette* will be under the new editorial management that begins today. First of all the *Gazette* will strive to be a newspaper. News is the mental food of the human race. It exhilarates the mind as wine and sustains, strengthens and builds as bread. By paraphrase, it is twice advantageous. It advantages him that gives and him that takes, or him that tells and him that hears. It takes every man around the world once every 24 hours; and, more marvelous still, allows him to stop and inform himself on the subject he happens to be interested in. When

J. N. Heiskell, photo portrait by Gray, 1904. Courtesy of UALR Center for Arkansas History and Culture.

> the humblest and poorest man unfolds a real newspaper he opens a window through which he may look out upon the universe. . . . This newspaper has outlived many lives. It begins a new one this morning.[12]

The brothers shared a journalistic pedigree. Judge Heiskell's father, Major Frederick S. Heiskell, had trained as a printer with his brother, John Heiskell, publisher of the Winchester (Va.) *Gazette*, before moving to Knoxville, Tennessee, in 1814.[13] Two years later, Frederick Heiskell founded the *Knoxville Register*.[14] The Heiskells were also card-carrying southerners: Judge Heiskell had served as a colonel in the Nineteenth Tennessee Infantry Regiment during the Civil War; his brother, Joseph Brown Heiskell, had served in the Confederate Congress.[15] From his childhood, the young J. N., known as "Ned" to the family, was interested in newspapers and magazines.[16] During young Ned's years at home, the family received the morning *Memphis Appeal* as well as the evening *Public Ledger*.[17] He loved reading and writing as well as politics and government. He began "publishing" a family newspaper, *The Jolly*

Fellowship, when he was ten.[18] The paper lasted just two issues, was written in pen and ink on notebook paper, and recounted the happenings of his family and neighborhood.[19] "In politics this paper will be strongly democratic," he wrote in *The Jolly Fellowship*, foreshadowing the *Arkansas Gazette* under his leadership.[20]

After being educated mostly at private academies in Memphis, J. N. Heiskell entered the University of Tennessee in 1890. There was then no formal course of study in journalism, and he studied languages, mathematics, and physics. But the day after his graduation in 1893, he took a job at the *Knoxville Tribune* as a reporter. "My beginning salary was nothing a week, and I'm not sure I was worth much more than that," he recalled later.[21] Following that came stops as reporter and city editor at the *Commercial Appeal* in Memphis and with the Associated Press in Chicago and Louisville, Kentucky, before the opportunity arose to purchase the *Gazette*.[22] The family's patrician point of view and the brothers' journalistic experience boded well for the new ownership.

In 1902, the *Arkansas Gazette* was on financially shaky ground, and the journalistic quality of the paper itself was suspect. The new owners commanded a new policy by which the business office would not influence editorial policy—an early example of their commitment to quality journalism. J. N. Heiskell then announced a goal: "We are going for ten thousand circulation." Allsopp, always careful with a dollar, answered: "We are going broke."[23] That was his conservative business response to most of the journalistic changes the Heiskell brothers wanted to make.[24] Indeed, the frugal Allsopp saw the newspaper as a business; the Heiskells saw it differently. J. N. Heiskell believed that a newspaper should not be considered a property but rather an institution—the difference between civic responsibility and business. That conflict of philosophy from the early part of the century would return to haunt the *Gazette* in its final years under remote corporate ownership.

Circulation had been about stagnant since 1884, but by 1906, the new owners had nearly doubled the numbers they inherited to twelve thousand.[25] The Heiskells set about making improvements immediately. All advertising material would be thus labeled.[26] The plant had to be completely modernized, and because the newspaper itself did not reflect the best standards of national journalism, that had to change. Slowly but surely, the Heiskells achieved those goals.[27]

With the addition of a Monday issue on November 20, 1906, the eighty-seventh anniversary of the publication, the *Gazette* was published year-round. That would mean, Heiskell wrote, that it could take responsibility for publishing "an absolutely continuous record of current history."[28] He believed the *Gazette* was duty-bound to become "the record of current history in Arkansas."[29]

Other firsts reflected the Heiskells' ongoing commitment to journalistic quality: On October 11, 1908, the paper featured the first half-tone engraving; on October 24, 1908, came the first sports page, followed two months later by the first society page. In fact, the news became departmentalized as a rule instead of being placed willy-nilly.[30]

Another improvement was physical, substantial, and public. The Heiskell brothers commissioned George R. Mann, J. N. Heiskell's father-in-law, who had designed the Arkansas State Capitol, to design a new building. The three-story Beaux-Arts building, built by Peter Hotze, went up at the northeast corner of West Third and Louisiana Streets in 1908, with the name of its tenant—*"Arkansas Gazette"*—chiseled in stone. Although the newspaper is no more, the building remains, more than one hundred years later.

While the newspaper's first cartoons predated the Heiskell purchase, the family added the first regular Sunday comics section in 1906. In 1907, the *Gazette* became the first Arkansas newspaper to print its Sunday comics in color. In 1909, "Mutt and Jeff" became the first daily comic strip.[31]

To Heiskell's chagrin, advertisements were staples of the *Gazette*'s front page when the family arrived, and it took years for him to win that quality journalism battle with Allsopp. First, they removed ads from the top half of the page. According to Heiskell's front-page 1972 obituary in the *Gazette*, "It took a harder fight and several more years to get the ads off the front page altogether, because the business office resisted throwing away thousands of dollars worth of advertising income merely to gratify the Heiskells' aesthetic tastes."[32] Again, the Heiskell branch of the local ownership resisted the route to easy money, preferring quality journalism to profit for profit's sake. The *Gazette* featured a separate business page by 1925. The Sunday Magazine arrived in 1930. Commemorative editions marking the one-hundredth anniversary of the paper's founding on November 20, 1919, and the state's centennial on June 15, 1936, were issued as bound magazines.[33] The *Gazette*'s editorial page under J. N. Heiskell reflected his progressive views and cosmopolitan interests.[34] The newspaper trumpeted Arkansas news, hiring correspondents in every county[35]—a commitment to quality journalism that was its own reward.

While J. N. Heiskell was the dignified, proper, widely traveled patrician, his younger brother was "flamboyant, impatient and volatile," according to coverage of the one-hundred-fiftieth anniversary of the paper's founding.[36] The rough-and-tumble printers, editors, copy boys, janitors, and bookkeepers were more readily able to identify with Fred than with the reserved J. N., holding the former in "virtual worshipful regard."[37] According to one *Gazette* legend, Fred Heiskell once threw the governor of Arkansas down the back stairs after he came to the newsroom to get election night returns,[38] almost certainly cementing his popularity among *Gazette* journalists for generations.

The brothers made a rare team, as recalled in the *Gazette*'s sesquicentennial coverage:

> Fred Heiskell, with scant effort, merged the clans of the business office, the assorted mechanical departments, the carriers and street salesmen into a tribe. By unspoken arrangement, J. N. Heiskell was the sachem, Fred the medicine man. The *Gazette* still is a single organization. The clans still enjoy some internecine bushwhacking but it is a united front to the world and empire-building just isn't tolerated by the chieftains or the "Indians."[39]

As good local owners guided by the principles of quality journalism, the Heiskell brothers reinvested their earnings into the newspaper to improve its profitability and viability. This was a two-fold operation. Fred was responsible for the news, and J. N. paid attention to the broad picture—the finances and the needed technological improvements. This made the team of the Heiskell brothers a real contribution to Arkansas journalism.[40]

J. N. Heiskell had never been to Little Rock prior to the family's purchase of the *Gazette*, so the new owners arrived with no agenda other than the newspaper. Arkansas itself was a poor, rural state that was heavily dependent upon farming and too dependent in its farming practices on cotton. Segregation was a fact in every aspect of life, and education, in many places, was hit-or-miss. Although there would be some attempts at political reform during the early part of the century, the Heiskells arrived during the reelection campaign of Governor Jeff Davis, who would provide J. N. with his first editorial foe in his adopted state. Davis, a populist Democrat, served from 1901 to 1907 and was Arkansas's first three-term governor. (Coincidentally, no governor until Orval Faubus in the 1950s would equal that record.) Davis's time as governor, however, was marked by divisiveness as he pitted Arkansas's rural residents against the city-dwellers, proclaiming in a speech: "I had rather eat turnip greens, hog jowls and cornbread with you fellows out here around the wagon than go into the hotel and eat with the high-collared crowd."[41] He stood against corporations and turned to racial demagoguery to win three terms as governor. He spoke in favor of lynching and once promised to "fill the penitentiary so full of niggers their feet would be sticking out of the windows."[42] These attitudes were anathema to the genteel Heiskell, who, while generally reflecting the prevailing racial views of the time, was also steeped in fairness and spent much of his editorship trying to improve Arkansas and its national reputation.

Davis's enmity against the newspaper preceded the Heiskells' purchase. As one Heiskell biographer wrote, while Davis railed against most of the state's publications, he held special scorn for the *Gazette*, which he called "that old red harlot." He added: "I had rather be caught with a dead buzzard under my arm or a dead pole cat."[43] He christened his enemy editors as "squirrel heads." Although Heiskell was mild at first in his editorial comments regarding Davis, that changed after the governor called the *Gazette* "a Republican sheet," and his forces later put out word that the *Gazette* was "thoroughly subsidized." The accusation "apparently enraged Heiskell," and the battle was on.[44] They skirmished throughout Davis's years in the statehouse, including his remarks defending lynching during a luncheon meeting honoring President Theodore Roosevelt during his 1905 visit to Little Rock, prompting the president's outrage. Heiskell kept up the editorial barrage, in 1906 declaring, "The demagogue is one of the most serious problems of American life. . . . In his arraying of class against class, in his creating prejudice and enmity against any man who succeeds in a business enterprise, in his misleading of honest people into believing they are suffering great wrongs at the hands of certain interests, he works incalculable harm—and all for the sake of an office for himself."[45] One story Davis told crowds was that if his young son turned out to be above average in intelligence, he hoped he would become a minister. If he turned out to be average, he hoped to make him a lawyer. "But if he's a complete idiot, a man who just doesn't have any judgment about anything, God help us, I'm going to send him up to Little Rock to be the editor of the *Arkansas Gazette*," he said.[46] From the statehouse, Davis ran for United States Senate; despite the *Gazette*'s opposition, he was elected by the legislature, and Heiskell's criticism followed him to Washington in 1907, where the blustery style that had made him wildly popular in Arkansas proved to be a hindrance. According to the *Encyclopedia of Arkansas*, even after Davis apologized for his "intemperate rhetoric and breach of senatorial etiquette," the national press portrayed him as "a wild-eyed, backwoods buffoon."[47] Heiskell believed Davis's reputation was harmful to the state, and his criticism of the politician ended only with Davis's death two months before the end of his first senatorial term (he had already been reelected) on January 3, 1913. In an ironic twist, outgoing governor George Donaghey appointed Heiskell to fill Davis's seat on a short-term basis. Heiskell thus succeeded his old enemy, serving from January 6–31, 1913, when a successor was elected. Heiskell apparently had no interest in the permanent appointment, saying that working editors and publishers had no business in politics because it stifled their editorial duties.[48] In Senator Heiskell's only address before the Senate, he took up for his state:

> [I]t has been the singular misfortune of Arkansas to be misused, misadvertised, misunderstood, and misinterpreted. . . . Arkansas needs nothing more than to be known for what she truly is. And Arkansas asks nothing more than that her own and veritable voice, the voice of an enlightened and progressive, God-fearing and God-serving people may be heard before the Nation and the world.[49]

Newspapers nationally remarked on the irony of the Heiskell appointment, as illustrated in these words from the *Newark (N.J.) Journal*: "No public man in the entire history of Arkansas ever had a greater aversion for newspapers and 'squirrel-headed editors' than did Senator Davis and he would turn over in his grave if he knew a newspaper man was occupying his seat in the Senate."[50]

Ironically, the *Gazette* group bought its younger rival, the *Arkansas Democrat*, in 1909 but sold it two years later. With the high standards of their journalistic philosophy, the Heiskells believed that competition was better for community newspapers.[51] During those early skirmishes with Davis, Heiskell and the *Gazette* fought other battles, too. He wanted to make his adopted home a better place, and one of the best ways to do that, he thought, was to lead the effort for a public library. He editorialized that it would "fill one of the greatest voids in our municipal life."[52] As to its need, he said: "If what you don't know would fill a book, you need a library card."[53] It was a long, drawn-out battle against budgetary priorities for the city, and ultimately, private contributions—including $50 by Heiskell[54]—helped the cause, resulting in the library's opening on February 1, 1910. Heiskell, who served on the library board from 1907 until his death, carried Library Card No. 1[55] and borrowed the first book from the library.[56] Heiskell also campaigned editorially for a library for black people as well.[57] He originally believed that a branch of the white library in the black neighborhoods would better serve that segment of the population, Thompson explained. But Harry S. Ashmore, who joined the *Gazette* in the late 1940s, just as the race issue was becoming a major one in the United States, recounted the evolution of the older man's thinking: "[W]hen a younger board member persuaded him to visit the colored branch and Mr. J. N. saw its gross inequality he readily reversed himself. Any man of any color who wanted to read a book should be encouraged to do so, he said."[58]

In his early years as editor, Heiskell showed his belief that the right ideas, properly understood by the electorate, would ultimately win out. He editorialized for such progressive causes in Arkansas as city planning, the direct election of U.S. senators, civil service protection for police and firefighters, the merit system for postmasters, the abolition of capital punishment in favor of life imprisonment, the humane treatment of inmates, the eight-hour workday, restrictions on child labor, improved public schools, a state highway system, and the diversification of agriculture beyond cotton.[59] He opposed demagoguery and blatant racism and was rooted in common sense and the belief in the power of knowledge.[60] As the biographer Thompson recalled, "His belief was that if his readers could only be made to understand a problem they would reach the correct solution. When they did not, he regarded it as a failure to have the matter properly understood, and his response was not despair, but a determination to keep showing the way."[61]

As a man of reason, Heiskell was in no hurry for the United States to join the Great War when it broke out in Europe in 1914, but over the next two years, he began to see that neutrality was likely impossible. Once President Woodrow Wilson signed the declaration of war, Heiskell used his editorial voice to promote the war effort and loyalty to the nation.[62] But he refused to allow his newspaper to become part of "the army of hysteria," adding, "The *Gazette* will strive now and henceforth to keep its equilibrium and will not bend to every gust of wind. Wars are not won by hysterical people."[63]

When the *St. Louis Republic* merged with the *St. Louis Globe Democrat* in 1919, the *Gazette* became the oldest newspaper west of the Mississippi River, but Heiskell was quick to write that his paper's sheer age would not be enough to satisfy the public "if it does not serve good food."[64]

Over the years, J. N. Heiskell took great pride in the *Gazette*'s role as the state's newspaper of record and insisted upon proper grammar in its pages. Under his leadership, the newspaper became what one *Gazette* reporter called "a very literary journal," attracting many bright young journalistic talents who were often later lured away by the nation's elite newspapers—the *New York Times*, *New York Herald-Tribune*, *Chicago Tribune*, and *Philadelphia Inquirer*, among others.[65] Heiskell also amassed one of the state's best collections and libraries of Arkansas-related materials and used them as the basis for the paper's Chronicles of Arkansas series.

In an early editorial, he reiterated that the paper would "pursue in its daily life a building up instead of a tearing down policy."[66] With his philosophy of quality journalism and his own previous journalistic experience, he believed in the factual, nonemotional approach of the Associated Press as a model for how his paper should report the news.[67] He believed news should take precedence over editorials because people must have knowledge before taking action. His editorials were for the most part explanatory, providing context for the news.[68]

"The greatest service an editor can do his readers is to explain things that would not be clear otherwise," he wrote.[69] He tried to avoid personal attacks, even with Governor Jeff Davis, preferring instead to focus on issues, ideas, and policies, but he made it clear that a newspaper should not hesitate to take on public officials who were guilty of official wrongdoing.[70] The Heiskells were careful not to use their positions with the paper for personal benefit. When Fred Heiskell was mentioned as a candidate for the state Constitutional Convention in 1917, the newspaper's editorial failed to tout him. The subject was never again mentioned in the paper, and Fred Heiskell lost the election.[71]

Heiskell became a booster of his adopted state and city and began to view defending the state against out-of-state newspapers that spread false information about Arkansas as his main job. He believed strongly in a free press and in shining a light on problems so that public attention could solve them. As an editor, Heiskell was independent, and he used his newspaper as a forum for competing ideas. He favored a conservative news policy—no sensationalizing the news to attract readers.[72] Years later, the *Gazette* under Gannett ownership would buck that conservative philosophy—to the paper's detriment. Heiskell brought to Arkansas journalism what Thompson called "an intellectualism, enlightenment, and sense of noblesse oblige."[73] His editorial style appealed to reason, principle, fairness, moral duty, civic pride, loyalty to state and nation, law and order, planning, and good manners. He avoided emotional arguments, prejudice, and nativism.[74] He was a member of a committee that opposed the enactment of Arkansas's "monkey law" that banned the teaching of evolution in the schools.[75] Indeed, in many ways and on many subjects, J. N. Heiskell and the *Arkansas Gazette* were a progressive, moderating influence on twentieth-century Arkansas.

James Street, who worked as a lower-rung editor under the Heiskells in 1926, recalled the newsroom reacting to a warning that the *Gazette* might be mobbed in answer to a Heiskell editorial. While Heiskell sat at his desk writing another editorial in longhand, his staff "barricaded themselves with six-shooters and sort of hoped for the fracas that never came," Street remembered.[76] Street said he learned from Heiskell that "a nickel pen, a penny point, and a well of good black ink are mightier than pistol or purse."[77] The *Gazette* was known for restraint, avoiding so-called Second-Coming headlines for lesser stories, so when it did use big type, for such events as the sinking of the *Titanic*, various wars, and a Little Rock lynching in 1927, its readers got the message.

With Little Rock police looking on that year, a mob lynched a black man named John Carter, who was accused of assaulting a white woman and her daughter. The mob then dragged the body around the streets of the city and burned it. It was one of the most notorious incidents of racial violence in Arkansas history. Under Heiskell, the *Gazette*'s front-page headline read:

With Officers Making No Attempt at Restraint
Mob Burns Negro's Body and Creates Reign of Terror

Heiskell's front-page editorial criticized the police and called on them to take control[78]—another example of an independent ownership committed to quality journalism and community leadership.

The Heiskell brothers appeared to have little in common except for the newspaper. Street called Fred Heiskell "a gregarious man who loved a laugh and a neat tipple of good whiskey." J. N. Heiskell was, for most of his life, a teetotaler. The staff idolized Fred, considering him, as Street remembered, "our Gunga Din, a better man than we were, and Mr. Ned was Buddha."[79]

Street recalled that the 1927 lynching coverage led to the mob threat; Fred Heiskell told the staff that any fight would be management's and that no employee would be involved, but Street wrote that that warning didn't sit well with the working men. "Who was he kidding? That night the boys fortified themselves with .45s and a little moonshine and strutted around like heroes."[80]

But the boys lost their hero, J. N. Heiskell lost his beloved younger brother, and the *Gazette* lost its managing editor on March 31, 1931, when Fred Heiskell died of a heart attack at his home. He was just fifty-five. According to the next day's *Gazette*, after the first edition telling of the loss went to press, employees gathered for a moment of silence in tribute to a "damned good guy" and "a friend of all who stood there."[81] A page-one tribute called it "the saddest news that ever came out of the editorial rooms of the *Gazette* since the oldest members of the staff came onto the paper."[82] Allsopp paid tribute on page one as well: "As a newspaper man he had no superior in the South. His judgment in news matters was phenomenal, and in emergencies he was most resourceful. His sudden passing away is a terrible shock to his associates, an irretrievable loss to the *Arkansas Gazette*, as also to the newspaper profession generally."[83] W. F. McGuire, who had been foreman of the *Gazette*'s composing room for eight years, was quoted in the paper (with one of the *Gazette*'s distinctive style spellings): "A true friend of the printers has been taken from us and we are sad. An employe of Fred Heiskell did not feel as if he worked for him, but with him."[84]

Nationally, newspapers praised Fred Heiskell for having put in place a system of newsgathering for state elections that got results to *Gazette* readers first and for conducting an agricultural advancement program that benefited the state economically.[85] The *Commercial Appeal* in Memphis credited him

Fred Heiskell, undated. Courtesy of UALR Center for Arkansas History and Culture.

with "large vision, keen insight and sound judgment" in, together with his brother, elevating the *Gazette* to high stature both in the South and the nation:

> A lover of life and the good things of life, he always maintained a democratic idea toward people and things. He was ever cheerful and filled with the joy of living. He met success with equanimity and he builded upon it to higher things. In his newspaper work his friends were numbered from the bottom to the top of society and all of them will mourn his passing.[86]

Within the state, local papers praised him in death. The *Baxter Bulletin* called him "one of the trio that has made the *Gazette* one of the greatest newspapers of the country."

> Under his editorship the *Gazette* has had an influence that few papers enjoy, and it has always been used for the best interests of the state. He insisted on uncolored facts in both his news and editorial columns, and it was on this foundation that he built a great newspaper. He was humanly democratic in spirit and was able to

> impart this spirit into his newspaper, which has given it a greater influence among its readers probably than any other state paper in the country.[87]

Fred Heiskell's death also brought a message of condolence from President Herbert Hoover.[88] The Heiskells and Allsopp had proven to be generous to their employees, sometimes to a fault. At Fred's death, nearly half the newsroom employees owed him varying amounts from $2 to $100 each, as did a large percentage of workers in the backshop. Not one of them reneged on those debts even after J. N. Heiskell forgave them. Workers who retired before Social Security and fringe benefits programs were fully funded were retained on the payroll.[89] It is almost impossible to imagine that kind of employer-employee relationship in the era of long-distance corporate ownership.

Although the line of demarcation between the editorial and news departments had been clearly drawn by the brothers early in their tenure, after Fred's death, J. N. Heiskell took on more newsroom duties. But Fred Heiskell's personality dominated the newsroom's customs and style for decades after his death. According to the newspaper's sesquicentennial coverage in 1969, the brothers and Allsopp teamed "to make the *Gazette* a force for good, a force for progress, a mouthpiece for all worthy minorities, a champion of a region that was suffering an acute inferiority and persecution complex. These goals were achieved largely before Fred Heiskell died in 1931."[90] The philosophy reflected that of a quality independent ownership.

Unsurprisingly, J. N. Heiskell was conservative in his philosophy of newspapers. In a report to the Southern Newspaper Publishers Association annual meeting in Asheville, North Carolina, in 1935, almost certainly railing against the era's growth of chain ownership, he compared a newspaper to a restaurant —quality of the product, whether it be food or news, would be the determining factor in the entity's success or failure. "You may be able to high pressure a man into subscribing for your paper, but you can't high pressure him into appreciation of it, or into regarding it as an indispensable part of his daily life."[91] While acknowledging the growing importance of entertainment to the news consumer, he cautioned his colleagues against relying too much on the comics and other feature material, maintaining that if it does so, it is failing as a newspaper. He also took aim at publishers, saying that if they insist on their editor being "reduced to the ignoble status of a floor-walker and glad-hander for the Advertising Department, his spirit and enthusiasm may be killed, and even his respect for his own newspaper may be destroyed."[92] "Every owner, every publisher, who in miserly or merely misguided way denies his Editorial Department proper personnel and equipment should ask himself how far removed is his newspaper from one of those bell ringers and Fuller brush men known as a Shopping News."[93]

Even in the 1930s, Heiskell believed that a newspaper should serve as the conscience of its community.

> He who is actually a newspaper's editor is its voice and soul and the keeper of its conscience. Choose him with care and circumspection. Arm him with freedom. Equip him with the tools of his trade. Grant him reasonable time for his work. Fortify him with your confidence. Then may you enjoy the rewards that come to a newspaper that speaks with intelligence, sincerity and conviction and that lights the way for good citizenship to follow.[94]

Heiskell's warnings reflected the growth of chain ownership in American journalism. The number of chain-owned newspapers grew from 62 in 1910 to 311 in 1930 (comprising 15 percent of American dailies), and that growth would continue—560 (32 percent) in 1960, 1,158 (70 percent) in 1986, and 77 percent of all papers in 2000.[95] Even in 1935, Heiskell saw the potential dangers of the trend and solidified his own philosophy of quality journalism at the *Arkansas Gazette.*

As the improvements continued at the *Gazette*, Heiskell began to hire more and more college graduates, many of whom had studied under Walter J. Lemke at the University of Arkansas. Lemke had been hired by the UA in 1928 to write publicity and teach journalism classes. A formal journalism department was established there in 1930;[96] it now bears his name.

As rumblings about the war in Europe in the 1930s commenced, the war industries geared up in the United States, and newspapers made the most of their opportunity. Even though the first competition from radio had begun to emerge, newspapers were still the major source for information. Heiskell and the *Gazette* installed a six-unit Goss printing press capable of producing 37,048 page copies an hour. Another addition was an Associated Press Wirephoto machine that would bring images of the war to Arkansas breakfast tables. But the Japanese bombing of Pearl Harbor on December 7, 1941, signaled a change of plans for all Americans, including those at the *Arkansas Gazette*. Starting with the peacetime draft in 1940, newspapers across the country began to suffer from staff shortages, and women began to fill the jobs formerly held by men. With major shortages in newsprint, however, newspapers found it more challenging to deliver the news.[97]

But the biggest impact of World War II on the *Arkansas Gazette* was the loss in late 1943 of J. N. Heiskell's son, Carrick, who had been groomed to take over for his father at the newspaper. While it is impossible to know what the *Gazette* would have been like had he lived to lead it, it is unlikely that Harry Ashmore would have landed there, at least in the position he did, and without Ashmore's influence, the *Gazette* might not have taken the stance it did regarding the desegregation of Central High in 1957. Almost certainly that stance would not have been so forceful. Had his son lived to become editor, in all likelihood J. N. Heiskell would not have remained as involved with the paper as he did for the rest of his life. Carrick Heiskell, like Ashmore, was close to his brother-in-law, Hugh Patterson, so the younger generation might still have prevailed over J. N. Heiskell's Victorian sensibilities, but Ashmore's standing as an outsider—albeit one with deep southern roots—helped to deflect some of the criticism that came, and his departure after the crisis subsided hastened the *Gazette*'s recovery from its time of trial.

J. N. Heiskell had married Wilhelmina Mann of Little Rock on June 28, 1910; they had four children: John Netherland Jr., Carrick, Elizabeth, and Louise. John Jr. was severely retarded and died a few months before Carrick in 1943.[98] Carrick White Heiskell was born July 1, 1917, and graduated from St. Mark's School at Southborough, Massachusetts, in 1936 and Harvard University in 1940. He joined the *Gazette* staff, working as a reporter

Carrick Heiskell, undated. Courtesy of UALR Center for Arkansas History and Culture.

and later as assistant city editor, and married Bertha Forbes in Little Rock on September 14, 1940. Three months after Pearl Harbor, he enlisted in the Army Air Force.[99] While training in Waco, Texas, he wrote a letter to his parents and sisters as a Christmas present:

> My greatest regret is that I will not be there at home to celebrate the Christmas with you. But, then, there are millions of others in the same situation and we are all in this thing together. My Christmas present for you is still in the future. Some day, I and thousands of others like me, will be able to give you a peaceful world again where we can all live our own lives again in freedom and happiness. And it will come to pass soon. We are right and we cannot fail.[100]

Carrick Heiskell earned his commission and wings in February 1943 and trained further in Michigan, Tennessee, and Utah before being assigned to the Army Transport Service in India. In a letter to his sister, Effie, J. N. Heiskell wrote: "Carrick is now having what will apparently be his last training before going on foreign service. It is a very sobering thought for me that the time seems so near. The planes at this field are the biggest he has ever flown in. They go more than 200 miles an hour and fly at 20,000 feet, which means oxygen for the crew."[101]

While Carrick Heiskell, in letters home to his father, seemed resolute and in some ways excited about his foreign service, he was also a realist:

> There are some things I want you to attend to just in case anything happens to me. Bert is entitled to a payment from the government equal to six times my base pay plus flying pay in event of my death. She can also collect all the back pay owed me, plus a pension of $50 a month. All this is over and above my insurance. But she has to make an application for this money—it is not an automatic payment. Also to get my insurance promptly she should have copies of mine and her birth certificates. Be sure she gets these.[102]

Once in India, Carrick Heiskell found himself working long hours, enjoying the planes, and complaining good-naturedly about mail service, food, and his bungalow accommodations, among other things, in letters home:

> I like these planes more and more each time I fly them. It's a real experience just to be in one of them. Every time I go up I wonder that so much weight can overcome gravity. I'm afraid I'm leaving you a lot of things to take care of at home. But watch out for Bert for me. She thinks about herself so little that she forgets to do the things for

> herself she should. I couldn't stand to have anything happen to her. Or to you.[103]

In a November 21, 1943, letter to his parents, Lieutenant Heiskell wrote of bad weather and his hope to get in as many flights as possible before monsoon season started. "It is beginning to look like my stay in India is a quarter of the way finished already," he wrote. "I hope so."[104]

However, he died eight days later, on November 29, 1943, when he crashed while piloting an army transport plane between India and China in the area known as "the Hump."[105] As had been his uncle Fred nearly thirteen years prior, Lieutenant Heiskell was eulogized on the pages of the *Gazette*:

> What is there to say? He was our good comrade in the confraternity of work and interests that makes a newspaper's staff a kind of family. In the few short years since he joined us to begin the career which war cut short, he had won our esteem and respect by his abilities and character, and our warm liking by his human qualities—his unfailing sense of fun, his modesty and his ready friendliness. The elder among us had observed with keen interest his progress in mastery of our craft and had formed high hopes for his future, as those nearer his own age had enjoyed his companionship in hours of duty and hours of relaxation. We all felt a thrill of pride when he joined the Air Force. We all followed him in our thoughts through each stage of arduous training and shared his triumph when the silver wings were won. Since he went overseas to the perilous service assigned to him in the Far East, we have waited eagerly for every bit of news that came back. And now has come this news. Words are made futile. To say that all our hearts are heavy with grief is but a feeble expression of what we feel. Yet what else is there that can be said? This is Goodnight, Carrick—Goodnight for the last time from your comrades of the city room. And may God rest the soul of a gallant gentleman.[106]

Again, messages of condolence poured in from all over the state, this time including one from Governor Homer Adkins.[107] Not surprisingly, the loss hurt J. N. Heiskell deeply, but typically, he determined to move forward. "I have suffered the greatest loss that could have befallen me but I must do my best to carry on, as I know Carrick would want me to do," he wrote.[108] In another letter, he wrote, "My boy held my hopes for the future and he will always be my strength and inspiration."[109] A year later, he wrote his sister Grace: "This is the anniversary of the saddest day in my life, the day the telegram came from the

War Department."[110] He remained affectionate with his daughter-in-law, who had also worked as a reporter at the *Gazette*, mentioning her in letters to his sisters. Twelve years after young Carrick's death, on May 13, 1955, Heiskell wrote to his daughter-in-law, congratulating her on the news that she and her new husband were expecting a child:

> Wilhelmina and I were rejoiced to hear the news. We can understand what a baby will mean to you and Curren. A child of a marriage is more than a child. It is fulfillment. It is something spiritual. It binds the father and the mother as nothing else can. It makes them partners in the greatest and most valuable of all possessions.[111]

By April 9, 1946, when the second member of the *Gazette*'s triumvirate, business manager Fred Allsopp, died, the newspaper was in much better shape than it had been when the group bought it forty-four years earlier, despite the personnel and paper shortages that hit all newspapers during wartime. Daily circulation had allowed the *Gazette* to become Arkansas's newspaper of record. Its reporters were by then typically college graduates. Circulation and advertising increases had allowed the local family ownership to modernize the plant and commission a new building, and a new printing press and Associated Press Wirephoto machine enabled the *Gazette* to print photos from the war. Readers found newspapers to be invaluable.[112] In fact, weekly newspapers in Arkansas showed a 12.6 percent increase in circulation in 1942; dailies averaged a 12 percent increase.[113] Indeed, Allsopp's conservative accounting practices and financial integrity had turned out to be a perfect match for the Heiskells' journalistic principles and commitment to quality journalism.

Under the three men, the *Gazette* never missed a payroll or laid off an employee for financial reasons.[114] Allsopp had planned to retire from the *Gazette* on May 1, 1946, but died three weeks earlier. In his statement regarding his retirement, he wrote:

> I am firmly convinced that when W. E. Woodruff started the *Gazette* he was inspired from on High. I am further convinced that it was providential that the mantle of editorship fell on the shoulders of a man of such high attainments and noble sentiments as Mr. J. N. Heiskell. While I believe there is a Divinity that shapes our ends, I don't know why I should be an humble instrument of Providence, but my heart and soul tell me that when I became connected with the *Gazette*, it was a destined event, so great has been the influence on my life.[115]

Fred Allsopp obituary, Arkansas Gazette, *April 11, 1946. Courtesy of UALR Center for Arkansas History and Culture.*

Having outlived his original partners as well as the son he had groomed to be his successor, J. N. Heiskell, at seventy-three, was left to look to the future of his paper alone. His leadership had turned the *Arkansas Gazette* into a well-respected newspaper nationally and a beacon of influence on the state. Coming events would test him, the newspaper, and Arkansas.

CHAPTER THREE

1947–1959: A New Triumvirate Takes Control

J. N. Heiskell, Hugh B. Patterson, and Harry S. Ashmore Face the Crisis at Central High

BY THE END OF World War II, J. N. Heiskell's leadership had allowed the *Arkansas Gazette* to achieve a level of quality it had not come close to since its founding in 1819. Its brand—a commitment to quality journalism—had been firmly established by the time Heiskell became the sole survivor of his original business partners (following the deaths of his father, brother, and Fred Allsopp) and had to overcome the loss of the son who was to have been his heir. By the end of the war, Heiskell was forced to reassess his plans for the future of the oldest newspaper west of the Mississippi. Although not what he had envisioned, the postwar *Gazette* would stand tall during its greatest trial and become one of the country's most honored and respected newspapers. A new triumvirate would build on the legacy of fairness and community spirit established by the first one as the *Gazette* led the state through its most notorious crisis toward a moderate position on the race issue. Harry Ashmore and Hugh Patterson would build on and extend Heiskell's commitment to fairness.

The end of World War II signaled the beginning of a time of progress for Arkansas, as it did for much of the United States. The postwar years saw the expansion of electricity, which in turn helped the recruitment of industry to the state. White business and political leaders embraced the economic changes, and some returning servicemen, after their years fighting the Nazis, even began to question segregation, one of the pillars of the society they had left to go to war. But many of the state's established leaders had a hard time dealing with the emerging civil rights agenda at home that a new generation of black leaders began to work toward. However, with little controversy, Silas Hunt became the first black student admitted to the University of Arkansas

Law School in February 1948,[1] pioneering the desegregation of higher education in the South. Sid McMath succeeded Ben Laney as governor in 1949 as part of the GI postwar revolt against the state's political machines, signaling the beginning of a run of progressive governors that also included the early years of Orval Faubus, although later events would make his progressivism a little-remembered footnote of history. The most famous of those progressive Arkansas governors wound up in the White House after the 1992 election. McMath's election heralded real change in a state that had not progressed as most others had in the twentieth century. Ernest Dumas wrote that McMath's political skills "awakened yearning by people for real progress and reform."[2] Not surprisingly, based on J. N. Heiskell's first editorial in 1902, that progressivism was evident in the pages of the *Arkansas Gazette* under its local family ownership. But as with the changes nationally, the *Gazette*'s progressive stances would not come easily or without a sometimes-heavy price. Despite the harsh consequences, however, Heiskell reiterated that the *Gazette* would make the same choices if it were faced again with the same situation. On multiple occasions, he alluded to St. Paul when he said a newspaper "must have dedication. It must fight the good fight. Above all else it must keep the faith."[3] Clearly, his was a brave call in the face of enormous economic pressures.

Besides the devastating effect on his family, the death of Lieutenant Carrick White Heiskell during World War II had broad ramifications for the *Arkansas Gazette*. There would be no direct family successor. One was possible, however. J. N. Heiskell's elder daughter, Elizabeth, had worked on the *Gazette*'s editorial page during World War II while the men were off to war, but her request to remain on after they returned was denied by her father. As one Heiskell biographer reported, the old man's younger daughter, Louise Heiskell Patterson, remembered that her sister "wanted to remain on in some capacity after the war, and Daddy wouldn't let her. She would take away a man's job. He wanted educated daughters, but he didn't want (them) to do anything with it."[4]

Although not exactly what he had planned, Heiskell had another family option that proved acceptable to his Victorian philosophy. Louise Heiskell had married Hugh B. Patterson Jr. in 1943. He had served as a major in the army during the war and had worked in commercial printing before that, including some time as a traveling salesman of printing supplies.[5] "The only male in the family with the proper background was my father, who had married my mother during World War II," their son, Carrick Patterson, explained. "He had been in the graphic arts industry. He sold printing, basically. During World War II, he had gotten a lot of management experience."[6]

Hugh Patterson was named national advertising manager when he came to the *Gazette* in 1946, but Heiskell continued his search for an editorial successor. While at the American Society of Newspaper Editors meeting in Washington, D.C., in the spring of 1947, he attended a panel discussion. On the panel was a young Harry Scott Ashmore, editor of the editorial page of the *Charlotte (N.C.) News*. Ashmore impressed Heiskell, who invited him to Little Rock for a sizing-up session. Heiskell hired the younger man as editor of the editorial page in September 1947[7] after Ashmore had turned down offers from newspapers in Richmond and Atlanta.[8] He was named executive editor the following year. Ashmore was a South Carolinian and a Nieman Fellow who had a reputation as a moderate-to-liberal thinker, particularly on the race issue. Gunner Myrdal's 1944 book, *An American Dilemma*, had crystallized Ashmore's thinking on the race issue as he returned to journalism following his service in World War II. Ashmore felt the South "needed to change with the changing times or face change being forced on it from outside the region."[9] Like Governor Orval Faubus, who would become his adversary, Ashmore believed race would become a defining issue of the time. Although by no means popular, Ashmore's message was at least somewhat palatable because it came from someone with a southern ancestry traceable to colonial times.[10] One Heiskell biographer described Ashmore's powerful writing style as "truly thought-provoking and conscience-prodding" even if his message was not wholly accepted in the region.[11] After he added executive editor to his title, Ashmore took leave from the *Gazette*—with Heiskell's and Patterson's blessing—to compile a report for the Ford Foundation research project. His first book, *The Negro and the Schools*, a report on the dual system of education in the South, was published on the eve of the 1954 *Brown v. Board of Education* decision,[12] which overturned the 1896 "separate but equal" doctrine of *Plessy v. Ferguson* and declared school segregation unconstitutional. Advance copies of Ashmore's book were given to members of the Supreme Court.[13] The *Gazette* thus boasted the country's best-informed editor on the race issue.[14] Patterson said all this put the *Gazette* "in the best position to put the problem in Southern and National perspective."[15]

Patterson, meanwhile, was being groomed as publisher, an office "left vacant for more than forty years until the Heiskells were satisfied that they had turned up one of their own with proper qualifications," Ashmore recalled. He said Patterson proved to have not only the necessary skills for the job but also a healthy dose of stubbornness, which helped. "He was able to ease the suspicion of modernist heresy with his ultimate Southern credentials—descent from a long line of Scotch-Irish Presbyterian ministers, teachers and lawyers, and a birth certificate that identified him as a native of Cotton Plant, Mississippi," Ashmore wrote.[16]

Patterson was named publisher in November 1948, becoming the first person to hold that title under the Heiskell ownership. He modernized the *Gazette*'s equipment and created an accounting system that other newspapers followed. One of his most important contributions, though, was his shepherding of the consolidation of ownership of the *Gazette* to the Heiskell family. To do that, he successfully fought off an attempt by stockholder Witt Stephens, whose family would go on to found the investment firm Stephens Inc., to obtain a controlling interest.[17] On November 27, 1948, Heiskell announced in the paper the purchase of the "common stock" of William C. Allsopp and Mrs. Fred W. Allsopp, paying $750,000 for the 25 percent *Gazette* stock that was not already under the family's ownership.[18] Patterson, who had handled the negotiations, was announced as "chief business executive of the *Gazette* with the title of publisher" in the same edition.[19] Other accomplishments of the newspaper under Patterson's leadership included more sections and news services and the addition of color comics, *Parade* magazine, and stock tables.[20] The commitment to quality journalism thus continued under the second generation of Heiskell family ownership.

During the transition to the new triumvirate, Heiskell's philosophy of newspapers continued to shine through, as reported by *Time*: "In a time of corporate, impersonal journalism, doughty old John Netherland Heiskell is a holdout. The lean and gimlet-eyed boss of Little Rock's *Arkansas Gazette* snorts at the notion that a newspaper is just a 6% investment; it is first of all an institution, says he, and only incidentally a business."[21] In an era of increasing chain ownership of newspapers—the number of chains had doubled from 1920 to 1940 (31 to 60), and the number of newspapers owned by chains had more than doubled (153 to 319)[22]—Heiskell continued to illustrate a marked contrast between chain and family proprietorship. Although family ownership alone does not guarantee such an enlightened philosophy, even the most well-meaning corporation still looks first at the bottom line. In fact, in a January 1946 speech to the Little Rock Rotary Club, Heiskell had reiterated this idea, recalling that from the beginning, founder William E. Woodruff had established the *Gazette* to be "an invaluable record"—and sometimes the only one—of the state's history.

> The convention which wrote the constitution on which Arkansas was admitted to the Union in 1836 kept no journal and the *Gazette*'s reports are the only record of the proceedings. Those who are carrying on W. E. Woodruff's paper today regard the *Gazette* as a public

> trust. They are legally the owners of the property, but they are primarily trustees for the public to whose service every paper should be dedicated. The sincere purpose is to serve the state and the nation and to make the *Gazette* a record and a chronicle, a prophet and a voice.[23]

Heiskell's philosophy stood out even then amid the growth of chain ownership in American journalism.

In 1983, on the occasion of his thirty-fifth anniversary as publisher, Patterson remembered that his biggest problem at the *Gazette* upon becoming publisher was the same problem that faced much of the country—rebuilding in the postwar economy. "The staff was depleted during the war years and the physical plant was in need of modernization," he said. Part of the strategy included a "bold" plan in 1950 to raise the price of its Sunday paper 50 percent—from 10 cents to 15 cents. Patterson recalled that most of that increase went to expenses—newspaper carriers and a magazine insert—but two cents were able to go back into the product. With the Sunday circulation of 110,000, that meant an extra $2,200 per week for the paper. "That was 'just enough to provide an edge,'" Patterson said. "That marked the beginning of a period of building."[24] The move illustrated the family's ongoing commitment to quality journalism.

Patterson's older son, Carrick, said that as a manager, his father faced some difficult battles as the son-in-law of the editor and principal owner. "He hadn't been a newspaper person, and I think he may have felt like an outsider in some respect," Carrick Patterson said.[25] But Patterson and Ashmore were aligned philosophically and socially as well as in age and background, making them a powerful two-thirds of the new triumvirate. William (Bill) Rutherford, the newspaper's final managing editor and a longtime newsroom employee, wrote that the younger soldiers had been through the war years; "they sensed the tide of changing racial patterns, and they believed that it was their duty to prepare the readers of their newspaper for it."[26] Heiskell, however, saw segregation as a practice that enabled whites and blacks to live peacefully.[27] Hugh Patterson described his father-in-law's views on race:

> He had always been taught to be a champion for, well, civil rights doesn't seem to be the appropriate word now, but due process, legality, all that kind of business. Yet it was recognized that his father, having been a colonel in Longstreet's army, you know, had sort of engendered a feeling of racial superiority or whatever. Separate but equal and not conceding that it was not equal and never was and never would be under that theory.[28]

Again almost certainly in response to the rising tide of chain ownership, Heiskell chastised his colleagues at the Southern Newspaper Publishers' Association convention in Florida in 1948. He castigated them for their failure to recognize the importance of editorial columns and their unreasonable demands on editors that resulted in insufficient manpower and the resulting uninformed editorial policy "and then complained that editorials were not read and therefore, no money should be spent on them."[29] Ashmore added management of the newsroom to his duties when Heiskell changed his title to executive editor in 1948. "He wanted an executive editor for the first time," Roy Reed said of Heiskell's motivation for the change.[30]

Ashmore, who took another leave of absence in 1955 to work as a civil rights adviser in Adlai Stevenson's presidential campaign,[31] began to make subtle changes in the *Gazette* that, in hindsight, were significant. In 1946, the *New York Times* had begun omitting racial designations in stories unless a reference to race had a purpose. The move was unusual enough to merit coverage by *Time* magazine.[32] One of Ashmore's changes at the *Gazette* was the use of courtesy titles for blacks. In 1952, a survey of thirty-four southern dailies found that just half were using courtesy titles for blacks or regularly running black news.[33] Ashmore recalled that early in his stay in Little Rock, when he suggested to Heiskell that the *Gazette*'s style regarding courtesy titles for blacks be changed to use them for all women and drop them for all men except for a few specifics—president, governor, the clergy, and the dead—it marked his first conversation with Heiskell about a specific racial matter. Heiskell acquiesced, but Ashmore thought the reason was more because of the awkwardness the established policy wrought—not to correct an injustice. "[He] was a meticulous grammarian who could see that the style forced clumsy convolutions in the use of his beloved English language," Ashmore recalled.[34] Under Ashmore and the *Gazette*'s editorial leadership, Arkansas bypassed the Dixiecrat ticket in 1948, helping President Harry Truman to reelection despite Arkansas governor Ben Laney leading the conservative revolt against the Democrats. The Dixiecrats were committed to states' rights and maintaining segregation.[35]

On June 27, 1952, J. N. Heiskell was feted with a celebration at the Country Club of Little Rock to mark his fifty years as editor of the *Arkansas Gazette*. Among the many congratulatory notes and telegrams he received for the accomplishment was one from the White House and President Truman. According to the newspaper's coverage, more than one hundred of the state's "distinguished citizens"—clergy, merchants, bankers, utility executives, newspapermen, physicians, jurists, and other old friends—marked the occasion at the country club.[36] Mark Ethridge, publisher of the *Louisville (Ky.) Courier-Journal*, recounted what made the *Gazette* under Heiskell "a truly regional newspaper with an equally great editor": fairly told news, uncorrupted and incorruptible editorial positions, a strong editorial policy that did not shout but instead persuaded, and reasoned, mutual respect between the editor and the public. He reiterated that the *Gazette* had a "sense of responsibility, that the *Gazette* is an institution; that it is not a crusader in the classic sense, but in a civilized and temperate way with a lack of emotion." He concluded: "Newspaper men know Mr. Heiskell as a proponent of good things for Arkansas and as one who has blocked the paths of things not so good."[37] In his remarks, Heiskell again reiterated his philosophy of ownership when he compared a newspaper and its editor to the community's conscience, a metaphor he would use for the rest of his life: "The one question then is whether he must be adjudged guilty of default on his obligation to a community and betrayal of his mission and his opportunity; or whether he can look his judges in the eye and ask discharge from his labors with the words: 'I have fought a good fight. I have finished my course. I have kept the faith.'"[38] He had hit upon the theme that would take the Old Gray Lady through her darkest hour just five years later. Independent family ownership would allow her to hold on despite great financial loss.

Heiskell had tended to agree with Senator Harry Truman's views on race as an issue of justice, not social equality. Despite favoring social segregation, Heiskell, like Truman, believed in fairness and justice for all despite race.[39] And when Truman became president and moved toward equality of treatment to get that equality of justice, Heiskell was able to, in good conscience, hire Ashmore,[40] who had been described in *Time* when he went to the *Charlotte News* as one of the few southern journalists identified as liberal in the national press.[41] So Heiskell knew what he was getting. As *Arkansas Publisher* put it, he "had hired a Southern liberal who had been a Nieman Fellow at Harvard to work for what Heiskell called 'a conservative paper which sometimes disappoints conservatives.'"[42] James O. Powell wrote in Heiskell's obituary that Ashmore's liberalism was no cause for surprise or angst for his new boss.[43] As for Ashmore, he understood Heiskell's personal preferences, realizing that the older man's values were different from his, having been shaped and fixed during a time and in a place that the younger man knew only from stories.[44] But Ashmore had become convinced that segregation's days were numbered, first in public education. "The contrast between white and Negro educational facilities reflects no credit upon the South and has seriously weakened our defense of segregation," he wrote in 1948 in response to Truman's civil rights proposals.

> The willingness of most Southern whites to give the Negro a fair share of our limited public funds is genuine, but it has not been

> matched by performance . . . . [The solution] calls us now, as it did in 1865, for courage, complete devotion to our highest ideals, and self-sacrifice. But until we turn to it we will continue to be vulnerable to every zealot and every political opportunist—inside the South as well as out of it—who would use our weakness for his own ends.[45]

Even before the battle with Faubus, this statement harkened back to Heiskell's row with another governor, Jeff Davis, in the early 1900s. It also foreshadowed the *Gazette's* editorial stance in 1957 that stressed the supremacy of the federal government in all matters of law, recalling the realities of the Civil War.

Heiskell had hired Ashmore just as race was becoming the defining issue of the time. The younger man had hoped to land at a paper where he could make a difference in coverage of this issue, and he found such a situation at the *Arkansas Gazette*.[46] In 1954, his foil appeared in the guise of Orval E. Faubus, a relative newcomer to Arkansas politics who came down from the hills of Madison County to plunk down his fee on the final day of filing to run against Democratic governor Francis Cherry. Faubus ran as a liberal, attacking Cherry's record on welfare.[47] It was a nip-and-tuck race until Cherry's people intimated that, based on his three-month attendance at Commonwealth College, a left-wing institution outside Mena, as a youth, Faubus was a communist.[48] Reed, who wrote Faubus's biography, recalled that Ashmore saw the charge as "an egregious case of red-baiting and unfair tactics" to bring up something twenty or thirty years in the past. "Lord knows, Orval Faubus was anything but a communist in 1954," Reed said.[49] Faubus at first tried to deny that he had attended the school but changed strategy after some community leaders, including Ashmore, Henry Woods, and Edwin Dunaway, advised him to make a tear-jerking radio speech, claiming innocent involvement that was quickly rectified after he realized what Commonwealth College really was. Ashmore, the wordsmith, wrote the speech, which was credited for turning around the race in Faubus's favor and causing a backlash against Cherry. Faubus won the primary and the general election.

Said Michael Dougan: "Of course the irony in all of this is that by putting Orval Faubus in the governor's office, Ashmore inadvertently had created the person who was going to symbolize opposition to progress and desegregation in Arkansas and become his biggest political enemy."[50] No one could envision that "the Faubus the state had elected was not the Faubus it would for so long have," Dougan wrote.[51] In fact, Faubus's father, Sam, had been a card-carrying Socialist who had circulated petitions years earlier for such initiatives as women's suffrage, old-age pensions, and the abolition of the poll tax,[52] and he gave his son the middle name Eugene in honor of the Socialist leader Eugene V. Debs.[53] Although they would be overshadowed by the Little Rock Central crisis, Faubus initiated several progressive accomplishments during his tenure in the statehouse, including improvements in public education; the establishment of the Arkansas Children's Colony, the first institution for underdeveloped children; expansion of state parks; and the paving of hundreds of miles of highways.[54]

When the *Brown* decision came down in 1954, Ashmore and Patterson were ready for it, but a story retold in the *St. Louis Post-Dispatch* in a tribute to Heiskell after his death illustrated the old man's dilemma. It recounted Heiskell watching a news service teletype revealing the news of *Brown*. "He turned to a colleague and said, 'Richmond has fallen'—and immediately began his own form of Reconstruction."[55] Heiskell's words from February 23, 1929, came back to haunt him: "You never can tell when the whirligig of time is going to whirl around and do some gigging."[56] Indeed, it must have been extremely difficult for an old man to watch the foundation of much of his whole way of life begin to crumble. And when it finally fell, it must have been devastating for him to realize that America had, essentially, passed him by. To compensate, he fell back on the other reliable precept of his life—adherence to law and order.

The opinion of the majority of southerners was vehemently against *Brown*, reflecting a common belief in segregation after the practice had been entrenched through generations. Little Rock, though, was an unexpected battleground in the school desegregation fight. As a borderline southern state, Arkansas had appeared to be ready for the gradual desegregation of its largest school district in the months leading up to the opening of the 1957–1958 school year. Desegregation had previously occurred with few problems in Charleston and Fayetteville, in the northwestern part of the state. In Hoxie in northeast Arkansas, it did proceed with strong local leadership despite outside interference—but not interference from the statehouse. Little Rock, though, was a state capital and thus much more high profile, and Faubus, who by then was aiming for an almost unprecedented election to a third two-year term as governor, seized on the issue he hoped would solidify that reelection.[57] Jim Johnson, Faubus's more conservative Democratic opponent in 1956, agreed that Faubus's response was a political move. "He needed some turmoil," Johnson said. "I'm convinced that he was playing the gallery—what is the most opportune thing that could come of this? Well, I knew him for the political opportunist that he was. I never doubted that."[58]

Not surprisingly, it was difficult for Heiskell to accept the new society the *Brown* decision portended. He was a firm believer in segregation, having known nothing else for all of his nearly eighty-five years. He was not a typical racist, although he held a patriarchal view of race relations. Patterson, regional chairman of the National Council for Public Schools, got into a bit of trouble with his father-in-law when he was quoted in a wire service story while out of state agreeing with the *Brown* decision as "the only decision that could have been made" in the fundamental matter.[59] Ashmore wondered, perhaps jokingly, if Patterson would be fired.[60] A family meeting convinced Heiskell of the strategy he and his paper should take. Jerry Dhonau, a *Gazette* reporter during the Little Rock crisis, remembered a conversation with Louise Heiskell Patterson several years later in which she recalled a family gathering near the time of the crisis. She said she and her husband had had to work on her father to get him to agree with the proposed stand. The winning argument was that his grandchildren should not have to grow up in a society that was racially unjust.[61] As recounted by the Heiskell biographer Rutherford, Louise Patterson said later that the incident marked the first time in her life she had really stood up to her father. "I said I could not raise my children in an atmosphere of fear and hate, that the whole world was changing, that this was going to come whether we liked it or not and I had to have my children in a position to accept, and to live with it, and that we had to go along with it and encourage it. I think he was so dumbfounded that I stood up to him that he really didn't know what to say."[62] Enlightened family ownership thus allowed for the evolution of philosophies for the greater good.

Several entities were in agreement with the Little Rock School District's plan for gradual phased-in desegregation in the months heading into the 1957–1958 school year. Those included the mayor, school board, superintendent, NAACP, and leading businessmen, including Ashmore, Patterson, and Heiskell, as well as one of Little Rock's two black newspapers, the *Arkansas State Press*.[63] *Brown*, though, was by no means popular, and by the eve of the new school year, word had circulated that Faubus was going to make a move to stop the planned desegregation. Roy Reed, who at the time was a young reporter for the *Gazette*, recounted the September 1, 1957, incident as Ashmore reported it later to him:

> Something was afoot. Harry asked to meet with Mr. Heiskell and Hugh Patterson downtown at the *Gazette* office. I should say by this time, Harry and Hugh had become great friends. They took the lead in making sure that the *Gazette*'s editorial position was the right one—law and order, no mobs in the street, obey the court orders—which at the time amounted to being the pro-integration stand. The three of them gathered for this meeting in Mr. Heiskell's office on the

> Sunday before school started on Tuesday and, as it turned out, before Governor Faubus called out the National Guard the next night to surround Central High School, to prepare for how we're going to treat this—what are we going to do? And as Harry recounted it to me, he said to Mr. Heiskell, "I know in my own mind what would be the right course for the paper to take, the stand that we should take, the editorial position. But it's not my paper. You stand to lose a lot of money. This is going to be an unpopular decision if we do this. It's not my decision to make." And Hugh was backing him up, and he knew exactly what stand Harry was talking about. And as Harry told it, the old man listened patiently and heard them out, and then he had a swivel chair and he turned the chair so that he could look out his window down Louisiana Street, and when he turned back around, he said, "I'm not going to let those people take over my town." And that was the answer that Harry and Hugh wanted. And that set the stage.[64]

After Faubus called out the National Guard to keep the nine black students out of Central in September 1957, Ashmore articulated the issue editorially not as one of segregation versus integration but as the supremacy of the Constitution of the United States in all matters of law.[65] Suddenly, it was a state versus federal government question,[66] and this made it easier for Heiskell to bear. Years later Ashmore recalled that with Heiskell's memory running back to Reconstruction, the older man knew that the consequences of such an action would be "a period of disorder that would end only with the second occupation of Little Rock by United States army troops, and beyond that immediate tragedy an embittered political struggle that would divide and dispirit the populace."[67] And he was right. When President Eisenhower ordered the 101st Airborne to Little Rock to enforce the law, it marked the first occupation of an American city by federal troops since Reconstruction.

With the nation and the world looking on, the *Gazette* newsroom excelled under the pressure. Reed, who was a reporter at the time, said he had never seen a newsroom more alive than it was that fall. "That's the kind of atmosphere that generates exceptional reporting because everybody is operating at one hundred percent capacity all the time," he said.[68] Charles Allbright, who wrote the *Gazette*'s "Our Town" column in 1957, recalled it as a strange, scary time, but ultimately a rewarding one. "There was a real feeling of knowing you were doing something right," he said. "We knew if we were going down, it would be for the right reasons. I have great admiration for Mr. Heiskell, who had nothing to gain but being right."[69]

Although the *Gazette* was praised internationally, it paid a heavy price at home, with "a huge number of white people all over the state" turning against it because of the editorial stance, Reed remembered.[70] Within two weeks of the September 4, 1957, front-page editorial "The Crisis Mr. Faubus Made," circulation dropped by twenty thousand. It had surpassed the one hundred thousand mark only a few weeks earlier. "The switchboard was jammed, people were trying to cancel their subscription," Gene Foreman, a *Gazette* reporter at the time, recalled.[71] Opponents organized boycotts, and mobs attempted to prevent trucks from delivering papers.[72] Jerry Dhonau, then a young reporter, recalled hearing the dollar loss from the crisis at $2 million. "I thought that spoke volumes of J. N. Heiskell and the owners, Hugh Patterson, Louise Patterson, to be willing to accept that kind of monetary loss for basically a principle," he said.[73] Such quality family ownership was willing to look beyond the heavy losses to the bigger picture.

It was a difficult decision for Heiskell in other ways as well. Socially, he faced criticism from friends—sometimes aimed strategically at Ashmore. Included in a 1958 Christmas card to him was the note, "What punishment my beloved Little Rock is taking! Wish I were there to 'scrap' with Harry Ashmore!!! But do remember me to Hugh!"[74] Financially, it was much worse. Ashmore called it an escalation from "skirmishing" to "guerilla war" as the *Gazette* stood alone while the opposing *Arkansas Democrat* "would play it safe and grow fat on our blood. . . . [Heiskell] had to bear with prudent friends who came to warn him that he had passed beyond considerations of financial loss, and that his newspaper faced extinction. If he felt panic, or entertained doubt, we never knew it."[75]

As the outsider, Ashmore took most of the heat for the *Gazette*'s stand. He was dubbed "Public Enemy No. 1" by the White Citizens Council of Arkansas,[76] one of many similar organizations established throughout the South to resist the implementation of the *Brown* decision. Ashmore wickedly explained that he had become "in the wonderful lexicon of our muted time, a 'controversial figure.'"[77] But Patterson took his share of criticism, too. Louise Patterson told Rutherford of an incident at the Country Club of Little Rock when her husband was confronted by someone who said, "We admire you and Mr. Heiskell, but that Ashmore . . . " As quoted in Rutherford, Louise Patterson recalled that her husband then blew up. "He said, 'I don't know what you're thinking. You either think that Mr. Heiskell and I are stupid and dupes of this man, or are not standing up for what we believe in by letting him go ahead and do it when we don't believe in it. Now which is it?"[78]

In his oral history, Reed remembered Bob Douglas, another former *Gazette* newsman, calling Ashmore "one of the great con artists" of journalism for getting Heiskell to endorse a stance of which he did not really approve.[79] Another *Gazette* reporter from the era, Patrick J. Owens, wrote following Heiskell's death that the greatest irony of the crisis was that the older man remained a segregationist pretty much until the end,[80] but the author argues that Heiskell's conscience would not allow himself or his newspaper to obstruct society's progress. He disagreed with that progress personally—even arguing with Ashmore's successor, James O. Powell, when, after the crisis passed, the *Gazette* editorialized in favor of desegregating Little Rock's public swimming pools.[81] But he was realistic enough to realize that he could not keep desegregation of society from happening. The *Saturday Review* described Heiskell's stance as allowing the evolution of American policy to occur orderly, safely, and with respect for the law.[82] Family ownership was the major factor in the *Gazette* getting there.

Faubus, on the contrary, was unwilling, at least politically, to let society progress in such a way. When he was first elected during the gubernatorial race in 1954, he drew criticism from the *Gazette* when he called desegregation the biggest issue in the race. Reed said that Faubus guessed early on that at the right time, the issue "eventually would elect a governor of Arkansas. He matter-of-factly told a small gathering of campaign associates at the Marion Hotel one day in 1954 that if he could find a way to capitalize on the race issue, 'they'll never get me out of office.'"[83] Ultimately, Faubus was elected to six two-year terms. In an October 1957 letter, Heiskell called Faubus's actions in pursuit of a third term a tragedy for the city and the state. "The *Gazette* has suffered from the emotionalism and prejudice that have been aroused," he wrote. "We feel, however, that the *Gazette* has gained new stature and respect."[84] To Heiskell, integration of the races was a problem that could not have a perfect solution. The best society could do, he believed, was to be sure that thoughtful citizens made the decision—not the radicals on either side. "The U.S. Supreme Court didn't consult me when they made their decision," he said. "I believe it would have been better if they had consulted some people in the South."[85]

Ashmore recalled that the *Gazette* "stood virtually alone in insisting that the Constitution must prevail."[86] Circulation ultimately fell by nearly twenty thousand (20 percent); many local businesses dropped advertising, and the *Gazette* was the subject of threats and intimidation. A local segregationist group, the Capital Citizens Council, organized a boycott against businesses that advertised in the *Gazette*, sending an anonymous letter to fifteen hundred local merchants. David Bluthenthal of the Gus Blass Company, Arkansas's largest department store, sent a copy to Patterson on December 11, 1957, with the note: "Here is a letter received this morning that I think is worthy of your waste paper basket."[87] The newspaper printed it and an answering editorial on the front page on December 13.[88] The letter read, in part:

> The *Arkansas Gazette* has identified itself with integration of the races. When white people think of Negroes in our schools and bayonets in our backs, they automatically think of the *Arkansas Gazette*. Before long your store will be identified with this class. The white people will soon be saying, "The *Gazette*, supported by (firm name), is cramming the Negro down our throats." . . . There is a rising tide of race feeling—in fact a revolution is beginning in the South and Little Rock. Your store and all stores that advertise in the *Arkansas Gazette* will be placed on one side or the other. This is your notice to make your own choice.[89]

The letter was signed, "An Indignant Group." The answering editorial clarified the *Gazette*'s position as having "never advocated integration."

> On the contrary, the *Gazette* has consistently supported every legal effort to maintain the social patterns of segregation, and will continue to do so. . . . Until and unless the court decision in this case is reversed, the Little Rock School Board's program can be halted only by naked defiance of the law. This the *Gazette* has opposed, and will continue to oppose. To do less would, in our judgment, be to invite a state of anarchy. Since violence erupted at Little Rock Central High School, the issue before our people has not been segregation or integration, but law and order. The refusal, or inability, of local law enforcement agencies to carry out the directives of the court inevitably brought about the use of federal force—a situation the *Gazette* did not invite, but warned against and used all its influence in a vain effort to prevent.[90]

For all their courage, Ashmore, Heiskell, and Patterson stopped short of advocating integration. In hindsight, it is easy to criticize this decision as a weakness of spirit, but when placed in the time and place, the law-and-order stance was likely as far as they could go. Certainly, Heiskell would have had a harder time with it than Ashmore and Patterson.

The editorial called the letter writer representative of "a small group of extremists who seek to rule this city by terror, coercion and boycott of the sort typified in this anonymous letter."

> This newspaper is their immediate target, but it is not their only one. They have used the same technique of slander, vilification

> and abuse against the respected members of the Little Rock School Board and its officials and attorneys, against the successful candidates for the new City Manager Board of Directors, against the ministers of the city's leading churches, and against some business firms—in short, against any person, public or private, who has taken a firm stand for law and order and condemned the mob rule which they advocate. The *Gazette* does not believe that this revolution will succeed. But we do believe that the people of Arkansas should be aware that it is under way—and should understand what its ultimate cost could be, not to this newspaper, but to all of us.[91]

The boycott failed because the newspaper's large advertisers, particularly department stores, refused to join it. In fact, in February 1958, the state of Illinois, for the first time, ordered advertising in the *Gazette* to promote tourism. In a letter to Patterson, J. R. Work of Evans-Work Advertising Agency in Springfield, Illinois, wrote: "The responsible people of Illinois have long admired the courageous editorial policy of the *Gazette* and this advertising is, I believe, a modest expression of this regard."[92] In his response, Patterson wrote: "Ours has not been an easy editorial course, as you know. Honesty and forthrightness have their penalties. . . . We are also grateful that the sometime questioned newspaper virtues also have their rewards."[93]

Once the decision was made to urge Arkansans to follow the federal mandate—even though many in the state, including the old editor, did not agree with *Brown*—Heiskell was unwavering, although readership and advertising declined precipitously, and across town the *Arkansas Democrat* reaped the benefits. Through March 1958, the *Democrat*, which under its own local family ownership had "carefully avoided" taking a stand in the crisis, according to *Time*, gained more than six thousand readers for both its daily and Sunday editions, pulling within twenty-eight hundred of the *Gazette*'s daily circulation and ahead by three thousand on Sunday.[94] Patterson called the competing paper "a virtual house organ for the Governor and the white Citizens' Council."[95] Leon Reed, the longtime circulation director for the *Gazette*, said in 1967 that the *Gazette*'s numbers fell to 82,860 daily and 93,039 on Sunday from an average circulation of more than a hundred thousand. Circulation losses ran as high as $40,000 a month. Within a month's time, one-third of the newspaper's dealer and carrier organization was gone, and within ninety days, the entire setup had to be replaced.[96] Ultimately, the Heiskell family suffered a reported loss of $1–2 million—roughly the equivalent of $13 million today—before things settled down and the *Gazette* regained its status as the top paper in Arkansas.[97] The family ownership was rewarded for being patient and principled. Patterson told the *New York Times* in May 1958 that he believed some of the local advertisers, while not willing to take a public stand on the matter, showed their support by keeping their business with the *Gazette*.[98]

Heiskell, who turned eighty-five on November 2, 1957, might have easily distanced himself and laid the blame for the unpopular stand on Ashmore and Patterson as the younger, more progressive soldiers, but he would have none of it. He said multiple times that except for one day when he missed work, he read every editorial before it ran, thus implicitly giving his approval.[99] "Harry is a bold man," Heiskell said another time. "My editorials would have been more restrained but they would have stood for the same thing."[100] Roy Reed said Heiskell would write to those who complained, "If you have a problem, it is not up to Mr. Ashmore or somebody else, I am editor of this paper. I am responsible."[101] Heiskell's obituary in the *Gazette* in December 1972 recalled talk at the time in the community that Ashmore and Patterson were taking advantage of him and pushing their views as his. The older man wanted to publish a full personal endorsement of the newspaper's editorial stance, but he was talked out of it.[102] Bob Douglas, news editor during the crisis, said he was told that Heiskell wanted to include a final sentence in one editorial that would have placed blame for the crisis on the Supreme Court and the NAACP but that Patterson talked him out of it.[103] Patterson argued that such a deflection of blame would only dilute the paper's position. "To say to the mob . . . that it was not our fault would raise the level [of agitation]," he said.[104]

Although Heiskell wasn't a typical racist, he did have racist tendencies, but they were hidden beneath the veneer of patronage. Reed said Heiskell "thought it was the white person's responsibility to look after these unfortunate human beings who couldn't really look after themselves."[105] Heiskell was always quick to clarify his paper's stance during the crisis. "We opposed Governor Faubus' use of troops to defy a federal court order and we opposed mob violence," he said. "We have stood for better opportunities for negroes but we have never advocated integration."[106] Ashmore said that Heiskell did not consider desegregation to be either desirable or necessary. "He was able to convince himself that you could achieve racial justice, social justice, within the limits of a segregated society," Ashmore said.[107] During the crisis, Heiskell told the Associated Press at a meeting of the Southern Newspaper Publishers Association that the *Gazette* was promoting order—not supporting integration. He continued the conscience theme: "These things have not been pleasant but there comes a time when a newspaper man has to decide whether to follow his conscience or material considerations," he said,[108] reflecting the values that had made the *Gazette* a twentieth-century journalistic success story.

In a letter to his sister Effie, Heiskell wrote, "The *Gazette* is having to combat blind prejudice and unreasoning hate. All this is part of a newspaper's life."[109] Still, it must have been difficult for an old man to watch his whole world and much that he had believed in for eighty-five years crumble.

For its stance urging the people to follow the court's ruling, exhorting law and order, obedience to the court order, and no mobs in the street, the *Gazette* was awarded two Pulitzer Prizes on May 5, 1958. The gold medal "for disinterested and meritorious public service" went to the newspaper "for demonstrating the highest qualities of civic leadership, journalistic responsibility and moral courage in the face of mounting public tension during the school integration crisis of 1957." The Pulitzer Prize for distinguished editorial writing went to Ashmore "for the forcefulness, dispassionate analysis and clarity of his editorials on the school integration conflict in Little Rock."[110] The *Gazette* thus became the first newspaper to be awarded two Pulitzer Prizes in the same year for coverage of one event.[111] The public service citation continued: "The newspaper's fearless and completely objective news coverage, plus its reasoned and moderate policy, did much to restore calmness and order to an overwrought community, reflecting great credit on its editors and its management."[112]

Harry Ashmore, J. N. Heiskell, and Hugh B. Patterson in the Gazette *newsroom, May 1958, following the announcement that the* Gazette *had won two Pulitzer Prizes in 1958. Courtesy of UALR Center for Arkansas History and Culture.*

Following the Pulitzer announcement, Heiskell reiterated his newspaper's stance and the reason he was able to live with it: "My father spent four years defying the U.S. Government in the Civil War, but never defied it after the war was over. I'm not an integrationist—I'm a conservative. But it is unthinkable that the governor should use the State Guard to try to nullify the order of the [United States] Supreme Court."[113] Writing in the *Syracuse Herald-Journal*, Alexander F. Jones said the phrase "meritorious public service" was the understatement of the year.

> There isn't a finer example of the operation of a free and unafraid newspaper in the history books than that of the *Arkansas Gazette* when the governor of the state was using force to defeat the courts. . . . [W]hen the chips were down, and at an age when most men are either in their graves or their dotage, [Heiskell] emerges as a giant—one of the men for whom the authors of the American Constitution created a free press in the very first amendment. He and his newspaper and his colleagues are a beacon for us all.[114]

Heiskell, though proud, took the news of the Pulitzer awards with the same even temperament that he had taken the controversy. On May 6, the day after the awards were announced, he walked into Ashmore's office after reading proofs of the editorials that would run in the next day's edition. "Harry," he said, "I don't want to say anything grouchy after the jubilation of yesterday—but these editorials are dull."[115]

Not everyone in Arkansas took pride in the Pulitzers. Two months later, under the headline, "The Greatest Honor of All," the *Arkansas Democrat* ran a house ad that appeared to be in response to the Pulitzer announcement:

> The greatest honor which can be bestowed on any newspaper is the acceptance it enjoys and the endorsement of its policies by the people living in the area it strives to serve. Such acceptance on the part of the public evidences that the newspaper is close to the people it serves and reflects the opinions and thinking of the majority of the citizens in its circulation area. The *Arkansas Democrat* is highly appreciative of the honor which the people of Little Rock—North Little Rock—Pulaski County—Little Rock's 26-County Retail Trading Zone and throughout Arkansas have bestowed on it in making it the first newspaper circulation-wise and their popular choice.[116]

The ad claimed higher circulation for the *Democrat* in the city and retail trade zone with a total paid daily circulation of 86,925 and total paid Sunday circulation of 100,905. The tag line called the *Democrat* "Arkansas'

Most Popular and Fastest Growing Newspaper."[117] The *Democrat*'s ownership thus proved that family proprietorship alone was no guarantee of quality journalism.

Besides the Pulitzers, other honors rolled in for Heiskell, Ashmore, and the *Gazette* for their coverage of the crisis. In November 1957 the paper received Sigma Delta Chi's "Courage in Journalism" award and a special citation by the Associated Press Managing Editors Association. In March 1958, Syracuse University's School of Journalism awarded the paper its Medal and Citation for distinguished service to journalism. Besides the Pulitzers, May also brought the first Columbia Journalism Award from the Columbia Graduate School of Journalism, which Heiskell said marked one of the greatest days of his life.[118] As a newspaper owner, he was technically not eligible for a Pulitzer Prize.[119]

The Mothers League of Central High, another segregationist group, declared May 29, 1958, to be "Liberation Day" from federal invasion when the National Guard troops were released from federal duty. The group announced a sarcastic "Recognition Award" for the newspaper, presenting the resolution to *Gazette* reporter Jerry Dhonau and photographer Rodney Dungan as representatives of the newspaper when they came to cover the meeting. Heiskell, Ashmore, and Patterson were recognized "for betrayal of Little Rock, Arkansas, and the Southland." The citation mentioned the awards the *Gazette* was receiving "in New York, Washington, and other far-removed places" and declared it would make public the group's award "so that people everywhere may know in what low esteem said newspaper and those listed are held by their home people."[120]

However, the local notoriety hardly stopped the paper from receiving other honors. In July the Elijah Parish Lovejoy Fellowship of Colby College for courageous journalism was awarded to the *Gazette*; the Freedom House award, "for devotion to principles—for courageous and responsible journalism in a time of crisis" followed in October 1958.[121]

At every event, Heiskell reiterated the *Gazette*'s stance and vowed that despite the hardships, he and his paper would make the same decision again because it would be impossible not to do so and remain faithful to his editorial beliefs—including that of the newspaper as conscience.[122] His remarks at the Freedom House dinner in New York on October 14, 1958, summed up his philosophy of the crisis and of journalism itself:

> [M]aterial losses and abuse and misrepresentation may well be borne for the recompense of the respect of right-thinking people . . . Every newspaper must come to judgment and accounting for the course that forms its image and its character. If it is to be more than a mechanical recorder of news; if it is to be a moral and intellectual

> institution rather than an industry or a property, it must fulfill the measure of its obligation, even though, in the words of St. Paul, it has to endure affliction. It must have a creed and a mission. It must have dedication. It must fight the good fight. Above all else it must keep the faith.[123]

Heiskell family ownership had made possible such an editorial philosophy. The old man's conscience was rewarded by the reaction of friends and admirers. To celebrate the Pulitzers, the largest crowd then ever assembled in the history of Little Rock's Marion Hotel—925 people—recognized the newspaper and its leaders.[124] Mrs. Adolphine Terry, a prominent Little Rock liberal, had praised Heiskell early in the crisis, saying she had admired his wit, integrity, and information, but she had criticized his conservatism until then. "And now, he has made his paper a tower of strength with his eyes on the future and not in the past," she wrote,[125] affirming his family ownership. Congratulatory letters and telegrams poured in from readers and editors from across the country, including one from the *Richmond Times-Dispatch*'s Virginius Dabney, who was "far from happy" over the *Brown* decision but "profoundly grateful" to Heiskell and Ashmore for their journalistic integrity. Ashmore responded with characteristic wit: "I keep hoping that ultimately this madness will pass and all of us in the South can get around once again to important subjects like sex and whiskey." Heiskell responded to a congratulatory letter from R. L. McGrath, managing editor of the *Seattle Times*: "Our paper was made the target of angry words and reprisals, but they are outweighed by the approval of people whose opinion we value most, as well as by our confidence that we followed the sound course."[126] Editorial praise flowed in newspapers and magazines throughout the United States and beyond.[127] According to the *Saturday Review*, a journalist from outside the state said of the oldest newspaper west of the Mississippi: "The *Gazette*, God bless her, is justifying for every newspaper in the country the guarantees of free speech in the Constitution. This is the kind of situation where they separate the men from the boys and the great newspapers from the ones that just set type."[128] The *Wichita Beacon* wrote:

> It is easy enough for a Yankee paper to take a strong stand on things that are happening in Arkansas. It is far from easy for an Arkansas editor to do so. In the long run [t]he *Gazette* policy will strengthen the paper. Today, however, there are undoubtedly hot-blooded Faubus adherents who are raising merry hell with the editor. No editor likes to make enemies. Sometimes he must make enemies because he believes in something. Hurrah for the *Gazette*.[129]

Ashmore recalled telling Heiskell's daughter Elizabeth after the turmoil that he feared her father's role in the 1957 crisis would never be fully appreciated. Her response was, "I suppose so. But, you know, if we knew the truth I suspect we would find he enjoyed it."[130]

David Pryor, who would serve as governor of Arkansas from 1975 to 1979 and United States senator from 1979 to 1997 and who had begun his career just out of the University of Arkansas as a young newspaper publisher in Camden, explained the leadership of the *Arkansas Gazette* for the state during that era:

> The *Gazette* was a voice of reason, and I've always thought that the independent newspapers of our state . . . the small dailies and weeklies out there, those little newspapers made us different. They made us progressive. They had the courage to speak out many times, and they spoke out when they had to and when they needed to. But the thing that gave them courage, I think, what gave them courage, was knowing they were in the wake of the mother ship. And the mother ship was the *Gazette*.[131]

Patterson has perhaps never received his due for his contribution to the *Gazette*'s stand in 1957. Bill Rutherford wrote that Patterson "took more arrows than bouquets" as many critics saw him as more the owner's son-in-law than "an embattled publisher who also was standing on principle." But in 1987, quoted in Rutherford, Ashmore gave his old friend solid credit: "Hugh was the one who was gung ho," he said.[132] Indeed, the two younger soldiers won the generational battle with Heiskell. As Ashmore remembered it, again quoted in Rutherford:

> I think that he never could see the situation the way Hugh and I saw it. . . . And he simply found it very difficult, having grown up in a totally segregated society, one in which the question really never had arisen. I think he had a strong sense of justice. He recognized when it could be pointed out to him that the segregated society was inherently unjust and that blacks were not receiving equal treatment. [On] any specific case of inequality, I think, he had no hesitation. When it came to the social question which was involved in the school case, I think he found that hard to accept, but he did accept it. He certainly never, never took any position with me that restrained the position we were arguing editorially throughout that period.[133] . . . It was always my argument that what we were talking about was not integration; we were talking about desegregation. We were talking

> about removing the legal barriers and then what would follow would be a relatively gradual process of people actually accepting in the social situation an equality of treatment, but that could not be done by law. You couldn't change the hearts and minds of men by law, but by law you could remove the barrier. This also was Martin Luther King's argument.[134]

The *Gazette* under Heiskell, Ashmore, and Patterson was one of a handful of southern newspapers that advocated moderation, tolerance, and obedience to federal law during the desegregation crisis and the ensuing civil rights movement and inspired a new generation of journalists. Others included the *Atlanta Constitution* under Ralph McGill and Eugene Patterson; *Delta Democrat-Times* of Greenville, Mississippi, under Hodding Carter Jr.; *Tuscaloosa News* under Buford Boone; *Norfolk Virginian-Pilot* under Lenoir Chambers; and *Lexington (Miss.) Advertiser* under Hazel Brannon Smith. Each of those journalists won Pulitzer Prizes for editorial writing.[135]

After the rocky 1957–1958 school year, the turmoil continued, with Faubus closing the Little Rock schools in 1958–1959 rather than accept desegregation. But on May 26, 1959, an election swept out Faubus's allies on the Little Rock School Board, and the schools reopened on August 12, 1959, effectively ending the ongoing crisis.

Ashmore had said after the Pulitzer announcement that he was confident the *Gazette* would recover from the crisis and emerge from the ordeal stronger than ever.[136] A few weeks after the schools reopened, sensing that his work was done and believing that his ongoing presence would hamper the *Gazette* in that recovery, Ashmore left the newspaper and what he called his role as "personal devil" of Faubus[137] to become a consultant at the new center for the Study of Democratic Institutions, established by the Fund for the Republic, at Santa Barbara, California, and, concurrently, as editor-in-chief of the *Encyclopedia Britannica.* Heiskell hated to see Ashmore's move. "He has served this newspaper and this state well during a difficult period," he was quoted as saying in the *Gazette*'s coverage of Ashmore's departure. "His decision to accept the position with the center actually was delayed on his own motion for more than a year because of the school situation here."[138] In a handwritten note, Heiskell wrote: "Harry Ashmore is leaving the *Gazette* for what looks like a dream position with the Fund for the Republic, of which he is a director. The organization is moving to Santa Barbara, California, which I suppose is an especially desirable place of residence."[139] Ashmore's departure was cause for celebration among some Arkansans, eliciting this response from Louis Graves, editor of the *Nashville (Ark.) News*:

> Few Arkansans agreed 100 percent with Harry Ashmore, whose liberal political philosophy and support of the 1954 Supreme Court decision concerning school segregation was not in accord with public thinking in the state. But few will deny that the *Arkansas Gazette* editor since 1947 had great courage and a skill with editorial matter, skills which were recognized in the award of the Pulitzer Prize. . . . In the wake of his resignation from the *Gazette*, it can be said that his readers knew where he stood when the pressure was the greatest and in his convictions he was unyielding in the face of majority disapproval. Politically, he was and is too liberal for us when it is our conviction some conservatism must be restored to national government if we are to survive as a Democratic nation, and we have disagreed with Harry Ashmore, but our disagreement must be leavened with some admiration for his ability and courage.[140]

The J. N. Heiskell family ownership had allowed Harry Ashmore, in building on the legacy of the family's commitment to quality journalism, to change Arkansas history. But any thought that Ashmore's successor might moderate the *Gazette*'s editorial tone was short-lived. On September 27, 1959, the *Gazette* announced Ashmore's replacement on page one. James O. Powell had been associate editor of the *Tampa (Fla.) Tribune*. Powell called the *Arkansas Gazette* "a desirable place for an ambitious young liberal newspaperman to go."[141] With the blessing of the Heiskell family ownership, he would continue Ashmore's liberal legacy. To many, that proved to be comforting; to others, including Governor Orval Faubus, it allowed them to continue to curse the Old Gray Lady. "The *Gazette* seldom endorses any cause or action unless it is atheistic, immoral, or pro-Communist," Faubus once said.[142] Having survived the worst of the crisis, the *Gazette* under Heiskell ownership would see its unpopular stance vindicated and come back stronger than ever.

CHAPTER FOUR

1960–1970: The Aftermath of Central High

FOLLOWING THE CRISIS at Little Rock Central High, the *Arkansas Gazette* under Heiskell family ownership continued to stress quality journalism. Over the decade of the 1960s, that quality would lure back most of the readers who had defected because of their anger over the editorial stance from 1957. In the decade following the Pulitzer announcement, the Heiskell family ownership continued to invest in the newspaper, improving both news and sports coverage, and maintained the *Gazette*'s role as the state's voice of progressivism. Once Orval Faubus finally left the governor's office in 1967, the *Gazette* under Heiskell influence played a major role in the development of progressive politicians who were able to help the state overcome the black eye suffered because of the crisis at Central High. James O. Powell, who replaced Harry Ashmore as the *Gazette*'s editorial page editor, recalled Dale Bumpers, eventually a two-term governor and four-term United States senator, contending that the *Gazette* was what made Arkansas politically moderate and so different from its more right-wing southern neighbors such as Louisiana, Mississippi, and Alabama.[1]

After Little Rock Central, the battles of the nation's civil rights movement moved on to other cities in the South—Montgomery, Greensboro, Anniston, Birmingham, Oxford, Philadelphia, and others. Central High had taken its toll on Arkansas and the *Gazette*, but as time passed and tempers cooled, the state eventually moved on toward that more progressive future, and the *Gazette*, under Heiskell family ownership, used its moral authority to lead the way, even when the cause was not popular. It had been battered but stood firm in the face of conflict beginning in 1957, and J. N. Heiskell reiterated for the rest of his life that were it ever faced with a similar predicament, the *Arkansas Gazette* under his stewardship would not hesitate to take the same stand in "the crucial choice between the safe and easy way and the hard and hazardous course that is the line of duty." Any criticism, he maintained, was actually validation that his newspaper had done the right thing.[2] By the end of the decade, he would be proven right.

As the 1960s began, the *Gazette*'s circulation numbers remained behind those of the *Arkansas Democrat,* 88,027 to 85,979 daily and 104,546 to 96,826 Sunday, as reported to the Audit Bureau of Circulations.[3] But with the crisis at Central High fading into memory and the *Gazette* continuing its recovery from the damage, Heiskell took some time for travel and personal celebration. At eighty-seven, and after everything he and his newspaper had endured for the last three years, it was well deserved. In February 1960, J. N. and Wilhelmina Heiskell spent some time in the Caribbean—Antigua, Barbados, and the Bahamas were among the stops.[4] In April, he wrote that he planned to give his wife a Mercedes-Benz automobile for a golden wedding anniversary gift.[5] In June, the Heiskells sailed from New York on the *Mauretania* for a European vacation. "This may be my last trip to Europe and if plans go through it will be a grand fling," he wrote.[6] After landing in Le Havre, France, they continued an itinerary that included stops at Nice, Genoa, Rome, Florence, Stuttgart, Berlin, Luxembourg, and Reims before they sailed home on the *Liberte.*[7]

The *Gazette* was in good shape a year after the crisis ended, although some ill will would remain for years. As the memory of the crisis faded, the *Gazette*'s circulation rebounded and eventually dominated the other paper's.[8] The *Gazette* regained the daily lead, 87,869 to 87,526 by 1961[9] and took over the Sunday lead, 102,203 to 100,753 by 1962.[10] By 1965, the *Gazette*'s lead had stretched to nearly twelve thousand daily and eight thousand Sunday.[11] By 1970, the *Gazette* dominated, 110,096 to 79,959 daily and 128,026 to 96,381 Sunday.[12] The postwar years were generally a period of growth for American newspapers, and after the vestiges of the Central High crisis passed, the *Gazette* was probably healthier than most as it continued to grow despite the increasing competition from television and the national trend toward suburbanization of newspapers. In a private nationwide poll of publishers, in fact, the *Arkansas Gazette* ranked twenty-first on a list of the top American daily newspapers. The *New York Times* headed the list. The *Gazette* ranked ahead of such larger papers as the *New Orleans Times-Picayune, Portland Oregonian, Chicago Sun-Times, Philadelphia Inquirer, Dallas Morning News, Minneapolis Tribune, Richmond Times-Dispatch, Atlanta Journal, Des Moines Register, San Francisco Chronicle, Wall Street Journal, Detroit News, Hartford Courant, New York World-Telegram and Sun, Oklahoma City Oklahoman, Cincinnati Enquirer, Memphis Commercial Appeal, San Francisco Examiner, Houston Post, Sacramento Bee,* and *St. Petersburg Times.*[13] Michael Dougan, Arkansas historian, said the newspaper improved in quality after 1957 because Heiskell "continued to hire the best talent available and give it the freest range. So the *Arkansas Gazette* entered its last decades as good as any newspaper could be in a time when newspapers, and especially good newspapers, were becoming more and more irrelevant to American life."[14] As the *Democrat*'s circulation advantage faded and it, like afternoon papers across the country, faced the daunting competition of a vibrant and growing television news cycle, the *Gazette* solidified its unusually healthy status.

The *Gazette*'s reputation was not built entirely on the Little Rock Central crisis. For years, reflecting its principal owner, it had been known as a paper with high standards of literacy, thanks to Heiskell's protectiveness of the English language.[15] Ernest Dumas, who came to the *Gazette* in 1960 after graduating from the University of Missouri, said the newspaper was unusual in the South. "It was a very literary journal and had that reputation, so people were eager to work at the *Arkansas Gazette*," he remembered.[16] He said he had admired the newspaper's principled stand and courage in 1957, which had made him want to work there.[17] Like Dumas, eager young journalists from all over the country, including Patrick J. Owens, Pat Crow, Bill Whitworth, Gene Foreman, Charles Portis, Jim Barden, Richard Allen, Jim Bailey, and Chris Kazan, to name just a few, made their way to the newspaper; many eventually moved on to some of the country's largest and most prestigious newspapers and magazines, including the *New York Times*, *New York Herald-Tribune*, *Philadelphia Inquirer*, *Newsday*, *New Yorker*, *International Herald-Tribune*, and others.[18] "An ambitious young reporter knew if he did well at the *Gazette*, he could move on to another paper without any trouble," said Roy Reed, who went on from the *Gazette* to a long career with the *New York Times*. "That's one reason that the *Gazette* was so grieved when it died because it was not just local people who grieved. They were all over the country, scattered everywhere, and they all had a special feeling about the paper."[19] Others, like Dumas and Bailey, made their careers at the *Gazette* and remained there until the end.

True to the philosophy of the Heiskell family ownership, even after Ashmore's departure, the *Gazette* continued to be Arkansas's voice of progressivism. In a tribute after Heiskell's death, Owens, one of those *Gazette* alumni who had moved on to bigger papers, wrote that Ashmore's legacy lived on at the *Gazette* long after he left, pointing to a March 1965 editorial that commented on the murder of Mrs. Viola Liuzzo in Alabama by the Ku Klux Klan, nearly six years after Ashmore left the paper: "The American people have had all they will bear: Their minimum requirements now will surely be a swift and sure implementation of voting right guarantees and the strictest surveillance of racial terrorism permissible within the concepts of the Constitution. It is up to Congress and the President to translate the national will into action."[20]

The *Arkansas Democrat*, which had seen great benefits from the *Gazette*'s stance during the crisis, found those benefits to be fleeting. "As the crisis faded and people began to forget, the [*Gazette*'s] circulation began to grow again," Dumas recalled. "Sometime in the early 1960s it surpassed the *Democrat* and moved far, far ahead."[21] Arkansans loved or hated it, but large numbers of them read it. In a special section celebrating the one hundred fiftieth anniversary of the paper's founding, Bill Lewis wrote: "*Gazette* subscribers, indeed, seem to take an almost proprietary interest in the morning newspaper; they may praise or curse it, but they find it almost as necessary to their life style as breath itself. Few readers are indifferent to it."[22] Indeed, it was not difficult to know where the paper stood editorially on almost any issue, as Lewis wrote: "In modern times, it has served as a kind of collective conscience, always reflecting the liberal and progressive approach that conflicts—violently, at times—with public sentiment."[23] In an interview, Lewis called the relationship the *Gazette* had with its readers "indefinable." "It was a very conservative state, and the *Gazette* was always a liberal newspaper," he said. "How it managed to stay alive so long, I have no idea, except people could get mad about the editorials and still want the content."[24] In 1969, he wrote of a complaint frequently heard about the paper: "You can't live with it, and you can't live without it."[25]

One thing Arkansans could not live without—even during the dark days of the Little Rock crisis—was Orville Henry's coverage of the University of Arkansas Razorbacks. Henry had arrived at the paper just out of Little Rock Central in January 1942 as a copy boy,[26] "a scrawny, underweight, dour-visaged lad," as Sam Harris described him in the paper's sesquicentennial coverage.[27] Harris recalled that Henry worked his way into a sportswriter position, where he was encouraged by sports editor Ben Epstein and managing editor Clyde (Count) Dew to "develop his own style, write complete accounts of sports events and to qualify controversial judgments."[28] After Epstein left for a job with the *New York Daily Mirror*, Henry became sports editor of the *Arkansas Gazette* on October 9, 1943.[29] Most of the men in the newsroom had gone off to war or were about to, and newsprint was rationed, so he had little to write about except some high school sports and little space in which to write it, but he "turned out more housewritten sports copy for the *Gazette* than was printed in all of the other Arkansas newspapers combined," Harris wrote.[30] After Ashmore's arrival, the *Gazette* gave more space to sports, and Henry became the media guru of the Razorback program as it moved into the modern era. His friendships, first with football coach John Barnhill and later, especially, Barnhill's successor, Frank Broyles, along with his comprehensive coverage of the program, helped the Razorbacks become a statewide obsession (and Arkansas a one-team state) and cemented himself and the *Gazette* as the authority on Razorback football. More than anyone else, Henry was credited with being the *Gazette*'s savior in 1957. Dumas recalled: "We had lost a fifth of our circulation, but it clearly would have been a lot more had it not been for Orville Henry. There were tens of thousands of people in Arkansas who read the *Gazette* for Orville Henry, who told you what you had to know about the Razorbacks."[31] Dougan said the *Gazette* had generally been considered to be "a leftist, pro-Communist, integrationist rag," when in reality most of its stances simply reflected mainline progressivism. Still, "Many readers would have loved to have gotten rid of it, but they had to keep it on account of the strength of its sports department," he said.[32] The *Gazette*'s reputation in sports journalism grew as the fervor for the Razorbacks did throughout the 1960s. Jerry McConnell, a sportswriter of the era, recalled subscribers coming up to him while he was on out-of-town assignments to tell him that the only reason they continued to take the *Gazette* was for its sports coverage. The high school football coach at Clarendon told him that the school board had ordered the teachers to stop taking the *Gazette* during the crisis and that only three people in town remained as subscribers. But those three copies were passed around so much that "that's the most worn-out, dog-eared paper. Everybody still read it; they just read the same copies." The family ownership recognized the importance of the sports section. McConnell said after the crisis the sports staff was given more resources—space and personnel—as a reward for its role in helping the paper overcome the hard times.[33] Those resources helped the newspaper's overall quality continue to improve. When the Razorbacks played in the 1960 Gator Bowl following the '59 season, the paper sent the entire sports department to Jacksonville, Florida, for the game, but only Henry and McConnell had to work. The rest got to enjoy the game. Back home, managing editor A. R. Nelson, news editor Bob Douglas, and city editor Bill Shelton put out the edition.[34]

Bill Lewis, the longtime general assignment reporter, stressed that the *Gazette* under Heiskell was a newspaper of record, calling it "poppycock" that its coverage was slanted. "Even if something I wrote conflicted with editorial policy, it ran," he said. "[I]t was an institution that [people] could rely on even if they hated the editorial page with a purple passion."[35]

The newspaper's ongoing quality continued to be recognized in the decade following Central High. On June 28, 1961, the National School Bell Award of the National Education Association went to the *Gazette* for "distinguished state or local reporting or interpretation of education." Heiskell received the John Peter Zenger Award in 1964 for "distinguished service in Freedom of the Press and the people's right to know." Leland DuVall, the newspaper's business and farm editor, was cited for "excellence in reporting and interpreting business and industrial news" by the Independent Natural Gas Association of America. On April 14, 1966, Heiskell received the Elijah Parish Lovejoy Award for "courage and integrity, fearlessness and long devotion to journalism."[36] On September 15, 1966, Sigma Delta Chi designated the *Arkansas Gazette* a historic site for leadership in state and civic affairs. It had previously made Heiskell an honorary fellow in 1958.[37]

Like newspapers across the country, the *Gazette*'s November 23, 1963, edition was filled with news of the assassination of President John F. Kennedy. That day's editorial read, in part:

> The loss is real, and the dismay genuine. More than any other of the free world's leaders, President Kennedy was the most nearly irreplaceable in his time and place, as Churchill and then Roosevelt had been in their earlier time and place. This was partly because of what America has meant—and continues to mean—to the hopes of the free world, but only partly. It also was because of what the man, Kennedy, meant to America—regardless of how many or how few of us were capable of realizing it in time.[38]

Such sentiment foreshadowed the despair that followed the *Gazette*'s own death twenty-eight years later. The loss of the president was poignant in Arkansas; Kennedy had been in the state only weeks earlier to dedicate Greers Ferry Dam on October 3. At his death, the Blass Company took out a half-page ad on the back of the A section that featured the Twenty-third Psalm.[39]

Under Heiskell ownership, the *Gazette* spoke out during the rest of the turbulent decade, which included the Vietnam War, the growing hippie and drug culture, the ongoing struggles for civil rights, and the ensuing riots, as reporter Wayne Jordan remembered.

> You're talking about an absolute social revolution. People did not have any moral compass. It was a crisis in the American system of government and the American way of life. You had to have someone to lead you to make sense of this. The *Arkansas Gazette* made sure that its readers had some kind of idea of what was benefiting them and what was their enemy and what was causing the turmoil in their hearts and in their minds, trying to give them moral direction.[40]

The *Gazette* thus responded as Arkansas's voice of progressivism. By 1964, the memory of the Little Rock Central crisis was beginning to fade, and the readers were coming back thanks to the quality of the newspaper and its editorial leadership. "The *Gazette* was easily the most outspoken daily paper in the South on racial issues," Patrick Owens wrote in *Newsday* after

Heiskell's death, but the strong positions "involved many a tense tussle with Editor Heiskell." But not all of them. During the Freedom Summer campaign in Mississippi, after the murders of civil rights workers James Chaney, Andrew Goodman, and Michael Schwerner, the *Gazette* editorialized harshly under Heiskell's headline, "Three Lost Men and a State's Well-being."[41] The *Gazette*'s Ernest Dumas and photographer Larry Obsitnik were the first media people on the scene when an accidental fire killed fifty-three civilian workers near Searcy while they were converting a Titan I silo to accommodate a Titan II missile in 1965. The incident became a major national story.[42] For years following the crisis, the *Gazette*'s state capitol corps had to work under the handicap of Governor Orval Faubus's rule that no news was to be released on the *Gazette*'s morning-publication cycle. Instead, press conferences were called for 8:30 A.M., which allowed the afternoon *Democrat* to get the story first. But the *Gazette*'s Ernest Valachovic beat the *Democrat* on 90 percent of the stories, Dumas said, by relying on career people at the state capitol and not Faubus appointees. "They would leak stuff to him," Dumas said. "Faubus was not pro-*Democrat*; he was anti-*Gazette*."[43]

As expected, the *Gazette* supported Kennedy's Democratic successor, Lyndon B. Johnson, in the 1964 presidential election against Republican senator Barry Goldwater. President Johnson thanked publisher Hugh B. Patterson following the endorsement, writing: "Through your newspaper, you have served your State and your Nation long and well. I will rely on your strength and your wise counsel in the days ahead."[44] Those days would be marred by the Vietnam War and the ongoing strife that engulfed the American people during the era. After originally supporting the United States government's involvement in Vietnam, the *Gazette* ultimately switched sides and editorialized against the war, enraging the right wing.[45] Powell recalled that the paper followed the lead of Arkansas senator J. William Fulbright, an early critic of the war. The *Gazette* was early to criticize army lieutenant William Calley, who was convicted of twenty-two counts of murder in Vietnam's My Lai Massacre, although public opinion across the country defended him. "We were opposed to what he'd done, but you didn't criticize the U.S. Army or a soldier, whatever they'd done," Powell remembered.[46] With the 1968 assassinations of the Reverend Martin Luther King Jr. and Senator Robert F. Kennedy adding to the nation's ongoing unrest, the *Gazette* continued to advocate unpopular stances, supporting school consolidation in Pulaski County and editorializing against Governor Orval Faubus and President Richard M. Nixon.[47]

In accepting the John Peter Zenger Award in January 1965, Heiskell titled his address, "The Newspaper: Keeper of the Community Conscience." In his introduction of Heiskell, Richard A. Harvill, president of the University of

Arizona, noted that Heiskell "never stood aside on any issue when he believed he was in the right."[48] In the address, Heiskell explained:

> Just as an individual may find his conscience put to test and trial and his courage challenged, so a newspaper may have to make the crucial choice between the safe and easy way and the hard and hazardous course that is the line of duty. If it finds itself embattled in time of controversy and crisis it can so acquit itself that reprisals against it translate into recognition of its courage and independence. Losses are gains, and words of denunciation are tribute and testimonial. For abuse, and for misrepresentation and material losses, there is recompense for a newspaper if it is known of all men that duty and obligation were rested in its keeping and were not betrayed. . . . There was reward not made with hands or spoken human voice. There was reward in conscience satisfied and the sense of duty done.[49]

Again, Heiskell represented the best of local family ownership. With each award announcement, editors and publishers from across the country—*Daytona Beach News-Journal*, *Washington Post*, *Tampa Tribune*, *Kansas City Star*, *New Orleans Times-Picayune*, *Des Moines Register and Tribune*, *Oregonian*, *Minneapolis Star and Tribune*, and *Atlanta Constitution*, among others—sent notes of congratulations. The *Constitution*'s Ralph McGill wrote to Heiskell: "I think it is the concensus [*sic*] of all Southern newspapermen that you are the chief figure in our pantheon of heroes."[50] James Russell Wiggins, editor of the *Post*, wrote that the *Gazette*'s "noble performance has made editors throughout America stand taller and take more pride in their profession."[51] Clark R. Mollenhoff, the Pulitzer Prize–winning Washington correspondent for the *Des Moines Register and Tribune* and *Minneapolis Star and Tribune*, wrote of his increasing admiration for the "great courage that it takes for publishers and editors to take a firm stand in the face of great economic pressures in the home community. . . . [Heiskell's selection for the award] will again emphasize the importance of steady courage at the editor and publisher levels. It is a point that must be made often."[52] As he had done so many times before, Heiskell exhibited many of the qualities of the best sort of family ownership.

A note from Evelyn D. Law, who read about the Zenger award in the *New York Times*, included these words: "If there was just one similarly brave newspaper editor in Mississippi perhaps there wouldn't be such a terrible situation there and perhaps those three young Civil Rights workers wouldn't be dead."[53]

On September 15, 1966, Sigma Delta Chi, the country's largest and oldest journalism society, formally designated the *Arkansas Gazette* as a historic site in journalism, just the twenty-fourth such designation. An aluminum plaque was unveiled outside the *Gazette* building with these words: "This marker is placed here to honor the *Arkansas Gazette*, oldest newspaper west of the Mississippi, and John Netherland Heiskell, editor since 1902. Under Heiskell's editorship the *Gazette* has exemplified his belief that the integrity of a newspaper and its responsibility to provide sound leadership are obligations to be fulfilled at all costs, whatever the pressures of an inflamed public opinion."[54] Sigma Delta Chi president Raymond L. Spangler, editor and publisher of the *Redwood City (Calif.) Tribune*, remarked at the day's luncheon that "'strong men weep when a newspaper dies.' If so, 'then the vigorous life of the *Arkansas Gazette* and your noted career as its editor must give them pleasure today,'" adding that the word "character" summed up the essence of the success of the *Gazette*.[55] Mark Ethridge, former publisher of the *Louisville Courier-Journal*, was twenty years prescient in his remarks, saying that in an era of absentee ownership, chain newspapers, and "letting the columnists say what the editorials should say, it is refreshing to find a newspaper independently owned, recognizing and using the full potential of the editorial page to benefit its own community."[56]

In 1967, the *Gazette* announced an increase in its advertising rates. Witt Stephens, the long-ago *Gazette* stockholder who was by then president and chairman of the board of Arkansas Louisiana Gas Company and one of the most powerful men in Arkansas, wrote publisher Patterson an unusual letter, congratulating him on the rate increase because it would make for a higher-quality newspaper. "It is impossible to run a newspaper like you do without additional rates," Stephens wrote. "As far as our company is concerned, we feel it is money well spent."[57] Patterson responded, noting the unique communication between advertiser and newspaper: "To say simply that it is appreciated would not begin to express our joyful and grateful reaction. You can be quite sure that it will be our purpose to try to continue meriting your good opinion."[58] Roy Reed called Patterson "every editor and reporter's dream of what a publisher should be," unlike "money-grubbing bottom-liners who don't care about quality." He said as publisher, Patterson understood that he was in charge of a great institution and that his job was to see that the paper made enough money so that its journalistic quality would continue and it would not have to skimp on expenses for the news product. Reed called Patterson a friend of the newsroom who did not meddle. "He stayed out of our hair," he remembered. "He was the kind of publisher every newspaper deserves and ought to have."[59] Jerry Dhonau, who moved from reporter to editor of the editorial page over his career at the *Gazette*, called Patterson the best publisher he ever worked for.[60]

The third generation of the Heiskell family arrived at the *Gazette* in 1968 when Carrick Heiskell Patterson, the son of Hugh and Louise Patterson, brought his Stanford degree back home. While he had worked summers at the newspaper, he came back this time intending to stay as the eventual heir apparent to succeed his grandfather as editor, although he remembered that after his return he was a "very, very, very junior reporter for quite a while."[61]

The major event marking the one hundred fiftieth anniversary of the paper's founding was the 1969 publication of a 428-page history of the early years of the newspaper by Margaret Smith Ross, the *Gazette*'s historian and author of the newspaper's popular Chronicles of Arkansas series. Ross had been hired as one of the few staff historians on a newspaper because Heiskell "was very conscious of the paper's role as the oldest newspaper west of the Mississippi, and that the study of history and the lessons to be learned from history were very important to the general education of a person who wanted to be a knowledgeable person, a competent person," Carrick Patterson said.[62] The book covered the years 1819–1866 and was intended to be the first volume in a series. In the foreword, Heiskell wrote of the close tie between the *Gazette* and the state. "The pages of this history tell the story of a newspaper and the related story of a Territory and a State," he wrote. "One could not be told without the other, because the newspaper wrote a continuous record of events, and discussed through the changing years the issues that filled chapters in the annals of Arkansas."[63]

Under Heiskell influence, the *Gazette* was a major force in the development of progressive Arkansas politics as the state eventually sloughed off the Faubus years and became known for its powerful representation in the United States Congress, first under Senator J. William Fulbright, a vocal critic of the Vietnam War. James Powell named Fulbright, Winthrop Rockefeller, Dale Bumpers, David Pryor, and Bill Clinton as central political figures in twentieth-century Arkansas history. Hugh Patterson remembered Fulbright saying he did not think he could have had the legislative career he had in the Senate if not for the longtime enlightening influence of the *Gazette*.[64] Unsurprisingly, during the years following Central High, the *Gazette* continued to oppose its old foe, Faubus. Following his election in 1954, however, the *Gazette*'s lack of support notwithstanding, he was reelected in '56, '58, '60, '62, and '64. Among Faubus's accomplishments were expansion of educational, public welfare, and economic development services to help recruit industry, but the shame of the Little Rock Central crisis would haunt the state for years to come.[65]

The political climate changed when Faubus decided against running again in 1966. Rockefeller, the transplanted New York Republican who had run against Faubus in '64, ran again in '66. After Faubus's retirement, the Democrats nominated Jim Johnson, the well-known, unapologetic segregationist firebrand who had challenged Faubus from the right in 1956. In the '66 campaign, the *Gazette* bucked its history to side with Rockefeller, editorializing:

> [The absence of party allegiance] is a point of major importance to the *Arkansas Gazette*, a newspaper which, with scant exception [a brief, unmentionable lapse during Whig years], has been Democratic in its philosophy and party orientation for nearly 150 years. . . . It is not Democrat vs. Republican; it is simply Johnson vs. Rockefeller. . . . We believe the election of Winthrop Rockefeller would mean the beginning of a new era.[66]

As quoted in Reed, Heiskell called the shift in support "a necessary interlude . . . when Winthrop Rockefeller made Republican reform more desirable than Democratic lassitude."[67] Years later, Johnson remembered that the *Gazette* "never stopped pounding my candidacy."[68]

Espousing a progressive agenda, Rockefeller was unlike the typical Arkansas Republican, and the *Gazette* editorialized that a Rockefeller victory would eventually help the Democratic Party find its way back from the Faubus years.[69] Rockefeller won with 54 percent of the vote to become the first Republican governor elected in the state since Reconstruction.[70] The day after the election, the *Gazette* praised Arkansas voters for repudiating racism, putting an end to the Faubus political machine, and electing "a moderate Republican whose ambitions and values offer great promise for the state."[71] During his tenure, Rockefeller shut down the casinos in Hot Springs, pushed through prison reform, and established an independent parole board. In April 1968, he was the only southern governor to hold a public memorial service after the assassination of Dr. Martin Luther King Jr., doing so on the steps of the Arkansas State Capitol.

Again with the *Gazette*'s support, Rockefeller was reelected in 1968, this time over Marion Crank, a longtime associate of Faubus. That year, Arkansas voters also sent the Vietnam War critic Fulbright back to the U.S. Senate, choosing him over the conservative Jim Johnson in the Democratic primary, and went for Alabama governor George Wallace, the independent candidate, for president. Rockefeller lost his 1970 bid for a third term in the statehouse to a Democratic newcomer, Dale Bumpers, who, with the full aid of the *Gazette*, continued the progressive agenda Rockefeller had attempted. "The *Gazette* had a tough time between me and Rockefeller," Bumpers said. "They had been strong Rockefeller supporters."[72] In the end, party loyalty won out in the *Gazette*'s choice in 1970, but the paper praised Rockefeller's accomplishments for years. "[I]n 1970, we supported Dale Bumpers, but that was because he had reformed—he and Rockefeller, together, in effect—had reformed the Democratic Party," James O. Powell, the *Gazette*'s longtime editorial page editor, remembered. "When Bumpers took over the Democratic Party, it became what it ought to be. Rockefeller was the great reforming catalyst."[73] In fact, Rockefeller, who had declared a moratorium on executions when he took office, used executive clemency on December 29, 1970, following his defeat by Bumpers, to commute the death sentences of all fifteen men on Arkansas's death row.

The *Gazette*'s 1966 assertion that a Rockefeller win then would eventually turn out to be good medicine for Arkansas's Democratic Party had proven to be true. Bumpers said he could not have been such a successful governor without the newspaper's support.[74] A string of progressive Democrats succeeded him, beginning with David Pryor, who, like Bumpers, wound up serving multiple terms in the United States Senate. Along the way, the *Gazette* was by their sides, advising, criticizing, and praising the new, post-Faubus era in Arkansas.

Pryor said the *Gazette*'s priority of progressive politics under Heiskell ownership gave such politicians a voice and an advocate, something that was not true in many states. He called the *Gazette* the state's voice of moderation and progressivism and recalled that its support on issues was not guaranteed just because it had favored a particular candidate in an election. "Once they made a decision, boy, they were tough," he said. "They were formidable if they took out after you. [Longtime editorial cartoonist] George Fisher could sizzle you good."[75]

Although certainly no liberal Massachusetts, as a border state, Arkansas was also no reactionary Mississippi or Alabama, either. Historians and others have remarked on the irony of the shame of an ugly school desegregation hullabaloo happening in what had been, with the notable exceptions of Governor Jeff Davis and Justice Jim Johnson, among some others, a politically moderate state. "Insofar as the integration crisis was concerned, the whole tragedy there was that we didn't deserve that," Bumpers said. "We were not a racist state, not like some states in the Deep South were, and the fact that that was so politically contrived was just a tragedy. We deserved better."[76] In the decade or so following Central High, Powell said there was an increasing liberalism in the pages of the newspaper as its editorial writers, still under Heiskell family ownership, dealt with segregation as a moral issue at the heart of society. "That transition was pretty typical among liberal newspapers in the South," he said.[77] While the *Gazette*'s stance in 1957 had been for law and order—not for integration—Powell said that as time went by, it became possible to discuss the racial situation in philosophical rather than legal terms. "The passage of time helped, but it was hard to overcome," he said. "All of us stuck to safer arguments for some years."[78] Ultimately, the *Gazette* under Heiskell ownership supported both the Civil Rights Act of 1964 and the Voting Rights Act of 1965,[79] signifying the evolution of attitudes of Heiskell and his editorial staff.

Although late, the newspaper eventually began to put its platitudes into practice. Whereas the *Arkansas Democrat* had hired Ozell Sutton as the first black reporter for a white-owned daily newspaper in Arkansas—and the first in the South—in 1950,[80] it wasn't until 1968 that the *Gazette* hired Wadie Moore Jr., who became its first black newsroom employee when Orville Henry hired him in the sports department. Moore recalled that he was unaware of his pioneer status, although he noticed "all the eyes looking at me when I walked through that second floor."[81] Although his comrades in sports quickly accepted him, it took longer for those in other departments to do so. About a year after his hire, he said, the ice was broken in the newsroom when Matilda Tuohey, one of the paper's early female reporters, shared her Sunday night popcorn with him.[82] "But I always had an ace in the hole, and that was Hugh Patterson," Moore recalled. "[The publisher] told me the day I walked in if I had problems to come see him. But I never did." The problems came from the outside. While answering the phone, "*Gazette* Sports," Moore got a few threats, and someone shot through his windshield while he was on assignment in north Arkansas.[83]

By January 1963, desegregation had come to Arkansas lunch counters, hotels, restaurants, and movie theaters, and Robinson Auditorium, the Little Rock Zoo, Arkansas Arts Center, public parks, and golf courses followed. By the end of 1963, Little Rock had integrated public services. School integration, however, was minimal and slow. ACORN (Arkansas Community Organizations for Reform Now), an interracial umbrella group with an emerging social justice coalition, formed. Arkansas liberalism in the civil rights era was mostly in Little Rock and around the University of Arkansas, and the *Arkansas Gazette* under Heiskell family ownership was a prominent leader.[84]

Despite all the successes, however, the Heiskell family ownership made some errors that would ultimately prove costly. For all of its prosperity, with the benefit of hindsight, the *Gazette* of the 1960s perhaps should have looked more to its future rather than becoming complacent in the aftermath of the Central High crisis. Having overcome a real threat to the newspaper's existence, Heiskell family ownership should have paid more attention to further improving the newspaper—infrastructure, for example—for quality's sake instead of being snookered into comparing it to its feeble competition. Such a comparison led to what would ultimately be a false sense of security and a tendency toward smugness and complacency that would eventually come back to haunt the Old Gray Lady.

Still, as Roy Reed, who left the newspaper for the *New York Times* in 1965, remembered, there was a special feeling about the *Arkansas Gazette.*

> We knew that it was a special place. We knew its history, the oldest newspaper west of the Mississippi, that the Heiskell family had owned it since 1902. That one family had been in charge of this newspaper for the unfolding of most of the twentieth century. But beyond that, we were trained in how to feel about our work. This is not just a way to make a living. It is not just a craft, manufacturing a product. It was almost a religious calling—and we all felt that. We pretended to be cynical, but we were not. We felt deeply that this newspaper had a reason for being, and it was to provide information. We were not to make mistakes. A lot of us were not terribly religious, but I think to a man and a woman, the people in that newsroom understood that to make a mistake in print was a sin, and you didn't do it. Of course we did, but you were awfully embarrassed about it. We paid the price in shame if we made a mistake. It was not just another place to work.[85]

As the decade of the 1960s ended, the *Gazette* had rebounded in circulation, advertising, and stature to the point that it was in the strongest position of its life, unquestionably the dominant newspaper in Arkansas, a strong moral compass for the state, and one of the country's leading publications. A quote from the newspaper's 1969 special section commemorating its sesquicentennial would prove to be relevant to the future of journalism: "In an age of emphasis on brevity and telegraphic style, when space is money and reading time a premium, the *Gazette* remains one of the few newspapers of the nation that does not stint on depth reporting, granting however many column inches are necessary to tell the full story."[86] Bill Lewis, known as a prolific writer, said under Heiskell family ownership, management never encouraged him to keep a story short. That would turn out to be one of his great conflicts with Gannett.[87] In the difficult 1960s, though, the newspaper was rewarded for bucking popular trends. After the turbulence of the decade, J. N. Heiskell would approach his centennial birthday as the grand old man of Arkansas; the *Gazette* was his Old Gray Lady.

CHAPTER FIVE

1970–1974: Mr. Heiskell's Death and the Transition of Ownership to the Patterson Family

AS THE 1970S DAWNED, both the *Arkansas Gazette* and the state were in far better shape than either had been when the Heiskell family entered Arkansas journalism in 1902, and much of the credit for both trends was due J. N. Heiskell, the editor and principal owner. But as he neared his centennial birthday, he and everyone else knew there was no way to stop the coming transfer of ownership to his heirs. He could only hope that the next generations had learned their lessons well. Through nearly seventy years of Heiskell family ownership, the *Arkansas Gazette* had stood for quality journalism and been the voice of progressivism in the state. As editor, J. N. Heiskell had battled governors, advocated progressive reforms for his adopted state, risked his family's livelihood for a principle, overseen the growth of his Lady from six thousand subscribers to a six-figure list, and become one of the country's most respected newspapers. Through it all, the old man had been the constant—the conscience of his newspaper, as he believed a newspaper should be the conscience of its community. In many ways, he had already outlived his time as he buried first his father, then his brother, and, finally, two sons, but he was malleable enough to, if not completely embrace, at least accept the changing American society that had, in many ways, passed him by.

At ninety-eight, Heiskell retained his title as editor. He had cut a distinctive figure in the newsroom since his arrival in 1902, with his tall, slender, conservatively dressed presence and gold-rimmed glasses.[1] Jim Bailey, the longtime sportswriter who arrived at the newspaper in 1956, called him "the living embodiment of the *Gazette*."[2] The Victorian Heiskell was unfailingly polite to his employees, always addressing them as "Mr. Foreman," "Mr. Reed," etc.[3] Gene Foreman, a young reporter during the 1950s, remembered him as a "paternalistic boss who wanted to take care of his staff."[4] Margaret

Ross, the newspaper's historian who worked closely with Heiskell, called him "a very courtly, formal man, mild mannered and very courteous," although he could be "quite demanding, and was a terrible nit-picker on occasion."[5] He never smoked; only late in life had he acquired the habit of a daily glass of sherry.[6] Although neat with his clothing and grooming, he maintained a notoriously messy office and desk, which was always piled high with newspapers, books, and correspondence, as was almost every piece of furniture in the room, prompting his wife to scold him that such clutter had to be a health hazard. He responded with characteristic wit, telling her: "Perhaps, my dear, that's why I died so young."[7] As he aged, he used a magnifying glass to read.[8] Roy Reed repeated the legend that when one new employee needed a typewriter, someone remembered that there was one in Heiskell's office. Although Heiskell disagreed, he acceded to the search, which yielded "two typewriters and the body of a reporter who'd been dead for eleven months."[9]

With his Victorian sensibilities, Heiskell had his taboos regarding what should not be on the front page of the *Arkansas Gazette*, always conscious of the fact that people often read it at the breakfast table. Among those taboos were pictures of snakes and dead bodies.[10] Bob Douglas, who spent more than thirty years at the *Gazette* in various newsroom positions, recalled that Heiskell would take a daily nap at the Little Rock Club, which then offered nap rooms, and that he only quit driving after he was well into his nineties.[11] Carrick Patterson remembered that his grandparents, while better off financially than most Arkansans, nevertheless lived lives of service, being conscious of the newspaper as a public service organization. "The newspaper was reasonably successful," he said. "But if you compare his wealth, his family's wealth, to that of many newspaper barons around the country, you would find that in fact the *Gazette* reinvested the majority of whatever profits it made into really quality employees and tried to keep the place reasonably modern in terms of equipment."[12] Such a strategy had played a major role in the *Gazette*'s attaining the status it had by 1970. Indeed, the family did not have other major financial holdings besides the newspaper, a fact that would hamper them in later years in their competition with the Hussman family and ultimately force them to sell to Gannett.

Heiskell came to his office daily until his ninety-ninth birthday and worked from his study at home after that, having his wife or secretary read the *Gazette*, the *Democrat*, and other papers to him after his eyesight failed him.[13] He sent memos and spoke to editors by phone, once advising James O. Powell that the editorials were "again" getting too long.[14] The wit, though, never faltered. At ninety-nine, his doctor pronounced him in perfect physical condition prior to a six-week vacation in Greece, adding that his kidneys were good for another twenty years. After a short pause, Heiskell asked the doctor, "And what am I going to do after that?"[15] Ross recalled that the old man was never profane except when it was essential to his point and wrote the story of the *Gazette* librarian once putting down the phone and reaching for the almanac after a caller wanted to know the world's highest dam. "Mr. Heiskell supplied the answer, 'GOD Dam,' in a voice so soft that it was heard only by a nearby reporter," Ross wrote.[16] After a rash of crimes involving homosexuality broke after the *Gazette*'s deadline, Heiskell posted a note on the newsroom bulletin board: "Christian civilization in Arkansas has reached a low level when these horrible, revolting sex crimes continue to be committed on the *Democrat*'s time. JNH."[17]

One of Heiskell's last public appearances came in 1971 when he shared with Mrs. David D. Terry the Brotherhood Award of the National Conference of Christians and Jews.[18] Ross said that although he continued to come to the office until his ninety-ninth birthday, his duties were so light that only his status as principal owner of the company kept him employed. "He did continue to send in his [editorial] paragraphs every few days, and to phone the office with his comments and suggestions, but this did not happen as often as it sounds like," she wrote in response to a scholar seeking information about centenarians. Ross called him "a militant grammarian" who resisted changes in the language that might reflect a breakdown of high literary standards. "He never used slang of any kind, and particularly deplored journalese," she wrote.[19] The historian Michael Dougan agreed that even in his latter days, Heiskell paid enormous attention to individual issues of the newspaper, calling in people who made grammatical mistakes or who in some way offended his sense of style. "The ultimate contribution of Heiskell to the newspaper was his commitment to a style and integrity to the product," he said.[20]

Dale Bumpers entered the Arkansas governor's office in January 1971, putting the Faubus years further into memory. James O. Powell contended that Bumpers helped the Democrats become what they should be in the state. And the *Gazette* under Heiskell family ownership encouraged the transition. In his first term, Bumpers was able to shepherd the first significant tax increase in the state since 1957 when he got an increase in the income tax—the first time since it was created in 1929—even though it required a three-fourths majority of the legislature. Powell, the *Gazette,* and the liberal Bumpers were of like mind: "I became more liberal after I turned forty, sometimes notoriously so," Powell said. "I like to think I got smarter as I got older."[21] And Heiskell allowed that. Whereas the *Gazette* had to couch its support for the 1957 desegregation of Little Rock Central in a law-and-order stance, by the 1970s, it could afford to be more obviously liberal about desegregation, dealing with it as a moral issue at the heart of society. In fact, Powell won an argument with Heiskell when the *Gazette* editorialized in favor of desegregating Little Rock's public swimming pools.[22] The state's voice of progressivism grew stronger with the passing years.

On November 2, 1972, Heiskell turned one hundred. To celebrate, the *Gazette* published an eight-page supplement honoring its grand old man. Bill Lewis, who wrote much of the copy, said the project had to be a secret because Heiskell would have refused both the honor and the expense.[23] James Powell remembered that by that time, the *Gazette* was simply the dominant newspaper in Arkansas.[24] Audit Bureau of Circulation figures for 1972 showed the *Gazette* with daily circulation of 108,752 to the *Democrat*'s 75,010 and Sunday numbers of 131,485 to the *Democrat*'s 93,390.[25] "Everything had worked out well, so his family pitched a centennial birthday party for him at the [Country Club of Little Rock]," he said. "I like to think that everybody who was anybody in Arkansas was there."[26] The guest list included four generations of the Heiskell family, Harry Ashmore, Senator J. William Fulbright, Governor Dale Bumpers, bankers, attorneys, businessmen, state and national leaders, E. K. Gaylord, owner of the *Daily Oklahoman* and *Times* at Oklahoma City, who was just a few months younger than Heiskell, and every employee of the *Arkansas Gazette*.[27] More than seven hundred fifty people greeted Heiskell, who had seemed to rally from the boredom he found in his retirement, the unproductivity of which chafed him. Orville Henry, the *Gazette*'s sports editor since 1943, remembered greeting him: "I almost had tears in my eyes, and he grinned. And he said, 'Well, Mr. Henry, you and I have become a couple of old fogies together, haven't we?'"[28] James Powell recalled the grand evening: "Mr. Heiskell, although not that strong at the time, although he seemed to be very well, sat there, and a parade of people came by and wished him well," Powell remembered. "The next morning, he suggested that I might prepare his obituary should he die on the *Democrat*'s time."[29]

Newspaper reporters and television journalists, many from out of town, were in to interview him for a couple of weeks before and a few weeks after the birthday, "and he was in very good spirits and seemed to feel very good," Ross said.[30] The last was Robert Carey, manager of the Little Rock bureau of United Press International. In that story for *The Quill*, published after his death, Heiskell said that newspapers often do not act in the public interest. "Newspapers have advocated strong stands on things that were primarily to the owners' advantage," he said. "Newspapers are human institutions, not perfect and not God-like."[31] Heiskell's own words even then stressed the importance of the quality of a newspaper's owner.

J. N. Heiskell at his centennial birthday celebration, fall 1972. Courtesy of the Arkansas Democrat-Gazette.

By early December, though, he was flagging. Ross said he didn't seem to be sick but just awfully tired. The day after Christmas, he went to the hospital for the second time since his birthday and died at 12:15 P.M. on December 28, 1972, at St. Vincent Infirmary. According to the obituary in the *Gazette*, the unofficial cause of death was "congestive heart failure caused by a general degeneration of the circulatory system in advanced age."[32] Hugh Patterson was quoted in the *Dallas Morning News* that Heiskell had been alert during the morning and wanted the newspaper to be read to him before his heart stopped.[33] In the obituary, Powell dwelled on the *Gazette* as a family institution and the heritage that Heiskell was passing on to his heirs.[34] Little did he nor anyone else realize how critical those factors would become to the Old Gray Lady's final nineteen years. No one could anticipate then an *Arkansas Gazette* without Heiskell family ownership.

Ross said on the surface, it appeared that Heiskell had set his own deadline. "Most of his friends and his family seem to agree that he was simply hell bent on living to be one hundred, and having accomplished that goal and enjoyed its afterglow, he neither expected nor tried very hard to live longer . . .

except, of course, not to spoil the family's Christmas by dying on or just before that day, Christmas being a very big time in their family," she wrote.[35]

Coincidentally, that day also marked the death of another longtime *Gazette* legend, police reporter Joe Wirges, who was so closely tied to the newspaper that he was called "Joe *Gazette*." Wirges had joined the newspaper as a copy boy in 1913. He left in 1916 but returned a year later and was there a total of forty-nine years before he retired in 1966. He was friendly with law enforcement officers across the state and was, according to his *Gazette* obituary, "a confidante of criminals and prisoners, an observer of scores of executions, a photographer and a man who was reputed to have a sixth sense about crime that often enabled authorities to solve crimes and to nip planned prison breaks in the bud."[36] Heiskell's obituary led the paper on December 29, 1972; Wirges's was played at the bottom of page one, along with coverage of the funeral of former president Harry S. Truman.[37]

Heiskell was buried at Mount Holly Cemetery (coincidentally also the burial site of William E. Woodruff, founder of the *Arkansas Gazette*) in Little Rock on December 30, 1972, following a twenty-minute funeral that drew about three hundred mourners to Trinity Episcopal Cathedral. Wirges's funeral was held four hours earlier to allow *Gazette* people to attend both. The *Gazette*'s coverage of the Heiskell funeral included messages of sympathy from, among others, Joe M. Dealey, publisher of the *Dallas Morning News*; the Executive Council of the International Typographical Union; and Rodrigo Madrigal Nieto, president of the Inter-American Press Association and publisher of a San Jose, Costa Rica, newspaper.[38] As expected, Heiskell's death brought an outpouring of responses. The congratulations of the centennial birthday gave way to sympathy and loss. Governor Dale Bumpers said:

> Mr. Heiskell dedicated the adult portion of his 100 years to serving all the people of Arkansas. He was first and foremost a newspaperman of the highest order, but he was also a great humanitarian who had the courage to champion unpopular causes which he believed to be in the state's best interest. He was a man of strong conviction. He set high standards of excellence for himself and demanded the same of his colleagues and employees.[39]

Tributes flowed in newspapers across the state and the country—*Russellville Daily Courier-Democrat, Dallas Morning News, Arkansas Democrat, Conway Log Cabin Democrat, Boston Herald American, Pine Bluff News, Benton Courier, North Little Rock Times, Pine Bluff Commercial, Searcy Daily Citizen, Newsday, Detroit Free Press, Abilene (Texas) Reporter-News, St. Louis Post-Dispatch, Miami News,* and *Charlotte (N.C.) Observer,* among others.[40]

The *Arkansas Democrat* compared his death to "the closing of a major street, the demolition of a special building or the damming of an important river" and said that Heiskell was the reason it had "always found the *Gazette* to be a tough but honorable competitor." In fact, the *Democrat's* coverage of Heiskell's death praised him for the absence of so many of the negative traits of today's newspaper owners in the age of corporate journalism:

> Mr. Heiskell had no interest in accumulating great wealth and making vulgar displays of it. Another thing that set him apart from many of his peers is that he was not an empire-builder, a monopolist bent on controlling communications in this or any other area. No one was prouder than he was of the fact that Little Rock is one of the few cities in America that still have two locally-owned, independent daily and Sunday newspapers.[41]

The *North Little Rock Times* ran a George Fisher cartoon of Heiskell walking up the masthead of his newspaper to heaven under the quote by Ralph Waldo Emerson: "An Institution is the Lengthened Shadow of One Man."[42] Patrick J. Owens, a former *Gazette* reporter, wrote in *Newsday* that Heiskell's "ancient, wintry smile was as good a reward as I've ever received for a job well done. His stout-hearted defense of a principle dear to his heart was a joy to hear if you happened to agree with him and a judgment just short of cosmically dreadful if you happened to think he was full of beans right then."[43] Roy Reed, who by then had gone on to the *New York Times*, remembered, "We all kind of worshipped the old man. We understood and appreciated who he was."[44]

Letters of condolence poured in for the Patterson family. Witt Stephens wrote to Hugh Patterson that his father-in-law's death had left a void that would never be filled in Stephens's heart, Little Rock, or Arkansas: "No citizen of this community has stood so steadfast for what he considered to be best for Arkansas," Stephens wrote. "His influence will be felt for another century beyond the hundred years he lived."[45] David W. Mullins, president of the University of Arkansas, telegrammed that "Arkansas has lost one of its first citizens. The nation's cherished principles of a free and concerned press have lost one of their great champions."[46]

However, not all of the correspondence was positive. Harmon L. Remmel, in his letter to Patterson, expressed his sympathy but quickly inserted his family's disagreements with the *Gazette's* political stance over the years, ordering the cancellation of his family's subscription that had dated to the late 1890s because they could no longer abide the liberal editorial stance: "Further, the nearly total alliance with *The New York Times* and various of its 'news affiliates' is more than I, an Arkansan, can further tolerate," he wrote. "A long time, but it has now come to an end."[47]

Senator J. William Fulbright eulogized Heiskell on the floor of the United States Senate on January 18, 1973, calling him "one of the most remarkable men in the country," "a great humanitarian and a great newspaper editor." "He and his newspaper have made a strong imprint on Arkansas and set the standard for the high quality of journalism that has been prevalent in the State," Fulbright said.[48]

Bill Lewis, the longtime general assignment reporter, credited Heiskell as the force that made the *Gazette* a great newspaper—one with a soul. While as publisher Hugh Patterson had kept an eye on the financial side, "Mr. Heiskell said, 'To heck with finances,'" Lewis remembered. The attitude illustrated a key part of Heiskell's success. Lewis continued: "[The *Gazette*] took care of its people and they did their best to take care of it." He said he didn't know of any other editors in Heiskell's mold. "He was such a patrician character, but as long as you were doing the right thing, he didn't care who you were."[49]

By the time of Heiskell's death, his newspaper had completely recovered from the last vestiges of the Central High crisis and was in the most dominant competitive position in its history.[50] It had stayed true to his editorial philosophy, which he had reiterated on the occasion of his fiftieth anniversary as editor in 1952:

> A newspaper is indeed primarily and properly a moral institution even though it has a commercial function in its sale of papers and advertising. . . . It is true that a newspaper may dominate its field in circulation and advertising when its integrity and decency are notoriously suspect. But there is a leaden character about the dollars it piles up. Or as the Scripture says, its gold and silver are cankered. Another thing distinguishes a newspaper. It is the legal property of one or more individuals, but in spite of their legal title they hold it as trustees for the public. If they fail to fulfill their character of trustees their paper will be tolerated rather than respected. . . . The man responsible for the destiny of a newspaper must make daily accounting to his community and to his own conscience. And at last he will have written the record of his stewardship and he must make final accounting. He cannot use as a means of measurement the financial success he has had or the size of circulation or volume of advertising. It is as if he entered the confines of a tribunal where sat judges, stern in judgment but just and righteous and tolerant within the bounds of conscience and duty. The one question then is whether he must be adjudged guilty of

> default on his obligation to a community and betrayal of his mission and his opportunity; or whether he can look his judges in the eye and ask discharge from his labors with the words: I have fought a good fight. I have finished my course. I have kept the faith.[51]

After December 28, 1972, the Patterson family, which over the years had consolidated majority ownership from J. N. Heiskell's siblings and later from Louise Patterson's sister, would be charged with maintaining that philosophy and the legacy of the Heiskell-owned *Arkansas Gazette*. It was a daunting task, as Hugh Patterson wrote in response to a sympathy telegram: "The family was prepared to be philosophical about his passing, of course, and were grateful that he remained alert and in reasonable health and comfort until the end. But after such a long and fruitful life, it is difficult to get used to the idea that he's not still around."[52] That was true for Arkansas as well, but time marched on.

Hugh Patterson remained as publisher. Carrick Patterson was news editor when his grandfather died; his younger brother, Ralph, had left the *Gazette* for a local advertising agency, but he would return to the paper in the years to come.[53] Hugh had thought that Carrick might end up as editor and Ralph on the business side.[54] Carrick Patterson recalled having been very close to his grandfather, with whom he shared an interest in photography, and remembered a favorite Christmas gift from him—a camera. Carrick Patterson also recalled the old gentleman's formal manner and frequent quips, often at his grandson's expense.[55] Carrick Patterson had worked at various jobs in the newsroom for years before joining the paper full-time after his graduation from Stanford. He said he thought he could learn more hands-on about the newspaper business at the *Gazette* than he could at any journalism school, so he took his degree in music; he toyed with the idea of a music career before coming back to the family business. He remembered that his last name earned him no favors from his superiors in the newsroom, recalling that his colleagues and bosses refused to give him special treatment, insisting that he earn his place. "I didn't get to feel smug about much," he said. "People thought I was smug, but I wasn't."[56] Looking back, he said if he had it to do over again, he probably would have gone to another newspaper to avoid the awkwardness of being the publisher's son in the newsroom. "It was inevitable that I would rise through the ranks faster than a normal person off the street," he said. "It messed up the orderly process and caused some resentment."[57] One of those who had some resentment was Bob Douglas, who was managing editor. He eventually left for a teaching position at the University of Arkansas after Carrick Patterson became executive editor over him. Douglas said he thought publisher would have been a better position for the younger man.

> The more authority he got [in the newsroom], the worse he was. He influenced his father, and his father influenced him the wrong way. He sort of reinforced some of the bad decisions Hugh made, like killing stories, good stories. As long as I was dealing with Hugh, we could work it out. I could usually persuade him that we needed to do something. . . . Carrick came along and, of course, when he became executive editor, he was a notch above me and there was just no trying.[58]

Years later, Carrick Patterson said he regretted the tension between himself and Douglas, whom he remembered as being generous in teaching him. "We were friends, and to have him have lingering resentment about that is awful," Patterson said. "I wish I could go back and do it differently."[59] In hindsight, those were some of the early mistakes made by Heiskell's heirs.

As assistant managing editor, Carrick Patterson had overseen the revamping of the *Gazette*'s women's section, with its emphasis on society and brides, into "Omnibus," a more broad-reaching features section. He said he thought the writers in the old women's section were underutilized for their talent, and he didn't think the society column "Among Ourselves" was appropriate for a liberal-leaning newspaper. Those changes caused resentment in the newsroom—and with his own mother—but "Omnibus" remained.[60] He shepherded the *Gazette*'s transition from typewriter and paste pot to the computer age in 1973–1974. Following the *Detroit News* and *Chicago Tribune*, the *Arkansas Gazette* was the third newspaper in the country to adopt the Hendrix computer system "at extreme cost." "Overnight, the first edition improved," Patterson remembered, citing the ease of the computerized editing of typographical errors. "There was some harrumphing about getting rid of the typewriters, but we picked up some time and streamlined the production."[61]

Max Brantley, who came to the *Gazette* in 1973, said he thought then it was a serious newspaper, an important newspaper, and its civil rights stance had been a powerful lure for him. He remembered some of the giants in the newsroom who were his mentors in the early 1970s: city editor Bill Shelton, whose "forbidding presence," "towering integrity and great skills" helped make the *Gazette* what it was; managing editor Bob Douglas, another man of few words; George Fisher, the editorial cartoonist who "should've won a Pulitzer Prize"; and his personal hero, Ernest Dumas, "utterly fair, well-informed—one of those paragons of journalism." Brantley, whose *Gazette* career ended only with the death of the newspaper, said the building was full of people who could have worked anywhere.

> There was a core of supremely talented people who weren't there just to have a job. They were there because they wanted to work at

> the *Gazette*. Most were Arkansas natives, and most felt at least a spiritual kinship with the spirit of 1957. They were there on a mission as well as earning a paycheck.[62]

One of those was Bob Lancaster, who arrived at the *Gazette* in 1973 after a Nieman Fellowship to revive the Arkansas Traveler column. He said, "I probably bought into the *Gazette* legend—kind of like everybody else did. . . . At that time, I guess, it was probably the best editorial page in the world. Really."[63]

In late 1973, with the economy struggling, the *Gazette* raised its subscription rates, but again Witt Stephens sent Patterson a note of support, as he had done in the decade before when it had raised its advertising rates: "You can't put out the kind of service and the kind of newspaper that you are publishing without the rates being comparable to the service," Stephens wrote. "I think we are all better off than we would be if we have a poor paper a few nickels cheaper. I congratulate you."[64] Part of Patterson's response reflected the *Gazette*'s partisan progressive viewpoint: "I suppose no one can predict where this inflationary spiral will end, and there certainly appears to be little hope while the Republicans are in power," he wrote.[65]

Early in their ownership, though, the Pattersons faced a crisis from within. The second attempt to unionize the newsroom came about in 1974, and many of the big names of the newsroom signed their union cards. "[W]e were a pretty noisy bunch of Bolsheviks," sportswriter Jim Bailey remembered, chuckling.[66] Brantley recalled the unionization attempt as a real test of Douglas's leadership. Ironically, Douglas had been one of the strikers during the first attempt to unionize with a chapter of the American Newspaper Guild in 1949. He walked the picket line for a year and a half then before taking a job in North Carolina and eventually returning to the *Gazette*.[67] But in 1974, he was management and thus on the other side. Douglas said the newsroom was justified in asking for raises, but the Nixon wage and price controls made it difficult for management to give them. The vote for the Newspaper Guild ended in a tie, which went to management and ended the attempt.[68] Brantley recalled that Douglas took the unionization attempt as a personal affront after many of his longtime friends in the newsroom joined the movement. "That left a bad feeling that never went away," Brantley remembered. "Bob Douglas never forgave some of the people he thought he had nurtured for voting against him."[69] Good raises did, however, come shortly after the Guild attempt.[70]

After J. N. Heiskell's death, the Patterson family would be charged with continuing for a second generation its patriarch's ownership style, which had been marked since 1902—no matter what the cost—by a commitment to quality journalism and a progressive voice. Looking back years later, Powell said the importance of a newspaper's family ownership such as the Heiskell-Patterson clan could not be overestimated. "There may be a great array of reporters and commentary writers, editorial writers who express the views or cover the stories in such fashion as to make the newspaper great, but the owners have to support it and have to stand still for all the bitter criticism and sometimes lose a lot of money," he said. "You've got to have the owners behind it, and I think that's true of any of the great newspapers that have existed in the history of this country."[71] Indeed, under Heiskell family ownership, the *Arkansas Gazette* had, as reported in J. N. Heiskell's obituary, risen from a "struggling, obscure country newspaper" to "a position of honor and respect among the great newspapers of the nation."[72] Heiskell's belief of the newspaper as conscience of its community had served his Old Gray Lady well, but the family ownership's second generation would be tested in coming years by changing economic realities and a reinvigorated cross-town challenger.

CHAPTER SIX

1974–1986: A Change Atop the *Arkansas Democrat*, the Ensuing Newspaper War, Antitrust Lawsuit, and Sale to Gannett

BY THE MID-1970S, the *Arkansas Gazette*'s only real competition in Little Rock, the *Arkansas Democrat,* like afternoon newspapers throughout the United States, was struggling to remain viable as women entered the workforce and the evening news on television became a staple in American homes, lessening the relevance of any evening publication. In fact, the *Democrat* had seen the temporary gains it had made at the *Gazette*'s expense following Central High erode; by 1974, the *Gazette* once again dominated the circulation numbers, 114,970 to the *Democrat*'s 69,498 daily and 140,475 to 91,664 Sunday, according to Audit Bureau of Circulation numbers.[1] The struggles of afternoon papers were just another factor in the shrinking numbers of newspapers nationwide. In 1923, five hundred American cities had competing newspapers; that number had dropped to ninety by 1953 and was down to just thirty-four in 1974.[2] With such trends, it is not difficult to see how the mighty *Arkansas Gazette* could become complacent, but the Patterson family—and eventually the state—would pay a dear price twelve years later for that complacency when they were forced to sell to the Gannett Corporation. Their first major mistake was underestimating the competition.

The beginning of the end of the *Arkansas Gazette* came with the arrival of a thin, bespectacled son of another of the state's newspaper families. Walter Hussman Jr., twenty-seven, was named publisher of the *Arkansas Democrat* in 1974, and he would prove to be a brilliant, unyielding adversary for the Old Gray Lady after Hugh Patterson refused his request for a joint operating agreement (JOA). The *Gazette* thus faced a perfect storm—a dogged competitor and ownership that was too conservative and slow to respond to a reinvigorated challenger who was more than willing to compromise his journalistic principles and squander his family fortune in the single-minded pursuit of what some might call revenge.

The March 4, 1974, edition of the *Arkansas Democrat* brought the announcement that that newspaper had been bought by the Hussman family, which owned small monopoly newspapers in south Arkansas in Camden, Texarkana, Hot Springs, Magnolia, and El Dorado.[3] The Hussmans, however, were not held in the same esteem by the Arkansas journalism community that J. N. Heiskell had been. Walter E. Hussman Sr. had married the daughter of C. E. Palmer, who had owned all five newspapers; before Palmer's death, Hussman bought the *Camden News* from his father-in-law in an attempt to branch out on his own. After Palmer died, Hussman consolidated the Palmer properties under his Camden News Publishing Group, eventually reorganizing them into WEHCO Media (for the Walter E. Hussman Company) in 1973.[4] The family also owned the CBS television affiliate in Texarkana/Shreveport[5] as well as, since the 1960s, cable television systems in several cities: Hope, Camden, and Hot Springs, Arkansas; Vicksburg, Mississippi; and Longview and Kilgore, Texas. The family was borrowing money to build more cable systems in 1974.[6]

Arkansas media scholar Michael Dougan recalled that the heirs of August Engel, faced with declining circulation and rising costs at the *Arkansas Democrat*, put that newspaper up for sale after his death.[7] Walter E. Hussman Jr., who had earned a journalism degree from the University of North Carolina and an MBA from Columbia and whose first job was as a reporter for *Forbes* magazine,[8] encouraged his father to enter the Little Rock market.[9] The young Hussman had been lured back home in 1970 from his *Forbes* job as his father was contemplating retirement and the future of the family company. The older man told his son that if he returned home to work in the family business and later decided he didn't like it, he could always return to New York. "But if you decide you want to stay [in New York] for a long time, we'll probably sell these businesses," the son remembered his father telling him. "'I don't want to wait until I'm seventy or older to decide whether someone in the family is going to run the business.'"[10] Hussman Jr. acceded to his father's wishes and went on to hold several jobs within Camden News Publishing. As he remembered it, his father was "in charge of everything," and he was charged with "trying to learn everything."[11] Then the family learned the struggling afternoon *Arkansas Democrat* in Little Rock was for sale.[12] After their success turning around the *Camden News*, the younger man recalled being intrigued by the prospect of taking on a larger rebuilding job in Arkansas's state capital with the ideas he had learned during his Columbia education. "I said, 'As long as we're in the business of journalism in Arkansas then the ultimate would be to have a newspaper in Little Rock,'" he recalled. "That would be a wonderful

Walter E. Hussman Sr. and his son, Walter E. Hussman Jr. Courtesy of the Arkansas Democrat-Gazette.

thing if we could own a paper there, and if it could be a really well-regarded and financially successful paper, that would be terrific."[13]

But the Hussman family did not enter the Little Rock market without serious reservations, including downward trends in advertising and circulation for the *Democrat* as well as the strength of the *Gazette*. Max Brantley, who came to the *Gazette* in 1973, called that newspaper's competitor at the time "a shell of a newspaper," very small, declining in circulation, advertising, and news coverage. "It was a classic evening newspaper," he said.[14] He recalled Bill Shelton, the *Gazette*'s city editor, assigning general assignment reporter

Bill Lewis the obituary for the *Democrat.*[15] Ultimately, the Hussmans decided to take the chance. In so doing, they would eventually change the course of Arkansas history. "[B]ecause our whole family had been in Arkansas in the newspaper business for decades, it was worth a try," Hussman Jr. remembered.[16] The sale price was $3.7 million.[17] The younger Hussman was named publisher.

The goal of the new owners in 1974 was to be a comparable alternative to the dominant *Arkansas Gazette*. They set a self-imposed deadline of three years to get the business turned around—making money and reversing the advertising and circulation trends. Although it had been profitable not too many years before, by 1974 the *Democrat* was losing money. "[I]t it had been profitable for many, many years, so it had lost money only four or five years by the time we bought it," Hussman Jr. said.[18] He recalled that in the early 1960s, the *Democrat* had had about the same daily and more Sunday circulation than the *Gazette*, the aftermath of the 1957 Central High crisis.[19]

Max Brantley said he knew little of the *Democrat*'s new leaders except their ownership of other media companies, which meant they had money to be competitive. That was one key difference between the Hussmans and Pattersons. WEHCO was a chain; the Pattersons owned only the *Gazette*. "They gave evidence from early on that they were going to be at it for a while," Brantley said of the Hussmans. "And I thought there was at the *Gazette* on the part of some people an unhealthy inclination to dismiss the challenge, to not take them seriously."[20] Indeed, the Hussman chain was not well respected in Arkansas journalism. The monopoly status of each of its small dailies guaranteed low wages and little motivation to strive for improved quality.

Hussman recalled many problems with WEHCO's new property, including the lack of an aggressive advertising staff, the unionization of one-third of the workforce, and a philosophy of willingly following the *Gazette* instead of breaking stories.[21] Upon Hussman's arrival in Little Rock, he went around to meet advertisers and civic leaders, many of whom told him they found the *Gazette* to be arrogant. "Maybe they didn't agree with the editorial policy, but we found a receptive audience for a more reinvigorated *Arkansas Democrat*," he said. "We didn't even think we could be a comparable alternative right off the bat." Instead, their goal was to become a "necessary complement"—not a substitute—for the *Gazette*.[22]

The first hurdle for the new owners was to win a union election to keep the new property in line with their other corporate holdings, which were nonunion—with their monopoly status, not a surprise. The International Typographical Union was trying to organize newsroom employees about the time the Hussmans bought the paper. Hussman Jr. remembered that the new ownership spoke frankly with *Democrat* employees, telling them that the union's "archaic work rules" would be a problem for the new owners' attempts to improve the newspaper. Their message was that with WEHCO's other holdings, employees would not need a union to ensure such benefits as good healthcare and profit-sharing plans.[23] The strategy worked; newsroom employees voted, 31–15, to give the new owners a chance.[24] More good news for the Hussmans followed in the first year of ownership: Circulation and advertising turned around; Hussman elevated Bob McCord to executive editor and praised his leadership. "But every month I looked at the profit-and-loss statement, and the more business we did, the more money we lost," he said. "It turned out that our operating expenses—mainly because of all the union work rules and restrictions—we couldn't make money by bringing in more business."[25] From 1975 to 1977, most of the newspaper's four unions chose to no longer be represented by their unions. The pressmen, composing room, stereotypers, and mailers had been unionized.[26] Hussman Jr. called the decertifications a huge vote of confidence for the new ownership.

> I told them honestly, "We can't make any money the way things are set up now. And if we can't make any money, none of us have any hope. Me, you, and all of us don't have any hope of having a job here." They all came around.[27]

The *Democrat*'s losses lessened as the new ownership focused internally. "We had reduced the losses down to a fairly small amount by 1977," Hussman Jr. said. "But . . . while we were focusing internally, the *Gazette* was just getting stronger and stronger, gaining more advertising, gaining more circulation, and we were losing market share."[28] He recalled that the *Democrat*'s daily circulation fell from 65,000 when the family bought it to 56,000 by 1978. Meanwhile, the *Gazette*'s circulation had grown from 116,000 to 126,000. "They were becoming more and more—which they already were, but even more so, they were becoming the primary buy," he said.[29] The *Democrat* was, like radio, a complementary buy.[30]

The Hussmans' self-imposed deadline of 1977 arrived. Although the new ownership had shown improvements in circulation, advertising, and the reduction of production and operating costs from more than $100 to about $20 per page, the dramatic improvement had not translated to the bottom line.[31] By the end of the year, the *Democrat* had a daily circulation of just 51,916 (28 percent of the readership market) and Sunday numbers of 96,278. The *Gazette* stood at 132,519 daily and 160,292 Sunday and held 81 percent of advertising share.[32] So Hussman Sr., who had not been as enthusiastic as his son at the purchase,[33] reminded the younger man of their agreement. He told his son that while they had made "a valiant attempt," with the financial losses and lost market share, "'It's time to come to grips with that reality,'" Hussman Jr. recalled. "And at that point we decided that it hadn't worked and we'd try to get out of this investment."[34]

Patterson's response would, ultimately, lead to the death of the Old Gray Lady.

By 1977, afternoon newspapers were in even worse shape than they had been when the Hussman chain bought the *Democrat* three years earlier. Hussman Jr. recalled that it would have been easier to sell the paper in '74 than it was three years later. "[O]nce an experienced newspaper operator had come in and operated it for three years and now they wanted to sell it, well, that made it more difficult to sell," he said.[35] So the family decided to try instead for a joint operating agreement with the *Gazette*, in which the papers would combine some operations to share costs and reduce operating expenses—but still retain editorial independence. "And let's not make any bones about trying to get a good financial deal or the best deal or whatever," Hussman said. "Let's just try to get out."[36] So Hussman Jr. called Hugh Patterson to talk about the possibility of a JOA. As he recalled, he told Patterson:

> We got into it for laudable reasons. We wanted to have a voice in Little Rock. We had been in the newspaper business for years, and we hoped to make money. We haven't been able to. We had hoped to be more competitive with the *Gazette*, and we haven't been able to do that successfully. It's time for us to recognize that, and we're willing to do a JOA. We're willing for the *Gazette* to be the dominant newspaper, and the *Democrat* to be the secondary newspaper. We're not asking for fifty-fifty or anything like that. We will agree to whatever terms you think are reasonable.[37]

But Patterson told him his family wasn't interested.

Hussman remembered being shocked that any company would not jump at the chance to eliminate its competition. "I couldn't believe he wasn't interested," he said.[38] So he told his father they had to make Patterson an offer he couldn't refuse. Their second offer included concessions in distribution area and publication cycle, but they did have a minimum number required for the profit-split plan. With the *Gazette* clearing $2 million annually with the potential "to make far more than that," the Hussmans wanted to split the first $600,000 in profits so that they could cover their obligation to the Engel heirs from when they bought the paper. Their payment on the $3.1 million note was $295,000 annually for twenty years. After the first $600,000, they proposed giving the *Gazette* 90 percent of the profits.[39]

But Patterson again said no.

So Hussman got a copy of all twenty-some JOA agreements from the U.S. Department of Justice and said he crafted the most favorable one in the United States for the larger paper.[40] He then took the offer back to the *Gazette* publisher a third time. This proposal gave the *Gazette* 100 percent of the profits until it had matched its earnings of the previous year. After that, the papers would split the next $600,000 equally (to cover the *Democrat*'s note payment). Then the *Gazette* would receive 90 percent of the remaining profits. Hussman said he thought, "That way he's guaranteed—he'll always make as much as he did last year, and that will address that concern."[41]

Patterson's response?

Not interested.

One of the key differences between the two newspaper families was revealed in his explanation:

> I didn't want to have a thing to do with Hussman. I just disapproved their outlook on life to begin with. . . . [T]hey had cut corners every way they possibly could have over all the years, in the operation, with suppliers, machinery people. We'd get the reports on those things, so I just didn't want to have to be involved in it, and I didn't think we had to be. I tried to persuade Walter that he could make adjustments of his own in the operation, that he could just decide to go after them and limit his circulation and all to try to develop more retail business and what not and at least be reasonably profitable.[42]

Carrick Patterson, Hugh Patterson's son, said he was barely aware of the Hussman proposal at the time, but he understood why his father made the decision he did. In most other cities with JOAs, the afternoon papers eventually lost their viability because people simply did not want them anymore. "And it became a financial drain on the operation as a whole," Carrick Patterson said. "My father didn't think that that was fiscally responsible."[43]

Bob McCord, then the executive editor of the *Democrat*, said he spoke to Patterson on Hussman's behalf about the possibility of a JOA. But Patterson, who had worked with McCord to create a chapter of the Society of Professional Journalists in Little Rock, told his friend he had no intention of bailing out his competitor. "This young man came to town with his daddy's money, and he thinks he is going to win," he told McCord. "I don't think he will." McCord said Patterson was convinced the *Gazette* would prevail.[44] In fact, any reasonable person would have been. Hussman said he figured that Patterson thought the *Democrat* was about to go out of business. "And if we go out of business, he is better off than if he has to share ten percent or $300,000 or whatever," he said. So the Hussmans began exploring how to close the *Arkansas Democrat.*[45] "It was conceivable to [the Pattersons], and very plausible, that we would not be able to sell the newspaper to anyone else," Hussman said.[46] But the son was bothered by the family's failure—its first unsuccessful business in three generations.

> When you come to grips with total failure like that, you really start thinking, is there anything we could possibly do? And you start thinking, well, maybe we ought to really consider doing some things we'd never even considered before, because what's the down side? If you fail doing that, well, you're going to fail if you don't do that, absolutely, if you're thinking about shutting the newspaper. . . . Risk-taking becomes a lot easier when you're confronted with total failure.[47]

In retrospect, Carrick Patterson credited Hussman's tenacity and his willingness to ignore the economic realities and commit the resources to try to make the *Democrat* profitable. "And I wouldn't be a bit surprised—although he'd never said this, certainly, to me or maybe to anybody else—if he didn't have just a little bit of ego tied up into it, as far as being turned down on the joint operating thing," Patterson said.[48] In a later interview, Patterson reiterated: "Hussman, a proud man, of course, and a very wealthy man, evidently resented that quite a bit, so he made the decision to go head-to-head with the *Gazette.*"[49]

Although there was no exact duplicate situation, he found some ammunition in several different places that featured competitive situations: the *Chattanooga Free Press*, an afternoon paper that eventually surpassed its morning competition; the *Dallas Times-Herald*, which switched from afternoon to morning publication; Tulsa, which featured a JOA that charged advertisers $7 per column inch to advertise in one paper and $8 an inch for both; and Winnipeg, Canada, which offered free want ads.[50] He cobbled together a strategy that would make the economics the same as if there were a JOA in Little Rock—a shockingly illogical money-losing proposition. "We could say, 'We'll just charge you a dollar an inch if you'll duplicate your *Gazette* ad in the *Democrat*. Not if you run different ads,'" Hussman said. That price was enough, he said, to cover the *Democrat*'s newsprint and ink costs, but the very idea that valuable retail advertising would be sold for a dollar an inch remains amazing. Hussman said he believed for the *Democrat* to be a real alternative to the *Gazette*, it had to put out as big a paper as the competition. The Chattanooga newspaper had featured a bigger news hole with a heavy emphasis on local news. The *Dallas Times-Herald*, an afternoon paper, published a morning edition outside its city zone. Despite the free want ads, the Winnipeg newspaper had seen its classified revenues increase. The key pieces in the Hussman strategy became adopting the free want ads modeled after Winnipeg and charging $1 an inch for duplicating major retailers' ads.[51] Hussman Jr. apprised his father of the plan and got him to agree to give the venture one final shot for the *Democrat* to become a true alternative to the *Gazette*. "And if it won't work, I, for one, would feel much better about saying, 'We tried everything. We tried it all,'" Hussman Jr. recalled.[52]

He said prior to deciding on the new strategy, he had talked with Patterson about selling the *Democrat* to the *Gazette* but that Patterson had told him he would "need to create a public monument to the fact that you've been a failure." Hussman said he did not understand what Patterson meant. "I thought, 'Okay, a public monument. Do I need to go build something down here in the Metro Center Mall?'" he remembered. "I guess what he was trying to say there is that we not only had to admit to being a failure, but we had to convince the Justice Department that we couldn't sell the newspaper to anyone else." That would have satisfied federal antitrust requirements—an ironic foreshadowing. "And if we could show them we couldn't sell to anyone else, then he would take it," Hussman remembered.[53] Patterson never offered a price, and Hussman maintained that if they proved that no one else was willing to buy their newspaper, his family would have lost any negotiating standing it had with the Pattersons. "[W]e were going to admit we had failed when we shut the newspaper down," Hussman said. "[S]o we really didn't think that was a viable way to proceed."[54] Patterson's refusal to buy his competitor harkened back to the Heiskells' 1909 purchase and sale two years later of the *Democrat*. According to the Heiskell family's journalistic philosophy, competition was better for community newspapers.[55] It was a completely opposite philosophy to that of the Hussman family, whose other newspapers were all monopolies. Nearly thirty years after his overture to Patterson, Hussman insisted he had not been insulted by the older man's "public monument that you've been a failure" answer. His frustration, he maintained, was in not being able to convince the older man to accept the JOA.[56] That frustration likely stemmed from what others would later describe as Patterson's having "high-hatted" the younger man, something he would never forget.

So the Hussmans decided to go for broke. They implemented their final plan in December 1978, first by offering free want ads to individuals.[57] While commercial accounts still paid the regular rates, the free ads brought more traffic to the *Democrat*.

Not everyone agreed with the new strategy. Bob McCord, the *Democrat*'s executive editor, was the most obvious skeptic. "He didn't want me to leave, and I really didn't want to leave either, except I knew I didn't want to be there when the end would come," McCord said.[58] Hussman recalled that McCord told him he should "get somebody in here who would really believe in this, who could think they could really challenge the *Gazette* and really put out as good a newspaper as the *Gazette*."[59] McCord eventually wound up at the *Gazette* in 1981 as an associate editor in charge of creating an op-ed page.[60] More than thirty years after McCord left the *Democrat*, there is discrepancy about his successor. Hussman recalled that McCord suggested John Robert Starr, who had been the Associated Press bureau chief in Arkansas but by then was pursuing a Ph.D. at the University of Tennessee.[61] McCord, however, remembered it differently, recalling that he suggested a couple of Arkansas newsmen then working at newspapers outside the state. Hussman interviewed both, McCord said, but didn't think either was right for the job, and he kept asking about Starr, whom Hussman ultimately hired as managing editor in 1979.[62] "I realized he had a real competitive streak, and that's what we really needed," Hussman said, adding that other factors in the hiring were that Starr, a veteran Arkansas newsman, knew the state. "We needed somebody from Arkansas to be the editor of the newspaper," he said.[63] Although WEHCO was a corporation, albeit privately held, it was local enough to realize the significance of such a hire; Gannett years later never would.

In 1978, the *Democrat*'s news hole increased by 60 percent, the newsroom staff doubled from fifty to one hundred, the paper started running color every day and intentionally tried to run more pages than the *Gazette* so that it could call itself "Arkansas's largest newspaper." Hussman agreed that with the *Gazette*'s circulation advantage, the moniker was a stretch, but he said the *Democrat* had to promote anything it could because the underdog did not have much to promote.[64] Another salvo in the early days of Arkansas's newspaper war occurred when the *Democrat* switched to morning publication beyond the metro area. The afternoon paper continued in Little Rock for a few months until Hussman decided to focus all his resources on a morning publication cycle and went morning statewide.[65] That decision was applauded in the *Democrat* newsroom. Meredith Oakley, then a reporter there, remembered feelings of elation and jubilation when Hussman made the announcement. "We were extremely excited about it because we were young and we were hungry," she said. "We didn't know any better."[66]

Carrick Patterson said Hussman's strategy of offering retail advertising for $1 an inch, which drew the presence of major department store ads to the paper, helped to legitimize the *Democrat*. But "[t]hat was like a tenth or less of what it was really going for, and it was much under the cost of production," he said.[67] To combat the *Gazette*'s circulation advantage, Hussman implemented a Total Market Coverage strategy, which meant delivering Wednesday's edition to every household in central Arkansas.[68] Carrick Patterson also said another advantage the *Democrat* had was its implementation of a High Profile section, thus garnering the bride and society news that the *Gazette* had relinquished with its earlier shift to Omnibus.[69]

Brantley recalled Bill Shelton, the *Gazette*'s legendary city editor, keeping a list early in Arkansas's newspaper war comparing the content of the two papers. Shelton's philosophy was that the *Gazette* had to not only match but also beat the *Democrat* on everything—more details, better stories.[70] But the overall *Gazette* response to its invigorated rival was an abstract one. The Pattersons did not increase the size of the paper or the staff, likely seeing no real need to do so, Hussman's presence notwithstanding. "And there was still a certain self-satisfaction about our relationship that I think was unhealthy to us and that we paid for dearly as the years went by," Brantley said.[71] The roots of that attitude came, ironically, from the *Gazette*'s greatest triumph. After everything the paper had survived in 1957—boycotts, opposition campaigns—it had emerged stronger than ever. "Really, the owner of some small south Arkansas newspapers was going to be a threat to this great institution, the oldest business in the state of Arkansas?" Brantley explained. "I can see why people would have that view; it's not crazy to have that view—it just turned out to be wrong."[72]

ABC numbers for the two papers, in fact, showed that in 1979, the *Gazette* was more dominant than ever, with daily circulation of 127,997 to the *Democrat*'s 56,000 and a Sunday lead of 154,601 to 103,501.[73] Brantley said he thought Shelton responded to the *Democrat* in exactly the proper way, but the strategy quickly became impossible because of Hussman's commitment to increase the *Democrat*'s news hole and news staff—at whatever cost—and the Pattersons' injudicious decision not to try to match it.[74] Brantley recalled being nervous about the competition from the late 1970s and growing more nervous with every passing year. "I hated not responding to stories," he said. "I hated just being silent when they would break some story or cause some public stir."[75] Deborah Mathis, who had worked at the *Democrat* before the Hussmans bought it and later spent several years in Arkansas television news where she covered the newspaper war, recalled asking Patterson what he thought of the *Arkansas Democrat* and his responding, "They have a perfect right to exist." She said she found that to be a dangerous statement.

> I thought it was a little haughty and dismissive and I was surprised by it, because even though I wasn't very sophisticated at the time in terms of political correctness, I knew that wasn't too smart to say that. Even if you're kicking your enemy's rear, it usually isn't

> a good idea to go taunt them. And I found that a taunting kind of statement. And I think if that's the way he really felt, it bore some bad fruit later on because I think the *Gazette* may have become too dismissive of the *Democrat* right from the start.[76]

Mathis said she also interviewed Hussman and found him to be eager, earnest, determined, and energized, in contrast to Patterson's being "disappointingly relaxed about it."[77] Oakley, the *Democrat* reporter, found that attitude to be prevalent among her older, more stable and settled competition. "I wouldn't say they were young and hungry at all," she said of the *Gazette* staff. "They were pretty sedate and pretty self-satisfied with things."[78]

Jim Bailey, one of the stalwarts of the *Gazette* sports department who said he thought the *Gazette* was at its peak when he arrived in 1956 until well into the 1970s, said several of his colleagues in the newsroom agreed the *Gazette*'s family ownership was not prepared for what would become one of the fiercest newspaper wars in American history.[79] "They claimed that the Hussman newspaper group had all these other media assets—newspapers, TV stations, radio, so on—and they did," Bailey said. "But they could've had some if they'd wanted to over the years."[80]

Sports was an area that the *Gazette* dominated, despite the *Democrat*'s advantage in space. Orville Henry, the legendary sports editor, had correctly foreseen from the 1950s that the University of Arkansas Razorbacks would be the wave of the future in statewide sports coverage. After Arkansas's newspaper war began, he gave up his day-to-day editing duties to move from Little Rock to Fayetteville in 1983 to be closer to his beat. Henry said Hussman and Starr gave the *Democrat*'s sports staff resources "to do a lot of spectacular things that we were not able to do. And this is where they hit us first, and they did because, I believe, they knew that sports was the strength of the *Gazette*."[81] Henry said neither Hugh nor Carrick Patterson was a match "for anybody who was so stubborn as Walter Hussman and such a wild animal as John Robert Starr."[82] Another difference between the two papers' sports sections was that the *Gazette*'s sportswriters were more established than those at the *Democrat*—and remained so. "They knew all the coaches and all the coaches knew them, whereas the *Democrat* was always starting over with young fellows, and by the time they began to get their feet on the ground and know their way around, they were gone and another young fellow was in," Jim Bailey said. "The *Gazette* had a better pay scale and therefore more stability, not that *Gazette* staffers were getting rich."[83] In fact, Wadie Moore, the first black newsroom employee at the *Gazette*, said he didn't see a newspaper war in the sports section. The *Gazette* went about its business, "busting our butts."[84]

The addition of Starr, however, changed the game. His ego would match—perhaps even exceed—Hussman's. Meredith Oakley, who had gone to the *Democrat* as a young reporter in 1976, called the bombastic Starr one of the finest newsmen she had ever known.

> Lots of personality, certainly, and that was something that the newspaper needed at that time, but he had a nose for news. I liked him. You didn't have to walk on eggshells with Bob Starr. You could talk back to him and not worry about collecting your pink slip at the end of the day. A lot of people were intimidated by him, but anyone who had the nerve to walk up to him or into his office was welcome. A lot of people were intimidated by him and didn't like him for that reason.[85]

Bailey recalled that Starr "relished a fight," particularly with the *Gazette*.[86] Carrick Patterson remembered that the attitude had personal roots—just like Hussman's. Starr had been working at the AP during the Little Rock Central crisis and had been "kind of an apologist for Orval Faubus." *Gazette* management had "tattled on him" to the national AP office, and Patterson said Starr bitterly resented the *Gazette* and the Patterson family for that, so his role as battler of the despised Old Gray Lady was perfectly suited for him. "He might not have thought of himself as a Faubus apologist, but I think any objective person would say that he was," Patterson said. "He was angry, and this gave him a forum for that anger."[87]

Starr was, in fact, disliked by many in the Little Rock newspaper market. Michael Dougan, who wrote *Community Diaries: Arkansas Newspapering, 1819–2002*, called him one of the most polarizing people in Arkansas journalism in the late twentieth century.[88] Bob Lancaster, who had written the *Gazette*'s Arkansas Traveler column in 1973–1974 after a Nieman Fellowship before going to the *Philadelphia Inquirer* for four years and then returning to his home state, left the *Democrat* when Starr was hired there. Lancaster said he "knew too much about Bob Starr to be able to work for him in good conscience."[89] Lancaster called Starr "pompous and single-minded in his dedication to destroying the *Arkansas Gazette*. . . . He was just a phony and I didn't like him and I knew I couldn't work with him," he said.[90] Those feelings continued long after Arkansas's newspaper war ended. After Starr's death on April Fool's Day 2000, Lancaster wrote of him in his column in the *Arkansas Times*, which by that time had become a weekly newspaper:

> [T]hose he picked on usually really were superior people, and he knew it, and thought his association with them by his attacks on

> them in the paper might elevate his own standing (at least in his own mind), like the pug fighter who beards the real contenders in the hope they'll admire his spunk enough—or be sufficiently annoyed by it—to accept him in a manner of speaking into their circle. . . . [H]e was one of that breed of lowborn characters who find their identity in life and take their only real pleasure in committing sophomoric attention-begging malicious mischief against the high and the mighty, or against anyone discerning enough to have figured them out.[91]

Bill Lewis described Starr as "an SOB in many ways."[92] Jerry McConnell said: "He was probably a really good newspaperman, and I never liked him very well."[93] Added Max Brantley: "It was not hard to dislike Bob Starr. I think he liked being disliked."[94]

Hussman, however, praised Starr's common sense, news judgment, and managerial skills.[95] Their common enemy in the Pattersons also drew them together. All was going well at *Democrat* headquarters at Fifth and Scott until Hussman picked up a copy of the May 1979 edition of *Arkansas Times*, then a monthly magazine, that featured on its cover a color photograph of Starr dressed in combat gear with a knife in his teeth, squatting on a *Gazette* newspaper box with the headline, "I'm Bob Starr. I'm declaring war on the *Gazette*."[96] Brantley said Starr consciously wanted to be seen as the embodiment of the *Arkansas Democrat*. "He gladly crouched on top of a newspaper box, took off his shirt and was wearing a vest or something and put a big knife between his teeth and said, 'I'm the gorilla coming at the *Gazette*.' And again, it got a lot of attention."[97]

The genteel Hussman recalled being shocked. Starr had not bothered to tell his boss his plan, which made the publisher uneasy. He said he vehemently disagreed with the metaphor of Arkansas's newspaper war as an alley fight, reiterating that the *Democrat* was not out to kill or maim the *Gazette* but was instead trying to compete and save a dying newspaper. "This is not a message we want to convey," he remembered thinking.[98] Although he may not have wanted to convey that message, it was probably accurate. The *Arkansas Times* cover, he maintained, showed "totally the wrong image of what we were trying to do," and he said the irresponsible stunt hurt the *Democrat*.[99] Despite the progress that had been made under Starr, whom he called almost the perfect person for the job, Hussman said he considered firing him over the incident. Instead, he had a serious talk with Starr, who was "sort of contrite," Hussman recalled.[100] He maintained the magazine cover gave him his first indication of Starr's ego.[101]

John Robert Starr on the infamous 1979 Arkansas Times *cover. Courtesy of* Arkansas Times.

But Oakley, who would work closely with Starr after moving to the editorial offices, maintained it wouldn't have bothered Starr had Hussman fired him.

> Starr would've just said, "Kiss my ass, goodbye," which may have been a large thing in the success of their relationship. "Yassa, massa" wasn't Bob's style with Walter or anyone else. I don't think he was deferential to Walter or anyone else. He was respectful. They didn't clash often, but I think on the few occasions they'd clash, they'd talk it out, and Starr probably won as many as he lost.[102]

Looking back after Arkansas's newspaper war was over, Hussman said it was a good thing he had not followed his first instinct because Starr knew Arkansas well.[103] That would ultimately contrast with the Gannett managers who were brought in to the *Gazette* from afar who never knew, nor, it seemed, cared, much about Arkansas. That philosophy would prove to be a major factor in Hussman's ultimate victory in Arkansas's newspaper war.

Over time, the *Democrat* under Starr began making progress in advertising and circulation. The huge losses began lessening. And then Starr wrote a column. Hussman said he thought the occasional column from his editor could be a good addition, but Starr took it to the extreme, cranking out seven a week. "I said, 'I didn't hire you to be a column writer. I hired you to run the newspaper,'" Hussman recalled telling his editor.[104] But the workaholic Starr, whom Hussman called "very energetic, very enthusiastic,"[105] did both, despite Hussman's concerns about the lack of separation between news and opinion and the unusual situation of having someone who directed news coverage also commenting on the news. The publisher feared Starr's column crossed the line, and it did. Hussman thus allowed his journalistic principles to be compromised, but he was, in fact, rewarded for it. Starr's column would prove to be another decisive factor in Arkansas's newspaper war. He wrote simply, identifying himself and his newspaper with everyday Arkansans, many of whom still remembered the *Gazette*'s unpopular stance during the Central High crisis. Max Brantley recalled the immediate results of Starr's column:

> He had a knack for going for the jugular. Politicians were afraid of him . . . and if he wasn't picking on some politician . . . he was picking on the *Gazette* the rest of the time, and of course we took it personally. And some of the stuff he wrote—I mean, he wrote columns making fun of Carrick Patterson's weight. That's how bad it got. He could be about as classless as they come. But very effective.[106]

Hussman said Starr's column positioned the *Democrat* as the "fearless champion of the little guy." But it was never antibusiness, he said. In fact, the *Democrat*'s readership studies showed that readers perceived the underdog paper—not the liberal *Gazette*—as siding with everyday Arkansans and the *Gazette* as more in line with the establishment. "It was kind of interesting," Hussman said. "His column did end up creating a reputation for the *Democrat* that we'd never contemplated."[107]

Bob Lancaster, who worked at the *Gazette* twice and left the *Democrat* when Starr was hired there, called him "the mucker pose personified." "You struck the 'mucker pose' when you tried to appear stupider and tougher and more abrupt than you really are," Lancaster said. "They want to show they're rough, tough sons-of-bitches, too."[108] But Starr's column became one of the most popular things in the *Democrat*. Jim Bailey said Starr gave the underdog newspaper something it had never had before—an identifiable force. "Whether you liked him or not, people wanted to know, 'Gosh, what'd that crazy Starr say today?' 'Did you see what he said about Orville?'"[109] Jerry Dhonau, who was by then an editorial writer at the *Gazette*, said Starr's columns were unnecessarily personal in their gigging of the competition and for that reason he was not well regarded.[110]

But as the underdog newspaper trying to make a comeback, the *Democrat* needed to attract reader interest, Hussman said, and Starr's column certainly did that. Hussman called it "very fearless, beholden-to-no-interests whatsoever, muckraking in a way," the kind of column that had been missing from both Little Rock newspapers.[111] However, the blurring of the lines between news and opinion forever bothered him, he said, although in the situation he faced—with a quarter of the revenues of his competitor and trying to build circulation—"you probably experiment with some things like that or acquiesce in some things that maybe you wouldn't if you were the only newspaper in town and you were making money."[112] Ultimately, though, he also sacrificed his journalistic principles to do so.

Hussman said he often disagreed with his editor's column, but he found that acceptable philosophically since it did not run on the editorial page.[113] Instead, it ran on the op-ed page (called "Voices") and was often caustic, skewering politicians, newsmakers—and, as Brantley said, the *Gazette* and its employees. Hussman said he complained to his managing editor that those references were self-serving and may have hurt the *Democrat*'s cause. "I don't think it rubs well with people; it sure doesn't rub well with people in Arkansas," Hussman said. "I just think it created a lot of curiosity in the *Democrat* and made people say, 'Gee, I need to read Bob Starr because I'm not going to read what he's writing anywhere else. I may disagree with it, but I'd like to read what he has to say.'"[114]

Dougan likened Starr to Jeff Davis, the controversial Arkansas governor with whom J. N. Heiskell had tussled during the early days of his family's ownership of the *Gazette*. "He was an extremist for extremists," Dougan said of Starr. "His value to the *Democrat* during the war was in attacking the *Gazette* and making it, as Davis had done before, an object of ridicule."[115] Ernest Dumas remembered that Starr kept up an almost steady drumbeat against the *Gazette*, both through his attack columns and in the news coverage he directed. When Starr would make a speech at the Kiwanis Club or someplace, he "would denounce the *Gazette* and tell what terrible people we were, and they would cover those stories at some length," Dumas said. "And Walter Hussman would go make a speech about the newspaper war, and there would be these thorough stories in there about how terrible the *Gazette* was." Dumas said as far as he knew, no one from the *Democrat* ever called the *Gazette* to get its side when reporting such stories.[116] The brazen disregard for journalistic principles was shocking. Such practices run completely counter to standard journalistic practices, and even the fact that they took place during Arkansas's fierce newspaper war cannot condone their use. Simply, the Hussman-owned *Democrat* did not have the same commitment to quality journalism that the *Gazette* had under Heiskell family ownership. Dumas said that although it was dispiriting for *Gazette* employees to read such stories and to think that readers might believe the allegations, Hugh Patterson's edict was that the *Gazette* would not respond. Gannett would continue the same philosophy.[117] Both would gamble that journalistic quality would make the difference in Arkansas's newspaper war. Both would lose that bet.

Despite their dubiousness, all the points in Hussman's strategy began to work. Circulation jumped significantly, and in 1980, the *Democrat* was the nation's fastest-growing newspaper.[118] Hussman said he thought some of the trend could be traced to the *Gazette*'s stance on Central High and the arrogance of his competitor's business operations and advertising staffs. He said Arkansas readers liked the idea of a challenger for the *Gazette*, which had been dominant for so long, so they and advertisers supported the underdog.[119]

Nate Allen, who had been based in Fayetteville as a *Gazette* sportswriter since 1976, said Starr's significance in the war could not be overstated. "It was like one day [Starr] said, 'We're number one,' and the *Gazette* believed it," he said, mentioning the attention Starr got from "taking potshots" at Orville Henry. "[I]t seemed some at the *Gazette*, not just the new regime, started doing the same."[120] Jim Bailey said the *Gazette* had been "going so good for so long, we were on automatic pilot waiting for the *Democrat* to throw in the towel. And when they went the other way, we had a real tough time getting off of automatic pilot."[121] Senator David Pryor said many Arkansans felt the *Gazette* was resting on its laurels. "It truly was a voice of moderation and progressivism, but a lot of people felt it became arrogant and elitist," Pryor said.[122]

The staid Old Gray Lady found it difficult to respond to her competitor's attacks. Max Brantley said the paper "for years and years and years took the high road, that we would not respond to Starr, that we would commit good journalism as we understood it to be. . . . [T]here was sort of an official ignore-them policy."[123] Should the *Gazette* have answered? Brantley said that was a difficult question. "Clearly, it helped them develop by ignoring them," he said. "And whether we'd have been hammered for getting down in the dirt with them had we done it earlier, I just don't know."[124] Carrick Patterson said the *Gazette*'s putting out a good newspaper was not enough to keep advertisers totally loyal to it because they were driven by economics.

> If you have a chance to buy advertising for a dollar an inch, versus fifteen dollars an inch, you're going to do it. And they also did a pretty good job over there at the *Democrat* of identifying interesting things to report on. They didn't do as good a job of covering the traditional news of record, perhaps, as we did, but they covered for that to some extent by having . . . interesting stories about what

> people were doing and what was going on. . . . So, to say it was totally economic competition is wrong, but that was the key factor, the economics.[125]

Ernest Dumas, who had joined the *Gazette* in 1960, remembered that the staff had been convinced by Hugh Patterson and others that it was just a matter of time before the *Democrat* would fold. "And then after several years and the *Democrat* began to grow, we really began to get apprehensive about it," Dumas said.[126] Brantley reiterated that the *Gazette* always had a superior staff, but it was hamstrung in various ways, such as when the *Democrat* began emphasizing investigative-style reporting, which resulted in a few public officials losing their jobs after the newspaper exposed their wrongdoings, even though the methods used screamed yellow journalism. "[W]e were not really generating those kinds of stories ourselves," Brantley said. "I don't think you can [over]estimate how valuable that was in making the *Democrat* a talked-about commodity in town." Starr, who had assigned the stories in his role as managing editor, would then comment on them in his column,[127] again contradicting every rule of responsible journalism. Bill Lewis, who had joined the *Gazette* in 1956, remembered a too-prevalent attitude at the *Gazette*, from the top down, to act like the competition didn't exist, a strategy he said he never understood. "They began to make inroads very soon thereafter, and it got to be pretty serious," he said. "We knew we had a fight on our hands."[128]

Part of the *Gazette*'s answering strategy was to hire some of the *Democrat*'s better people.[129] As managing editor in the 1970s, Bob Douglas had hundreds of applications from bright young journalists across the country because a paper with the reputation of the *Gazette* could hire the very best people. As Arkansas's newspaper war heated up, many of those applications came from *Democrat* employees.[130] Ernest Dumas recalled that during the '60s and '70s, the *Gazette* had applications "from nearly everybody who worked at the *Arkansas Democrat*," and Douglas and other top management at the *Gazette* delighted in cherry-picking the competition's best people, particularly as Arkansas's newspaper war cranked up. "It didn't make any difference if we had perhaps better applications from somebody else, we'd hire people from the *Democrat*," Dumas said. "I think at that point, it had become so personal."[131]

The *Democrat* under the Hussmans positioned itself as the conservative alternative to the more liberal, progressive *Gazette*, moving more in stride with the political philosophy of most everyday Arkansans. But while the underdog paper's new regime saw improvements in many facets of the organization, such as circulation, single-copy sales, and advertising revenue increases, the most important one went the other way. The *Democrat* lost more money in

1979 than it ever had under Hussman ownership—$5 million. The losses brought the entire WEHCO company into the red.[132] It marked a reversal of trends from the earlier years of Arkansas's newspaper war. Hussman said the *Democrat* lost about a million dollars during his family's first year of ownership and cut those losses in half by 1977. He recalled countering his parents' concerns about the staggering monetary losses by pointing to the rising circulation and advertising numbers. He told them, "We're really having to force-feed this thing to resuscitate it. We don't have a big enough share of the market to be able to profitably operate, because we've got to add on enough expenses so we can go out and cover those same meetings the *Gazette* is covering—so we can have those delivery routes in Crossett and places where the *Gazette* delivers."[133] The fixed costs required to compete with the dominant paper led to the losses, Hussman explained. For example, the *Democrat* didn't make any money off coverage of a Benton City Council meeting and had to pay the reporter's salary, but after it established such essential coverage, readers would eventually recognize that there was a different voice than the *Gazette*'s that would ultimately attract subscribers. "So there's a lag there," he explained. "You have to add the fixed costs first before you can start covering those costs with extra and new revenues."[134] Whatever the reason, it would seem to have been an irrational response for a businessman playing with his own money. He said he remembered by the end of 1979 thinking "like you've gotten on the back of a tiger, and the tiger's started running through the jungle and he's running so fast, how do you get off?"[135] He said it was hard to consider giving up with the increases in revenue, circulation, and acceptance, and he was getting positive feedback from readers who wanted a morning alternative to the *Gazette*—not just a complementary buy.[136] In reality, he was also getting closer to the retribution he had likely craved after Patterson's perceived slight of him years before.

The Hussman family's conundrum was that for the first time since they had owned the *Democrat*, it was succeeding in all matters of business except financial. So they adopted a short-term approach. "We just kept at it," Hussman said. "It started out like a ninety-day program; it succeeded; we did another ninety days and another, and so we get into '80 and '81."[137]

Advertising rates in the *Democrat* were still low because its circulation remained behind the *Gazette*'s. Hussman tried to increase his retail advertising prices from $1 to $1.25 an inch—the *Gazette*'s rate was $8 an inch—and was met with major resistance. He recalled many dark days when he wondered whether his company would make it. But after 1979, the reality of the losses set in, and he raised his prices.[138] When the *Democrat* went morning in 1979, it charged $3.60 per month for a seven-day subscription; the *Gazette*'s rate was $4.95. In early 1980, the *Democrat* raised its rates to $4.25.[139] Circulation employees resisted, but Hussman had a simple answer. If the increase backfired, the *Democrat* would go out of business. But if he didn't have the increase, it would go out of business anyway, so he felt he had no choice. "We have got to raise our prices, and if it works, great," he said. "And if doesn't work, then there's no hope."[140]

Once again, Hussman's desperate gamble worked. Circulation kept rising. In 1981, he raised the rates to $4.95 to match the *Gazette*'s. "Again, our circulation people protested, saying, 'We can't charge [the same rate] as the *Gazette*. The *Gazette* has been so dominant here for years, we'll *never* be able to do it.'" But he offered the same justification, and again he was right. "People were willing to pay for a better-quality newspaper," he said, calling the *Democrat* then a better, more interesting newspaper with more hard news and more local news than it had previously been,[141] although the *Gazette* remained a far superior publication journalistically and would until the end.

Hussman said by that time, Arkansas's newspaper war was draining all the profits from WEHCO's other newspapers. In fact, the company as a whole lost money in 1979 and 1980 and was plagued by interest rates as high as 21.5 percent in 1981. "We weren't borrowing money on the newspaper; we were funding it with cash flow from our other operations, but we had gone out and borrowed a lot of money on our cable TV companies, and we owed about $5 million in debt, the most debt our company had ever had in its history, and we were paying 21 1/2 percent interest," he explained.[142] The interest bill alone amounted to $1 million that year, he recalled, and WEHCO didn't have access to its cable cash flow for Arkansas's newspaper war because of restrictions the banks had placed on the loans requiring the company to keep its cable money separate from the newspapers. But interest rates eventually decreased, and with the arrival of HBO and CNN in the early 1980s, the cable business increased, giving Hussman some breathing room.[143]

Feeling the pressure, Hugh Patterson, in an effort to revamp the *Gazette* in 1981, brought in Bill McIlwain, former editor of the *Washington Star*, as editor. Carrick Patterson moved into the managing editor slot as Bob Douglas moved on to head the University of Arkansas journalism department. By that time, Douglas was convinced that the two papers were engaged in a real war, his friend and former *Gazette* colleague, Roy Reed, remembered. "Walter Hussman was putting up quite a fight, and it was sort of a worthwhile thing because both papers were probably made better for a while," Reed said.[144] McIlwain was tasked with grooming Carrick Patterson to assume the leadership role at the paper, but Max Brantley said he was "the first of many outsiders who came in and had an awful lot of pretty harsh things to say" about the Old Gray Lady.[145]

Under McIlwain, the *Gazette*'s features section improved, and designers came in to change the look of the newspaper. "One of the things he was not happy about, and it would be a theme that would echo and re-echo as subsequent new leadership came in, was that we were too boring, too stodgy, too concerned with matters of record, and not enterprising enough, and not colorful enough, and not in tune with everyday concerns enough, and we needed to have a whole lot more of that kind of writing in the newspaper," Brantley remembered.[146] McIlwain didn't last long, but many of his criticisms foreshadowed what the new Gannett leadership would say a few years later. Looking back, Brantley said a number of McIlwain's moves were not bad changes, including emphasizing the features section to appeal to readers' leisure time and creating a special assignment desk for enterprise reporting.[147]

One of McIlwain's moves was to hire McCord, the former executive editor at the *Democrat*, to create an op-ed page for the *Gazette*. McCord remembered Hugh Patterson saying he wanted him, based on his three years of working under Hussman, to help the *Gazette* win Arkansas's newspaper war. But after a few months, when Patterson had asked nothing, McCord approached the publisher, who told him, "[W]e have got this 'newspaper war' under control, and Walter is not going to last another six months. We are doing just fine." In Patterson's defense, Hussman's actions seemed to be doomed—he was in the midst of spending $42 million of his family's money to battle the *Gazette*. How could Patterson not think that saner heads would eventually prevail? Perhaps because he had worked with Hussman and understood him better, McCord disagreed with Patterson's analysis and told the *Gazette* publisher, "You have to fight fire with fire," but Patterson again declined to meet the challenge. In a later meeting, McCord, trying to anticipate Hussman's next move, advised prizes and free papers to boost circulation. Patterson and Leon Reed, the *Gazette*'s longtime circulation manager, again said no. "Finally, I said, 'You know, I think we ought to go back and think about a joint operating agreement so we can keep the two newspapers alive,'" McCord remembered. "Well, they just laughed at that. . . . 'Bob, you worry about things that we have under control.'" They told McCord that Hussman would run out of money.[148] Again, the prediction made sense; it just proved to be wrong. McCord was also critical of Patterson's decision to fire McIlwain. "They were clannish and didn't want an outsider coming in there and being the boss," he said. "I have sometimes thought that if McIlwain had stayed, things might have ended in another way—a joint operating agreement or maybe even the defeat of the *Democrat*."[149] The Patterson family's attitude differed from that of Heiskell's more than thirty years earlier when he brought in Harry Ashmore and made him executive editor.

The *Democrat*'s pattern of circulation price increases continued in 1982. Hussman's decision that year would make the *Democrat* more expensive than the *Gazette* in order to have more money to compete. The *Democrat* did an offset conversion on its press in 1982; the *Gazette* continued to use its letterpress. The offset yielded "fantastic" colors for the *Democrat*. "All that costs money," Hussman said. "We had to start getting more revenues—we just didn't have the money as a company."[150] Even though WEHCO's holdings included the five monopoly south Arkansas newspapers and the cable operations, and the Pattersons' only real source of income was the *Gazette*, Hussman reiterated that the *Gazette* was a bigger company in terms of the bottom line.[151]

The 1982 circulation price increase put the *Democrat* at $5.75 per month, a rate the *Gazette* quickly matched. Yet neither paper lost circulation. "People were willing to pay for a newspaper as long as it was a reasonable price," Hussman said. He said as the *Democrat* raised prices, its revenues increased even more.[152] From 1974 to 1978, the *Democrat*'s revenues had remained fairly flat at $5 million to $6 million a year, he said, while the *Gazette*'s revenues were increasing. Hussman said from 1974 to 1978, the *Gazette*'s annual revenues increased 50 percent to $22.5 million. His company, he said, stood at $23.6 million total before the $5 million loss in 1979. But with the more competitive (although inferior) product by the early 1980s, the *Democrat*'s share of revenues steadily increased.[153] The *Democrat*'s classified revenues ballooned from $800,000 per year in 1978 to almost $4.5 million in 1984. Hussman said the free want ads had brought much-increased readership to his paper, so more commercial advertisers wanted to be there, too. "We were able to raise our classified rates by larger percentages than we could raise our retail rates, because our classified section really gained a lot of readership," he said. "And readers would even look in our classified section before they'd look in the *Gazette*'s classified section, even though the *Gazette* had more circulation."[154]

The phenomenal success of the free want ads had allowed the *Democrat* to increase its share of revenues from less than 20 percent of the market to about 36 percent.[155] As the *Democrat*'s classified revenues increased, the *Gazette*'s decreased. Ernest Dumas recalled that in order to offset the losses, the Pattersons began to make reductions—shrinking the news hole, failing to replace departing personnel—anything to break even or make some kind of profit.

> So I think it was probably sometime in '83 they realized that this guy was not going to go away. He was willing to accept losses at the *Democrat* forever. The *Gazette* continued to be the dominant paper; it had the dominant circulation, all the way to the end. And it was

> still making money, barely, barely making money, but the raises were small for the staff; we weren't rehiring people, canceling features to shrink the expenditures.[156]

When faced with his bold new competitor, Patterson's conservative response had been a textbook example of the newspaper industry's slowness to respond to a threat—first with the advent of television and today with the arrival of the Internet. Obviously, it has been exactly the wrong response in each instance. In fact, Hussman's aggressive approach to competition—counterintuitive as it was—proved to be a far better strategy. Nearly twenty-four years after becoming the owner of the only statewide newspaper in Arkansas, despite layoffs, furloughs, and other cuts, he appears to have retained the wherewithal to respond at least somewhat similarly to the ongoing threat of the Internet and is now hailed as "a model for success in the digital age."[157]

With its increasing circulation, the *Democrat* was also able to raise retail advertising rates, helping increase its share of revenues even more. In April 1984, the Hussman-led *Democrat* made its first profit—$14,900.[158] Hussman's response also proved to be another right move in Arkansas's newspaper war. "So we took that $14,000 and divided it by three hundred-plus employees we had, and everybody got a check for about $42," he recalled. "[W]hat was $14,000 to us when we had years when we had lost $5 million?"[159] The reward for those who had helped get him there marked another difference in Arkansas's newspaper war. Hussman's loyalty would be returned. The *Gazette* under Gannett later tried to hire his single-copy circulation manager at a greatly increased salary, but the manager turned down the offer. When Hussman asked him why, he said the man told him, "Do you remember that $41.27 you gave me that time out of the first profits you ever made? I decided I was going to stick with you," Hussman remembered, adding that that reinvestment in his people turned out to be a valuable strategy for the *Democrat.*[160]

In May 1984, the month after the first profit, the *Democrat* cleared $50,000 and proclaimed—complete with employee-worn buttons—"We're in the black." Hussman said he thought the announcement was very discouraging for the Pattersons. "Here we had come from virtually going out of business to actually publishing a newspaper that was an alternative to the *Gazette*," he said. "[B]y then, many people felt like they really needed to read both papers." He said that by that point, there were things in the *Democrat* that were not in the *Gazette*.[161] Although the *Gazette* retained the circulation lead (120,000–80,000 daily), the *Democrat* had pulled much closer on Sunday. By 1986, the *Gazette* led on Sunday by just 2,000 subscriptions—157,000–155,000.[162] Bill

Shelton, the longtime city editor, said he thought the *Gazette* began its deterioration in the early 1980s, both in appearance and in the shrinking news hole. "In essence, we're almost converting ourselves into a *Democrat*," he said. "The time was when the *Gazette* had the space, and every story in town got in there first; the *Democrat* followed along."[163] Jim Bailey said Shelton told him years later that after the *Democrat* engaged, the *Gazette*'s main editors were brought together and told, "We're not going to do anything different." Shelton told Bailey, however, "But they did, from that day forward."[164] In football terms, the Pattersons played not to lose instead of to win. It was their misfortune to face a foe who ignored all the rules of the game and ran into the end zone on every play.

Carrick Patterson agreed that by that time, Hussman's strategy was working. "You have to hand it to the guy; it was pretty damn clever," Patterson recalled. "Except that he was spending more to do it than he was bringing in, and that's called an unfair business practice." The Patterson family, at least, thought so. "You couldn't sell a competing product for less than it cost you to produce it because that was an unfair business practice to your competitor," Carrick Patterson explained. He said his father had previously tried to get the Arkansas attorney general and the national Fair Trade Commission involved in Arkansas's newspaper war but had no luck. "So the last resort was to file a civil suit against him, which was done," Carrick Patterson said.[165]

On December 12, 1984, the *Gazette* filed a federal antitrust lawsuit against the *Democrat*, asking that Hussman be stopped from selling below the cost of production.[166] The *Gazette* contended that its competitor had violated the federal Sherman Antitrust Act and the state Unfair Practices Act by deliberately operating at a loss to damage the *Gazette*, using the profits from other Hussman companies (the five daily newspapers in Camden, El Dorado, Texarkana, Magnolia, and Hot Springs, two radio stations, a television station, and fourteen cable television franchises)[167] to try to establish a monopoly in Little Rock.[168] The Associated Press reported the *Gazette*'s contention that Hussman subsidized the competition with $50 million from the family's other companies.[169] The tactics at issue included the *Democrat*'s giving away a Wednesday newspaper to seventy thousand nonsubscribers for five years, giving away classified advertising to individuals, publishing a bigger paper than its rival every day regardless of revenue, cutting some advertising rates to a dollar an inch, selling all of the advertising one department store wanted for $500,000 a year, and operating at a loss.[170]

Max Brantley maintained that by any fair reading of antitrust law, the Patterson lawsuit made perfect sense:

> Hussman was giving away classified advertising; he was giving away valuable retail advertising for a dollar an inch to people like Dillard's. He had made a vow that he was going to run more pages than the *Arkansas Gazette*, no matter how much it cost. . . . It would be as if you ran a service station and a guy with huge wealth came in across the street and said, "I'm going to sell my gas for a nickel a gallon less than you do for as long as it takes to run you out of business." And so Hugh Patterson's family owned the *Gazette* and had no other real source of revenue to finance a campaign against a richer foe, so they filed an antitrust lawsuit.[171]

The *Democrat* contended that its tactics were unusual but not illegal.[172] John Robert Starr said of the *Gazette*, "They're crybabies."[173] Hussman denied in court that he had used any revenues from his broadcast companies to help the *Democrat*.[174] The *Gazette* asked for damages totaling $23 million to $123 million for alleged losses of potential advertising and lost value of the company.[175] Hussman said his company's net worth at the time was about $30 million, so if the *Gazette* had won a judgment—which would have been tripled in antitrust—it would have bankrupted his company. He called the *Gazette*'s case "a very novel theory of the antitrust laws," with the idea of a smaller competitor engaging in predatory pricing.[176]

> When we bought the *Democrat*, all our companies combined were smaller than the *Gazette* in total revenues, and when we decided to compete with the *Gazette* in 1979, all our newspapers were smaller than the *Gazette*. Our companies did prosper. Our cable companies started doing better. The *Democrat* started doing a lot better. Eventually we did pass the *Gazette* in size, but that was because of good management. And good luck.[177]

Predatory business practices—regardless of the jury's ruling—and dubious journalistic practices were also factors.

Powell said he thought the suit was "perfectly right."[178] The *Democrat*'s Oakley, however, said the filing of the lawsuit validated her newsroom. "It was like an injection of vitamins or amphetamines or something," she said. "If there were any doubt that this was the good fight, that proved it, because why else would they try to put us out of business, which is what that was all about."[179] Hussman said he was very surprised that the lawsuit was filed, citing the fact that the *Gazette* was still making money—enough, in fact, that the *Gazette* board had voted in December 1983 to give Hugh Patterson a $150,000 bonus, to increase his salary from $150,000 to $250,000, and to set up a bonus plan for 1984 that would provide bonuses to him of up to $100,000 a year, depending on profits.[180] Testimony from the trial revealed that in the year the lawsuit was filed, the *Gazette* posted its biggest revenue gain in modern times.[181]

Hugh Patterson hired Stephen D. Susman, a respected antitrust lawyer from Houston, Texas, as the *Gazette*'s main attorney. Susman told jurors, "We aren't saying that we are on the verge of bankruptcy or at the door of the poor house," but that the *Democrat*'s practices had caused $23 million in losses in profits to the *Gazette* and in the newspaper's worth.[182]

Hussman used Philip S. Anderson, who had been the *Democrat*'s attorney since 1974. Anderson, of the Wright, Lindsey and Jennings firm in Little Rock, "absolutely" was convinced that the *Democrat*'s practices were pro-competitive, not anti-competitive, because it had increased the competition between the newspapers, Hussman said, adding that Anderson's passion for the case was also a plus. "I think Phil is a better attorney than Steve Susman," he said. "He certainly didn't have Steve Susman's reputation."[183]

Carrick Patterson said his father made "a huge error" with his choice of attorney.

> Arkansas is a parochial state. We don't like outsiders coming in and telling us what to do, and we especially don't like Texans coming in. These were pretty competent lawyers and everything, but they were fish out of water when that trial began. This guy, the lawyer from Houston, opened his mouth, spoke for about two minutes, and I said, "We have lost this suit." And Philip Anderson, the *Democrat*'s attorney, who's probably much more aristocratic and non-typically Arkansan than these guys from Houston were, but still did this folksy stuff, and basically this jury of Arkansans believed the *Democrat*'s story, that it was okay for Walter Hussman to spend his money any darn way he wanted to, even if it was an unfair business practice. The facts were never in dispute. Indeed, they admitted, yeah, we did this free circulation; we did the free classifieds, we did the dollar-an-inch advertising; we did all that, but it's okay because it's Mr. Hussman's money to do with what he wants.[184]

Ernest Dumas remembered Susman coming to court every day "with this fine suit on and with a gold watch chain in his vest. . . . He was eloquent but aloof and arrogant, and the *Democrat*'s lead attorney . . . was down to earth, knew the jury, knew Arkansans." Dumas said Patterson should have hired "someone like [Arkansas lawyer] Bill Wilson, a great trial lawyer—no antitrust lawyer but somebody who had a feel for juries and wouldn't prejudice our case just by standing up there, which is what [Susman] did."[185]

Hussman said he thought with the loss of the lawsuit, there was a tendency to claim the *Gazette* had been outlawyered, but he disagreed, arguing that the facts of the case had hurt the *Gazette*. "First of all, to be engaged in predatory pricing, it's generally a bigger company that does it to a smaller company," he said. "This was the case where the smaller company was supposedly using predatory pricing against the bigger company."[186] He reiterated that the *Democrat* had made the Little Rock newspaper market more competitive—not less. "When people engage in predatory pricing, the market becomes less competitive, not more competitive," he said. "The facts were just on our side."[187] Ultimately, though, the tactics would lead to the death of the Old Gray Lady, but in 1986, no one could anticipate that.

Meredith Oakley, the *Democrat* columnist, agreed with Hussman that the facts were on their side. But she said her exultation at the verdict was tempered when she saw the look on Louise Heiskell Patterson's face.

> The woman was destroyed. You can't celebrate something like that. You can't celebrate tradition and legacy and birthright going down the toilet. And I'm sorry that the Pattersons mismanaged the newspaper, and I'm sorry that Gannett kept it on only as long as it needed to do to write it off as a loss and then liquidate the assets. All that is terrible, but the *Arkansas Democrat* didn't entirely bring that about by winning a newspaper war. It was a bad decision to sue the *Arkansas Democrat* because the evidence wasn't on the *Gazette*'s side. They should've fought it out the way we were fighting it, but they weren't street fighters, and I suppose we were. Or we became that because Starr was a street fighter, and he was captain of the ship at that point. They could've respected us a little bit, a little bit more. I'm not going to tell you I wasn't grinning like an idiot [after the verdict] because I was. But I was brought up a little short when I looked over and saw Louise Patterson's face, and as I understand, that was sort of the beginning of the end of [Hugh and Louise Patterson's] long relationship. They weren't together too much longer after that.[188]

In an interview after Arkansas's newspaper war ended, Hussman produced trial exhibits that showed in 1984, the *Gazette* had revenues of $32 million. The *Democrat*'s were $18 million.[189] Generally, he said, the property with larger market share uses predatory pricing to hurt the smaller property after it has become a nuisance, so the *Gazette*'s case was a "very maverick" reading of the antitrust law. "We at the *Arkansas Democrat* never spent in any single year as much as the *Arkansas Gazette* spent to produce their newspaper," he said. "The remarkable thing is that we were gaining market share and spending less money to do it." He said that was only possible by being more efficient. "And we were far more efficient than the *Gazette*," he said. "And we made better business decisions, and a lot of times made some better journalistic decisions than they did."[190] The *Democrat* may have been more efficient—the *Gazette* still had a unionized backshop—but any better journalistic decisions were few and far between. There was a reason, after all, that so many *Democrat* reporters and editors had their applications on file at the *Gazette*.

Hussman's figures from the trial showed that from 1974 to 1978, the *Gazette* spent $64 million to the *Democrat*'s $26 million. But to reinvigorate the *Democrat*, starting in 1979, WEHCO had to increase its operating expenses from $7.8 million the previous year to $11.7 million. The *Gazette* spent $20.7 million in 1979, slightly more than it had spent the previous year.[191] Hussman said the *Gazette* under the Pattersons never took him or the *Democrat* seriously. "'This is not going to last' was the attitude," he said. "And it probably wasn't a bad idea at the time to think it wasn't going to last."[192] From 1979 to 1984, his figures showed the *Gazette* outspent the *Democrat* by nearly $10 million every year.[193] Yet, despite the profitable year and Hugh Patterson's bonus, the *Gazette* claimed to be damaged. "[S]omeone expressed the fact that it must have been very frustrating for the ownership of the *Gazette* to have realized that they had the whole Little Rock newspaper market at one point, and they could have had ninety percent of the profits," Hussman said. "[L]iterally, we did almost go out of business." But by 1984, the *Democrat* had made the turn and was profitable and gaining market share. "And it looked like they'd <u>never</u> get rid of us now," Hussman said. "So someone expressed the opinion that maybe what the *Gazette* wanted to do was win in the courtroom what they had not been able to win in the marketplace." He said if the *Gazette* had prevailed, he would not have been able to pay the judgment. "We would have had to file bankruptcy or sold our companies, or we could maybe have settled the case by agreeing to close the *Arkansas Democrat*," he said.[194]

Brantley said he was nervous about the trial from the beginning because he sensed the outcome would be "powerfully important." But fifteen years afterward, he remained angry about the *Democrat*'s coverage of the lawsuit in its news pages, especially in the days leading up to the trial. He said it "should be in a textbook for dishonesty" as the *Democrat* wrote stories that stressed elements that were advantageous to the defense and none that focused on the advantages of the plaintiff.[195] "I'm quite sure Starr read the copy very carefully and read it with an eye toward making sure things turned out right," he said. "But this was a pattern that Starr followed. Where business interests intersected with journalism, business interests won out." As another example, he pointed to the *Democrat*'s habit of not reporting negative stories about Dillard Department Stores, which was both papers' single-biggest advertiser, or failing to report on Walmart's censoring some music because of content. "We wrote a story about it; the *Democrat* wouldn't touch it," he said. "So they were very sensitive to what the lifeblood of their operation was."[196]

Dumas agreed that the *Democrat*'s trial coverage was biased. "All of the developments that would seem to be favorable to the *Democrat* were reported, and comments, testimony that were not favorable did not get in the paper," he said. "Days when points were made that were damaging to the *Democrat*, you didn't see them in the paper, or else they were at the end of the story and played down."[197] Yet both agreed the *Gazette*'s trial coverage by George Wells was "painfully fair and balanced," to the point that Brantley remembered a couple of occasions of Carrick Patterson "swearing under his breath that, here we are writing it this way, and he knew that across town it was going to be presented in a different fashion. But that what had happened had happened, and George's account was a fair reading of what had occurred."[198] The Heiskell-Patterson family's commitment to quality journalism had, in this instance, come back to haunt them. A few blocks away, there were no such scruples.

Brantley recalled finding out by reading the *Democrat* that Hugh Patterson had taken four hundred thousand dollars out of the company in the preceding year in the form of a dividend.

> I thought, "Son of a bitch." That was a lot of money. . . . I was assistant city editor, making twenty-five thousand dollars a year, maybe twenty-six thousand dollars a year. Of course, the *Democrat* lawyers hammered it and hammered it and hammered it.[199]

Brantley later called that revelation the most critical factor leading to the verdict, citing post-trial interviews of the jurors by *Spectrum*, a Little Rock alternative newspaper. Despite the *Gazette*'s advantages in revenue and advertising market share, he said, its lawyers correctly predicted the newspaper was in a death spiral against Hussman. "[B]ut they put on their defense in a very good, thorough and aggressive manner, and they won," he said. "And it was critical, and I think everybody who followed it closely knew that when the suit was lost, the *Gazette* as we knew it was lost."[200]

Speculation abounded that if the Pattersons lost the suit, they would sell the *Gazette*. Ernest Dumas remembered that it was pretty clear to all that if the verdict went the wrong way, the Pattersons "didn't have the resources to continue to fight, and the paper was shrinking, and we weren't filling vacancies on the staff, every effort being made to kind of conserve resources, so we were all pretty bothered by it."[201] But Jerry Dhonau recalled that a possible sale wasn't dwelled on within the newsroom. "The journalists there just went on about their usual business trying to put out a good paper and didn't let that take on the importance that it does now in retrospect," he said.[202] Hussman said that, with Hugh Patterson growing older and the difficulties Carrick Patterson had had at the paper, "this is typically why newspapers are sold, is because of a management succession problem in privately held companies."[203]

Hussman said he thought it was a mistake for the Pattersons to file the lawsuit and that they would have been better served instead "to roll up our sleeves and we're going to start taking these guys seriously, we're going to compete with them" and make the internal operation more cost-efficient.[204] He said in retrospect, he agreed that the lawsuit was an effort to win back in the courtroom what the Pattersons had lost in the marketplace. "Maybe they did feel like we'd not played fairly and we'd gained our market share in some improper way," he said.[205] Bob Douglas, who by that time had gone on to the University of Arkansas as chair of the Department of Journalism, said he was convinced that the Pattersons could have beaten Hussman if they had chosen to fight. "Hugh was scared, too," Douglas said, adding that the elder Patterson didn't want to spend money on a fight. "He could have knocked them off in two years, I am convinced," Douglas said.[206] Powell, too, wondered years later if the Pattersons had kept going if they might have won. "I don't know whether the *Gazette* could have fought and fought and fought and survived or not, but I understand why they would decide to go that route rather than wind up in the poorhouse," he said.[207]

Mathis called the antitrust suit a serious miscalculation on the part of Patterson and the *Gazette*.

> I think the dismissiveness, the thinking that, we are the *Gazette*, we're mighty, we have the power, we have the reputation, we have the resources, etc., that all of that worked against them. They got too comfortable and too cozy with the power and the privilege they had and did not take this little puppy nipping at their heels seriously. When they did take it seriously, it was too late. That puppy had grown up into a pretty big dog and had a pretty good bite on him, and by that time, it was a little too late to start backtracking.[208]

With the lawsuit, perception made its first appearance in Arkansas's newspaper war. Hussman said he thought when the *Gazette* filed the lawsuit, people began to perceive the Old Gray Lady as vulnerable. "[I]t really opened people's eyes around the community, thinking, 'Gee, really, I hadn't been paying much attention to the *Democrat*; maybe I need to pay more, maybe I need to advertise in the *Democrat*,'" he said.[209] Arkansans found it shocking to think that the state's oldest newspaper might be run out of business, but if the *Gazette* believed that—as the filing of the lawsuit had suggested—maybe it was a possibility. Hussman said such thinking as "What if they do run them out of business, and we've only been running ads in the *Gazette*?" helped his cause. "In a way, they gave us some credibility that we couldn't give ourselves except from that lawsuit," he said.[210]

Hussman reiterated that he did not have access to his company's cable revenues during the early years of his newspaper war with the Pattersons. That was because the company was borrowing money to build the cable systems, and its agreement with the bank was that it could not take money out of WEHCO Video to use for the newspapers.

> So we didn't have access to any of the cash flow, revenues, profits or anything from our cable companies back in the 1970s, probably not until it was in the 1980s. In 1983 the cable TV company finally paid off all their debts. So, basically, when we bought the *Arkansas Democrat* in 1974, it was really our newspapers—we had access to revenues and profits from our newspapers, but not our cable TV companies. And then in 1978 when we decided to challenge the *Gazette*, we still didn't have access to the cable TV funds, either. In fact, in 1980 the cable companies owed more money than they had ever owed. They owed over $5 million. And then the prime rate went to twenty-one and a half percent. . . . But all that was just kind of part of our company that was carved out for cable TV that we didn't have any access to for funds for the *Arkansas Democrat*.[211]

The newspaper side of WEHCO included revenues of $11 million in 1974 when the company bought the *Democrat*. By 1978, the newspaper revenue of the company had grown to $16 million—virtually all in the smaller monopoly newspapers. Hussman said in that year, the *Gazette* was at about $22.5 million in revenues and WEHCO overall at $16 million.[212] In 1982, WEHCO's newspaper division was slightly larger than the *Gazette*.[213]

After twelve days of testimony and five and a half hours of deliberation, the lawsuit ended on March 26, 1986, when the jury found in favor of the *Democrat* on all four counts. Hussman recalled being relieved that he wouldn't have to leave town. "It was very gratifying when they delivered the judgment and we won on all counts," he said.[214]

McCord had considered the lawsuit a last, desperate try on the Pattersons' part. "I don't know anybody that thought it would work," he said.[215] But Gene Foreman, who had worked at both papers and called Hussman a friend, said Hussman's below-market-price sales of advertising financed by the profits from his other all-monopoly newspapers—which did not participate in such pricing—would seem to be prima facie evidence of predatory pricing. "I do think a fair jury would've found in favor of the *Gazette*," Foreman said, adding, however, that a jury was always a dice roll.[216] Bailey said he never thought the *Gazette* would prevail. "I felt pretty sure if the paper doing the suing is still leading in circulation and revenue, it'd be hard for them to win," he said.[217]

After the verdict, Hussman moved to recoup the losses from the ongoing war—more than $42 million since buying the *Democrat* in 1974, according to court documents[218]—that had been compounded by the $1.3 million it cost him to defend the lawsuit. The strategy was to eliminate circulation discounts. It was announced at the press building—where the *Democrat* had bought new presses during the lawsuit—that the *Democrat* had a bright future because it would be profitable. "We've gained a lot of market share, and hopefully we can gain some more market share," Hussman recalled of the announcement. "You employees—you've got a bright future here."[219]

A few blocks away, at Third and Louisiana, the Pattersons were looking at a very different situation—bleeding at every pore, with no strategy to change anything. Carrick Patterson said after the verdict there was no possibility the family could survive economically and still own the paper. "It became obvious then that we, as the ownership, did not have the economic forces to compete economically at the level that the Hussmans had established," so the family looked to sell.[220] Hussman said, though, that at first he did not think the Pattersons would do so. At that point, he said, there was some talk between the attorneys to maybe discuss another JOA, "obviously a very different JOA, that they might be concerned that they couldn't make a go of it and they felt after losing the lawsuit they might throw in the towel."[221] Again, that went nowhere.

Carrick Patterson remembered his family's dilemma:

> These tactics had been working. They worked great. It cost him millions and millions and millions of dollars, but it worked great. The *Gazette* was suffering; they couldn't raise advertising rates as much as they needed to. The commodity of newsprint kept rising in price. Employee salaries and newsprint—two major expenses for a newspaper—and both were going up. And you had to keep buying equipment at a newspaper. And you didn't just run down to the dime store and buy a press. It was a major multimillion-dollar investment. . . . More and more, people were wanting quality press work; they were wanting color. The *Gazette* was faced with having to modernize its press

> at a cost of millions and millions of dollars. By that time the computer equipment was absolutely necessary; you had to keep on top of that, too. You had to keep recruiting and retaining quality people—tremendous expenditures. So if you couldn't raise your advertising revenues either by rates or by volume or both to compensate, what were you going to do? The *Gazette* found itself in that situation. So very reluctantly, the alternative being going out of business—and we had more than three hundred employees who would've been out on the street—it was decided to try to find a buyer.[222]

He remembered that the family cried a lot of tears following the verdict. Fifteen years after the *Gazette* closed, he had to compose himself during an interview while recalling the situation.

> There was a great sense of responsibility to the people of Arkansas, to the employees, to the people who had supported us through thick and thin, to the employees who probably, a lot of them could've gone to much higher paying jobs in bigger markets but stuck with us. . . . It was your reason for being taken away from you, and not just taken away, but you almost had to involuntarily give it up. You had to be the one who said, okay, for the greater good, we're going to have to give this up.[223]

James O. Powell, who had succeeded Harry Ashmore as the editor of the *Gazette*'s editorial page in 1959, said the Patterson family had to decide whether to eventually lose money or make plans to sell to a major newspaper concern in order to save their fortune and possibly the institution. "The *Gazette* recovered completely from the [Central High] crisis and had never been stronger, we thought," Powell said. "But of course we did not know the kind of situation that we would get into."[224] Besides the possibility of bankrupting the paper and the family, Carrick Patterson said his family was not willing to allow the more than three hundred employees who depended on the *Gazette* for their livelihood to lose their jobs. "[T]hat wasn't something that we were willing to accept even for the ego of owning it for ourselves," he said. "We couldn't just let all those people be sacrificed, so the only other alternative, the legal one being exhausted, practically, was to find somebody with more capital, who could compete."[225] The economic realities of the mid-1980s assured that there would be no more family ownership of the *Arkansas Gazette.*

Several companies were mentioned as possible buyers, including the *Los Angeles Times-Mirror* group, Knight-Ridder and Ingersoll, among some others.

At one time in the past, Hugh Patterson remembered, someone representing the *New York Times* had sent word that if the Pattersons were ever interested in selling, that newspaper would like to talk. But up to that point, the family had never even considered a sale. "You can't imagine just how intense that was for the last two years before we finally sold the paper," Hugh Patterson said. "I'd wake up and try to fathom just what we could do and all."[226] By 1986, however, neither the *New York Times* nor *Times-Mirror* was a viable option to buy the *Arkansas Gazette*. The *New York Times* would wind up making a pittance of an offer—book value of $16 million—but the family never considered that to be a serious offer.[227] "They, I think, recognized to a greater degree than some what an undertaking it was," Patterson said of the *New York Times*. "[B] y that time, the *L.A. Times* had made the decision to go for the *Dallas Times-Herald* and the *Denver Post* and had made a mess of both of those things."[228]

Finally, the Gannett Corporation approached the family. Carrick Patterson recalled that Al Neuharth, head of that company, was nearing the end of his career.

> As he got older, he had sought legitimacy more and more and had purchased name papers in Louisville, Kentucky, and Des Moines, Iowa, and was trying to have a legitimate side. They'd been kind of business-as-usual type papers in most of their smaller markets, but they were sort of seeking legitimacy, so Neuharth came and said, "We'd like to buy the *Gazette* because we're trying to establish this almost separate division of quality newspapers, and we promise we'll keep up the quality, and of course we've got the financial clout and the business expertise that it'd take to keep this newspaper going, to keep your employees employed and keep this tradition alive."[229]

Hugh Patterson had met Neuharth at a Columbia seminar in the early 1960s, and the two had remained friendly over the years.[230] After Gannett bought the *Louisville Courier-Journal*, Hugh Patterson indicated that Neuharth said that the *Gazette* "would be another jewel in their crown. And I thought it was at a time when Al, really having fooled with all these smaller papers and running them on a kind of a formula basis, was really trying to achieve some distinction in the good paper field and what not."[231]

Max Brantley recalled that the *Gazette*, as a winner of multiple Pulitzer Prizes and with a nationwide reputation, was an obvious addition for the flamboyant Neuharth, who, to his credit, was not one to back down from a fight. "He paid what was a pretty good price to come in and buy Little Rock and try to win the newspaper war," Brantley said. "He was dead serious about competing, so that was a good thing."[232] The decision to sell was essentially

Hugh Patterson's, but everyone in the family realized the situation. Carrick Patterson said nobody wanted to sell to Gannett. He said he did not have much respect for the way the chain ran its newspapers. "But, either naïvely or for whatever reason, I thought that going with Gannett, with the assurances we'd been given, was better than shutting the thing down," he said.[233] Although Neuharth later denied having said it,[234] Carrick Patterson said he was in the room when the Gannett chairman promised "to keep the editorial page intact and to keep the spirit of the thing alive."[235]

> Everybody knew Gannett was just a corporate moneymaking-type thing. Except that they had made these moves in recent years in Louisville and Des Moines to try to attain some legitimacy, to invest in some big-name newspapers and try to do an excellent job. I'm not sure how successful I thought they were at that, but the fact is, that was their stated ambition, Neuharth's stated ambition. So, given the alternative, which was basically to rock on because there wasn't much else on the table, and given these promises, it seemed a reasonable risk.[236]

Hugh Patterson remembered that by that point, the family had few options.[237] Carrick Patterson recalled that it was disappointing and surprising to his father how little interest in the *Arkansas Gazette* there was among the country's respected, larger newspaper organizations,[238] but the fact illustrated how few competitive markets were left and how most chains were loath to spend money on any newspaper war. Carrick Patterson called Gannett "the only game in town. . . . It literally was Gannett or nobody at that time. There was no other choice."[239] The only possible alternative, which was not pursued by the family, was to draw back and operate the *Gazette* as just a central Arkansas newspaper, shedding the expense of newsprint, transportation, and so forth, that was necessary to circulate in areas that did not yield high advertising dollars. Carrick Patterson said that would have amounted to "trying to eke it out," but the problem remained that the *Gazette* needed a new offset press in order to print color.[240] With the paper up for sale, the Pattersons ordered a new press. "It had to be done," Carrick Patterson remembered. "You had to be publishing quality color, period. That's the way it was."[241] Max Brantley said everyone realized there were downsides to corporate ownership, but money wasn't one of them. "Gannett brought money," he said.[242]

While negotiations were ongoing with various companies, the *Gazette* worked to increase its circulation at any cost to attract the best possible buyer. Hussman explained that he knew a new owner would come in and look more at the circulation figures than the income statement, so increasing those numbers was the Pattersons' immediate goal. The *Democrat* had nearly caught the *Gazette* in Sunday circulation. "I think they said, 'Let's start discounting circulation with a vengeance. And let's do it to get our circulation numbers up,'" Hussman recalled.[243]

So in the aftermath of the verdict, the *Democrat* cut its circulation discounts and the *Gazette* increased its. Audited circulation figures for March 1986 showed the *Gazette* still retained the circulation lead, 121,000–80,530 daily and 156,146–149,758 Sunday,[244] but by the end of the third quarter of 1986, Hussman said the *Gazette* had increased its Sunday lead from what was once 2,000 to 15,000–20,000.[245] On October 30, the Pattersons announced that they had sold the *Gazette* to the Arlington, Virginia-based Gannett Corporation, the nation's largest newspaper chain. Gannett paid $51 million and assumed $9 million in debt,[246] with thirteen members of the Patterson-Heiskell families who owned shares in the company dividing the sale price.[247] Neuharth said the original asking price was too high "because it's always too high. Every asking price of every newspaper or anything else for sale is too high," but after a period of negotiation, the two sides came to an agreeable price.[248]

Gazette employees assembled in the newsroom for the 10:30 A.M. announcement, which was followed by a public press conference at the nearby Capital Hotel. The morning's events foreshadowed some of the arrogance that would come under the *Gazette*'s new corporate ownership. Brantley remembered: "Neuharth got in a limousine at the Capital Hotel so that he could arrive at the *Gazette* in a limousine, and for those of you who don't know, the Capital Hotel is one block from the *Arkansas Gazette*. But he took a limo ride to cover the distance." Brantley described Neuharth as "a very sharp, hard-charging guy" who told those gathered in the newsroom they would have the necessary resources to continue to fight Arkansas's newspaper war.[249] Despite his wariness of the new owners, Brantley was relieved by the deal.

> I was at that point so fearful about the *Gazette*'s future that I wasn't necessarily depressed by the news, although Gannett didn't have the best reputation in the world. I knew they had deep pockets. I knew that we didn't. I knew that, over time, Hussman, inevitably, with the antitrust suit won, could do anything he wanted to in this market, and he clearly demonstrated that he was willing to do it forever. The thought that somebody was coming in with unlimited money—I thought, well, better that than going out of business. I preferred to be optimistic although they brought a retinue of Gannett overseers who made everybody a little bit nervous by the way they were looking around.[250]

Neuharth set an optimistic tone in the press conference announcing the sale: "It is our hope and our expectation that we will preserve all the best of that and that we will add to the rest of that with an infusion of Gannett resources in terms of people, talent and other resources," he told the crowd gathered at the Capital Hotel.[251] In the newsroom earlier, he had assured employees that Gannett would "continue the *Gazette* traditions and professional standards," adding that "we not only preach but practice local autonomy."[252]

But it did not take long for that to prove to be false. Gannett's "deep pockets" became an ongoing theme. McCord recalled that Neuharth referenced them and told the gathered employees, "[Y]ou don't have to worry about the survival of the *Arkansas Gazette*."[253] Dumas remembered Neuharth saying: "The *Gazette* is going to be here from now on. We've got deep pockets."[254] Jerry Dhonau, editorial page editor at the time, recalled Neuharth saying, "We are with you for the duration."[255] Jim Bailey said in context, the sale was reassuring because "Gannett certainly wasn't the kind of corporation that was going to disappear overnight."[256] Wadie Moore remembered, "We all had a little taste of greed in us" and that everyone welcomed the "deep pockets."[257] John Brummett, a well-established state capitol reporter who had begun writing a political column in February 1986 as part of the *Gazette*'s answer to the *Democrat*'s Starr and Oakley, remembered thinking short-term:

Hugh Patterson, left, *and Al Neuharth at the press conference announcing Gannett's purchase of the* Arkansas Gazette. *Courtesy of the* Arkansas Democrat-Gazette.

> I so hated the *Democrat*. I thought, "There is no way we are going to lose this thing." I knew that Gannett had a less than solid reputation for journalism. I did not even want to think about what kind of paper they would put out if they won. I thought we had the best paper, we have the best history, the best tradition, the best people. And now we have all the money in the world. There was no way we were going to lose. I just did not want to even think about it. A lot of the other guys were turned off by Gannett. I knew it wasn't ideal. I really wasn't thinking about what comes after. I was thinking about winning the war.[258]

Dumas, also, didn't like being owned by Gannett. "We did not have particularly good notions about Gannett," he said. "It was kind of a bottom line [company], and the papers generally were kind of flashy, and the papers would shrink; the news hole would shrink, and they would be flashy but not very meaty newspapers."[259] But with the purchase, he said, the consensus was that one thing was certain: Arkansas's newspaper war was over. "Gannett, with its vast resources, will know how to squash this guy, and we may not like the product, but the newspaper will survive and maybe we could maintain the old *Gazette*," Dumas remembered thinking.[260] However, the "deep pockets" theme was not really true. Corporate accountability meant that the company expected the *Gazette* to turn a profit to keep its shareholders happy. Dumas remembered being surprised that Gannett would buy the paper in the first place because of the competitive market, which was anathema to a publicly held corporation.

> So when Gannett bought it, we thought, these are knowledgeable people, they know how to run a newspaper and make it profitable, and they know how to make it survive, but the truth was that they really didn't know that. Gannett and all the publicly held corporations, by that time, weren't engaged in competitive markets. They had a monopoly in virtually every town in America where they published either a weekly or a daily newspaper. So they didn't really have much experience in competitive newspapers. And that told on them.[261]

Even within Gannett, there was surprise at the purchase because Neuharth was not considered likely to get into the middle of a newspaper war, John Hanchette said.[262] Gene Foreman, who by then was at the *Philadelphia Inquirer*, remembered being disappointed by the sale. "I would've liked to have seen local ownership continue," he said.[263] Powell called the sale a sad development for the family and beyond.[264] Dhonau agreed. "[B]ut I understood that the Pattersons didn't have as deep pockets as Hussman and they had little if any other resources to call upon, so I think they felt they couldn't continue to go without more resources, and that was understandable," he said. "If the other guy has got deeper pockets, that's going to happen."[265] He recalled accepting the inevitable:

> The paper was going to be sold to somebody. Enough rumors had circulated by that time, and it was generally recognized that the paper was for sale. Most of us had hoped that the sale would go to Knight-Ridder or somebody else. Gannett may have been down the list. Pretty much down the list, to tell you the truth. I tried to look upon it in a positive way because there was no other way to look at it and hope that things were going to be okay.[266]

He said although Gannett's reputation was a bit suspect, *Gazette* people were willing to keep an open mind. "They were at least glad that the newspaper was not going to be shut down, that it was going to be sold, that it was going to continue to be published," Dhonau said. "So relief was a part of it."[267] Jim Bailey said he wasn't as down on the company's flagship *USA Today* as many of his colleagues were. He said he liked the national paper's graphic elements, but he thought it was "a poor substitute for a regular newspaper."[268]

Powell, who had become a columnist after retiring as editor of the editorial page and had worked with Neuharth when both were reporters at the *Miami Herald* in the 1950s, was optimistic about the new owners. "[T]hey were acquiring these great newspapers and, given the circumstances, it looked to me like a very good recourse," he said.[269] McCord said he thought most employees hated to see the Pattersons leave but believed Neuharth's assurances. "I was highly skeptical of all that from the very beginning, but I knew a little bit more about the Gannett operation, I guess, than most people did, so I never had any high hopes, but I never dreamed it would be as bad as it was," he said. "I just couldn't believe they would take a newspaper, the oldest newspaper west of the Mississippi, and turn it upside down like they did."[270]

Gannett's entrance into Arkansas's newspaper war also changed the game for Hussman and the *Democrat*.

> Gannett is not investing $60 million in order to have two newspapers in the Little Rock market. . . . I still thought two newspapers could survive. I thought that if we could make money—we had about thirty-six percent of the revenues when we started making money in 1984. Well, if we could make money with thirty-six percent of

> the revenues, maybe the *Gazette* couldn't make money with fifty-five percent of the revenues, but they could change their operation and they could be more efficient and not pay for all these costly work rules with the labor unions. We could both have fifty percent of the market and both make money. But when Gannett bought the paper, that changed the dynamics because obviously they were not buying the newspaper to have one of two newspapers in Little Rock. They were buying the newspaper to have the whole Little Rock market. So at that point we said, "Oh, this is not going to work, trying to sit here and make money. These guys are going to try to kill us, and we've got to respond."[271]

Whereas the war with the Pattersons had been a competition for advertising, Gannett brought a competition for circulation. In the war with the Pattersons, Hussman said the competition had been journalistic. "We were competing for readership, but it wasn't a circulation war, and circulation wars are documented in the history of newspaper publishing where one newspaper says, 'Get circulation [up] at all costs, no matter what it costs. Get circulation—drive your circulation higher than the other guy,'" he said. "And the *Gazette* had never done that, and we had never done that."[272] But with Gannett in the market, Arkansas's newspaper war would become a financial bloodbath. "It's just red ink everywhere because now you're cutting back into that circulation price, and there's no profit margin as there is in advertising," Hussman said. "You can cut your advertising rates twenty-five percent and you can still make money." That wasn't the case with circulation rates.[273] Hussman said he knew that the game had changed and that Gannett would force the issue so that there would be only one survivor, so he had to adapt his strategy. In order to gain circulation as quickly as possible, his company would be forced to look past even worse financial losses than it had faced in the first part of Arkansas's newspaper war.[274] Gannett had been able to get WEHCO's financial information from the public records of the antitrust trial, and Hussman said he was sure the company would try to quickly demoralize him after he had finally survived the long battle with the Pattersons[275]—at a cost of $42 million.

Underestimating the competition had cost the Pattersons dearly. With the sale, Hugh Patterson became a consultant to the newspaper and retired as publisher, leaving a legacy of "an overwhelming sense of integrity," his son said. "An unfair business practice to him, or cheating somebody or not paying a bill or taking an underhanded business practice of any sort, was anathema to him." He emphasized another of his father's standards that would come back to haunt the *Gazette* when Gannett later violated it. "He was very determined to treat advertisers the same; he would talk about the integrity of the rate card," Carrick Patterson said, referring to the sanctity of the newspaper's published advertising rates. "We didn't cut special deals for anybody."[276] Carrick Patterson, who acknowledged experiencing some difficulties in dealing with his father as publisher, also recalled the elder Patterson's often-overlooked voice in the decision that led to the *Gazette's* stance in 1957. "His integrity led him through that," Carrick Patterson said. "He was also in large regard the conscience of the newspaper for his time just as much as J. N. Heiskell had been for his." As had others before him, Patterson praised his father as publisher for foregoing the easy decision to maximize profits at the expense of improving the newspaper,[277] but in hindsight, Hugh Patterson had not done enough when he had the chance. Looking back, Max Brantley called Hugh Patterson a tragic figure "who made a decision, filing the lawsuit too early on the antitrust case, perhaps not responding as aggressively enough to the *Democrat's* challenge early on, turning down an offer from Walter Hussman to have a joint operating agreement of the two newspapers. The easy story is that Hugh made some misjudgments that ended the *Gazette* as we know it. Like a lot of easy stories, they're a lot more complicated than that."[278]

After the sale, Carrick Patterson remained as editor, solidifying the Heiskell family's third generation with the *Gazette*. But despite Gannett's assurances of local autonomy, under the new corporate ownership he would be unable to carry on his family's legacy of commitment to quality journalism and to being the voice of progressivism in Arkansas. Corporate ownership would sacrifice both those ideals in its relentless pursuit of profits at all cost and its detachment from the community it was attempting to serve. Patterson had considered trying to become publisher, but with the $60 million investment, Gannett decided it needed to bring in its own business people. That turned out to be fine with him. "We had some faults in our business operation, and I had great hopes that they would come in and clean up the business operation and do some aggressive selling of advertising, and everything would be cool," he said. "Well, they were freaking idiots, as it turned out."[279] Not only would Gannett, too, underestimate Hussman as a competitor, the company would also bring a stunning arrogance to Arkansas's newspaper war that would keep it from listening to its troops on the ground, further sealing the fate of the Old Gray Lady.

CHAPTER SEVEN

1986–1990: Gannett Ownership

WITH THE SALE of the *Gazette* to the Gannett Corporation, both parties in Arkansas's newspaper war became, technically, chain properties, but the purchase flipped Walter Hussman back into the underdog role he had played so successfully during his early battle with the Patterson family and would eventually make clear the lesson that engaged local ownership means far more than having a richer, larger absentee overseer. Gannett's purchase of the Old Gray Lady brought a major change in news philosophy from editor driven to market driven. That would ultimately undermine the newspaper's credibility. J. N. Heiskell had established a conservative news philosophy of emphasizing public affairs and government coverage, giving readers what they needed, and the eighty-four years of his family's ownership were marked by his sober, serious style. Gannett, to the contrary, favored giving readers what they wanted—more features, heavy emphasis on television and movies, less government coverage. With the *Gazette*'s established news and editorial staff augmented by an infusion of Gannett imports, the warring philosophies within would mark Gannett's time in Little Rock. Gannett arrived with a swagger, and the cocky attitude would continue until the company exited Little Rock with its tail tucked between its legs, having surrendered in Arkansas's newspaper war.

Until its death, the *Gazette* remained the quality paper in Arkansas, as evidenced by Arkansas Press Association contest results. Financial reasons, rather than quality, would make the ultimate difference in Arkansas's newspaper war. Hussman would prove to be better at guerrilla war tactics than would Gannett, which brought in a number of outside managers who, in their arrogance and ignorance, would try to force changes to the Old Gray Lady. Most of those outsiders failed to understand or appreciate the newspaper and the state, and their attempts to win Arkansas's newspaper war would be futile. There would even be ominous whispers of forcing a change in the *Gazette*'s vaunted progressive editorial stance. With the sale, the Heiskell-Patterson family's legacy of commitment to quality journalism and to be Arkansas's voice of progressivism would now be at the mercy of a distant money-grubbing chain with no knowledge of the newspaper or the state. It was a recipe for disaster.

By 1986, the number of chain-owned daily newspapers in the United States had risen to 1,158, a marked increase since 1920 (153 that year, 319 in 1940, 560 in 1960). As chain ownership increased, the number of independently owned newspapers steadily dropped (1,889 in 1920; 1,559 in 1940; 1,203 in 1960; 499 in 1986). When the *Arkansas Gazette* joined the ranks of chain newspapers in 1986, corporations owned 70 percent of all American dailies.[1] Upon its purchase of the *Gazette*, the Gannett Corporation was the largest media company in the United States with annual revenues of more than $2 billion and total newspaper circulation of six million. The *Gazette* became the company's ninety-third daily newspaper.[2] Gannett also operated eight television stations and eighteen radio stations and owned the largest outdoor advertising company in North America. When the transaction was completed, Gannett had operations in forty states and the District of Columbia, Guam, the Virgin Islands, Canada, Great Britain, Hong Kong, Singapore, and Switzerland.[3] In contrast, WEHCO Media, which owned the *Arkansas Democrat*, was then the largest media company in Arkansas. It had annual revenues of $67 million and total circulation of two hundred thousand among its six newspapers.[4]

Gannett had put together an incredible eighteen-year string—from 1967 to 1985—of ever-increasing quarterly profits. In fact, the company's manufacturing return on stockholder equity was 21 percent, compared to an average of 15 percent. Some of its properties had gaudy yearly profit margins of 30 to 50 percent.[5] While the company had tended to stay away from competitive situations, it had, earlier in 1986, bought the *Detroit News*, which was in a newspaper war with Knight-Ridder's *Detroit Free Press*. But it wasn't long before the companies there entered a joint operating agreement.[6] That didn't seem to be the company's goal in Little Rock, though, as it entered the market with a hefty lead in daily circulation (131,020 to 78,302), according to Walter Hussman in his history of the *Arkansas Democrat-Gazette*, as published on the newspaper's website.[7] Those numbers conflict with those Hussman himself estimated in October 1986 (120,000–85,000),[8] but regardless of the actual circulation, with the numbers so heavily in its favor, how could Gannett—like the Pattersons before it—not have been overconfident and arrogant as it took its place opposite Hussman on the front lines of Arkansas's newspaper war?

Indeed, Gannett's purchase of the *Arkansas Gazette*, announced the day before Halloween and closed on December 1, 1986, seemed to indicate the beginning of the end of Arkansas's newspaper war. Ernest Dumas recalled that it seemed to be an open-and-shut case that the giant Gannett would prevail over Hussman[9]—who, with his vast personal resources, did not really fit the role of David. Al Neuharth, chairman of the Gannett Corporation, was impressed with the new property. "[F]inancially, it had some difficulties because of the competitiveness of the market, but I thought that as a newspaper product serving the reader in the communities, it was excellent," he said. "We thought we could turn it around and win the war or we wouldn't have bought it."[10]

Hussman, however, recalled thinking, "This is a disaster. . . . [O]nce Gannett came in, the only reasonable rate of return for them was to be the only newspaper in the market."[11] At *Democrat* headquarters at Fifth and Scott, Hussman's team was quick to realize how much the game had changed. They began to think about their advantages: They called the *Democrat* "Arkansas' largest newspaper," but they knew that with its vast company resources, Gannett could match or surpass the *Democrat* in page count immediately. The *Democrat* offered free want ads, but Gannett could do the same. The only edge that the giant corporation could not match, Hussman's people surmised, was the fact that the *Democrat* was locally owned—albeit by a chain. "Well, that was cold comfort because in most surveys, people really don't care whether you're locally owned or not, they just want the best newspaper," Hussman said. "But since it was the only advantage we had, we decided we had to promote it, and we did."[12]

The *Democrat* staff, for its part, was not intimidated by the prospect of facing the media giant. Meredith Oakley, the political columnist, said she had no more respect for Gannett then than she did years later, referring in 2006 to the company's modus operandi as "McJournalism, fast food." As a member of the national board of the Society of Professional Journalists, she said she came into contact with "an awful lot" of people who worked for the company, "and they didn't respect Gannett either."[13] Hussman shrugged off the giant corporation's psychological salvos in the war. He realized, he said, that Gannett officials knew that their purchase of the *Gazette* would be demoralizing to him after the ups and downs of his war with the Pattersons. With their knowledge of his company's losses from the records of the antitrust trial, he said he knew Gannett officials were thinking, "Does he want to do this a third time and mount these huge losses? He's going to throw in the towel." He agreed that the thought was a reasonable assumption.[14] Not only was the sale demoralizing to him, he said, the *Gazette*'s order of a second press was, also; Gannett's $1.3 million purchase of an inserting machine was demoralizing; the addition of color to the Old Gray Lady was demoralizing; the adding on to the building was demoralizing. But the worst thing—by far—was the staggering financial losses after Gannett's purchase, the likes of which his company had never seen.

"But you know, we just didn't want to sit there and throw in the towel," he said. "After 1986, we'd been here for twelve years; we'd been through a lot to get to where we were, and we were going to give it a go and see if we could compete against them."[15]

Gannett brought in a transition team that included managers from various company properties. One of the members was Paul Borden, executive sports editor of the *Jackson (Miss.) Clarion-Ledger*. A few years earlier, Borden had been in the same situation that *Gazette* people faced in 1986. He had gone to work for the *Clarion-Ledger* in 1978 under Hederman family ownership. Gannett bought the paper in 1982. "It was actually a good move for most of us at the paper at the time because the family was going to take the paper back to the nineteenth century," Borden said of his Mississippi experience, illustrating the fact that in certain circumstances, distant chain ownership can be preferable to that of a local family. "Also, the new publisher was one of the two best I have ever worked for, and the new editor was a Jackson native who knew what he was doing."[16] In Little Rock, each member of the transition team was assigned a different segment of the *Gazette* with which to work. That portended the future. "Here were people from Louisiana, Mississippi, and, I think, D.C., going to tell *Gazette* people what kind of newspaper they should put out for the people of Arkansas," Borden remembered. "Kind of a cavalier, we-know-best attitude."[17] But Susie Miles Ellwood, who had been hired a couple of years previously by the Pattersons to work in marketing, said although she was not then impressed with Gannett's reputation, the company's transition team at the *Gazette* included "some really good people who I thought asked the right questions, and they particularly viewed those of us who were from Arkansas as people who were important to listen to. And I know during the course of that spent a lot of time talking to me, and I felt like they valued what I brought to the table."[18] In fact, Ellwood was one of the survivors of Gannett's time in Little Rock, escaping before the *Gazette* died and going on to a long career as a top executive with the corporation.

John Seigenthaler, publisher of the *Nashville Tennessean* and editorial director of *USA Today*, headed the transition team. Neuharth said he was his point person in negotiations for the sale and in installing management to succeed Hugh Patterson. "John Seigenthaler has the long-time reputation as a leading Southern, liberal journalist who was a friend of Harry Ashmore's, a good acquaintance of Hugh Patterson's, so he seemed to me to be the best qualified person at Gannett to handle that transition," Neuharth later recalled.[19] Neuharth said his directions to Seigenthaler regarding the *Gazette* were "to become the winning newspaper or surviving newspaper in Little Rock."[20] The chairman himself did not pretend to have the winning formula. He recalled that by then, he was supervising nearly one hundred daily newspapers in addition to a number of television and radio stations. "And no one who runs a corporation that size can or should pretend that he or she can get into details or specifics," he said. "He or she should set general goals and then hire the right people to try to make those goals work." With the purchase of the *Gazette*, Neuharth said he reiterated to Seigenthaler, company president John Curley, and chief of finance and administration Doug McCorkindale, among others, that the company's goal was for the *Gazette* to win Arkansas's newspaper war. "And then they had to figure out how to do that," he said. "The private and public commitment was to win the war in Little Rock."[21]

Jerry Dhonau, the *Gazette*'s editorial page editor, was one of the last of the *Gazette* department heads to talk to Seigenthaler during his transition visit. Dhonau received some disconcerting news during the conference when Seigenthaler told him that in his meetings with local business leaders, they had urged the new ownership to reverse the *Gazette*'s long-standing progressive editorial policies. Seigenthaler reassured Dhonau that his response to those movers and shakers was that that would not happen. "So I really appreciated that," Dhonau said. "And so they weren't changed, and we kept them until the bitter end."[22] But the fact that it was even brought up foreshadowed trouble. It had not taken long for the Heiskell-Patterson legacy to be threatened.

Other parts of the *Gazette* did not fare so well. Borden particularly recalled, as an example, the paper's television listings. One of the transition team members thought that a horizontal listing of programs was much superior to that of the *Gazette*'s existing vertical program listings with the stations at the top of the graphic. "So the change was made," Borden said. "The uproar from the readers was such the *Gazette* quickly had to go back to the old format."[23] It was a peek at what was to come, and what had been feared. The reporter Wayne Jordan remembered a Gannett reader survey to find out what readers thought of the company's newest property. Results showed that 70 percent approved of the newspaper. "That was the highest of any of the ninety papers in the Gannett company, and so what do they do? They immediately started tearing it away, tearing it down," Jordan said.[24] Deborah Mathis, who had worked at the *Democrat* before entering television journalism in Little Rock and Washington, D.C., had been one of the early broadcast reporters to cover the newspaper war between Hussman and the Pattersons. She said she was very upset about the sale to Gannett "because I knew that Gannett had a reputation of *USA Today*-izing as much as possible all the papers it had swallowed up, . . . and I was so upset because I knew what Gannett was going to do to it, what it had done to every paper it had touched." Whereas the idea for *USA Today* worked as a national paper with quick, short stories surveying the nation's news, the template was not appropriate for papers that were not national in focus—such as the *Arkansas Gazette.* "The world needs a lot of different ideas in order to make it a winner, not the same damn thing over and over and over again," Mathis said. "[F]irst of all, you're killing the uniqueness of the thing; it was the uniqueness of it to begin with that made it so, at least helped its popularity, and you're going to make it not unique anymore."[25]

The *Gazette*'s own coverage of the sale in October 1986 showed that whereas Gannett had made few changes to the *Des Moines Register*'s newsroom or appearance fifteen months after its purchase, in Detroit, despite early reassurances that there would be few management changes at the *News*, many of those top managers were swept aside a couple of months after the sale to Gannett.[26] Mathis compared the company's philosophy to a singer who tries to recreate one hit the rest of her career.

> You have to come up with a new idea; you have to reinvent the wheel to some degree. Gannett to this day doesn't seem to believe that, doesn't seem to get that. . . . You cannot just keep pushing the same thing and expecting every one of them to be, like, a wowie every single time, and Gannett to this day doesn't get that. It continues to try to press one model on all of its papers. And it killed the *Arkansas Gazette*. It killed the *Arkansas Gazette.*[27]

Neuharth, however, maintained that there was no Gannett formula. "Every acquisition was treated individually based on its community, its market, its employees, its past philosophy," he said. "Every Gannett acquisition was handled individually and differently, including the *Gazette.*"[28]

Many would disagree. State capitol reporter John Reed, among others, was critical about the editors Gannett would eventually send to Little Rock. He said the new ownership changed the newspaper and the atmosphere of the *Gazette* in many ways.

> They had their own ideas about how to run a newspaper, and I guess somebody at the Gannett Corporation realized that we were in the middle of a newspaper war, but they sure didn't act like it. I suppose the people they sent to Little Rock figured it out after a month or two in town, but I don't think anybody in Gannett headquarters ever figured it out. They sent a steady stream of idiots to Little Rock to run the *Gazette* into the ground. There might have been some decent business managers, but the editors they sent in—well, "idiots" is about the most charitable thing I can say about them. They didn't seem to understand the local market. They probably could do a good

job running a newspaper somewhere else, but they sure didn't do a good job at the *Gazette*, as history has proven. They shot the *Gazette* in the foot.[29]

Ernest Dumas remembered that Gannett poured money into the *Gazette* from the beginning. "If they wanted to do it, they could come in and outspend Walter Hussman, and they did that," he said. Salaries at the *Gazette* were already much higher than those at the *Democrat*, but Gannett expanded the staff and fattened the news hole. "The *Gazette* became a big, fat newspaper again, full of news, full of features," Dumas said. "They brought in a lot of new reporters."[30] Many of those Gannett hires were minorities and women, moves that were welcomed. And established reporters were used in new ways. Jim Bailey, the *Gazette*'s star sportswriter, covered all St. Louis Cardinals home baseball games in 1987 and, by the end of the season, road games as well through the World Series. Gannett News Service fed his coverage to the company's small papers in the Midwest. "I had a real good year in '87," Bailey said. "There were some nice guys at Gannett, but they were kind of alien to what we were looking for."[31]

By the time of the sale, WEHCO had paid off its cable television debt, enabling the company to use those revenues in Little Rock. Without that, Hussman said, his company might not have been able to stay in the competition through the shift in the war to a gain-circulation-at-all-costs battle that required his company to significantly increase its losses. "We were spending incredible amounts of money to gain circulation, and price discounting, which is so uneconomical," he said. "We needed every bit of the resources we could muster to stay in the fray."[32] One of the gimmicks was a Wingo-Zingo reader contest featuring a $250,000 prize that the *Democrat* tried to match for a while before Hussman made the wise decision to think long term instead of short term. "We finally said, 'This is nuts. Let's put our money back into the product, into better reporters and better editors. That's what's going to be more important in the long run,'" he said.[33] Bailey remembered that the newspaper war under Gannett boiled down to body counts, with one paper boasting of sending four people to cover an event and the other bettering that with six. "Hell, there probably shouldn't have been more than one," he said. "Both papers would ignore something, ignore something, ignore something, and then one day they'd hit what they called 'a package,' just blow it out—photos, stories, sidebars, two or three pages. Then they'd ignore it [again] for six months."[34]

In May 1987, Hussman said the *Democrat* lost more money than it ever had in one month. Although he has not revealed the specifics of his losses,

Hussman recalled being terribly discouraged and wondering when or if the pattern would ever end. "Have I kind of fallen into the trap that they're going to try to bleed us to death, and are they going to bleed us to death?" he remembered thinking.[35] The 1988 death of Walter Hussman Sr. added to the family's turmoil.

One of Gannett's first moves seemed to bode well as it brought in Bill Malone, who had been born in Arkansas, as its first *Gazette* publisher. Gannett could then say the *Gazette*, like its competition, was managed by Arkansans. But Malone, a company man, had a background in circulation—not news—and it did not take long for him to get crosswise with some old *Gazette* hands. Jerry Dhonau, then the editorial page editor, said Malone was not one of the better publishers he had worked for. "He didn't know diddly about news and editorial, and he didn't have an appreciation, I think, for the division of news and editorial," Dhonau said. "I've been on both sides and appreciate both, but Bill had a hard time."[36] Dhonau said Malone seemed to want to change a lot of things in the paper itself that he disagreed needed changing. He also remembered Malone as more conservative than the consensus of the *Gazette*'s editorial board and more concerned with the business aspect of the newspaper than the journalistic one—as would, perhaps, befit a circulation manager and a publisher. But without a good appreciation for the news and editorial aspects—as Hugh Patterson had had—he was lost. "There's no telling how much money they spent on promotions as opposed to the [journalistic] product," Dhonau said. "We got along okay, but he didn't have much journalistic sense."[37] However, Ellwood, who advanced to vice president of marketing after Gannett bought the paper, said Malone became her mentor, and she credited him for keeping her in the newspaper industry. She called him "a great circulator" and praised his Arkansas roots. "I think he felt some connection to the state, and we all felt a little more comfortable with him because of that," she said. "He just was a very, very nice man, and he worked hard."[38]

Carrick Patterson said while the company immediately contributed resources for advertising and circulation, there was also a disconcerting change at the top when Al Neuharth stepped down as chairman on April 1, 1989.[39] "It turned out, the people who were left there were not of his same point of view about keeping the *Gazette* the way it had been," Patterson said.[40] John Curley replaced Neuharth, who went on to head the Gannett Foundation. The transition was deeply disappointing for Hugh Patterson.

> From then on, their judgment in who to send in and how to try to deal with the thing was just flawed in just about every respect. [Malone] just had no concept of the editorial strength of the *Gazette*.

> Then the later ones tried to put it into the local formula edition of *USA Today* and that kind of business. . . . I called Al a couple of times and said, "I just don't know what to think because they are making every mistake you could make. They are offending people. They are offending the intellectual people from the university. I attend these meetings and they come cry on my shoulder, and there's nothing I can do."[41]

Hugh Patterson remembered Neuharth's response: "Well, they're just simply trying to Gannettize it." Patterson answered him, "Well, what they ought to be doing is *Arkansas-Gazettizing* more of their papers."[42] Neuharth said after he left his position, he never spoke to Curley about how the *Gazette* was run. "Since April 1, 1989, I have not had any involvement in any decisions, large or small, at the Gannett Company," he said.[43]

Hussman recalled a *New York Times* article on Arkansas's newspaper war that revealed a stark difference between the ownership of the two papers. The photographer asked him to hold up a copy of his free want ads. He agreed and remembered Malone telling him he had declined the same request because he "wouldn't be caught dead holding a copy of the free want ads." Hussman said he found that a telling comment. "[T]hey were doing free want ads because it was like an evil necessity," he said. "They really didn't want to do it; they didn't see the value of doing it." Hussman, however, was a big believer in the gimmick, which had allowed the *Democrat*'s classified revenues to increase from $800,000 to $5 million in about six years. He said he considered the free want ads to be a win-win-win situation: public service, financial boon to his newspaper, and builder of readership and circulation.[44]

One of the *Democrat*'s strategies was to change its motto, "Arkansas' Largest Newspaper," to "Arkansas' Newspaper," to emphasize the local ownership. "We were owned by Arkansans, managed by Arkansans, and we really promoted that, and that resonated with people in Arkansas, especially when Gannett really started changing the *Arkansas Gazette*," Hussman said.[45] How ironic that with years of hindsight, Hussman lamented any changes to the *Gazette*. After all, the *Democrat* under his ownership had spent years trashing the Old Gray Lady, making his stance seem hypocritical and a bit self-serving.

Newspapers were evolving by the mid-1980s, going more and more to color photography. The *Democrat* had already invested about $5 million in an offset press, and the *Gazette* had ordered its new press before the sale to Gannett. At the press conference announcing the sale, Neuharth was asked whether there would be changes to the *Gazette*'s format. "I hope not," he said, "but that will be up to Carrick [Patterson, the editor]. The format and content is outstanding and not only is it recognized that way nationally, but it is recognized by the readers."[46] Despite those assurances, over time Gannett seemed to tart up the sober Old Gray Lady, going far beyond what Neuharth had described as changes "in the normal course of events."[47] Hussman called that development "the best thing that ever happened to us."[48] Hussman's own focus groups indicated that there was nothing his newspaper could do to get *Gazette*-only readers to read the *Democrat.* He remembered the focus groups would say, "'Well, if the *Gazette* threw the newspaper on the roof for a month and I couldn't get it, maybe I'd take the *Democrat.* Or if they totally change the *Gazette,* its format, its content, maybe we would take the *Democrat.*"[49]

And that is exactly what would happen.

Deborah Mathis recalled several Gannett changes to the *Gazette,* including column width, type, and the addition of color. Although the color didn't offend her admittedly Luddite newspaper sensibilities, she was bothered by the superficiality of the changes.

> Why tinker? If you're not going to change the paper and improve the content, why are you going to change the form? Why are you so much about style? That's what bothered me. It's like, "Let's make it look different; let's don't make it be different, let's just make it look different." Why? For what reason? Just to do it. I always said that I thought Gannett's motto was, "If it ain't broke, break it."[50]

She said the attitude reminded her of people who, when served dinner, immediately pick up the salt shaker and start salting their food. "They haven't even tasted it yet," she said. "It may be oversalted already; it may be perfect—they don't know." She was bothered by Gannett's barreling in to change things before it had even had a good evaluation period.[51]

But there was also change to the content. With *USA Today* as its model, Gannett shortened stories and emphasized features at the expense of hard news, often putting those stories on the front page. Hussman remembered that many of the changes were so extreme, the newspaper did not even look like the *Gazette* anymore, so its hard-core readers began to consider taking the *Democrat.* "Gannett did for us what we couldn't do for ourselves by changing the *Gazette* so fundamentally that it put those readers in play where they would consider reading our newspaper," he said. "If Gannett hadn't changed the *Gazette,* I don't know if we would have ever caught them in circulation."[52] Despite the changes, however, the *Gazette* dominated the annual Arkansas Press Association contests once it began entering them in 1988. The *Gazette* swept the general excellence awards from 1988 to 1991. The *Gazette* won more total awards, too, winning twenty-eight to the *Democrat*'s twenty-five in

1989, thirty-two to the *Democrat*'s twenty-one in 1990, and thirty-six to the *Democrat*'s twenty-five in 1991. The *Gazette* also won more first-place awards in 1990 than the *Democrat*, eleven to six, and in 1991, sixteen to four. The *Democrat*'s only advantage in competing with the *Gazette* in the APA contests was in winning seven firsts to the *Gazette*'s six in 1989.[53]

As editor, Carrick Patterson almost immediately butted heads with the new outside Gannett management. "They decided that instead of bringing the place where they were experts, that is in advertising and circulation and whatever, that they would fool with the newspaper, with the editorial content," Patterson said. "Well, their idea of fooling with the editorial content was to have daily color comics." That move cost about $80,000 a year, he said—for nothing. No one had complained that the daily comics were black and white. Malone's determination to have daily color comics had another potential cost as well. Because of the way the press worked, only the front and back page of a section could be in color, so in order to have daily color comics, the *Gazette* needed to reduce its three pages of comics to one. Malone told Patterson to eliminate all but one page of comics. Patterson fought back. "You don't ever kill a comic unless you just absolutely, positively have to, because even the worst comic strip in the world has its loyal fans, and every one of them will call you if you eliminate it," he said. Ultimately, Gannett hired an artist to hand-paint the comics and, in the days before scanners, go through an elaborate process to separate the content into the component colors. "[A] nd nobody cared," Patterson said. "This was the kind of thing that they would do."[54]

There were other, more subtle pressures put on the *Gazette*'s newsroom. Gannett held internal contests for its newspapers, and judges graded the entrants on such things as length of average story and number of stories on page one. "[I]t turned out what you were graded on was not anything that we thought was anything that contributed to the newspaper's merit," Patterson remembered. "So we got low grades."[55] Jim Bailey recalled a critique of the *Gazette*'s sports section by someone at Gannett's White Plains, New York, newspaper. "His summation, and I'll never forget this, it was verbatim, 'This was bad, this was bad, this was bad, the fishing/hunting and outdoor section looked okay to me, although I didn't read it.' Wonderful critique," the wry Bailey said.[56]

Another misstep as Gannett meddled with content included the proposed elimination of the In the News column on the left side of page one. The column was a compilation of one-sentence summaries of news stories from outside Arkansas that had been one of the most popular features in the *Arkansas Gazette* since Bob Douglas created it during his days as wire editor.

Even some Gannett people disagreed with the proposal. "Of course, it was only the most popular feature of the front page and the most-read item in the paper," Borden recalled.[57] (In the News is one of the few things Hussman included from the *Gazette* in his new newspaper starting October 19, 1991. It remains in the left column of page one of the *Democrat-Gazette* today.) As editor, Carrick Patterson vetoed Gannett's move. Gannett's outside management also wanted to remove the river bulletin, part of the weather map that forecast the water levels of many of the state's rivers. "These people in Rochester, New York, and Washington, D.C. couldn't understand—what do you need a river bulletin for?" Patterson remembered. "Well, if you're raising cotton in east Arkansas, you darn well want to know whether the river's going to flood—but they didn't understand that."[58] Patterson recalled that rather than ask old *Gazette* hands why they ran a river bulletin, Gannett management instead simply demanded its removal. Again the *Gazette*'s local editor bucked the outside chain management. Another contention was a Monday business section. The *Gazette* had not had one, the theory being that businesses and the stock market were closed on Sunday, but Gannett wanted to add the section anyway. Patterson called such a section a fad of the times.

> There wasn't any advertiser interest. There wasn't particularly any reader interest. Oh, we came up with a pretty good Monday business section, but it was just more newsprint being put out. There was no advertising to support it, and staff resources being spent on it that could have been used for news that was actually of more, you know, compelling and more vital interest to the readers. But they said, "Well, you don't have to do the Monday business section, but we are not going to give you any resources to do anything else. So if you want any resources at all it's going to have to be for the Monday business section."[59]

Another battle between Patterson and Malone involved a proposed bill in the Arkansas legislature to expand the state sales tax, which at that time did not apply to newspaper advertising. Patterson recalled that, as a liberal newspaper, the *Gazette* had philosophically opposed unreasonable tax exemptions. "Really, it didn't make much sense for advertising to be exempt, so our thought on the editorial page was, 'Yeah, nobody wants to be taxed, but still, why should we not be taxed and somebody else be taxed? So yeah, we'll support it,'" he said.[60] Instead, publisher Malone ordered the staff to produce an editorial decrying the move to add sales tax to newspaper advertising. Patterson refused, to the point of insubordination. Malone, who told him he would speak to him about the situation later, apparently did call Gannett headquarters, which decreed that the *Gazette*'s editorial page would be left alone. Patterson said the incident might have hastened his demise. "Ultimately, we reached a compromise, and I feel bad about that because I did compromise," he said. "We just didn't write anything."[61]

Bob McCord said Gannett made many mistakes with the *Gazette*. "Some of the people they brought in were just not good at what they did," he said. "They knew so little about Little Rock and Arkansas except what they'd read in funny books."[62] He criticized the featurizing of news stories, calling it "amazing" some of the things that got on the front page, but he admitted Gannett improved the look of the paper.[63] John Reed agreed the company did some good things with the *Gazette*, citing in particular the pullout tab of legislative coverage he was a part of during the 1989 session. The stories were separated and enhanced by charts and photos.[64]

Early in its ownership, Gannett had Michael Gartner, the editor it had inherited when it bought the *Des Moines Register* (and who had since moved to the corporate office) critique a week of *Gazettes*. It did not go well for Patterson or his paper.

> [H]e wrote a critique that I just thought was—the technical newspaper term is "chicken-shit." [Laughter] He criticized the front page. He criticized the little "In the News" column . . . He criticized the weather map. He said, "The weather map's useless." He criticized the river bulletin. . . . It was vital information for agriculture and that sort of thing. He didn't understand that. Five or six pages of just nit-picking stuff, ignorant, shoot-from-the-hip stuff, I mean, and I say ignorant just because he didn't know the state of Arkansas and he didn't know what we were trying to do. Nobody asked what we were trying to do. They just said, "Oh, this is bad; this is bad; this is second rate; this is amateurish, this is . . ." We weren't used to people talking to us that way.[65]

Patterson said he reacted "very strongly."

> I wrote a very, very strong letter back, and the phone started ringing from Washington, and I was told how bad a mistake I'd make if I didn't show more tact. Another time I went to a national Gannett meeting in Washington, and they had the editors of *USA Today* there, and they were talking about how wonderful they were. And they were talking about their daily process of putting out the paper and that they were going to find the one story that they thought they wanted America to talk about that day, and they would put all their

> resources behind that. They would have a page-one thing about it; then they'd have a sidebar, and then they'd have editorials about it and op-ed. On the day I was there, there was some prizefight that was to take place. And I got up in the meeting and I said, "You know, that's very interesting what you're doing, but don't you think it shows a little contempt for your readers, that you decide on this frivolous thing that it's going to be the big topic every day?" And they sort of looked at me like, "Well, what's your point? Of course, that's what we're doing. Yeah, yeah, we have contempt for our readers, sure we do." Well, that wasn't popular for me to sass them like that. [M]y name was put down in a book somewhere.[66]

Paul Borden, the transition team member from Jackson who came to the *Gazette* as executive sports editor in fall 1987, said Patterson's days were numbered from that point.[67] Patterson himself said he could see a buildup to what would be his firing—including his betrayal by some longtime *Gazette* employees. "There were people who decided that Gannett was the wave of the future and that being loyal to Gannett, even abetting their obvious desire to get rid of the remnants of the family, which by then was just me, was the way to go," he said. "People who I had worked closely with and been friends with who decided that their future lay by not supporting me, I guess." He said it was obvious the outside Gannett management was marginalizing him. "They didn't make any progress in terms of the advertising and circulation, but messing with the newspaper, they were all for that," he said. "I made enough noise that they got rid of me pretty quick."[68]

Malone called him in for his annual evaluation and told him he was not measuring up and would have to improve or be gone. Patterson asked for specifics but was told, "You're just not measuring up." He said he realized then that his time at the newspaper was over, so he asked Malone if he could move up to the editorial staff until he could find something else. Malone agreed. After a few months on the editorial staff, the last Heiskell descendant left the *Arkansas Gazette* in 1988—after a family run of eighty-six years.[69] The move seemed to contradict the October 30, 1986, remarks of Neuharth, who had not by the time of Carrick Patterson's exit retired as chair: "The editors of the Gannett newspapers decide who to embrace, who to raise hell with, who to endorse, and there is no suggestion, no direction from Gannett," Neuharth had said upon the announcement of the Pattersons' sale to the chain.[70] In the same news story, Hugh Patterson had said he anticipated the *Gazette*'s principles could survive the sale to Gannett.

> I can readily imagine if a point ever came in this relationship where there was such a fundamental difference in view editorially from Carrick's point of view to that of someone who spoke for Gannett, that it was intolerable, then Carrick would say, "I'm no longer going to be affiliated [with Gannett]." I don't anticipate that is going to happen, but that is what I think of my son. And what I think of Gannett is that they would never put him in that position.[71]

Unfortunately, he was wrong about the outside ownership. Carrick Patterson said the newspaper went downhill from the point of his departure. "Not that I was all that great an editor, but I was compared with the people they brought in," he said.[72] He said the interference he put up against the new management was to have been part of the agreement between his family and Gannett. "It was supposed to have been the deal that what we're buying is your editorial product and news product, which you guys know better than anybody else how to do, and we're going to help you with the business management and the financing of the thing," he said. "Then the guy who made that promise left, and the guys who were left didn't keep that promise."[73] Obviously, Gannett did not live up to its promises even before Neuharth's departure.

What really angered him, Patterson said, was that he tried to go along with the new outside management.

> Even though I objected to the color comics, I figured out a way to do it. I never dropped the river bulletin, but other than that, I tried to do some of the things they wanted. I went to their meetings and all that. I tried to be a good soldier as much as I could and keep my personal integrity, which I'd learned from my dad. But they wanted more than I was willing to give, and they wanted their own people, which is understandable, I guess. And the promise had never been made that we're going to keep you forever. They promised that they'd maintain a great newspaper in the tradition [of the *Gazette*], but they never made me any personal promises except that at the end of the sale I'd be editor, and I guess after that it was up to them, and they made the decision they made. And from their point of view it was probably the right idea. And I don't claim that if I had been there that I would've saved the thing; I don't claim that by any means because I think it was bigger than any one person could've fought, and those who stayed behind fought as hard as they could under the circumstances, I'm sure.[74]

After Patterson left the *Gazette*, Gannett brought in Walker Lundy to be editor. Lundy, who had previously worked in editor positions at the *Detroit Free Press*, *Charlotte Observer*, and *Tallahassee Democrat*, had left his job as managing editor of the *Fort Worth Star Telegram* in September 1987 "to pursue other interests."[75] Max Brantley, the *Gazette*'s city editor, said no one knew much about Lundy except that he had been fired from his last couple of jobs, "which did make you wonder, but sometimes the owners are the problem there, not the person who got fired."[76] Although Lundy later said he didn't remember having said it, he made a lasting impression on his new employees during his first meeting with the *Gazette* staff, as Ernest Dumas recalled.

> We're all gathered in the city room for this announcement, and Walker Lundy was introduced and made a few remarks and said does anybody have any questions. And my recollection is that there was silence for a minute and finally Chuck Heinbockel, our business writer, spoke up and said, "Could you tell us something about your management style?" And Walker said, "Sure. The first thing you should know about my management style is that I know how to fire people. I'm used to it and I know how to do it."[77]

Brantley said although Lundy claimed later he did not recall saying that, a room full of people remembered it very clearly. In fact, Brantley said he learned that Lundy's philosophy was that a good newspaper fired about 10 percent of its staff every year, which "created a constantly improving newsroom staff and created a certain tension that drove more production," Brantley said. "I thought it was one of the nuttiest, cruelest views of employee management I'd ever heard of."[78] Dumas said the stunning remark was a terrible blow to newsroom morale. Afterward, Lundy wanted to get rid of many old *Gazette* hands and pressured Brantley, who would become his assistant managing editor, to do so. "He didn't want to do it himself, but he wanted Max to actually do the firing," Dumas said.[79]

John Reed, a state capitol reporter, recalled that for the troops on the ground, the pressure of Arkansas's newspaper war grew worse under Gannett. He said the original battle with the *Democrat* had been different. That was a tough but fair fight, he said, but the new outside corporate ownership brought the added burden "of having the idiots from Gannett who came into town from on high."

> When I say they were idiots, I'm being charitable because they were also assholes—lying, thieving, cheating assholes who cared no more about the *Gazette* than if it was a shoe store. I have more respect

Walker Lundy in the newsroom of the Gazette. *Courtesy of* Arkansas Times.

> for the reporters and editors at the *Democrat* [than the Gannett imports]. They are lying, thieving, shitty assholes, and if I could think of any worse names, I'd call them that.[80]

The vehemence of Reed's feelings is indicative of the passions involved in Arkansas's newspaper war. The bitterness remained palpable nearly twenty years after the *Gazette* died. Wayne Jordan, who had worked at the *Gazette* since 1966, said the Gannett years were the most miserable period of his life. The Gannett managers didn't understand news, he said, preferring "puff."

"Good, hard news, they weren't interested in it," he said, adding that management harassed him. "[B]ut I was determined that they weren't going to run me off, too."[81] Dumas said some of the old hands—like Jordan—who had been on the beat for several years became prime targets for Lundy. "He just thought they were not very lively; their copy was dull, and he wanted some bright, fresh, young writers, and he wanted [the old-timers] fired," he said. "And he wanted also, I think, to send a message."[82] The firings of such established employees would certainly shake up the newsroom.

Brantley contrasted the philosophy of that outsider with the local one espoused for so many years by the Heiskells and Pattersons.

> The *Gazette* previously had been a plantation; that is, the working conditions weren't always the best, but the overseers were fairly benevolent, and if you didn't screw up too badly you'd always have a home there. There's clearly a downside to that school of management, but it has a certain benevolence that was appealing, and it wasn't as patronizing as that sounds. I think there were people who were role players who were important to the newspaper who were not going to be page-one story writers for the *New York Times* but who brought value through their knowledge of Arkansas or for other reasons to the newspaper that didn't justify firing them. Those were particularly the types that Lundy honed in on because he thought those were job slots that if he could get rid of those people he could bring in superstars of some sort.[83]

Jim Bailey, who had joined the *Gazette* as a sportswriter in 1956, was among the first of the old-timers Lundy interviewed. He was about to head to Florida to cover Major League Baseball's spring training. "He thought that all the old *Gazette* veterans were just old entrenched mossbacks, no ambition," Bailey recalled. "He didn't know that for the better ones of them, it was a point of pride to work at the *Gazette*." Several months after Lundy's arrival, Bailey quizzed a *Fort Worth Star-Telegram* sportswriter, who was at War Memorial Stadium to cover an Arkansas Razorback football game, about Lundy. "Without batting an eye or even apparently thinking about it, he said, 'I do believe he is the most stupid son of a bitch I have ever met in any position of authority,'" Bailey recalled. "I began to swing to that view myself."[84]

Bill Lewis was another Lundy target. Lewis was known for producing lengthy copy—anathema to the Gannett philosophy. As the newspaper's main restaurant reviewer—although on a part-time basis along with his other general assignment duties—he remembered complaining to the editor when restaurant reviews by another writer began to appear. He said Lundy snarled back, "If I had the money I'd review five a week." Lewis, who had already had a heart attack and bypass surgery, said his stress level went sky-high under Gannett, and his cardiologist put him on three months of medical disability. "Lundy pounced on that and all over the office talked about what a lousy way to leave and used some really bad language," Lewis remembered.[85] He retired when his Social Security disability was approved and never went back to the *Gazette*. Malone later took him to lunch to hear his side of the story. "We sat there for two or three hours and I unloaded on him," Lewis remembered. "The last thing he said was, 'Would you like us to give you a retirement party?' I said, 'No, thanks.'"[86]

Jerry Dhonau, who had come to the *Gazette* in 1956 and, except for a couple of years in the 1960s while in graduate school had spent his entire career there, said some of Lundy's ideas were considered "off the wall" and that he was sometimes hard to get along with. "He had a reputation of being a quirky guy with quirky ideas," Dhonau said. "He caused a number of us a lot of grief." Dhonau remembered particularly Lundy's wanting to start a community columnist program, which would include a group of columnists from around the state who represented different demographic and ideological groups and who would write an op-ed column that would run periodically. Whereas the idea was interesting, Dhonau said the execution of it slipped quickly—along with the quality. "They were good people, but they weren't, certainly, journalists or writers," he said. "That went by the wayside, but it took a lot of people power and time and effort that might have been better used some other way for the paper."[87]

Bailey, who along with Orville Henry would eventually become the only sportswriters inducted into the Arkansas Sports Hall of Fame, said Lundy and Gannett did not know what to do with those he called "old *Gazette* rebels." They didn't fit the new regime, he said, but apparently management was afraid to run them off because they all had a following. "I guess if they had won the war, I'd have probably been on the street the next week," he said. "I was pretty sure that however the war fell, Gannett or the *Democrat*, I was going to be on the street."[88]

But Brantley said Gannett got too much of the blame for some of the changes to the paper itself. "Imagine, we put color photographs on page 1 of the *Gazette* and got nearly universal criticism for it," he said. "There's not a newspaper left in America, a conventional daily paper—even the *New York Times* has color on page one—but when the *Gazette* did it, we were 'tarting up' the old lady." He said the *Democrat* was in the enviable position of having it both ways. "They'd been running color on page one for years, but when we did it, that was just terrible," Brantley recalled.[89] One of the infamous examples was a large color photograph of the University of Arkansas at Little Rock dance team in its new body-hugging spandex uniforms. Ernest Dumas remembered Lundy's philosophy of using a color photograph on page one every day—news or feature. "They were trying to do that, and I don't think anybody thought they were sacrificing great principles to do so," Dumas said.[90] It so happened that Lundy was off the day of the UALR spandex incident, and it was Max Brantley who made the decision to run the photo. "Letters came pouring in and ever after that was cited as the downfall of the *Gazette*," Dumas recalled. "Max said he was the one who should've been fired."[91] But Roy Reed, among others, said it did not really matter whether Lundy was there that day. "I think to a large extent, Lundy was of the same mind as the Gannett managers of how to put out a newspaper," he said. "They made it pretty clear, 'You go along with our philosophy or leave.'"[92] Another Lundy fumble was believing John Robert Starr's criticism of the *Gazette*'s editorial staff that it did not run letters critical of the paper's editorial stance. That was not true, Dumas said.

> Lundy had just been there two or three months, and he read Starr's column and said, "Why don't we publish letters critical of the editorial page?" I said, "We do"; he said, "Starr says you don't." So I went back two months, maybe three months of the *Gazette* and *Democrat* and tabulated all the letters we'd published that were critical of our editorials and the same thing at the *Democrat*, all the letters that criticized the *Democrat*'s editorials. In that time period, there were something like twenty-three letters we published critical of our editorials, and in the *Democrat*, not a single one. In those days, there was really nothing in the [*Democrat*] editorials to object to. They were typically editorials criticizing the national debt or praising the month of April, beauties of April or October or something. There was really nothing much to get the people aroused one way or the other.[93]

James O. Powell, who had remained as a columnist after retiring as editor of the editorial page, was cut loose by Gannett in 1987 when the company "decided I was too expensive a luxury to have around," thus he never worked under Lundy. But he knew the new man's reputation at the *Gazette*. "No one I know on the *Gazette* thought much of Walker Lundy, and although I had no personal experience with him, that was my vague feeling about him," Powell said, pointing to a talk Lundy gave to journalism students at the University of Arkansas—where Bob Douglas had retired as chair of the journalism department and Roy Reed was still teaching. Lundy "said something to the effect he thought we should have fewer literate reporters," Powell recalled. "He didn't want educated, literate reporters." Instead, he recalled that Lundy wanted people who could go out there and get him a story. "And he got a lot of bad attention to that, at least in conversation among all the newspaper people," Powell said. "It was hyperbole, I'm sure, but it did not go over." He said J. N. Heiskell was probably spinning in his grave to hear of such a philosophy atop his beloved Old Lady.[94] Roy Reed said he and Douglas "came away appalled" by Lundy's philosophy of the news. "In a way, he was a very plausible choice for Gannett to turn into a Gannettoid," Reed said. "It's easy to be hard on Walker Lundy, but he was a master of landing on his feet."[95]

Douglas, the longtime managing editor who had moved on to the U of A to make room for Carrick Patterson, said Hugh Patterson told him that he went to Gannett headquarters after the sale and demanded that Douglas be brought back as editor. "Of course, Gannett didn't want to do that, and I think he nearly came to blows with somebody," Douglas said. The former editor was harshly critical of Lundy.

> Walker Lundy was an absolute fool. But he always lands on his feet, although Gannett had to let him go. He had the most sophomoric approach to news gathering. He led the paper one day with a kid who was dying of leukemia or something. A four-column headline. Leading the paper with a two-column picture close-up of him. Of course, those stories go in the paper, but lead the paper with something like that? That was just an example. And I kept hearing these stories from horrified staff members about the decisions he would make. So bad that even Gannett fired him.[96]

In their oral history interview, Reed and Douglas recalled Lundy's advice to the UA journalism students that readers ought to tell the editors what they want in the paper rather than have trained editors make such decisions—the unfortunate market-driven trend that continues and is indicative of one of the major philosophical battles within journalism today. Douglas said the idea eventually went with Lundy to the *St. Paul (Minn.) Pioneer-Press*. That paper's editorials "now are either written or dictated by the readers, the editorial position in that paper," Douglas said in 2000. "He was a fool."[97]

Lundy did, however, have his supporters. One was Susie Ellwood, the marketing executive who had preceded Gannett at the *Gazette*, who called him "a great newspaperman" whose every decision was from his heart and was something he thought would make the newspaper better. Although he made some bad decisions, she said, so does every other editor, even those who are local. "So I thought he had his heart in the right place and that he gave it his all," she said.[98]

Under Lundy, Brantley eventually became assistant managing editor in charge of the reporting staffs in the news and business departments. He said he worked reasonably well with the new man and understood what he wanted. "I was not a daily impediment to his philosophy because he was the boss, but I didn't always agree with him, and I particularly resisted this employee evaluation thing," Brantley said.[99] Lundy, he said, grew desperate to fire some people.

> Finally it had gotten to the point that we had a meeting one Saturday with several other editors, and he said, "I just want to know who you're going to fire." It was just really that simple. And I suggested somebody who was one of his particular pets just really to cause trouble; she was really not deserving of being fired. She was a newspaper politician who was always going behind people's backs to promote her stories and that sort of thing. She was not always a healthy influence in the newsroom, but she had talent, and I just really kind of did it to just get under his skin. He got red in the face and just about exploded, and that was more or less the end of the meeting. Later I was told by the managing editor that it was very close to my end. The good news was that he was fired before he fired me. So I got a few more years and he was shipped on to other places and later became a Pulitzer Prize–winning editor at the St. Paul newspaper, so everybody should view in context that I'm saying this about a guy who went on to far greater things than I did.[100]

Among Gannett's criticisms of the *Gazette* had been that the paper included too much "inconsequential" news, such as planning commission meetings and other such governmental coverage.[101] Brantley told *American Journalism Review*, "What they were looking for were the boy-howdy stories, in features and fashion and food."[102] Brantley called Lundy "one of those everybody-hates-government brand of editors" who preferred movie reviews to more traditional hard news. Brantley said the new editor shortened the length of government and other such stories and emphasized fluff pieces by new young reporters hired on by Gannett[103]—Gannettoids, as the old *Gazette* hands derisively christened them. Reporter Anne Farris said the conflict of philosophy between the Gannettoids and those who favored the *Gazette*'s sober style led to a division in the newsroom that had not existed before. Farris remembered that one Gannett editor told her she should never write above the comprehension level of a twelve-year-old. Farris, like Carrick Patterson before her, bucked the order. "I said, 'If they are reading at the comprehension of a twelve-year-old, let's educate them a little,'" she said. "We had lively debates over copy, and I was spending a lot more time protecting my copy."[104] She recalled front-page play of the obituary of Clara Peller, the actress of Wendy's "Where's the Beef" fame. That decision drew criticism by readers as well as many *Gazette* employees. Farris added that she got the sense that Gannett was bringing in people who did not know that Arkansas was a unique place. "And I think they were really trying hard to bring the paper around, and whoever was brought in didn't get long to do that," she said. "And to their defense, I don't know if anybody could've pulled it around."[105] John Reed, the state capitol reporter, gave an example of the poor news judgment: "a 23-year-old girl from California writing a fluffy piece about hillbillies," he told *American Journalism Review*. "Well, people in Arkansas aren't interested in this." Lundy disagreed, telling *AJR* that upon his arrival, the *Gazette*'s government coverage "didn't connect with our readers," thus his push to make such stories more reader-focused.[106] Dumas said the mainstay of the *Gazette*'s coverage—government—was in many ways an abomination to the Gannett formula.

> Gannett—and Walker, too, I think—thought, "That's not important. People don't want to read about that." Now, they liked the schools. They had polls, did surveys, focus groups—they really loved focus groups—and they'd have people come in and they liked school news, but beyond that they wanted stuff about movies and television. They wanted to know what's on television, so he wanted to beef up our coverage of television and movies, particularly movies. Walker himself loved movies, so when a new movie came to town somebody would have to go cover it and review it that night, and we'd try to get it in the paper the next day. No newspaper does that. But it was so important to them, we held up the paper to get movie reviews in the next day.[107]

Arkansas Times, then a monthly magazine, ran a cover story during Lundy's editorship with a photo of him under the tag, "Mellow Journalism." But Brantley said it was too simple to call Lundy all bad.

> He was a little wacky, a little loony, but he also had an eye for holes in stories. He was an old metro editor, and he could edit a solid news story well, and it's not true that he was entirely focused on movies and sports and frivolous things. I remember the happiest I ever made him with my own work was when I broke a story about a bill at the legislature to consolidate Pulaski County Schools. He stripped it across the top of page one, thought it was a great scoop and a very interesting story. He could be moved by government process stories, but only rarely, only very rarely.[108]

Dumas agreed that Gannett caught the brunt of the blame for the cosmetic changes to the Old Gray Lady that were going to come anyway. For example, in the 1980s, some color began to appear on section fronts and in color photographs. "[A] lot of old franchise readers of the *Gazette* thought this is not the real *Gazette*, this is *USA Today*, flashy stuff, and we want that good old hard-core reporting on public affairs for which we take the *Gazette*," he said. "So part of that rap that Gannett got, and Lundy too, was probably undeserved." He said the *Gazette* was in the process of moving to color before the sale. "We all recognized the paper needed to be a little more colorful and not sensational but presented in a little more attractive way," he said.[109]

Regardless, Hussman said Gannett's strategy "was a total disaster for them. It was a huge benefit for us."[110] Meredith Oakley said *Democrat* employees talked among themselves about how Gannett was "Gannettizing the *Gazette* and what a mistake they were making because people don't like their institutions changed dramatically, or drastically overnight." She said, though, that the Gannettization went far beyond updating the look and adding color.

> They were just bringing such drastic changes overnight to something that had been the same for decades upon decades. I'm not just talking about modernizing it and making it sleeker, but they did strange things. You would've expected that from the *Democrat*; we used to do strange things, too, when we were the underdog, like some of the crazy feature stories we would put on the front page above the fold. It's called a sexy story because it's going to catch the eye and make the reader want to pick it up and read the whole story. Gannett was doing strange things to the *Gazette*, and you don't expect that.[111]

She said the reaction of John Robert Starr, the *Democrat*'s editor with whom she worked closely, was "they're playing right into our hands." Starr, she reminded, had been an Associated Press reporter before becoming bureau chief in Arkansas. He had traveled the state, knew the *Gazette*'s readership, the product, and the audience for it. She said Starr never thought Gannett could win Arkansas's newspaper war. "We knew about the bank book and the deep pockets of Gannett, and that can be intimidating for people who don't have very deep pockets, but he always knew that Gannett could not win, not the way it was going," she said.[112] Dumas agreed that the local Starr exploited the outside Gannett ownership and management masterfully—and enjoyed doing it regularly in his columns, where he more often than not found some occasion to attack his competitor: "[T]he management of the *Gazette* was dishonest; the reporters were dishonest, we were unfair, news coverage was biased and deceitful," Dumas recalled. "He attacked individual members of the *Gazette* staff, reporters and editors and editorial writers." No matter their accuracy, the attacks, Dumas said, had some effect on the newspaper-reading public.[113]

Gene Foreman, who had worked at both the *Democrat* and the *Gazette*, agreed that because the *Gazette* did not change with the times during the last years of the Patterson ownership, some modernization was long overdue. In fact, he said, Harry Ashmore oversaw a 1949 makeover that made the paper more mid-century contemporary. But Foreman said Hugh Patterson and others felt that the *Gazette* would always be a good deal better than the *Democrat*, and consequently, "you don't fix what is not broken." That turned out to be a mistake; some modernization should have been ongoing. "Gannett tried to bring in things like color printing, color photography, overnight, and a conservative readership like the *Gazette*'s, a loyal readership, maybe should've been better prepared for that," he said.[114]

But Foreman said the Gannett changes went far beyond modernization almost overnight: Lundy's obsession with getting a color photo—any color photo—on the front page; a drastic change in news judgment from the previous sober selection of headline size and play. "As Bob Douglas said, 'We're telling people, here's what we think about the value of this story,'" Foreman said, adding that under Gannett, "the *Gazette* was trivialized."[115]

Senator David Pryor, himself an old newspaperman from Camden, watched the evolution of the Old Gray Lady under Gannett warily from Washington, D.C. He remembered thinking that it tried to get "a little glitzy." "I was worried when some of the older professionals, veterans, started sort of transitioning out from the paper, people who had made the *Gazette* what it was," he said. "I got concerned that maybe it was losing a little of its value."[116] Pryor was concerned enough that Gannett was trying to turn the *Gazette* into another *USA Today* that he reached out to Lundy with a phone call.

> I said, "You don't know me from Adam, but I'm Senator Pryor and I'd like to buy your lunch today." I took him over to Scott, Arkansas, to Cotham's. I thought maybe he needed to touch and be touched by some real people, real Arkansans. I think he was kind of amazed at that. All these old farmers would come up and visit with me, talk about their tractors, horses, mules, cows, chickens, and I'd introduce them to Mr. Lundy and I said, "This man's running the *Gazette* now." They all gave him a piece of their mind about what they thought should happen to the *Gazette*.[117]

But Gannett officials either failed to take the criticism seriously or brashly thought they knew better than Arkansans how to put out their newspaper. Bill

Lewis, who had originally been optimistic about the sale, said the company "seemed to have a death wish, seemed to want to commit suicide" in Arkansas. The management team it brought in, having been successful at converting other properties after Gannett acquired them, tried to implement the national formula that had apparently worked everywhere else, but Lewis contended the company totally disregarded the love-hate relationship the *Gazette* had with its readers. "[Readers] loved to hate us, but they still read it," Lewis said. "[Gannett] deliberately set out to ruin that relationship—and succeeded."[118] Lewis said Neuharth's early assurances of maintaining *Gazette* traditions proved almost immediately to be patently false. He recalled hearing Neuharth say, "We don't fix things that ain't broke." Lewis was aghast at what happened:

> You couldn't believe how broke the *Gazette* was if setting about fixing them was any indication of Gannett's policy. They ruined everything, and they brought in such bad people. Walker Lundy was one of the worst . . . editors I've ever seen anywhere. It just seemed like they were hell-bent on making the paper fail.[119]

Lewis remembered Lundy's belief that the only unifying factor in the country was television and that newspapers ought to be as much like that medium as they could, with short stories, graphs, charts, and many photos, things he called "razzmatazz and dazzle"—the complete opposite of what the sober Old Gray Lady had always been. "That's the main thing; they just seemed to have no perception of the *Gazette*'s nature and the relationship it had with its readers," Lewis said.[120] John Reed said the comparison to television meant "you had to read about six paragraphs into the story by the time some of their young feature writers had flowered up and backed into the lead. You had to read about six paragraphs into the story to figure out what it's all about."[121]

But the *Democrat*'s Oakley said after Gannett's purchase, the *Gazette* did start covering things it had never covered before. Whereas the *Democrat* had routinely covered meetings of the National Governors Association, the *Gazette* only did so after Gannett ownership, likely an indication of the Pattersons' attempts to save money during the newspaper war. The infusion of Gannett money enabled John Brummett, the political columnist, to travel nationally and the sports department to commit more fully to total coverage of its beats.[122]

Although some Gannett initiatives found favor among readers and old *Gazette* employees, many came with a price. Wadie Moore, the *Gazette*'s first black newsroom employee when he was hired in 1968 and who by the time of Gannett's arrival was the expert on high school sports in Arkansas, agreed that Gannett's deep pockets allowed for expanded coverage in that department, but the staff was happier under the local ownership of the Heiskells and Pattersons. "With Hugh Patterson and the family, there was a trust factor," Moore said. "Gannett had people running in and out, so the last two years, you just knew something bad was going to happen."[123] There was uneasiness even among the Gannett imports. Borden, the transition team member from the *Jackson Clarion-Ledger* who had joined the *Gazette* in September 1987 as executive sports editor and was called by longtime *Gazette* editor Bob Douglas "probably the best Gannett had," said Malone went behind his back to ask Henry Freeman, the first executive sports editor at *USA Today*, to critique the *Gazette*'s sports section. But Borden was unable to implement many of the suggestions.

> I pointed out that we simply didn't have the resources—the number of personnel—to do some of them. I didn't hear directly but heard later Malone didn't like that. When Walker later gave me a pretty good annual review, Malone put a note on it that he did not agree with it, though he never told me that. I just happened to find out and checked it out. You should have seen the sheepish look I got from the human resources department on that.[124]

Gannett also brought focus groups to the *Gazette* to supposedly get more input from readers, drawing withering criticism from some *Gazette* journalists. Mathis, for one, called herself old-fashioned, with her philosophy of news simply to tell readers what happened. "You don't like it; let's get to work and let's make some changes here," she said. "Don't blame me because I told you the truth about what happened."[125] McCord called the focus groups a public relations ploy. "There was no reliance on them," he said. "It was like me going to a meeting of dentists."[126]

Many Gannett moves outraged both readers and *Gazette* employees and played into the *Democrat*'s hands. John Reed remembered Lundy asking his opinion of how to win Arkansas's newspaper war. Reed told him he would not do it on the backs of the *Gazette* reporters, who were providing regular scoops, and instead pointed to the business aspects of the battle. "[T]he people in the ad bureau at the *Democrat* are winning this war, hustling on the streets," he remembered telling Lundy. Reed also criticized Gannett's promotional billboards that featured young Gannett imports—a young black man, Alvin Reed, and a young white woman, Phoebe Wall. Instead, Reed suggested those billboards should trumpet a well-established, trusted *Gazette* person such as Wadie Moore—who also happened to be black. "He was Mr. High School Football, high school athletics; every coach in the state knew Wadie Moore,"

Reed said. "Not somebody from Detroit who's been here six months." Lundy asked him, somewhat impertinently, "Will that increase our circulation by twenty thousand on Sundays?" "I don't know, but it's better than Phoebe and Alvin," Reed recalled answering.[127] Hussman agreed that, as with the Pattersons and the antitrust suit, Gannett's actions benefited his newspaper in ways that the *Democrat* could never have done on its own.

> They really changed the whole focus of the newspaper. They trivialized it in a way to the extent that they made it much more feature-oriented than hard news-oriented. . . . In my opinion, the reason the people in Arkansas loved the *Arkansas Gazette* is it was a very hard-news, serious, complete, comprehensive newspaper, and it might not have been the most exciting newspaper, the most interesting, but it was a very complete, serious newspaper. And Gannett at that point was really enamored with *USA Today*, and they really kind of turned the *Gazette* into a regional *USA Today* approach with a lot more feature articles. I remember the time they ran the mayor of Eureka Springs in a bubble bath with some rubber duckies. It just horrified *Gazette* readers; it horrified me as a *Gazette* reader that that was on the front page. I remember one day they ran a John Brummett column on the front page. They had never run a column on the front page in all the years. Doing things like that really alienated their readers, so as they went softer, we went harder, and so we were just moving into the niche that I think Arkansans normally appreciated in a newspaper because they'd been taught by the *Gazette* for years that that's what a good newspaper did.[128]

The changes, he said, disoriented readers to the point that they could not tell what was important anymore when they picked up the *Gazette*.[129] Again, though, the irony of Hussman's praising what the *Gazette* had always been—after he had allowed Starr and his *Democrat* to condemn it for years—is stunning.

Hussman said by 1988, Gannett was frustrated because, despite the influx of corporate resources, the *Democrat* was continuing to gain market share. The giant media company—and conventional wisdom—believed that Arkansas's newspaper war should have been over by that point, but instead, despite Gannett's heavy financial losses, the *Democrat* was gaining market share. "That's what gave me the encouragement to continue, despite losing all this money," he said. "This is my assumption: Gannett said, 'We've got to put this thing in fast-forward.'"[130] Although Hussman has never revealed his exact losses during Arkansas's newspaper war, they were in the tens of millions.[131]

So Gannett cut the *Gazette*'s subscription price from $2 a week to 85 cents per week. "[T]hat helped them for one or two quarters and then we went back to gaining market share on them again," Hussman said, adding that the move cost Gannett an extra $7 million a year in operating losses. As he had during his battle with the Pattersons, Hussman declined to match the price, he said, because he could not afford to do so. He called that decision one of the best he ever made. While his company could not afford to lose another $7 million a year, it could probably yield another $2 million, so he thought about where that money could best be invested and came upon the idea of improving customer service. "We should get more papers on the porch; we should knock on more doors and sell more subscriptions," he said. "Let them put their money into discounts and let us put our money into direct sales and service, and it turned out $1 or $2 million a year in direct sales and service was a far more effective strategy than $7 million a year in discounts."[132]

Among the *Democrat*'s customer service initiatives were maintaining phone lines for the free want ads from 7 A.M.–7 P.M. during the week, adding Saturday hours and classified staff, phone lines, and computers to ensure that callers to the *Democrat* had a shorter wait time than those calling the *Gazette*.[133] *Democrat* carriers already placed their papers on subscribers' porches, Hussman said, so people who took both newspapers would read his first because the *Gazette* was thrown in their yards. He called his decision "a classical, fortunate decision in marketing, or how to use limited resources."[134] In fact, he said the discounting wound up hurting the *Gazette*. Perception again made a difference. After an initial circulation bump leveled off for the *Gazette*, the *Democrat* continued to grow—it was named the fastest-growing newspaper in the country on a percentage basis, according to the ABC Audit Reports. Hussman had rack cards created promoting the *Democrat* as "America's fastest-growing newspaper." The *Gazette*'s racks proclaimed, "Now only 85 cents a week." "So what ended up happening, in people's perceptions, well, when they cut their price, it's like people started saying, 'Well, you know, the *Gazette* just isn't as good as it used to be. So I see why they cut their price,'" Hussman recalled.[135]

Jim Bailey said after a couple of years of the new ownership, he began to think Gannett would probably eventually lose Arkansas's newspaper war because the *Democrat* had taken months of Gannett's discounting and never blinked. "Mr. Hussman didn't really have anybody to answer to but himself," Bailey said. "Gannett had a bunch of nervous stockholders."[136] That revealed another of the major differences between public and private companies that would be one more factor in the outcome of Arkansas's newspaper war.

A showdown between the old *Gazette* and the new Gannett management came with the 1988 presidential election. Ernest Dumas said that while

Malone enjoyed the opportunity to return to his native Arkansas as publisher, he was a Republican whose wife had worked on Vice President George Bush's staff prior to the move. "He was upset, I think, by the *Gazette*'s editorial page," Dumas said. "They arrive at this paper and it's liberal and Democratic, every day critical of Ronald Reagan and the policies of the Reagan administration."[137] Because of Neuharth's promise to the Pattersons to retain the *Gazette*'s progressive editorial stance, Malone tried subtlety to influence it. Malone and Lundy began having weekly meetings with the editorial staff. Dumas said he thought Malone hoped that Lundy would try to use his leverage to influence the editorial writers' position. "Walker was kind of a liberal himself and was reluctant to do it and tried very subtly, but you couldn't use subtlety on *Gazette* editorial writers; we just acted like we didn't understand," Dumas said. "So there were some efforts made, very subtly, to change the editorial policies."[138]

Michael Dukakis was the Democratic nominee for president in 1988, with Bush as the Republican nominee. While the *Gazette* editorial writers were not wild about Dukakis—they believed him to be an intelligent fellow who would not be a great leader—there was no question among them that the *Gazette* would endorse Dukakis as the better choice. The editorial board met, as usual, with Lundy and Malone about a month before the election. "We talked about the endorsement and we all said, yeah, it's got to be Michael Dukakis," Dumas recalled. "We'll write about his frailties, but he clearly is the choice." He remembered Malone asking them, "Don't you think George Bush would make a great president?" And the editorial writers said no. "So he turned to Walker Lundy, and Walker would kind of fiddle around—he wouldn't take a clear stand—and said, well, they both have some good points and some bad points, and so it kind of rocked on," Dumas remembered.[139] Dhonau recalled that Malone, following a trip to Washington, "clearly and forcefully indicated to me that the editorial board should follow the lead of the *Washington Post* and not endorse."[140] About a week prior to the election, the board met again with Malone and Lundy, who suggested that the paper not take a stand. "We said no, you can't do that," Dumas said. "So they left us and we all wrote a little memo about it and Jerry Dhonau crafted an editorial endorsing Dukakis and sent it to Malone and Lundy." Lundy said Malone did not want the editorial to run and suggested another meeting, but the board stood firm that there was nothing further to discuss. "So Lundy left town, just disappeared, went off back to Florida to visit his family or something; he just disappeared," Dumas said. The editorial had to run in the Sunday edition prior to the election, but Malone could not find Lundy, so on Saturday afternoon before the election, Malone acquiesced and told Dhonau to run the editorial.[141]

One of Gannett's few positive moves in Arkansas's newspaper war was the appointment of John Hanchette as managing editor under Lundy in September 1988. Hanchette had won a Pulitzer in 1980 for his part in a Gannett News Service investigative series. A company man, he remembered being surprised that Gannett had jumped into such a newspaper war. He said he figured Neuharth "felt that it was one of those deals that if he turned it around, he'd be perceived as a huge genius. You know, that there was an old and honorable paper and it needed somebody with deep pockets, like Gannett had, to win that war."[142] Liking a challenge himself, Hanchette had campaigned for the managing editor position. He said he went to Little Rock with specific instructions from John Curley to strengthen the local news product. Nobody ever told him, he said, to worry about money. "We were able to hire when we needed somebody, and, hell, I don't know, I just knew we were losing ten to eleven, twelve million [dollars] a year," he said. "And I never got chastised for that—despite the rumors about Gannett, and my own assertion that it's a bottom line company."[143] He acknowledged some mistakes regarding story play, citing the UALR dancers in their spandex uniforms and the Clara Peller obituary, both on page one, and agreed the criticism was justified. "We just kept changing sections on people," he said. "I think that was the heart of the criticism." He would hear the talk socially: "You've got it just about right. Quit tinkering with it." Being more focused on content than design, he said he tended to agree with the critics, but "as far as I know we just kept changing it right to the end." Hanchette said, "I sort of sided with the readers on that one."[144] Susie Ellwood said Hanchette was one of the best things Gannett did to the *Gazette*, calling him a breath of fresh air. "He always stayed pretty much on an even keel," she said. "I just remember he had great judgment and he connected with the community and with us internally better than anyone else did."[145]

In an attempt to get to know the state, Hanchette made it a point to accept every speaking engagement offered. And he had a message—one party would win Arkansas's newspaper war because economics dictated that the state could not support two newspapers forever. But he said he had a hard time getting that message across to readers because they thought Gannett had all the money in the world and that Hussman was so proud he would never give up. "[And I said,] 'No, that's not going to happen. You've got to make a decision which paper you're going to support,'" he reiterated.[146]

One of Lundy's hires in 1989 was Deborah Mathis, the native Arkansan who, wanting to return to long-form journalism, gave up a career in television news on a gut feeling. Having worked for the *Democrat* before the Hussman regime, she knew Bob McCord, who by the 1980s was the op-ed editor at the

Gazette. With the *Gazette*'s editorial staff all older white males, she proposed to join the *Gazette* to bring a young, black, female voice to the Old Gray Lady. McCord told her he loved the idea and pitched it to Lundy, who took Mathis to lunch. She remembered that after hearing her spiel, he looked at her and asked, "How many can you write a week?"[147] Having reported on the newspaper war for Little Rock television stations, she was more aware of the stakes than perhaps any other Gannett hire. She said unlike his counterpart, Starr, Lundy never understood how to fight.

> John Robert Starr had the advantage of not having any scruples to hold him back. People who have manners, who have a sense of right and wrong, who know laws and believe in abiding by them, are at a decided disadvantage against people who don't have manners, who don't give a damn about the law, all that. Really, you have restrictions. Walker couldn't take on John Robert Starr because he was too much of a gentleman. He couldn't get down the way John Robert would. So it always looked like he lost every time he would try to respond to John Robert, and John Robert would just bait him, just bait him, week after week after week. And we'd go in there and tell Walker, don't respond to this. Walker would close his office door, let his blinds down, have his assistant hold all calls and sit in there and sweat over some column and try to take on John Robert Starr, and it would be like somebody with a feather coming after somebody with a bat. It would just be so frustrating, over and over and over again. I don't fault him for that because he was just too decent a man to do that kind of thing, and how do you fault somebody for being too decent? I just wish, again, that he had listened to us.[148]

Lundy also failed to listen to his managing editor. Hanchette said they butted heads on the same issue. He told his boss he was spending too much time letting Starr distract him. "He spent half his time writing a column to rebut Starr," Hanchette said. "Starr knew he could get his goat."[149] In fact, Hanchette said Starr gave him the greatest compliment he had ever received in print when, after the *Gazette* beat its competitor on a couple of stories, Starr christened the managing editor in his column "the Gannettoid spawn of Satan."[150] The *Gazette* had T-shirts made up featuring the phrase and distributed them to newsroom employees. Not surprisingly, readers perceived Starr as winning the war of words.[151]

Lundy wasn't the only Gannett manager who ignored Mathis's advice. She said she ultimately went to Malone's successor, Craig Moon, and gave the new publisher polite, sincere, unsolicited advice. His dismissive response made a lasting impression on her.

> I said, "I know you haven't asked for any advice on this, and I know you're probably tired of hearing people come to you and offer this to you, but can I just tell you I have nothing but the interest of this paper at heart? I just want to tell you, this is a different paper. People have a spiritual connection to this paper. You don't need to make some of the changes here that you've made other places. Please don't make these changes." I really was trying to be as humble, deferential as I could be since he hadn't asked for this advice, and I knew that he probably was fed up with it, but I was trying to let him know I am so sincere about this, and it's only because of the paper. Why would I care otherwise? What's in it for me to care? If he could have, I think he would've patted me on the head and said, "Okay, take your little butt out of here now." I didn't have much of an impression of him yet at that point, but I got one then, and I will always have that impression of him—as a total jerk.[152]

She remembered that upset readers wrote letters of complaint and canceled their subscriptions. Gannett never blinked, maddening in its certainty that its methods were the right ones for Arkansas's newspaper war. "Even when the writing was on the wall, they just thought, 'Oh, you people,'" Mathis said. "That was very disappointing to me."[153]

With that turmoil in the background, one of the major blows to Gannett's presence in Little Rock came in May 1989 with the loss of the *Gazette*'s largest advertiser, Dillard's. The Little Rock-based department store chain had spent nearly $2 million with the newspaper annually[154] but pulled out after a dispute over advertising rates and news coverage. Carrick Patterson described it as Gannett's violation of the integrity of the rate card. Under the Pattersons, the *Gazette* had offered volume discounts for advertisers—those buying more advertising got a cheaper rate per inch than those who bought less. "It's the same for everyone, no matter who you are, no matter what you are," Patterson said. "They messed with that and they undersold; they made a special introductory deal to somebody to sell them a rate less than Dillard's."[155] In its attempt to gain profits at all costs, Gannett shortchanged its largest advertiser.

Hussman recalled that after Gannett came to Little Rock, one of its early strategies in Arkansas's newspaper war was to start cherry-picking the *Democrat*'s advertisers. Gannett offered special, lower advertising rates to businesses that advertised in the *Democrat*. So the *Democrat* decided to try to match the *Gazette*'s "special" rate if the advertiser could provide proof—an invoice. "So we're not going to make special deals with people, but we've got to respond, and here's how we're going to respond and this is a way to respond uniformly and try to be fair with everyone," Hussman said. "All of a sudden we're getting lots of invoices, tons of invoices, because they're doing this with a lot of our advertisers."[156]

Sometimes, Hussman said, the *Democrat* would match the *Gazette*'s rate. Sometimes it would not. "We'd say, I'm sorry; we've got to charge more; we're a smaller company than Gannett," he said. "And if you go with Gannett and you keep doing this and they run us out of business, your rates are going to be a lot higher."[157]

The Dillard family did not particularly like the *Gazette*, Dumas recalled, although the Old Gray Lady was clearly the most effective way to advertise. "Seventy-five percent of his advertising was in the *Gazette*, although it was charging $9 an inch and the *Democrat* $1 an inch," Dumas said. "Mr. Dillard didn't like the *Gazette*'s liberal editorial policies."[158] In addition, the Dillard family was angered by a couple of news stories in the *Gazette*. The first was about a young family member who had stolen a car, carved up some yards with it while joy-riding, and gotten shot by someone who had fired on the car with a rifle. Brantley said the story was big news in Little Rock, and the *Gazette* covered it completely. The *Democrat*, on the contrary, managed to bury some of the key facts deep in the story.

> It was hard to put a story like that in positive terms, but such as they were able, they did. They treated it very carefully. There was certainly a great deal of nervousness about it because we knew we were dealing with King Kong. It's not that you're not going to cover the story, but you say, boy, these guys are big shots and they're tough and you'd better get it right. You always want to get it right, but when you know the other side has the ability to lower the boom on you, you REALLY are careful to get it right.[159]

Despite the many missteps Gannett made, at least in the Dillard's coverage, it retained the Heiskell-Patterson legacy of quality journalism.

The second—and final—strike was a news story run on page one about a dispute between Dillard's and its accounting firm over some tax liabilities. Max Brantley said neither paper was ever aggressive in covering the department store chain. "You couldn't cover Dillard's; they didn't talk to the press," he said. "The *Democrat* went beyond being non-aggressive to being very solicitous, to the point that they threatened to fire an advertising writer if she ever wrote something critical about their advertising again, as she once did."[160] In order to cover Dillard's to some degree, Brantley bought two shares of stock so that as a shareholder, he would receive the company's annual proxy statement. "Business reporting was kind of in its infancy in Arkansas then," he recalled. That year's proxy reported a legal battle brewing between Dillard's and its accounting firm over how some tax revenue had been accounted for, which potentially had some tax impact on the company. So Brantley gave the proxy statement to the *Gazette*'s business writer, Chuck Heinbockel, who wrote a story on it. Brantley recalled that Dillard's, true to form, refused to comment. The story wound up on page one, thanks in part to a slow news day and the fact that the *Gazette* was sure the *Democrat* would not have it. Brantley recalled the result:

> The next day, I remember clearly sitting at the city desk and somebody from advertising running through the newsroom saying, "We don't have the Dillard's ad yet, we don't have the Dillard's ad yet." Well, there would never be another Dillard's ad in the *Arkansas Gazette*. They never came back; they resisted visits by the head of the Gannett Corporation, John Curley; we did everything but shine their shoes, and they would never come back.[161]

He said Dillard's accounted for probably 7 or 8 percent of the *Gazette*'s annual revenue.

> I don't think there's any doubt that the news coverage was the last straw. But there had been other issues. There was a class of advertising that would get a lower inch rate than our single biggest advertiser, some curious circumstance like for a standby ad that would run only when some space opened up in the local edition, so that rankled them, and I think you put it all together and they were gone. Just like Dillard's is a market leader in a mall, they bring business to other stores in a mall—their presence in the newspaper brings other business. It was a crushing blow, and it was certainly critical to the final outcome of the newspaper war.[162]

Hussman said it was not unusual for an advertiser to pull its advertising over an editorial dispute but that it would usually return after emotions had cooled because it would be in the advertiser's best economic interest to do so. So after the Dillard's brouhaha, the *Democrat* plotted as to how best to keep the company from returning to its rival.

"We're not going to offer them any special deal not to go back to the *Gazette*; I don't think that would be the right thing to do, but we can show Dillard's how the *Gazette* has not been treating them fairly, and we can show them how they have very, very small advertisers that are getting a lower advertising rate than Dillard's, which is their largest advertiser," Hussman said.[163]

Hussman had already told William Dillard about Gannett's tactics. "He called me and said, 'Can you prove to me what you were telling me, that they offer lower rates to some people than they offer to me?' I said, 'I can prove it to you,'" Hussman recalled. He took *Gazette* invoices that several businesses had sent to the *Democrat* that proved that smaller advertisers were getting a lower rate than Dillard's. One was for Jimmy Karam's Men's Store. "It turned out that William Dillard and Jimmy Karam were friends, so it was easy for William Dillard to call Jimmy Karam and say, 'I've seen this invoice; is it legit? The *Democrat* didn't create this invoice, did they?'" Hussman recalled.[164]

Dillard moved his meeting with Hussman to an earlier time to accommodate an appointment on the same day with Gannett officials, who were trying to woo him back to the *Gazette*.

> So I went down to his office on Capitol and took my information and we went in the conference room, and I sat down and showed him. He said, "I've seen enough." At that point, his secretary came in and said the fellow from Gannett is here. He said, "Why don't you just stay here and let me go back to my office and take him to my office and once he's in my office, you can leave." So I think what happened is when the folks from Gannett came down they told him they weren't doing it. And then you had a double problem. Not only are you charging advertisers less than you're charging your biggest advertisers, but you deny you're doing it when he's just seen the proof you're doing it.[165]

Hussman recalled that Dillard had a plaque on his office wall referring to integrity as the most important thing in business. "And so that hardened his resolve to try to go it alone with the *Democrat* if he could," he said. "And then we made the decision to do something that made it easier for him to do that."[166] The *Democrat* started a weekend subscription package that included the Wednesday, Friday, Saturday, and Sunday editions—the four biggest advertising days of the week. "What this meant was Dillard's could run four days of the week and reach about as many customers as they reached with the *Gazette*, and they really didn't have to go back to the *Gazette*," Hussman said.[167]

And Dillard's did not.

Hanchette was at an American Press Institute seminar when Lundy called to tell him the news of the advertiser's defection. He remembered Lundy's low-key approach: "Something happened today I thought you ought to know about that might affect the future of this newspaper's viability," he told his managing editor.[168] But Hanchette added that he did not necessarily buy that explanation for the *Gazette*'s loss in Arkansas's newspaper war. "I think that the *Gazette* may have lost the war even before Gannett got involved in it," he said. "I think one of the key decisions, and I know Walker agrees with me on this, is Hussman's brilliant decision to give away classified advertising, which made it a real [losing proposition for the *Gazette*]."[169]

McCord said the Dillard's loss got a lot of attention at Gannett headquarters. "I think that rang a lot of gongs, not in Little Rock," he said. "Some big honcho flew in to fix it, and after that, I thought something might happen."[170] Dumas said while the financial loss was significant, perhaps more than anything else, the loss of Dillard's was a psychological blow that reverberated throughout the Gannett company. "They'd squire Bill Dillard to lunch, make all kinds of proposals but never could get that advertising back," he said. "I think it was at that point in the Virginia headquarters, Gannett began to think about getting rid of this paper."[171] The Dillard's decision caused some hard feelings that remain. Nineteen years after the *Gazette* closed, John Reed said he had yet to step in a Dillard's store since it had pulled its advertising. "They can place their ads where they want to, but I can shop where I want to," he said.[172] Carrick Patterson said his parents resented both Gannett and Dillard's.

> I didn't resent Dillard's at all; I thought Dillard's did the right thing from their point of view. Imagine underselling your biggest advertiser; imagine that. Of course they retaliated; of course they did. My mother thought, "Oh well, Dillard's should've been loyal to us"; well, no they shouldn't, either; it was a business relationship. Dillard's didn't care what kind of newspaper it was; they cared how many Guess jeans they sold. That wasn't what they were in business for. What we were in business for was to care about what the *Gazette* was like.[173]

Another more public disaster came three months later with the defection of longtime *Gazette* sports editor Orville Henry in August 1989—to the *Democrat*. Henry had become sports editor of the *Gazette* during World War II and had been the face of sports writing in Arkansas for generations. Ernest Dumas, among others, credited Henry in large part for the *Gazette*'s recovery from the ill will left by the Central High crisis.

> Orville Henry, understand, had been, perhaps more than anybody else, the *Gazette*'s savior in 1957. We lost perhaps a fifth of our circulation, but it was clear it would've been a lot more had it

> not been for Orville Henry because there were tens of thousands of people in Arkansas who read the *Gazette* for Orville Henry, who told you what you had to know about the Razorbacks, football and basketball. So Orville was literally worshipped by people. Down in El Dorado, when I went to work at the *Gazette* [in 1960], I had people stop me and say, "What's Orville Henry like?" So people could not give up Orville Henry, or couldn't give him up for long. They were upset about the editorials, but when football season rolled around, they'd re-subscribe.[174]

For years, Henry had taken potshots from Starr and others. Nate Allen, the Fayetteville-based sportswriter who worked closely with Henry, said some of those shots came from the *Gazette*—and not just from the new regime. "It seemed, too, that newcomers to the paper in the 1980s seemed resentful of the Razorbacks' prominence and seemed to think they could put their personal stamp on things by championing UALR as Arkansas's basketball team," Allen said. "Walker Lundy in particular seemed to think UALR hung the moon."[175] Allen recalled a deputy sports editor opening for which Borden interviewed Clay Henry, Orville's son who was then at the *Tulsa World*.

> Clay went to Little Rock just to interview with Paul, and a somewhat embarrassed Paul said he was told Walker Lundy now was handling the interview then was going to give Clay an editing test. Clay said Lundy asked him what the most important sports beat was in Arkansas. "The Razorbacks," Clay answered without pause. "The Razorbacks are king in northwest Arkansas," Clay recalled Lundy saying, "but in Pulaski County, our surveys say UALR is most important to our readers." "Where did you do the survey," Clay recalled saying, "the UALR gym?" "I see we have a difference of opinion," Lundy said, according to Clay. Clay agreed there certainly was. He declined the editor's test.[176]

Greg Henry, who had no ties to the state, got the job as deputy sports editor. Ironically, some would later blame him for Orville Henry's departure.

Brantley called Henry's defection a product of Gannett mismanagement and said the outside company never understood Henry's role in Arkansas. That was just one of its mistakes. Thirty years after Central High, Henry still had a legion of thousands and thousands of devoted readers. "Gannett thought he was old-fashioned, that he wrote too long, that his style of sports writing was over," Brantley said. "It was a terrible decision, and they treated him in a way that made him understand he wasn't that valued."[177] Earlier in the 1980s, Henry had moved to Fayetteville to be closer to the Razorback program, so he had given up his sports editor duties. Under Gannett, the copy desk, particularly young assistant sports editors who had come in from other company properties, would cut vast chunks from his copy. "They'd hired editors from outside that just simply thought he was an old guy who went on too long, and what they were doing was cutting the lifeblood out of the sports section," Brantley recalled.[178]

The newcomers, though, weren't the only ones who thought Henry was past his prime. He was widely perceived—even among some old *Gazette* people—as being the flag-waver and homer for the Razorbacks and Frank Broyles. However, Dumas, with whom Henry was close, said editing decisions such as those cuts and even not running the occasional column added to Henry's frustration.

> Orville would write a column that would start on the front page of the sports section and then jump over to an inside page for five or six hundred words, and people devoured this stuff. If you were a Razorback fan, you read that. It would jump twice, two thousand

Gazette *sports staffers Jim Bailey, Nancy Clark, Orville Henry, Wadie Moore, and Kim Brazzel prepare to cover the Arkansas Razorbacks in the 1987 Orange Bowl. Photo by Art Meripol. Courtesy of Wadie Moore.*

> words long, and you still read every word of it because that was Orville. So this guy would cut him back to four hundred words, a five-hundred-word column, and Orville was just seething and would complain about it. Finally, one day Orville's column was the column they ran the previous week. They ran it again. And this guy had just messed up; he'd forgotten to take out the old column and left it on the page and it ran again. Well, that was kind of the last straw for Orville.[179]

Henry himself indicated that more money and job security—signified by a contract—were his reasons to jump. "Gannett refused to give me a contract," Henry said. "They said they didn't sign contracts, except after I left, all at once, they signed two others to contracts."[180] He recounted a conversation with Lundy in 1988 when he was asked to put in writing his intention to stay at the *Gazette*. That, he said, planted the seed and made him think of his future after nearly a half-century at the paper. He decided he had to sell himself. "I am not leaving any friends except my people there," he said. "The paper is going to hell. There is no way the *Democrat* won't win this."[181] He said he figured that he was worth twice as much to the *Democrat* as he was to the *Gazette* because he would take some circulation with him, tipping the balance in the circulation aspect of Arkansas's newspaper war.[182]

Hussman had previously approached Henry through an intermediary to switch sides, but Henry was not interested then.[183] By 1989, though, he was. Little Rock financier Jack Stephens was the intermediary this time. Hussman said Stephens's call came out of the clear blue: "Jack Stephens called and said, 'Would you be interested in hiring Orville Henry?' And I said, 'Does the sun rise in the east?'"[184] Henry called Dumas and told him his plan to go to the *Democrat* the following Monday "unless the *Gazette* gives me a better deal and shows an interest in me." Dumas leaped into action.

> So I called Max Brantley at the *Gazette* and told him, "Orville Henry's going to leave because he's so furious at the way he's been treated." And Max said, "We can't let that happen," and so he went the next morning—they had a Saturday meeting—and he tells Walker Lundy, "Orville Henry is going to quit, going to go to the *Democrat*." And Walker says, "Well so what, do we care?" And Max said, "Hell, yes, we care," and persuaded him that that would be a disaster for the *Gazette* if Orville Henry left.[185]

Brantley convinced Lundy to craft a good multiyear package that would include a raise and a bonus for Henry. Dumas said Lundy tried to call Henry that weekend, but he called on his *Gazette* telephone line—not his personal line. "That line was upstairs, and Orville wouldn't answer the phone, and Ann, his wife, wouldn't answer the phone, and Lundy called three or four times over the weekend, got no answer, left a message, and so Orville on Monday had a press conference and announced he was going to the *Democrat*," Dumas remembered.[186] Hussman recalled that at their meeting, the first words out of Henry's mouth were, "I will go to work for you; let me tell you what I want, and if you agree to it, I'll go to work for you tomorrow." Henry was so frustrated at the *Gazette*, there were no negotiations. "We talked a little about the newspapers and why I thought it'd be good for him to come to the *Democrat*," Hussman said. "He would reach a lot of readers who didn't regularly read him, plus everyone knew him; he was such an icon in Arkansas sports."[187]

Years later, after leaving the *Democrat* when that contract ran out, Henry expressed some regret.

> I am not proud of everything about it. If I'd left the old *Arkansas Gazette*, there would have been some wrenching things. . . . You know what I thought about? Those marble steps to the back way of the city room, which is to our office. I ran up and down those things three at a time for many years, and I always claimed that they—over fifty years they had worn, then they turned them over, and I wore them out the next.[188]

Paul Borden disagreed that deputy sports editor Greg Henry played a big role in Henry's departure. Two days before the press conference announcing the move, Borden said, he and Greg Henry went to Fayetteville to speak with Orville Henry face-to-face to address their relationship. They left, he said, feeling that although there was not a lot of love between the two, Orville Henry was satisfied with the direction the *Gazette* sports department was headed.

> I don't think Orville had been happy for quite some time, probably because he didn't feel he was getting the respect he thought he deserved. But if I recall, we had pretty much turned over whatever space Orville wanted to him. That always seemed to be a big issue with him. I don't think he liked being edited. (That is what is known as an understatement.) If he wasn't getting respect, some of it was because of the way younger people look at their elders—what does that old fart know? I think Orville saw a new generation of people coming in who were not awed by his presence and stature. If you grew up in Arkansas, you rightfully had more respect for Orville and what he had meant to the state. These new people saw only someone

> of retirement age. I guess you can blame me for that one since many of the people I was hiring were from out-of-state.[189]

Borden said the tense relationship was compounded by the fact that too often Henry would write things that simply were not accurate. Some of the errors, he surmised, came from Frank Broyles, the Arkansas athletic director, "who would be wrong about something but whose word was the gospel to Orville," Borden said. "Orville simply wouldn't bother to check it out, so that would lead to problems."[190]

Regardless of the reason for the move, perception was the key issue again in Arkansas's newspaper war. Hussman said by 1989, Henry had passed the peak of his career, but he did have a following, and some people started reading the *Democrat* because of Henry's presence. "It certainly gave the impression to a lot of readers that, 'You know, gosh, I haven't been reading the *Democrat,* but maybe I need to be reading the *Democrat.* Even Orville Henry has moved,'" Hussman recalled. He said his newspaper was already gaining circulation. "I think it helped us more in perception than it did in circulation," he said.[191]

At the *Gazette* building, Jim Bailey, who had worked with Henry since 1956, said the icon's departure sealed the outcome of Arkansas's newspaper war because the *Democrat* could not have taken any symbol that signified the *Gazette* more than Orville Henry. Bailey said he had already begun to believe that the *Democrat* was going to outlast Gannett because of Hussman's determination—while Gannett could afford to lose, Hussman, the Arkansan, could not. "But after they got Orville, I felt like that was going to speed it," Bailey said. "I don't know how much it sped it up, but it sped it up some."[192] Wadie Moore, whom Henry had hired in 1968, called Henry's departure "one of the saddest days of my life." He blamed the Gannett outsiders for chasing Henry away—changing his copy, shortening it. "These people in the Gannett family, they didn't care about Orville," Moore said. "To them, he wasn't the legend that we all knew him as being."[193] He said Henry gave the *Democrat* its "first legitimate threat" to the Old Gray Lady. "That's when the word 'competition' finally came into play," Moore said. "Someone who can seriously change the tide in this game."[194] Brantley agreed that Henry thought he was not getting the respect he deserved. "There were plenty people at the *Gazette* who had the Gannett view of Orville Henry as kind of a dinosaur and quirky and who maybe needed a little editing, even," Brantley said. "But he was a marquis name, and what he said about the dynamics of the newspaper war was incalculable." The defection was a terrible blow, Brantley said, because if it could be Henry, it could be anyone. "All the old assumptions clearly didn't apply anymore," he said.[195] Roy Reed agreed that Henry's defection was one of the important negative events leading to the *Gazette*'s downfall—and another of Gannett's many mistakes.

> Gannett never understood how important he was. When they let him go, when they refused to do what it took to keep him there, it was a terrible blow to the morale of the *Gazette*. Orville's leaving was seen as the last straw. If they didn't have any more sense at Gannett than to let this man slip away, then this was a company that had no feeling for what's going on, what was important to the paper. I think that was sort of the beginning of the end of the *Gazette*.[196]

Dumas said the departure was unnecessary "and miserable, I think, for Orville over the years as well."[197] Ultimately, Henry left the *Democrat* after the newspaper war was over and the *Democrat* became the only statewide daily newspaper. "He was a tool," Brantley said. "He was used and chewed up and spit out as people tend to be."[198]

Henry's departure necessitated major changes in the *Gazette*'s sports department. Borden, Gannett's executive sports editor, first approached Harry King, the longtime Associated Press sportswriter who had started his career at the *Gazette* under Henry in the 1960s, to replace his old boss in Fayetteville. "It only took one sit-down interview for me to think, 'This newspaper is on shaky ground,'" King remembered. "They were looking for somebody to compete with what the *Democrat* was doing; I told them I didn't think I could do that."[199] When King declined the offer, Borden began to consider the opportunity himself. "I wasn't getting along with Walker Lundy, who was driving me crazy," he said. "I think Walker saw it as an opportunity as well." Borden replaced Henry in Fayetteville for the 1989 football season, working with Nate Allen, who had been in that sports bureau since the 1970s.[200] Greg Henry, Borden's deputy sports editor who came to the *Gazette* after working in Jackson at the afternoon *Jackson Daily News*, ran the department until Don Collins took over as sports editor. Collins, too, had worked with Borden in Jackson, but he came to Little Rock from *USA Today*. After Greg Henry left, another Gannett man, Don Hudson, came in to work under Collins. Although Gannett had a good reputation for hiring minorities, Wadie Moore said he thought management fought for several years not to move him into an editor's slot. He said officials told him they were afraid he would stop writing, but Moore said he never believed Gannett would promote him, despite its good track record of promoting minorities. "They generally would promote them in the North and bring them to positions in the South," he said, citing Hudson as an example. "I probably would've been stronger here" than the Gannett managers.[201]

Instead, the outsiders were able to be quickly moved as needed. Throughout the newsroom in the Gannett years, they often were. Gene Prescott, the longtime photographer who retired in 1989, put it succinctly: "The men that they hired in the management end of it, I thought were pretty stupid," he said. "I considered them nuts or crazy, or they were so intelligent they were just out of my ring." All of them had had numerous prior jobs. "What I never understood is these people who get fired all the time, how come they can go back to New York and get a management job when they're the way they are—how does that happen?" the sweetly naïve Prescott wondered.[202] Although harshly critical of Gannett management in general, John Reed said some of the company's personnel were good, such as Craig Durrett and Kate Marymont. "They were brought in to be low-level managers who were going to impose the Gannett way on us rubes from Arkansas," Reed said. "And they very quickly, because they were decent human beings, came over to our side."[203] Bailey summarized the revolving door of management: "It seemed like every sports editor they sent in was a little more inept than the previous one. It seemed like every executive-type editor they sent in was either a little crazier or more malevolent than the previous one."[204] During his tenure over sports, Collins shook up the established department. He fired Kim Brazzel, the *Gazette*'s longtime horse racing beat writer, and forced out Allen on the eve of the 1990 football season. Borden said he got the impression that he was targeting him, as well. "His problem was he had problems making decisions," Borden said of Collins. "He was a very loyal and effective assistant, a role he had played in Jackson both under me and my predecessor, but not a good sports editor because I think he was afraid of being responsible if a decision turned out bad."[205] Jim Harris moved from the Little Rock office to Fayetteville to replace Allen in the Fayetteville bureau.

In the aftermath of the Dillard's loss, there was more upheaval in top management. Craig Moon was named publisher of the *Gazette* on August 16, 1989, sending Malone to chairman status. Susie Ellwood, who remained with Gannett, said she thought Malone, a circulation man, had been "a little out of his element." "I think he looked to Gannett to guide him about what to do and when to do it," she said. "We did not become as successful, I think, as Gannett wanted us to under his leadership, not that it was his fault." She reiterated her belief that it might have already been too late to turn the tide.[206]

Moon came from the *Fort Myers (Fla.) News-Press*, where he was also publisher.[207] Keith Moyer, who had been executive editor under Moon at the *News-Press*, was named editor of the *Gazette* on March 6, 1990, replacing Lundy, who became a general news executive at Gannett Co., Inc.[208] Carrick Patterson, watching Gannett's revolving door of editors and publishers, was not impressed, pointing to Lundy's infatuation with getting a hero story on the front page every day. Sometimes there isn't a hero story. "So when you are in a position of trying to create something like that, you end up doing some pretty ludicrous stuff," Patterson said. "And they did."[209]

Despite the instability at the top, *Gazette* reporters and editors continued putting out quality journalism. Hanchette, who left as managing editor in summer 1990, remembered his fellow journalists being "awed" by the *Arkansas Gazette* at the 1989 American Press Institute. "They thought it was sort of a little local paper type thing, but there was so much news in it," he said. "We were covering everything that twitched." So was the *Democrat*, although Hanchette allowed that he did not like the way it covered things.[210] Under Lundy and Hanchette, the *Gazette* established five news bureaus around the state in Conway, Hot Springs, Fayetteville, Jonesboro, and Fort Smith to enhance statewide coverage.[211] One of the last great examples of the *Gazette*'s influence was the investigation into Democratic attorney general and gubernatorial candidate Steve Clark's expense accounts. Clark was considered the only real threat to Bill Clinton's reelection. Anne Farris, the reporter who took the lead in the investigation, revealed receipts for $400 lunches; ultimately, Clark dropped out of the gubernatorial race and was later convicted of felony theft for using his state-issued credit card to finance his lavish lifestyle.[212] The Heiskell-Patterson legacy of quality journalism still breathed. In fact, Ernest Dumas reiterated that until its death, the *Gazette* remained the dominant paper. "At the end it was a much better newspaper than it has historically been given credit for," he said. "It was the quality newspaper in Little Rock, but it was still a little frothier than it had been."[213]

> All these goofy competitions, award competitions, which I always thought were terrible things for newspapers to do, to enter all these contests, but they liked to do it. The *Democrat* started it and started celebrating its victories in all these contests, and the *Gazette* eventually under Gannett started entering these contests, too, and we were winning them all. Throughout the '80s, all the way up until the end, in these newspaper contests the *Gazette* was dominant, won maybe 75 percent of the awards and the *Democrat* maybe a fourth or a fifth of them. We were still covering state government and city hall and everything else like the dew, but it didn't make any difference—it was financial aspects that decided the newspaper war and not the news product.[214]

Hanchette said during his years there, the *Gazette* hired many people from the *Democrat*. As the better paper, it pretty much had its pick, and many

Democrat employees did not like Starr and wanted to bail. "[T]hat was a little intelligence operation that we set up," he said. "They would tell us people over there who were friendly to the *Gazette*. Of course the espionage went both ways."[215]

Wadie Moore, who became the *Gazette*'s final assistant sports editor after most of the Gannett imports moved on, said his department maintained a great staff. During his tenure in management, the *Gazette* sports section was a top-10 finalist in an Associated Press contest, he said. "You would think they would blast that all over, say, 'Congratulations, guys,' but you know, Gannett was not about sports," Moore said. "Gannett was about news." As an example, he cited the *Gazette*'s final sports editor, who backed into the job after Collins was fired and sent back to *USA Today*. "We received one sports editor because he closed the [news] desk early one night and a plane during Desert Storm from the Blytheville [Arkansas] Air Force Base went down and he didn't have it in the paper," Moore said. "So he became sports editor. That's the Gannett way."[216]

Despite the difference in quality, shortly after Moyer's hiring, the *Democrat* passed the *Gazette* in Sunday circulation. Hussman called that a huge development.

> I knew if we could ever pass them in circulation, the competition from their standpoint would probably be over because when they bought the paper, it was a circulation war. Whoever won the circulation war was going to win the newspaper war, and if they were going to come in and spend just with wanton abandon, on anything and everything, and yet we could still gain enough market share on them that we could pass them, they would probably give up. I had no idea they were losing as much money as they were. I knew they were losing a lot, but I didn't know how much. That was obviously pretty discouraging to them, too.[217]

As he had done when he made his first profit with the *Democrat*, Hussman chose to celebrate the milestone with a party, this time for more than a thousand people in the summer of 1990 at the Statehouse Convention Center with a big band and outdoor dinner.[218] "It's the first time it's happened in thirty years; it's the first time it's happened in our sixteen years of ownership, so we had a big party and celebrated," he said of the circulation reversal. "We invited all our advertisers and employees and celebrated."[219] The public announcement sent a message to Gannett that was received loud and clear.

After Moyer's arrival, Hanchette said he knew the new editor would want to bring in his own people. But he had continued to preach the same message throughout his time in the state—that Arkansas's newspaper war would not last forever, that only one side would win. He said readers saw both newspapers as striving and had a warm spot in their hearts for the *Gazette* because it was so old. But they also "had a cold spot in it, because it was owned by out-of-staters," Hanchette said. "They also viewed it as something traditional that could never go away."[220] Hanchette left a few months after Moyer was hired, and Bill Rutherford, who had worked his way up from copy boy at the *Gazette*, became its final managing editor. Hanchette said Moyer asked for no advice from him when he left.[221] That, too, speaks to the depth of the hubris of the outside company. Or maybe by that time, Gannett had already given up.

John Brummett, the former state capitol reporter who had become a political columnist, was one of the few old *Gazette* hands who benefited from Lundy's tenure. He had begun writing a news column—carefully separated from the editorial section—under Carrick Patterson's leadership in February 1986. Lundy gave him carte blanche to write opinion columns within the news section, and Brummett credited him for the improvement in those columns. "Lundy was just hateful to everybody and seemed to torment all the good guys at the *Gazette*," Brummett remembered. "He took a shine to me."[222] Malone, too, liked Brummett, as did the newcomers Moon and Moyer. "I may be one of the very few of the old-timers who liked Lundy more than the new regime," Brummett said. "That is almost blasphemous, to like Lundy more than anyone." Brummett said he thought Lundy was not as evil as some and was just odd, quirky—"quirky plus." "The new regime, I just didn't have any respect for them," he said.[223] He said he found Moon and Moyer to be "a couple of BMW golfers, corporate risers, without a great deal of sensitivity to their time or place here in Arkansas." He recalled attending a couple of Gannett functions at corporate headquarters prior to their arrival and being totally turned off by the experience. "It became clear to me that these really aren't very good guys," Brummett said. "Even if they won the war, this isn't going to be a good deal." After Malone and Lundy left, the new regime invited him to a managers' retreat at Red Apple Inn in Heber Springs, Arkansas. The experience solidified his original feeling. Brummett called it "the worst thing they could have done."

> I sat around and watched how inept they were. I sensed the frustration, and I knew that it was over. My motivation at that point became survival and fear. . . . I knew that I did not want to work for a sorry Gannett monopoly paper. I knew that I did not want to join [Gannett News Service] or *USA Today* and become part of the

> corporate culture and leave Arkansas. I knew what I do best, and what I wanted to do was what I am doing right now, learning about Arkansas. And I said, "Something bad is getting ready to happen. I have to take care of stuff. I have to find neutral ground and get out of here."[224]

Brummett left for the Arkansas Writers' Project and the monthly magazine *Arkansas Times* in October 1990.

> [M]y thinking was, "One, Gannett is not going to publish a very good paper here even if they win. Two, if they lose, they might find me a job, but I would have to relocate, and I don't want to do that. Three, there is no real nobility in this fight anymore. We are fighting for the Gannett Corporation."[225]

The thought revealed a stark contrast between the loyalty engendered by a local family ownership and that of a distant corporate chain.

However, Brummett said years later that what he was not sensitive to was the heritage of the *Gazette* as a major factor in the history and political culture of the state. "I came later to regret that I did not stay to the bitter end," he said. "It was futile, and it was sad."[226]

Brummett's departure was a particular blow to Gannett, which had identified him as a bright and rising star. Brantley, who would replace Brummett as columnist, said his colleague thought Gannett never understood the fight in Arkansas's newspaper war. "But shortly after he left, he realized weekly journalism didn't have the same kind of contact with the community that daily journalism at a big daily did, and he then struck a deal to contribute columns as well to the *Arkansas Democrat*, kind of completing the devastating blow, worsening by many magnitudes the loss," Brantley said. He said Brummett correctly intuited that the war's outcome would be bad for the Old Gray Lady. "Nobody, I think, really anticipated when it would be," Brantley said. "It always occurred to me that a five-year plan sounded about right, and it turned out that's what it was."[227]

Gannett had come to Little Rock in 1986 with the standard speech of chain acquisition, announcing, as media scholar Ben Bagdikian explained, its admiration and respect for the existing paper and proclaiming that the company "would never think of telling editors how to operate in this special and wonderful city."[228] Bagdikian explained three mandatory themes in every speech regarding such a purchase: "The new acquisition is a splendid paper that the outside company has no intention of changing; the chain acquired the paper in order to offer its larger resources for even greater service to the community; and the new owner believes, absolutely, completely, and without mental reservation in Local Autonomy."[229]

Gannett followed the script perfectly. At the announcement of the sale, Seigenthaler had said it did not matter what Gannett officials thought about the *Gazette*'s operations "because the company really does let local people run things."[230] He said Gannett did not have a standard it imposed on its publications.[231]

But Gannett's record in Little Rock failed to match its rhetoric.

Deborah Mathis said she believed Gannett's refusal to listen was based—in part—in prejudice. Had the property been the *Chicago Tribune*, the *New York Times*, or *Los Angeles Times*, she said, she believed the company would have listened more. "I think there was some kind of prejudice about oh, Arkansans, what do they know? We know better than they do; they're silly little ignorant people anyway, country people who don't know about the new way of doing things,'" she said.[232] While the attitude may not have been a conscious one, it permeated Gannett's presence in Little Rock, keeping the company from paying attention when any number of people—longtime *Gazette* staffers, community leaders, readers—tried to stop what was happening to their beloved *Arkansas Gazette*. They were ignored "at [the company's] peril," Mathis said.[233] Indeed, Gannett would pay a heavy price for its overconfidence, arrogance, and underestimation of its opponent in Arkansas's newspaper war, but the state would ultimately be the biggest loser.

From his position in the Little Rock advertising market, Carrick Patterson described watching the unfolding *Gazette* drama: "First alarming, then even comical at times," he said. "And then increasingly bizarre, just kind of like a bad dream will go from something that you can sort of say, I really think this is a dream, to this has *got* to be a dream, because nothing in real life really happens like that."[234]

But it was happening. And what was to come would be even worse.

CHAPTER EIGHT

1991: The Death of the Newspaper

THE GANNETT CORPORATION would turn out to be no better at ending its time in Little Rock than it was during its full engagement in Arkansas's newspaper war. It never understood the dynamics of the *Gazette*, the competition, or the state. Walter Hussman and John Robert Starr had felt slighted by the *Gazette* under Patterson family ownership, making Arkansas's newspaper war a personal one for them. For Gannett, however, the *Arkansas Gazette* was simply a business proposition. If Gannett lost the war, its managers would move on to other company properties, and in fact many would be transferred well before news of the company's deal with Hussman became common knowledge. If Hussman and Starr lost, they had nowhere else to go. With the benefit of hindsight, it is easy to see that the company's moves beginning in early 1991 added up to its planned exit from Arkansas's newspaper war, leaving the Old Gray Lady mortally wounded. But in the midst of the fierce battles, the signs were not easily interpreted. Ironically, Gannett continued to pour money into the *Gazette* even after the decision was made to give up. Perhaps that was done to guard the secret that the Old Gray Lady was, in fact, on her deathbed. Ultimately, Gannett would show contempt for its employees all the way to the end, as Arkansas's newspaper war would end abruptly on October 18, 1991, and company officials would slink out of town. Obviously, Gannett did not go out with honor, nor were Hussman, Starr, and the *Democrat* gracious winners. Arkansas would be the ultimate victim.

The ignominious end was all the more surprising given Gannett's strength when it bought the paper five years earlier. The company was riding high when it entered the Little Rock market on October 30, 1986. The *Gazette* became the ninety-third daily newspaper in the nation's largest media company, which also owned eight television stations, eighteen radio stations, forty weekly newspapers, and the Sunday supplement *USA Weekend*. In the fifteen months before the Little Rock purchase, the company had bought the *Des Moines Register*, the *Jackson (Tenn.) Sun*, the *Detroit News*, the *Louisville*

Courier-Journal, and *Louisville Times,* among other properties. The third quarter of 1986 saw an 8 percent gain in company-wide net earnings, the seventy-sixth consecutive quarter of comparative earnings increases, to $65,530,000.[1] But after a few years in the bruising Arkansas newspaper war, things changed. In 1990, although it still reported earnings of $377 million, the Gannett Corporation experienced its first yearly decline in revenues since it became a public entity,[2] despite revenues of $3–4 billion.[3] Company-wide, its newspaper revenues fell 6 percent in the first quarter of 1991; broadcasting and outdoor advertising revenues fell also, by 12 and 5 percent, respectively.[4] By that time, Gannett was entering the fifth year of its ownership of the *Gazette,* and Max Brantley said he had thought a five-year plan to show progress sounded plausible.[5] The company's impatience ultimately won out. Gannett had lost an estimated $20 million per year during its ownership of the *Gazette,*[6] and by 1991, there was no sign that it was making progress in the war against Walter Hussman and his *Democrat.* In fact, the *Democrat* was gaining strength, although it, too, had paid a heavy price. Hussman has never disclosed his losses against the nation's largest newspaper chain, but Gannett ultimately lost $108 million in its battle against him. His losses, he said, were significantly less but still in the tens of millions of dollars. "And, really, they were bigger for us than they were for Gannett because Gannett was such a bigger company," he said. "It was a much bigger sacrifice."[7]

Something had to give.

Gannett could not continue to justify to its shareholders why their profits were held down by the massive losses in Little Rock. Ernest Dumas recalled staffers getting nervous with the 1–2 punch of the loss of Dillard's advertising and the defection of Orville Henry in 1989. John Brummett's 1990 departure added to the plummeting morale, but Dumas said *Gazette* people were taken aback that the end came so quickly. "We thought maybe another year or two, they might try to do something," he said.[8] But with the perspective of time, he said he thought the decision was made to sell the *Gazette* to Hussman very early in 1991. Craig Moon, the relatively new publisher who had been named to the post on August 16, 1989, was another conservative Republican, Dumas said, and he, as Bill Malone had before him, became convinced that the newspaper's liberal editorial policies were hurting it in the war with the *Democrat.* A turnaround in those policies, Moon thought, would result in a "huge leap" in circulation and advertising. "[T]hey'd hear this out at the country club, the men's grill, the locker room, or whatever," Dumas said. "So Moon decided he was going to change it."[9] Gannett's public reassurances of local autonomy had obviously not been very binding.

Dumas recalled Hugh Patterson, the longtime publisher who had retired with the family's sale to Gannett, bemoaning many of the changes the Old Gray Lady suffered while under the yoke of her distant corporate ownership. "He said, 'By God, Al Neuharth told me, promised me, that they'd keep their hands off the editorial page.' Of course, he was pissed about some of the things that were going on," Dumas remembered.[10] He recalled Moon and his editor, Keith Moyer, announcing in January 1991 the implementation of a weekly conference with the editorial staff, at which the group would arrive at a consensus for the *Gazette*'s editorial stand on whatever the issues were. "We said, 'To hell with it,'" Dumas remembered.[11] When the time for the first such conference arrived, the editorial staff trooped down to the publisher's conference room. But Moon never arrived, and neither did Moyer. A secretary said both had been there earlier. Moyer's wife, Marilyn, who had been hired in the newsroom as a writing coach, called their home to find he had gone home sick, so the meeting was canceled. The pattern repeated itself twice more, and each time, neither Moon nor Moyer joined the group. "We say, 'Well, screw it,'" Dumas said. So for the final nine months of the Old Gray Lady's life, her editorial stance remained true to its liberal past. "Looking back, I think what happened is that was when they learned that Gannett had struck a deal with Hussman to buy the paper, and then what's the point?" Dumas remembered.[12] Moon and Moyer never asked to meet with the group afterward, and they never again meddled with the editorial page, Dumas said.[13]

But prior to that, Jerry Dhonau, the editor of the editorial page, remembered Moyer approaching him in early 1991 to suggest a modification of the paper's editorial policies. Dhonau said Moyer suggested that the editorial policy needed to become more conservative "to reflect the views of the railroad worker in North Little Rock," a result of reader surveys that suggested the *Gazette* was out of sync with its public. Dhonau said he was aghast at the idea.

> But it was clear that he didn't care. All he cared [about] was doing what the bigger boys wanted to do. I just flat resisted that. I knew that if we did that, the game was up, that this was no longer the *Arkansas Gazette.*[14]

When he refused the company's request, Dhonau said he expected to be fired. But even had such a thing happened, he maintained, "a clear conscience is a wonderful thing."[15] He said he had always found it difficult to communicate with the managers Gannett had brought in from the outside, and he found Moyer especially hard to talk to. He found the younger man's "railroad worker in North Little Rock" reference to be code for a repudiation of the *Gazette*'s editorial stance from 1957: "Should it revert to segregation and that point of view in order to get more readers than we had, because readers correctly knew that we were for the desegregation and so on, and he thought that was going to hurt the circulation, and it may have," Dhonau said.[16] Dhonau said he got the impression that there had been talk earlier about Gannett giving it a five-year run before reevaluating its presence in Little Rock. "That may have been his way of hinting at what was going to happen," he said. Looking back, Dhonau said, another sign that the end was near was that Moyer did not evaluate him that year, although Gannett was big on employee evaluations.[17] Dumas said that Gannett officials probably would have liked to fire the *Gazette*'s liberal editorial staff en masse, but they had to tread carefully lest they be perceived as staging a bloody coup. "[I]t would send a message everywhere that these guys were coming in and taking over, and they had said all along that the *Gazette* was going to be a local paper and local people—although they brought in these outsiders to run it," he said. With the *Democrat* hammering that us-versus-them theme daily, Gannett was forced to be a bit sensitive to such a message. And the editorial staff stood firm. "They'd pretty much have to fire all of us because it was clear none of us was going to yield on it," Dumas said.[18] Again, it was a case of corporate bungling. Subtle pressure didn't work, and Gannett was loath to use a two-by-four to make its point.

Ironically, even in early 1991, Gannett poured vast resources into the newspaper. Dumas remembered a thirteen-person crew covering the Arkansas legislative session. Coverage was presented in a tabloid section that included the work of several columnists, photographers, and reporters. Dumas recalled Gannett's commitment: "We're just, by God, going to just drive the *Democrat* in the ground with spending. We're going to cover them up. They want to talk about coverage. Well, we're going to cover the hell out of them,'" Dumas remembered.[19] He found the emphasis on governmental reporting refreshing after the frothier style of the Lundy regime and remembered Moyer's saying, "We're going to kick their asses."[20]

But Bob Lancaster, who by then was in his second stint at the *Gazette*, maintained that Gannett never had a chance in its battle with Hussman.

> Gannett's a corporation. They've got to make some money. They had some stupid ideas about how to make money, and they did a lot of monkeying with the paper, and I don't think that mattered much one way or the other. Whatever they did, they were in a bitter war. They were going to lose money until it was over, and they weren't going to do that indefinitely because they were a corporation that had other things on its mind. They didn't care about these old

> personal slights; they didn't care about the tradition of the *Gazette*. They tried to, but they didn't care. They were a company; they were supposed to make money for their stockholders, and you couldn't do it when the opposition was giving away their product.[21]

In fact, with the *Democrat* having seized the momentum in Arkansas's newspaper war against its Goliath-like competitor, Walter Hussman in 1991 bought a vacation home in Vail, Colorado. Hussman remembered an April 1991 phone call from Doug McCorkindale, Gannett's chief financial officer. "I think they said, 'Maybe we need to do something,'" Hussman remembered.[22] He said he was surprised, but once talks began, he could see that Gannett wanted out of Little Rock, and its officials knew Hussman, the Arkansan, was not going anywhere. "And the newspaper in Little Rock was a lot more important to me than it was to them," he said. "They tried to figure out how much money they could recoup by selling the newspaper."[23]

On the verge of his ultimate triumph in Arkansas's newspaper war, Hussman had a number of conversations with Gannett officials that spring. Signs portending the future were everywhere, but few at the *Gazette* realized their significance. Moon, who had been publisher only about eighteen months when he was quoted in the spring of 1991 as saying he would stay at the *Gazette* "until we win the newspaper war," left shortly after making that statement to become president and chief operating officer of the Gannett-owned *Nashville Tennessean*.[24] Hugh Patterson called Moon "a frivolous kind of fellow" and "not a man of very great depth."[25] Bob McCord christened him "the poorest example of a publisher" he had ever encountered. "He had no contact with the community," McCord said. "He did not lift one finger to ingratiate himself with the movers and shakers in this town, the advertisers, the politicians, or the people of the county."[26] McCord said he thought Moon figured out a few months after his arrival that the paper was doomed, so he bailed out to save himself. "I think we might have been close to winning, but Mr. Moon didn't see it that way," McCord said. Instead, he said, Moon was thinking about his own career with Gannett, "not about the *Arkansas Gazette*. That is the last thing he was thinking about."[27] But Susie Miles Ellwood, one of the *Gazette* employees who latched on with Gannett after it bought the Arkansas paper, said she didn't think Moon was there long enough to make much difference and that Moyer, who remained until the end, had good instincts but maybe "was a little too sophisticated for Little Rock."[28]

Ellwood, who by 1991 was the *Gazette*'s vice president of marketing, said she first heard rumors in the spring—months before most—that Gannett was going to do something with the paper. Maurice L. (Moe) Hickey became

Gannett's third publisher of the *Arkansas Gazette* on May 14, 1991.[29] That heightened the scuttlebutt, she said. "Rumors that it was going to sell, that it was going to close, that it was going to sell to another company—it was crazy," she said. "[I]t was a time of chaos and uncertainty."[30]

Although the rumors were not yet widespread, Deborah Mathis, who by then had joined the editorial staff, angrily remembered fifteen years later the uncertainty of the Old Gray Lady's final months.

> It was horrible. It was inhumane, when you see a whole staff of people being left in the dark, when the ship is sinking and nobody's even told the lifejackets are over here, those of you who can swim stand on this side of the boat—nothing, nothing. And in the meantime, all the captains are getting off. Craig Moon's ass was out of there. He was out of there early on, and I say now, those were invisible helicopters on the roof. That's what was happening. All of a sudden he and a few other people are being moved to Nashville or somewhere. Just all of a sudden, just coincidence, before all this starts coming down. Meantime, Moe Hickey, who is retired and gambling, I guess, every day in Las Vegas, is brought into town to go and hide out in the publisher's office, because he never was seen in the halls of the *Gazette*, he goes and hides out there, and I guess he's just mixing his poisons or something because all he's there to do is to kill us, or to oversee our death. And that's that. And he has no relationship with anybody. He's there to supervise the demise of the *Gazette*.[31]

Hickey did have that reputation. He had gone to work for Gannett in 1964 and eventually was publisher of the *Detroit News* during its war with the *Free Press*. He remained with the company until 1987, when he became publisher of the *Denver Post*, where he presided over the *Post*'s newspaper war with the *Rocky Mountain News*. He came out of retirement to take the job in Little Rock. At the time, *Arkansas Business* called him Gannett's "Mr. Fix-It" for his pattern of taking on trouble spots in the company, correcting the situation, and moving on.[32] In interviewing Hickey's former employees at the *Post*, Carrie Rengers of *Arkansas Business* found "dominance" to be a common word regarding him. "Ruthless" and "reckless" were common adjectives. Joe Bullard, managing editor under Hickey at the *Post*, told *Arkansas Business* that there was "not much room for dissent." Many of the same criticisms that had been aimed at Gannett in Little Rock were heard in Denver during Hickey's tenure—*USA Today*-izing the paper, trivializing the news. "The basic thrust of the paper under his leadership was trying to attract readers who honest to God didn't or couldn't read," Mike Rudeen, who had been entertainment editor at the *Post*, told Rengers.[33]

Upon Hickey's arrival at the *Gazette*, Dhonau received a delivery of black flowers from friends at the *Denver Post*. "That shows you how highly regarded Moe Hickey was," Dhonau said.[34] The friend, he said, knew what it meant to have Hickey hired as publisher. "They paid him a million dollars to come in and shut down the *Gazette*," Dhonau said.[35] Ellwood said although she didn't know Hickey personally, she knew his reputation based on the talk of others in the industry. His early actions in Little Rock seemed to confirm her feeling: he rented a car, apartment, and furniture. "Just all the signs—his wife didn't come with him, so I think it was clear that Moe Hickey was not going to be there very long, and the rumor mill was huge then, it was just crazy, so it was clear to most people that something was going to happen, although we didn't know what for sure," she said.[36]

In fact, by that point, nothing Gannett did seemed to have much effect on Arkansas's newspaper war. Management even had a hard time getting some of its initiatives through the staff. Jerry Dhonau, the *Gazette*'s editorial page editor who had tussled with Bill Malone and Walker Lundy over the 1988 presidential endorsement, faced another battle in 1991. One late summer day, after Moyer and Hickey had had lunch with Arkansas governor Bill Clinton, Moyer went to Dhonau's office and told him the *Gazette* should call for Clinton to run for president. By longstanding policy, Dhonau explained, the *Gazette* never urged any candidate to run for an office, and once Clinton or another candidate made such a decision, the paper often welcomed it—but not before. "When I told Moyer about this tradition and practice, he became livid," Dhonau said. "We had words, as they say."[37] He said the conversation convinced him that Gannett had an agenda.

> He stormed up . . . and threw open the door and shut it and started just really raising hell. "Why won't you do it?" I tried to explain to him that you don't do these things, that the *Arkansas Gazette* doesn't do these things. It didn't make any difference to him. It was clear that he was getting orders from Hickey, who, obviously, was trying to curry favor with Clinton because of Gannett and the presidential possibility. We had extremely sharp words, and at the end of that, I expected [to be fired] at any time. Of course, it was only a few weeks later that the paper went down anyway, so it became academic.[38]

Following that tradition, once Clinton made the decision to run for the White House, the *Gazette* published a long editorial cheerfully welcoming the announcement. But Dhonau said he never heard from Moyer again.[39] Dhonau said Hickey deserved his reputation as "the hatchet man"[40] and that a real chill settled between the two. "Hickey had a reputation of being a liberal ideologically," Dhonau said. "Actually, he just didn't care is what it turned out to be."[41] Dumas called Hickey "the undertaker."[42] John Hanchette, the Gannett import who had left his position as managing editor of the *Gazette* in the summer of 1990, called Hickey an able journalist. "But usually when he [came to] a paper, [it was] to wrap up things," he said. "That was an indicator to me they were going to [close the paper]."[43] Wadie Moore called Hickey "the managing editor of death." The move was typical of Gannett's strategy in Little Rock. "Gannett was sending so many people in and out, you never felt like you could trust the company," Moore said.[44] But Bob McCord, at least, was willing to give Hickey the benefit of the doubt. "I wanted so badly to get rid of Moon and get somebody who really knew what they were doing," he said. "[Hickey] saw me for a total sucker."[45] The *Gazette*'s op-ed editor called Hickey one of the smartest newspapermen he had ever known and said the *Gazette* was better during the five months under Hickey than it had been earlier under Gannett, but it didn't matter. Gannett had hired its man to get it out of Arkansas's newspaper war. "All the time he knew what he was there for, but nobody else did," McCord said.[46]

McCord said he thought up until the last minute that Hickey was fighting to save the *Gazette*[47] and later called him "the first real newspaperman" Gannett sent to Little Rock.[48] Afterward, he said he could understand his colleagues' ill feelings toward the *Gazette*'s final publisher. "He lied to them—and who likes to be lied to?" he said. "But I still say he was a good newspaperman, and if he was there running it, it might—might—have continued, but really, I guess I doubt it." McCord said he knew two newspapers could not survive in Little Rock long term, "particularly with the people [Gannett] kept sending here."[49]

Jim Bailey, the sportswriter, remembered a dustup between Moyer and the *Democrat*'s John Robert Starr in the spring of 1991. Before the e-mail era, the two fired insulting faxes back and forth to each other. "It went on for several hours," Bailey said. "They kind of degenerated into something as silly as, 'Your momma wears combat boots.'"[50] The crafty Starr proved yet again he knew how to play the latest round of Gannett imports.

In July 1991, Hussman flew to Washington, where he and Gannett came to an agreement to end Arkansas's newspaper war. But in order for the *Democrat* to buy the *Gazette* or its assets, it was necessary to prove that no one else would come forward to do so in order to satisfy federal antitrust laws, the theory being that if no one will come forward to buy it, then that company is going to go out of business anyway. "There's going to be a reduction in competition," Hussman explained. "It's going to be the same end effect as if Competitor A bought Competitor B."[51] He explained that according to antitrust law, if another potential buyer would operate the *Gazette* only for a month or two, that choice would have been preferable to a sale to the *Democrat* because it would have prolonged the competition in Arkansas's newspaper war.[52] So the *Gazette* would have to be offered for sale, and if no one else was willing to buy it, Hussman could. He said the Justice Department required that Gannett hire two different brokers to try to find someone—anyone but him—to buy the Old Gray Lady. By that time, he said, Gannett was losing $29 million a year in Arkansas.[53] But the situation became a Catch-22. "If you announce we're going to go out of business so we're trying to sell to our competition, it's sort of a self-perpetuating thing because then you start losing customers and you start losing employees and maybe somebody would've come in to buy it, but once that announcement's made, maybe nobody will," Hussman said. "So we had to sign our agreement where there was a $15 million liquidated damages [penalty] if either one of us disclosed the existence of this agreement."[54]

But word did trickle out slowly. McCord said talk in the building that summer was that Gannett was probably going to do something, either get rid of the paper or bring in yet more people—but better ones who knew what they were doing. He did not accept the possibility that the paper might be sold to Hussman. "I just didn't think it would happen, because Gannett had the money; they could stay there a long time," he said. "I was very out-thought by my friends there."[55] Ellwood, the VP of marketing, had been hired by the Pattersons in 1984 to work in marketing before the antitrust lawsuit and eventual sale, but she rose quickly under Gannett. She left the *Gazette* in July 1991—well before the rumors became widespread—to become a vice president for Gannett's Detroit Media Partnership. She said "survival" dictated the move. "I had changed career paths once and I didn't want to do it again," she said. "I certainly did not want to go to work for the *Democrat*, to be honest with you, so when it looked like it was clear that it was going to end, and I got the offer to stay in the industry and to go to another newspaper town, I took advantage of it, hoping that the *Gazette* would still exist."[56] A native Arkansan, she said she never gave up hope. "I couldn't imagine a day when the *Gazette* wouldn't exist," she said. "Even though you knew, all the signs were there that it was going to be over, I still, even when I'd already gone, I could not believe that it had really happened."[57]

Ernest Dumas remembered that it was not until August that word filtered into the community that Hussman had bought the *Gazette*. "It was all over the street and both newsrooms, but nothing was written about it," he said.

"We went to the managers at the *Gazette* and they said this is a rumor; a good newspaper doesn't write about rumors."[58] Mathis said she kept hope alive, but the rumors were everywhere by late summer after a report by Joe Quinn on KTHV Channel 11, Little Rock's CBS affiliate, that the *Gazette* had been sold to Hussman and would be closed. She and others went to Moyer, who denied the report, but she said other signs were there—people seen coming into town, meetings, rumblings on Wall Street.

> And every time we asked about it, we were told, no, no, are you crazy, what are you talking about? As if we were just nuts. And I remember saying to Keith Moyer, if the people in this room can't figure out the story, you need to fire everybody in here. These are reporters, for heaven's sake, this is what we do. How can you keep telling us there's nothing there? And down to the point where it was just all but in our faces, they were saying no, to the morning that, within a few hours, when they were going to be telling us that we were done, they were still saying no. They were still saying nothing had happened.[59]

She remembered one of her colleagues wondering, based on the rumors, whether he should go ahead and make arrangements for his son's dental surgery in case his insurance was lost, and another who wanted to know whether he should take another job offer. "None of them wanted to leave the *Gazette* if the *Gazette* was going to be there, but they needed to know if it wasn't going to be there," she said. "And I went in to Keith and said, 'These people have a right to know. Are they going to have a job, can they provide for their families, do they need to look somewhere else? Don't just do them like this." She said Moyer told her of the one considering another job, "Well, if he feels that insecure, he ought to go ahead and go." Even years later, his response—and what eventually happened—made her livid.

> This was within a couple of weeks, when the deal was pretty much cut, within a couple of weeks of it all ending. This was an injustice that people need to know about. This was a rotten way. If you ever have to close a newspaper again, America, this is the way not to do it. You do not do it in a way that destroys the faith of people, where people can't believe in any place they work in anymore because they know that with no notice, out of the blue, the rug can be pulled from under them. That's not the way you treat people, especially people who are dedicated the way the *Gazette* people were dedicated, who loved that paper, some like Ernie Dumas who had been there

> all of their working lives. You don't do that to people. You don't say, "Oh, you'll have to fend for yourself when the surprise comes down." It was cruel and unusual, and I hope it stays unusual because that is really no way of doing things.[60]

Dumas remembered that Gannett officials in Washington and Little Rock had no comment. But the weekend after the Channel 11 report aired, Bob Douglas, the former *Gazette* managing editor who had by then retired as chair of the journalism department at the University of Arkansas, called him with chilling news.

> He said, "It's true." I said, "Bob, Walter Hussman says it's a rumor," and [Douglas] said, "Trust me; I know what I'm talking about. I have unimpeachable sources who are in a position to know. It is true. The *Gazette* has been sold but it's pending in the Justice Department. The antitrust division of the Justice Department has to pass on it, but as soon as they do, the *Gazette* will close and it will become the *Arkansas Democrat-Gazette.*" But we could not pin that down. You had a denial across town, and you had the Gannett people saying nothing, but we pretty quickly presumed that it was the case.[61]

Max Brantley said he believed it when he first heard the Channel 11 report. So many things added up: Changes at the publisher and editor levels at the *Gazette*, the *Democrat*'s continued increasing circulation, the *Gazette*'s loss of the Sunday circulation lead. The March 31, 1991, Audit Bureau of Circulations Publisher's Statements showed the *Gazette* with the daily lead, 125,207 to 117,403, with the *Democrat* leading on Sunday, 236,093 to 222,072.[62] The numbers had trended downward for the *Gazette* over the last two years of Gannett ownership, from 142,568 daily in 1989, with the Sunday numbers down from 225,254 the same year.[63] Quality didn't matter. "By then we were winning the statewide newspaper contests year after year, but it didn't seem to be having any impact in terms of advertising and circulation," Brantley said. "It seemed to me that critical mass point had been passed."[64] Indeed, from the time the *Gazette* began entering the Arkansas Press Association contests in 1988, it dominated, winning the general excellence award for large dailies every year from 1988 to 1991.[65] But it made no difference.

Brantley said Gannett's no-comment stance about the rumors spoke volumes. "Gannett's silence chilled me to the bone," he said.[66] Hussman denied the rumors. "We now know he was lying," Brantley said. "He could've said, 'I have no comment,' but he said flatly, 'It's not true.'"[67] Dumas remembered

Hussman's assertion that the rumors had been started by the *Gazette*'s circulation department. "That didn't make any sense; it was nonsense, but that's what they said," Dumas said, adding that Hussman's comments seemed to be a denial. "And after all, he was a newspaperman, and he would tell the truth."[68] Once the story did hit the *Gazette*, Hussman did not return phone calls seeking comment, later citing the $15 million liquidated damages penalty if either side leaked the secret. He said it was the only time in his career when a reporter called that he could not comment. "I felt like being in the newspaper business, I should comment," he said. "That was the odd situation we were in."[69]

Arkansans could not believe the rumors were true. Roy Reed, by then teaching journalism at the University of Arkansas, remembered thinking, "This can't be."

> Denial, absolutely. How could the oldest newspaper west of the Mississippi River just die? That's not going to happen. And then slowly it became clear, hey, maybe it can happen. Maybe it can. Maybe it will. And by God, it did.[70]

The denial carried over into the *Gazette* newsroom. Bob Lancaster said he thought Brantley was kidding when he first told him the rumors. "And I didn't hear anything more about it until they were breaking out the whiskey bottle," Lancaster said.[71] Brantley said many people simply could not conceive that the *Gazette* might lose Arkansas's newspaper war and be sold to Hussman. "Even the day when they turned off the computers, Bill Rutherford [the longtime *Gazette* news editor who had become its final managing editor], I don't think he believed it," Brantley said. "He hadn't been told, and I really don't think he believed it."[72]

However, Wadie Moore was another *Gazette* employee who did believe it. The *Gazette*'s high school sports authority, he usually worked all night on Fridays during football season to finish his Sunday high school package before joining the crew covering the University of Arkansas Razorbacks on Saturdays. He said he had already moved most of his records to his home by that September. About 4 A.M. one Saturday that fall, he saw Moyer cleaning out his office. Moyer had not realized anyone else was there. "I'm back there working (in the Sports Department), and I see the lights on in the newsroom, and he's got boxes stacked up fixing to haul them out," Moore remembered. When Moyer realized Moore was there, "he just smiled, didn't say a word, and I went on by," Moore said. "We never talked about it."[73] Moore said that September, he received an offer to come to work for the *Democrat.*

He declined. Another offer came about a week before the end, but again he turned it down, although he knew the death was near.

> I couldn't have walked out on the people I'd been with for twenty-three years. That was family. I'm more of a man than that. I'd rather go the rest of my life without a job and just do odds and ends. I never could've lived with myself had I taken another position and money and [given] up that one moment to go out with the people I cared about. I wouldn't have done that for nothing in the world. The *Gazette* was family. If our doors are going to close, I'm going to walk out with my family.[74]

That feeling summarizes the difference between the outside Gannettoids, who had been bailing for months, and the local family—ownership or staff—who chose to go down with the ship.

Especially frustrating for the *Gazette* staff was management's edict that the paper would have no news coverage of the rumors, even that a television station had reported them. Brantley said a friend put him in touch with a source in the Justice Department who confirmed in early October that the sale was under review. "But I couldn't name the source, and I was not allowed to run that column," he said. "I did not stand on principle and quit because I thought the end was near and I wanted my severance package."[75]

The rumors reached well beyond the state. Senator David Pryor, whose career had begun as a newspaperman in competition with the Hussmans in their hometown of Camden, said he had been worried for some time, particularly by the transitioning out of people such as Orville Henry who had made the *Gazette* what it was. He said he had thought businessmen Witt and Jack Stephens might step forward to buy the paper, but there was apparently no interest on their part. "I'd always heard that the new owners of the *Gazette*, normally they would not allow any entity that they owned, any business that they owned, to lose money for over a year, or maybe two years, but they were not going to sit there and let it continually lose money," Pryor said. "That was concerning, to a lot of people and me, but I had no idea about the timetable."[76] Dumas said eventually, Congressman Bill Alexander from Arkansas's First District confirmed through his sources in the Justice Department that the rumors were true.[77]

A group of employees, including Dumas, Brantley, Anne Farris, Scott Morris, Scott Van Laningham, and Michael Arbanas, formed to pursue a possible employee buyout in an attempt for the *Gazette* to survive as an independent newspaper.[78] Dumas called it a "little silly rear-guard action" inspired by a few examples, including the *Kansas City Star*. "Of course, it was just silly because we couldn't have pooled all our assets and raised $10,000 among us, all of us, but we'd read someplace where a newspaper pension fund could buy the paper," Dumas said.[79] Farris said the motivation was twofold: to avoid succumbing to the *Democrat* and to get rid of Gannett. "[W]e weren't very particular," she said. "We were willing to take whoever came up with the money." But meetings with possible investors went for naught. "[I]n every case their sentiments were that if their pocketbook wasn't talking, they would have loved to have done it," Farris said. "They wanted to maintain the *Arkansas Gazette* as a tradition in Arkansas, but as a businessman, it was impossible."[80] Brantley said no one was willing to buy a company that was losing tens of millions of dollars annually "against a guy who is willing to spend an unlimited amount of money. Didn't exactly look like a good buy for anybody."[81] The coalition's efforts did, however, enable the *Gazette* to begin reporting on its impending demise. The group held public rallies and meetings "at which we said we believe the sale is imminent and we're attempting to gather support to stop it," Brantley said. "That became a public news event for which there were named sources."[82]

Mathis said she let it be known that she would take any measure to help save the paper, so "because I was so verbal, I think they put me on the team."

> I was pissed all the time. . . . I was very verbal with the management there, with my colleagues there. Anybody in town knows I always feel comfortable with the truth. It's lies that make me edgy; I can talk the truth very comfortably, and I feel protected by truth. I was angry at Hussman for trying to swallow up our paper and for unleashing his dogs [Starr] on us. I was very angry at Gannett/*Gazette* management for, again, the horrible, unconscionable way it managed this. We even said, "We don't want you to tell us what the deal is; we know enough about the real world to know that these things have to be held in confidence and particulars have to be kept quiet, but can you just tell us off the record, just so we can plan our lives, is there a possibility that the paper is going to be sold?"[83]

But every approach—anger, pleading, whining, laughing—was dismissed "as if we were out of our minds," she said. "And it wasn't even, 'We can't talk about that,' which would've been a tacit yes. It was like, 'What do you mean? Where did you hear that?' As if it were preposterous. All the time it's in the works."[84] Fifteen years later, she remained visibly angry at the way Gannett handled the closing.

> You just don't do that to people. There's no need to do that kind of thing to people. I understand that a lot of the managers we talked to were being tyrannized by the corporate mother, and so I don't necessarily blame the Keith Moyers and those for doing that—although I do blame them, for at some point, even a soldier can say, "I refuse to follow those orders," so I think at some point he could've found a way to be candid with us or at least given us some kind of heads-up. Maybe then again, they just assumed, "They're talking about it all, they probably know; we don't have to verify it." But it would've been decent of them to do that.[85]

Dumas said someone in the Save the *Gazette* group ran into Harry Thomason, the Hollywood producer of the popular television series *Designing Women* and a native of Hampton, Arkansas, in a Dallas airport. He expressed an interest in the effort. "He said, 'I don't have much, but I'd be happy to be an investor. I'll do anything I can to save the *Gazette*,'" Dumas remembered.[86] KARK Channel 4, Little Rock's NBC affiliate, reported in the fall that Thomason said he could not get Gannett to return his calls. Television coverage later reported that Thomason told radio station KARN he had talked to Gannett but signed an agreement not to say anything. After an employee meeting on October 10, Thomason told reporters:

> I certainly wouldn't mind owning a piece of the oldest newspaper west of the Mississippi. This thing might have gone too far before everybody realized what was happening. . . . I would certainly be interested in contributing some financially myself, but it's hard for me to be the leader of this group because I live in California and I've got to go back to a show tonight, but there are some other people in the community stepping forward. . . . Time is running out. I think it's a matter of, if not hours, days only.[87]

Before he left, Thomason told reporters, "I seem to go about jousting at windmills quite a bit."[88] But with Thomason's financial help, the group hired Little Rock lawyer Walter Davidson of the Davidson, Horne & Hollingsworth law firm. Brantley said Thomason also assisted the effort by working with Hillary Clinton, who got a letter from Walmart saying it might consider doing some advertising in the newspaper. Brantley said through all the efforts, the *Gazette* employees found out who their friends were.

> [P]eople [thought] the inevitability of newspapers was such that this was no big deal. We tried to reach people like Rosalyn Carter on

> the board of the Gannett Corporation and Carl Rowan on the board of the Gannett Corporation, and the response was mostly, "What are you going to do? There's no such thing as two-newspaper towns anymore; this is inevitable." And we now know the deal was Gannett went to Hussman and said, "Listen, you buy us; we buy you—it doesn't matter to us; it's got to be a one-newspaper town." And he said, "Fine, I'll buy you," and it was pretty much that simple.[89]

But *Gazette* employees didn't leave without a valiant—if late—fight. The public rallies continued; the group sold Save the *Gazette* T-shirts and pins to finance the effort and appealed to readers and Arkansans. At one late rally, which drew five hundred supporters and covered much of Louisiana Street outside the *Gazette* building during the noon hour October 16, Brantley told the crowd: "No savior may appear; our cause may be hopeless, but I want everybody here to know that we go out of this with our heads high. We don't go out down on the bottom; we go out on top. . . . Ultimately the person who will decide if two voices remain in this city is Walter Hussman. Call him. Write him."[90]

KARK reported that while Hussman hadn't commented to local media, he had told the *New York Times* he would close the *Gazette*. Brantley continued at the rally:

> It's something that the state doesn't want to lose, never mind the twenty-two-hundred of us who will be out of work if this place closes. . . . We're a family. We're proud of each other, and if this newspaper doesn't survive, its spirit and its role in history will. Long live the *Gazette*.[91]

Mathis was more defiant when she addressed the rally: "And so we are saying today if she goes down, we go down with her, proud to have been a part of something so excellent, so vital, so brave. . . . I daresay that any one of us, if we thought our departure from this paper could save it, would gladly and promptly leave." Her voice quivered as her final message to Hussman was interrupted by a cheering, weeping crowd:

> To Mr. Hussman, may we say this: You may have the presses. You may have the photo labs. The word processors are yours. But you will not and may not have the spirit of the *Arkansas Gazette*. That spirit—that spirit belongs to the people of Arkansas, and *we* are taking it with us.[92]

Watching a video of her address fifteen years later, she said it had not been difficult. As a writer, she said, any time she had felt anything passionately, it had always been easy to write. "It was heart-felt, and it was hard-felt, but it was easy to write it and easy to say those things because I meant them so much," she said. "And I still mean them, and I still feel that way."[93]

Amid all the turmoil, the *Gazette* staff continued to put out a paper every day. David Smith, one of the business writers, wrote most of the news stories about the situation. Brantley wound up getting in a couple of columns in the final days about the efforts to save the paper. "In times of great stress, I think what you do is do what you normally do," Brantley said. "That's the best way to cope."[94] In the final days, Bob McCord was in Memphis working on a story about the first black mayor of that city. It was late in the day when he finished his interviews, so he decided to stay overnight and return to Little Rock the next morning. But as he was working on the story from his motel room, he got a phone call with word that the paper was going to be sold. "I said, 'Oh now, let's don't start that again.' They said, 'Yeah, it's here this time.'" He said he was so nervous he packed up everything late that night and returned to Little Rock.[95] In Fayetteville, Roy Reed found those autumn days painful to watch. Bob Douglas was well connected and knew day by day and hour by hour what was going on with the Old Gray Lady. "He knew the last day was happening," Reed said. "It was a terrible thing, and all we could do up here was just watch."[96]

Many ordinary Arkansans felt the same way. KARK Channel 4 reported on scores of pieces of mail coming in to the paper. Brantley said on camera: "The main thing they're saying, and I don't have an answer for, is please tell us what we can do to save the *Arkansas Gazette*, and it's so frustrating to get asked a question you can't answer." He reported that one ninety-year-old woman wrote that her father had taught her to read out of the newspaper and that she was three years ahead of the other children in her class when she got to school "because I'd learned to read in the *Gazette*." Brantley said, "They break into tears and I break into tears. It's very sad." There were also humorous letters. He reported one that suggested forming a group with the acronym SUFFER: Save Us From Further Editorial Rubbish. Another suggested selling newspaper war bonds; another wanted to fire a few of the *Gazette* employees the author disliked. A writer in Hazen wrote, "Arkansas doesn't need to be forced to get its news and comments from just one paper and one rabid editor." Still more: "I can't imagine Arkansas without the *Gazette* as the independent voice of reason, moderation and responsible journalism," and "Though we've not always agreed on every issue, I've always respected and enjoyed the *Gazette*."[97] In his column, Brantley wrote of calls of support from Cherokee Village, Eureka Springs, Russellville, Crossett, Benton, Camden, Conway, Magnolia, and "everywhere a *Gazette* box or a *Gazette* carrier delivers this newspaper," and, poignantly, of the retired *Gazette* employees who turned out to support the efforts to save the newspaper. "Many offered to work free, if that's what it would take," Brantley wrote.[98] Not many corporate entities would elicit such feelings and loyalty.

Dumas said he thought the Save the *Gazette* insurgency stalled the sale of the paper for a while, since the existence of a potential legitimate buyer would negate the deal for the Justice Department.[99] How legitimate the group was as a potential buyer, however, was suspect. The group met with Walter Smiley, a Little Rock businessman who was head of the software development company Systematics who had emerged as an adviser. Fifteen years later, Brantley said there was still great debate about Smiley's role in the effort. "He insists his motives were pure and he was just trying to be helpful and bring his business expertise," Brantley said. "I think a lot of the people involved in that look back at it and think that Smiley's aim was to end that effort as quickly as possible by telling us repeatedly and over and over that it wouldn't work."[100]

Brantley said Smiley had been quoted previously as saying that Arkansas's newspaper war had been bad for business in Little Rock and bad for the community because competing newspapers were turning out all kinds of stories, and by definition, news is generally bad.[101] Of course, one-newspaper towns are good for business owners who only have to advertise in one place, but the lack of competition can wreak havoc on advertising rates. Smiley felt, Brantley said, that Little Rock needed more good news and less conflict coverage. "He takes great exception to this view that his role was really there to try to hasten an end to any dispute, but I know that's how a lot of us felt," Brantley said. "Certainly his opinion had some influence on the decision, although it was not the determining one."[102]

Under a confidentiality agreement, the group got a look at the financial papers regarding the *Gazette* that one of the newspaper brokers had put together in the attempt to find a buyer. Brantley said those numbers were part of the reason the group decided not to move forward. But they were not the only reason. Davidson told the group that Hussman and/or Gannett could sue the individual members for interfering with the sale if they were not really serious. "We might be held liable for millions of dollars of losses," Dumas said. "I don't know how much they were losing a day, perhaps a million a day between them, and nothing looked promising for us."[103] Brantley said such a lawsuit could have bankrupted everyone. "I think in retrospect, that was something that was not a real threat, but it sure scared the heck out of us at the time and dampened our enthusiasm a great deal," he said.[104]

So on Thursday, October 17, the Save the *Gazette* group had the attorney Davidson notify the Justice Department that it was no longer attempting to buy the paper. The letter read, in part, "We regret to report that due to the current market structure and the inability, short of expensive and complex litigation, to return the market to a realistic state, our clients have concluded that these efforts have been in vain.[105] "The odds are against this effort due to the *Democrat's* position and unabated business practices."[106] Brantley said they figured then that the Old Gray Lady's final day would be Friday, October 18. "We presumed the deal would be that the paper would close immediately and that Hussman would make sure the agreement included no chance for us to put out a last newspaper," he said. "[Hussman] blames that on Gannett, but it was within his power as the owner of the surviving entity to let us take our mule and sidearm home, and he didn't do that."[107] Mathis had a friend in one of the *Gazette's* business offices tell her that week that severance packages were being prepared. She went to McCord, who was editing the Sunday, October 20, editorial pages, and told him what she had heard.

> He got on the phone—I was standing right there—and called Moe Hickey. This is Bob McCord, a senior editor at the paper, a nationally renowned man, great man, earnest man, picks up the phone, calls his boss to ask him, "I just got word that there may not be a paper on Sunday and I need to know whether I'm wasting my time or not." Moe Hickey would not tell him. [McCord] said, "Moe, would you please just give me some word, do I need to keep doing . . . " He would not tell him. So we went and told Jerry Dhonau, editor of the editorial page, who had the presence of mind then to write the "fought the good fight" editorial. Because we all had a sense, just in case they did what ultimately they did do and not allow us to print, knowingly, a final edition, he was going to make sure he had that say, and he wrote a beautiful editorial.[108]

The editorial, titled "Goodbye and Thank You," read:

> Assuming the widespread and undenied reports are true, the *Arkansas Gazette* soon will bid farewell to a state it has known and praised and criticized and loved intensely for almost 172 years. It is not a pleasant thought, but this institution will take leave with its head high and its conscience clear.
>
> We are indebted to those of you who have been with us through the decades. You are a part of this newspaper. We hope you have felt that we were a part of you. Let us all cherish that memory.
>
> In the end, it was the reality of changing economic times that contributed to this sad day. A much bigger contributor, however, was the pattern of business practices by one man of inherited wealth who clearly was determined at all costs to prevail. Hard business

> decisions by our competition may have silenced the *Gazette*'s voice but they have not diminished the honesty with which it has spoken or reported the facts of Arkansas's public life. This has been a business—the oldest in this state—and it simply has not survived in the counting house.
>
> As our faithful readers know, this also is the oldest newspaper west of the Mississippi River. Arkansas's history has been written in its pages. Difficult times have come and gone, but the *Gazette* has firmly held to a solemn commitment to report what it thinks should be reported and state what it thinks about the facts, without fear or favor.
>
> That we have not been perfect in either endeavor is self-evident, but we can confidently state that we tried diligently and believe we usually succeeded. Our readers have always come first. Our regret is in not having the opportunity to continue serving them.
>
> Arkansas is a wonderful state with warm and caring people. It has a long and hard agenda ahead of it if it is to be blessed with prosperity. Education in all its facets must be improved even more than it has advanced in recent years. Arkansas must find a way to lift the poor and afflicted. It must resist the dark forces of bigotry and exploitation.
>
> Arkansans should demand the most of their leaders. Timidity must be replaced by courage and daring, the willingness to risk being wrong. This is a tall charge, but a state that does not set high standards for itself and its leaders surely will never approach them.
>
> As for the *Gazette*, if undenied reports are true, we will not be around to monitor their progress, but instead we must hand the challenge to others. To those Arkansans, we would say it is worth the honest effort and the goals are well worth the seeking.
>
> We will take our leave mindful of the words of St. Paul, who wrote: "I have fought a good fight, I have finished my course, I have kept the faith." We believe the *Arkansas Gazette* has kept the faith and we are proud to have had the privilege for almost two centuries.[109]

The references to St. Paul harkened back to J. N. Heiskell's words describing his paper's stance during the Central High crisis. Dhonau recalled the process that led to his decision to run the editorial. He and others had gotten nowhere in trying to get a clue from Gannett management what the future held for the *Gazette*. "I frankly asked Moyer at one point, and he wouldn't talk to anybody," Dhonau said. "None of the Gannett people would talk to

Gazette people."[110] He said he finally reached the conclusion on Thursday, October 17, that something was very likely to happen, so he sat down to write. "Emotionally, it may have been hard to write, but it was well thought through," he said. "I just gambled that that was going to happen." He said that time, he would have been glad to have been wrong.[111]

Among the editorial board, McCord voiced the only objection to running the farewell editorial. As things turned out, he agreed Dhonau was wise to do so. "Sure, I was a fool about it," he said. "And I was the only one in the building, I think."[112] Dhonau said he didn't want Gannett management to think the editorial board was going behind its back by running the editorial, so he showed it to Hickey in advance. "He made some small suggestion," Dhonau remembered. "He didn't say, 'Don't run it.'"[113] He said that was the only time he had actual contact with the *Gazette*'s final publisher. "Editorially, the *Gazette* had kept the faith long nurtured by Mr. Heiskell and others," Dhonau said.[114]

So the October 18, 1991, edition of the *Gazette* included Dhonau's editorial, two letters lamenting a future without the *Arkansas Gazette*, a final column by Brantley detailing the struggle to keep the paper alive and thanking those who had expressed support, and a front-page story by David Smith with the headline, "*Gazette* employee buyout fails," accompanied by a color photograph of flowers and notes left at the Mount Holly Cemetery grave of William Woodruff, founder of the *Gazette*. The cutline was from one of the notes: "Mr. W: We loved your newspaper for 172 years . . . We're just so very sad it was not loved enough today so people in the next 172 years [would] have it."[115] In 2005, Brantley said: "It still almost makes me cry to think about it. I know it did that morning when I saw it because I knew it was the end."[116] George Fisher had not finished the final editorial cartoon, but in the days to come, he completed it live on a television newscast—the eagle from the *Gazette*'s masthead, with a tear running down its cheek—and sold copies of it as a memento to fans of the newspaper.

For several days, the *Gazette* building had been under surveillance by photographers from the *Arkansas Democrat*. "It was one of the most classless things that John R. Starr did, and that's a pantheon of classless things, but that was one of the worst," Brantley said. When people left the building carrying their belongings, the *Democrat* employees would photograph them. "They were treating the property as if it were theirs," Brantley said. One *Gazette* employee got into a tussle with a photographer, shoving the camera in his face and giving the man a black eye. "I don't condone violence, but I understand what motivated it," Brantley said. "We were being treated like criminals."[117]

Friday
Partly cloudy; warm
Highs 80s; lows 40s
Details/15A

Arkansas Gazette.

Arkansas's First and Largest Newspaper

Final ★ ★ ★ ★

172nd Year, No. 333 · Little Rock | Oldest newspaper west of the Mississippi | October 18, 1991 · 35 cents

In the News

■ **Jimmy Swaggart**, back in the pulpit a day after his son said the television evangelist would step down because of another scandal involving a prostitute, announced in Baton Rouge, La., that he had gone back to preaching because God told him to do so.

■ **Marvin Mitchelson**, the longtime celebrity lawyer who said he thought he had seen it all in marital wars, disclosed in Los Angeles that he was representing Dr. Gloria Uboh-Abiola, a prominent New York physician, who wants to divorce Nigerian businessman M. K. O. Abiola on the ground that he has at least a dozen other wives.

■ **David Kay**, a senior U.N. inspector, told members of Congress that Iraq's nuclear know-how was so sophisticated that it could resume its shattered atomic weapons program unless blocked by constant foreign inspections.

■ **Peter Lauriat**, a Superior Court judge, made permanent in Boston an injunction that prohibits anti-abortion activists from blocking access to Massachusetts clinics, warning that violators face up to 30 months in jail.

■ **Leonard Cheshire**, a World War II British flying ace and founder of a disaster relief organization, said in Washington that his group planned to sell pens and pencils containing metal melted down from dismantled U.S. and Soviet missiles.

■ **Roger Craver**, a longtime fund raiser for Senate Democrats, canceled their contract, contending that the handling of the Clarence Thomas Supreme Court nomination was an affront to women.

■ **President Bush**, who will be in Hawaii Dec. 7 for ceremonies marking the 50th anniversary of the Japanese attack on Pearl Harbor, also will visit Japan, Korea, Singapore and Australia on a Far East trip starting Nov. 26, the White House announced.

■ **Pope John Paul II**, speaking at a Mass attended by 100,000 people in Campo Grande, Brazil, attacked widespread birth-control programs in Latin America's most populous country and accused government officials of undermining the Brazilian family by promoting them.

■ **Joseph Anderson**, a U.S. dis-

Gazette employee buyout fails

Leaders believe sale to rival, closing near

By David Smith
Gazette Staff

Efforts to put together an employee-investor purchase of the *Arkansas Gazette* "have been in vain," a Little Rock attorney told the Justice Department Thursday.

The concession apparently clears the way for the rival *Arkansas Democrat* to purchase the *Gazette*, members of the employee-investor committee said. Leaders of the employee committee said they believed the sale could occur at any time. Most of the committee members believe that will mean the *Gazette* would cease publication after almost 172 years.

Walter E. Hussman Jr., owner of the *Democrat*, and the Gannett Co. Inc., owner of the *Gazette*, have declined to comment on any of the rumors since they began seven weeks ago. Hussman did not return a reporter's telephone call Thursday.

Walter Davidson, a Little Rock attorney with the firm of Davidson, Horne and Hollingsworth, sent the letter to the Justice Department on Thursday. He was hired by *Gazette* employees last week to study the possibility of an investor group buying the *Gazette*.

Both Little Rock businessman Walter Smiley and Los Angeles television producer Harry Thomason studied the financial possibilities of bringing together investors to buy the *Gazette*.

"We regret to report that due to the current market structure and the inability, short of expensive and complex litigation, to return the market to a realistic state, our clients have concluded that these efforts have been in vain," Davidson said in the letter.

In an interview later Thursday, Davidson said: "I think everybody is more or less anticipating that

See GAZETTE/10A

■ Photographer injured/10A

AT GAZETTE FOUNDER WILLIAM E. WOODRUFF'S GRAVE: "Mr. W: We loved your newspaper for 172 years. We're just so very sad it was not loved enough today so people in the next 172 years [would] have it." — Readers of the Arkansas Gazette

Insights sought to killer

Texas man seemed to hate women deeply

By Mark Wrolstad and Todd J. Gillman
Dallas Morning News

BELTON, Texas — George Hennard had a "very violent temper" and wrote that women were evil. And he was a "beautiful son."

After the massacre Wednesday at Killeen, Texas, that ended in his suicide, Hennard left investigators searching for who he really was and whether a deep-seated hatred for women was behind his attack.

Police said the focus of their investigation was Hennard's references to "treacherous female vipers" and menacing ramblings in a letter he mailed last summer to a neighbor woman and her two adult daughters in Belton, population 12,500.

Hennard had "an evident problem with women for some reason," Killeen Police Chief F.L. Giacomozzi said at a news conference Thursday afternoon. "But not all women."

Hennard killed 22 other people, 14 of them women.

See TEXAS/7A

■ House votes down assault weapons ban/7A

Bush pledges to heal hurts

Women's, rights groups bashed

By Ellen Warren
Knight News Service

WASHINGTON — President Bush on Thursday pledged to help heal a nation rubbed raw by the divisive Clarence Thomas hearings, even as he berated civil rights and women's groups who opposed his Supreme Court nominee.

Bush said he was "troubled" by the "graphic sex" discussed on the top-rated televised Senate committee hearings, concluding that the senators should have heard the sexual harassment allegations in a closed-door session.

Bush said, however, that some good could emerge

The final edition of the Arkansas Gazette, *October 18, 1991. Courtesy of Donna Lampkin Stephens.*

On Friday, October 18, *Gazette* employees were nervous but busy working on the next day's newspaper. Wadie Moore was a morning guest on a Little Rock radio station, as usual, to preview that night's high school football games. Moore recalled the host wrapping up the segment by saying, "Well, Wadie, I guess we'll see you next week." He answered—on air—"I have a feeling this may be my last day in the newspaper business." Moore left the radio station at 7:30 A.M. and went straight to the *Gazette* building to start preparing for that night's high school coverage. He left about 9 but stopped by the desk of Nancy Clark, a former sportswriter who by then was in the features department. He told her he thought something would happen that day and asked her to call him when it did. Two hours later, she called and urged him to return to the office. "I just knew something was going to happen that day," he said. "I don't know why."[118] Jim Bailey went to the office about 10:30 A.M. to pick up his paycheck and was there when the computers shut down. Jerry Dhonau said the blank screens finally confirmed everything. "You knew that was it," he said.[119] Ernest Dumas was in the midst of writing an editorial. "I just thought it was some kink in the systems, but we found out immediately that they were dead all over the building," he said.[120] Word came down that all employees were to gather in the newsroom for a meeting in the early afternoon. In the interim, with no computers to work on, people started visiting, telling stories—and breaking some office rules, Bailey recalled.

> For several years, there'd been a ban on smoking in the building except for designated areas. And of course, you're never supposed to be drinking. Well, while we were sitting there waiting back in Sports, five or six or eight of us fired up cigarettes. Somebody brought in a bottle, some Cokes, having some drinks back there, and Keith Moyer, the . . . editor that went down with the ship, every time he'd come up that hallway that came past the Sports Department, we were right there at the edge of it, and four or five of us would blow as much smoke at him as we could, hoping he'd say something. He didn't.[121]

Brantley said the closing was "brutishly handled." He had cleaned out personnel files from his desk the day before but didn't put them in a *Gazette* dumpster "because I figured they'd root through those, too, which they did." Instead, he had taken the files to a convenience store a few miles away and thrown them in a dumpster there. "It was nothing—minor stuff—but it was notes about employee evaluations and that sort of thing, and I just didn't like the notion of somebody at the *Democrat* pawing through notes about human beings that had worked for me, which is exactly what they did after they took over the paper," he said.[122]

Gannett officials set up a lectern with a speaker in the newsroom for the announcement, but the meeting was delayed a couple of times. People gathered, some standing on desks, and told stories as in an impromptu wake. Some brought in video cameras to record the day for history. Many wore their Save the *Gazette* T-shirts that had been sold to help finance the proposed employee buyout. Brantley remembered they just told tales—some funny, some sad. "It was a room full of young people," he said. "I was only forty-one at the time—seems like forever ago. I had quite a work life ahead of me."[123] Lancaster remembered Leroy Donald, a longtime *Gazette* employee who was then business editor, coming around pouring drinks in paper cups and telling his colleagues it was a done deal. "They were trying to figure out, how I could sneak my personal files out of the office without getting arrested, because they had cops there to keep you from taking anything out," Lancaster said. "I did finally get some stuff out, and I still wouldn't say what it was because they'd probably send a truck over here to get it."[124]

When the announcement finally came, Hickey stood before the assembled newsroom and finally admitted what everyone already knew: "Ah, this is our last day, and I just got the word from Doug McCorkindale just a few minutes ago."[125] Deborah Mathis called that the final insult. "So we didn't even get the grace of a last edition," she said.[126] McCord said he, too, felt cheated by not being able to put out an official farewell edition.[127] He said Hickey had a taxi waiting for him outside on Third Street that day.

> His wife had left the week before, and he had a reason for that, too. But when he went to work that morning he had packed up everything, and he got a cab and the cab sat outside. His little speech was six or seven minutes, and then he turned it over to the business manager, and he walked right through everybody and went out the door. We thought he was going to his office—no, he was going to the cab. No one ever saw him again. See, he'd done this many times. And not just for Gannett, for other companies too. Because he had been a fine editor and he knew how to lie about the thing. He was getting paid; it was his work.[128]

Hussman said Gannett had within its power the authority to print an official final edition, but under the terms of the deal, WEHCO Media did not.

> You either buy assets or you buy the stock in a company. You can buy the stock and you take on all the liabilities. But we didn't know what their liabilities were because we weren't privy to them because the Justice Department wouldn't let us see any of their financial statements and contracts. . . . The *Gazette* could have published a final edition. Gannett could have operated the paper one more day and let them do that. But I was not willing to buy the *Gazette* and operate it for a day because if I had bought the *Gazette* and operated it for one day, I would have been buying the stock in the *Gazette*, assuming all their liabilities, and not knowing what those liabilities were. I was only willing to buy their assets.[129]

The laughter and nostalgia of the newsroom gathering quickly turned morose, and the room was filled with weeping, hugging colleagues. When *Democrat* officials announced that *Gazette* employees were "invited" to apply at that newspaper, the gathered employees jeered and yelled. Mathis remembered being furious and turning to Dumas and Doug Smith, her colleagues on the editorial board. "I said, 'Guys, it's been great.' And then I cried because it broke my heart," she said.[130] And there was anger. She remembered Hickey coming in, "flanked by two odd-looking people, tells us that that was it, and when we walk out, it's an armed camp—they'd moved in at every place, armed guards."[131] Years later, those memories were still fresh. Brantley remembered all

Gazette employees being checked as they left the building for the final time to make sure they were not taking any company property with them. "It was one of the most dehumanizing and insulting things that I've ever been through," he said. "I couldn't get out of there fast enough."[132] Dhonau also called it insulting. "We were not treated well, either by Gannett or the *Democrat*," he said.[133] Dumas remembered the employees being told they would have until 5 o'clock that afternoon to remove their belongings before the building would be closed and they would have no further access to it. "So security guards surrounded the building; there were security guards in the hallways, and they piled a bunch of boxes in the lobby on the first floor for those of us who had a lot of stuff to get out," he said. He had suffered back problems previously and had personally bought a more comfortable desk chair, for which he remembered paying $80 at Budget Furniture. But when he wheeled his chair out of the building and into the alley behind it, one of the security guards stopped him. "He said, 'That's a company chair; you've got to leave that here,'" Dumas recalled. "I kind of exploded. I was kind of tense anyway, so I said some nasty things to him, something like, 'Arrest me,' and took my old chair to the car."[134]

The armed guards' treatment of Fisher, the gentle cartoonist, especially infuriated Mathis. "I saw him packing up and shaking his head in disbelief, and then they told him, 'You can't take those brushes,' and he said, 'Those are mine.' They asked, 'Do you have a receipt?' The guy had the brushes fifty years or whatever. It really broke my heart," she said.[135] She had taken her belongings home the day before, so she spent the rest of the afternoon hugging and visiting with friends.

> I just knew it was coming down. Again, we were reporters. We can dig out the facts. All we wanted was the courtesy of some affirmation, which I don't think was asking too much. You're not demanding, you're just asking, would you please just tell us what the truth is—that's all you're asking for, and they refused up to the minute that they announced it.[136]

Mathis said the presence of the security guards confirmed that Hussman never understood that spirit of the *Gazette* she had so eloquently spoken of at the rally.

> I said, "What do you think we're going to do, trash the place? We love this place. We fought for this place—do you think we're going to trash it now?" But it no longer belonged to us; it belonged to the *Arkansas Democrat*. It belonged to Hussman. So they were going to make sure that we didn't hurt it. But that just showed me how they

> never understood what it meant to us. We would never have hurt it. They didn't have to have a soul there. They could've saved that expense and that insult because we would never have hurt it even when it was being taken away and given to somebody else.[137]

Wayne Jordan, who had been at the *Gazette* for twenty-five years by then, was moved by a feeling two days before to pack up his personal belongings. "I can't tell you how sad I felt," he said. "Walking out of that historic building that night was really a traumatic event for me."[138] As he left for the final time, the personnel director, Barbara Carter, tossed him the *Arkansas Gazette* watch he was to receive in December to mark his quarter-century with the paper.[139] Dumas said Starr later wrote in his column about the booty *Democrat* officials found when they went through drawers and wastebaskets "like vultures" after the last *Gazette* employees left the building.[140]

With the deal, the *Democrat* bought the contracts of Richard Allin and Charles Allbright, the *Gazette*'s humor columnists, but almost all of the remaining *Gazette* employees were immediately out of work. Max Brantley said that meant seven hundred full-time employees had their lives torn apart.

> [A]nd they weren't given much hope for the future, really. The *Democrat* sent out job offers to, I think, maybe three people, and invited people who wanted to apply to apply, but that wasn't exactly a warm, open-door policy. Gannett said it would have a little seminar for people about future employment opportunities, but it was a time of great uncertainty for an awful lot of people, many of whom depended on that job there for every bit of their livelihood. It was a very sad day.[141]

The sensitive Allbright was shell-shocked. He had been in Michigan that week visiting his daughter, arriving back in Little Rock the afternoon of October 18. After landing at the airport, he came by the *Gazette* office to pick up his mail only to see his colleagues trooping out the back door with their belongings. "It was an incredible spectacle to me," he said. "Only then did it hit me that this is really happening. It is over."[142]

It didn't take long for Starr and others from the *Democrat* to visit the site of their triumph to enjoy the spoils of victory. McCord said the man who had replaced him at the *Democrat* when McCord believed that paper would never win Arkansas's newspaper war came to his office at the *Gazette* on October 18, 1991.

> I was putting things together. John Robert Starr walked through the building, and he came up to my office because he really wanted

> to lay it out on me and growl and what have you. And I had written something that I thought was pretty good, and people would've enjoyed reading it, and I said, "Why don't you take this and use it? For Pete's sake, don't put my name on it. Just take it over there and run it if you want to." He said, "Well, I'll take a look at them," or something like that, and of course they never published either one.[143]

In Washington, Senator David Pryor was getting phone calls from Arkansas about what was going on. He said from afar, the situation sounded like the storming of the Bastille. He called it a takeover. "It was kind of an ugly day," he said. "I think most *Gazette* employees would say it was one of the low days of their lives."[144]

In some of the television coverage of that day, Starr said he was sorry to see the *Gazette* go and that October 18, 1991, was a sad day for Arkansas. *Gazette* employees never bought the attitude; in fact, Bob Lancaster called it a lie. "How many years had he spent with that objective? That was a single-minded pursuit of that day. In his later years he was very intent on rewriting his own personal history," Lancaster said.[145] Although he said he didn't see Starr going through the trash at the *Gazette* that day, he believed it.

> They were there in spirit anyway. It doesn't really matter if they were physically there or not because their presence haunted the place even if they weren't there physically. And there aren't many things that I know for certain in this world, but one is that [Starr] was not sad about the *Gazette* going under. That was his greatest moment. I think it's probably comparable to these soldiers who go slaughter innocent families—he was there to preside over his great accomplishment. He had killed off a worthwhile institution. He wasn't sad at all. He was proud of it. And he did spend several years after that gloating about it. . . . But the one thing I'm sure of is it was not sincere. He was happy and Hussman was happy.[146]

When Starr died on April Fool's Day 2000, Little Rock television coverage lionized him as a major hero of the newspaper war. Lancaster, by then writing for the *Arkansas Times*, which had converted from a monthly magazine to a weekly newspaper, answered that coverage with a scathing obituary column. Six years afterward, he said he never believed he was too hard on his old nemesis.

> Oh, no. He's dead. He couldn't do anything while he's dead to atone for his old sins. Mostly I heard from people who didn't like Starr, either. I don't know how you could defend him anyway. [The

> column] was pretty nasty. I think I used all kinds of synonyms that I knew for the word "scoundrel," and I think that's really what he was, was a scoundrel. I didn't like him from a long time ago. I had left the *Democrat* because he came, so it wasn't anything new.[147]

Meredith Oakley, who worked closely with Starr at the *Democrat*, said she was kept totally out of the loop regarding the sale. In fact, she said, she was at a national convention of the Society of Professional Journalists when the end came. Starr later apologized to her for not tipping her off. She said after she found out her publication would be called the *Democrat-Gazette*, she added a hyphen and "*Gazette*" to the affiliation on her convention nametag. "That's how I announced it to the world of journalism," she said. "They were pretty impressed."[148]

Lancaster reiterated that although he thought the *Gazette* was doomed with the loss of the antitrust suit, he was sure that Hussman, Starr and others gloated over their October victory.

> I just don't think [the *Gazette*] ever had a chance, because on the other side, you had two people, the publisher and the editor, who were dedicated to one idea, and that was they were going to kill the competition, no matter what it took. They didn't care what it took. They didn't care how much money they spent; they didn't care about anything except that one thing, and it was because both of those guys felt like the *Gazette* at one time or another had slighted them and had made them feel small, and it probably had, and they just couldn't get over it and they weren't going to get over it and they probably still—I don't know Walter Hussman, but I would guess that he still hasn't got over it. So he just, you know, he couldn't get over it, but he could get even, and that's what he did.[149]

Hussman said after the $68 million purchase price was wired to Gannett headquarters that afternoon, he gathered his employees to congratulate them.

> That's when I thought, "This is incredible." I told them I'm really proud of you people. You're the reason the *Democrat* survived; you're the reason we prevailed. It wasn't money. Absolutely, it wasn't money. My dad told me one time one of the greatest liabilities you can have is you can have too much money. I didn't know what the heck he was talking about. I really understand what he was talking about now. If you have too much money and you just throw it around thinking money's going to solve the problem, you can get led down a false path and you don't succeed.[150]

He cited the figures he was able to glean from the *Gazette*'s balance sheet and income statement only after the Justice Department approved the deal: *Gazette* assets (property, plant, equipment) of $49 million to the *Democrat*'s $20 million; 1990 operating expenses of the *Gazette*, $57.2 million, to the *Democrat*'s $46.9 million.

> They were spending $10 million more a year in annual operating costs. We never spent as much as the *Gazette* in any year. In fact, during the seventeen years we competed against the *Gazette*, they outspent the *Democrat* by $160 million. During the twelve years we competed with the Patterson ownership, the *Gazette* spent $110 million more than the *Democrat*. During the five years we competed against Gannett, the *Gazette* spent almost $50 million more than the *Democrat*.[151]

He said the ultimate difference in Arkansas's newspaper war was simple. The stakes were much higher for his side than they were for Gannett. "[T]he people at the *Democrat*—if we lost the newspaper competition, they were going to lose their jobs—including a lot of the upper-management people," he said. "If the *Gazette* lost, [Gannett officials] got transferred."[152]

At the press conference following the announcement of the closure, Hussman explained the deal:

> Basically today the Gannett Company permanently suspended publishing operations of the *Arkansas Gazette*. And they have, shortly before we had this press conference, notified all the employees there that they've been terminated. We have acquired all of the *Gazette*'s assets here. We are not buying the *Gazette* as a business, as a going concern. Frankly, we can't afford it. And basically, Gannett decided that they were going to leave Little Rock and they decided they were either going to, A, sell the *Gazette*, or B, close it. But we told them that if they were going to close the *Gazette*, that we very much did need, would like to buy their assets. . . . I grew up reading the *Arkansas Gazette*, like many of you did. It was a far better newspaper than the *Democrat* for many years. We cannot let that name die, and we don't intend to. And so effective tomorrow, the first edition of the *Arkansas Democrat-Gazette* will be published. Some people say, well you folks won the newspaper war, and I'm not sure that's really the accurate way to characterize it. I think we survived the newspaper war.[153]

On KARK's newscast that night, anchor Margaret Preston reported, "Emotions ranged from partying in the *Gazette* newsroom to crying on the streets outside. . . . [*Gazette* employees] videotaped their last meeting together, giving each other words of encouragement and telling old war stories."[154] Preston reported that within minutes of the official announcement, the locks in the building were changed. In the night's newscast, one of the locksmiths said on camera, "I was told anyone here from the *Gazette*, I was supposed to ask them to leave."[155]

Gazette employees and supporters gathered on Third Street in front of the *Gazette* building that night for a hastily organized candlelight vigil in memory of the oldest newspaper west of the Mississippi River, which was a month away from its one hundred seventy-second birthday. Hundreds of people filled the street. Speakers included George Fisher, the cartoonist; Pat Lynch, a local liberal radio host; former governor Sid McMath, and Lieutenant Governor (and future governor) Jim Guy Tucker, who delivered a message from Governor Bill Clinton, who had only weeks earlier announced his run for president. Video cameras recorded the vigil.

Said Fisher: "As we left this place, just having been told that it had been sold, they had guards at every door, on every floor. They were changing the locks. Ladies and gentlemen, that's pretty brutal."

Preached Lynch: "In the Irish tradition, a wake is not a sad event if the deceased has lived a good life and a full life and a virtuous life and a noble life and a life worth emulation."

Added McMath: "It's a pleasure to be here with you this evening and to pay tribute to a great old lady."

Said Tucker: "We will miss you intensely. The state of Arkansas will miss you, and personally and on behalf of Governor Clinton and on behalf of our state, we say to all of you we deeply appreciate your years of service, your faithfulness, your tradition, and we will miss you more than we can ever say. Good night."[156]

Brantley called it a bittersweet moment. "But I was already moving on at that point," he said. "Nothing was going to bring that back. It was just over."[157] Moore, who had awakened that morning planning his usual October Friday night routine of covering a high school football game, nearly passed up the vigil, but the woman who would later become his wife convinced him he needed to go. Others, however, couldn't face it. Bill Lewis, who had retired in 1989, had tears in his eyes in 2006 when asked about it. "I couldn't . . . couldn't do it," he said. "It was too much for me."[158] Carrick Patterson also didn't attend.

> It wasn't me anymore. It was not for me to come in there. I think I would've been resented, even, because the people who had

> been going through the Gannett stuff for almost two years then [after Patterson's firing], they had their own thing going. They didn't need someone like me down there. That was old news. They fought the battle, well, maybe on Gannett's terms, but to some extent on their own terms. I didn't want to intrude on their grief. I had my own grief, of course. It was dead to me when I got the famous, to me, "performance evaluation." I would've done anything I could to help them, but my help certainly wasn't wanted, and it was a separation that had already happened to me, but it was a devastating, devastating day for me. . . . It's a cliché to say thank goodness somebody wasn't here to see something, but thank goodness my grandfather wasn't here to see it.[159]

Although he had closely followed the story all that fall, Roy Reed said the death of the *Arkansas Gazette* was still shocking to him. "Even up to the end, I had some hope that something would be worked out," he said. "But all of us should've been a little skeptical from the beginning when Al Neuharth showed up after making his great promises, when it came time to go to the *Gazette* building two blocks down the street and he had the limousine pick him up. That should've told us something."[160]

The first edition of the *Arkansas Democrat-Gazette* was published on October 19, 1991. The name was jarring to many, including Carrick Patterson, although he said that by then, Gannett had so transmogrified the *Gazette* that it was no longer recognizable to him.

> So it wasn't like suddenly losing your mother and having an evil stepmother come in. There had been a series of progressively worse stepmothers before you got to this last one as the *Gazette* had deteriorated under the Gannett yoke. But to see *Democrat* and *Gazette* on the same nameplate—it hadn't really sunk in to me that they were going to do that, that they were going to use both names, until I saw it. I said, "Oh, shit."[161]

Hussman said the name was the *Gazette*'s biggest asset.[162]

> We felt we wanted to perpetuate the *Gazette*'s name because the *Gazette*'s got a great history, a great heritage, and that that ought to be part of the name of the newspaper. I know that seemed to offend a lot of people who worked at the *Gazette*, but I don't think it offended a lot of readers, maybe some, and we feel like we need to continue that part of their heritage. Not only winning the Pulitzer Prizes in 1957 but being the oldest newspaper west of the Mississippi, et cetera. And

> when you look at the *Arkansas Democrat-Gazette*, in so many markets the exact same thing has happened, a hyphenated name, and journalistically, we wanted to carry on the tradition of both newspapers. Business-wise, it made a lot of sense, too, because when the people who were hard-core *Arkansas Democrat* readers picked it up, they saw *Democrat*, and when the people who were hard-core *Gazette* readers picked it up, they saw *Gazette*. They saw the In the News column down the left-hand side; they saw their favorite columnists, Allin and Allbright. We felt like Arkansas will be better off if the surviving newspaper in Little Rock has as large a circulation as possible and still remains a statewide newspaper, so that was part of the reason for coming up with the hyphenated name.[163]

The first edition of the *Arkansas Democrat-Gazette* included the dual name separated by the *Gazette*'s symbol, an eagle holding a banner with the phrase, "Regnat Populus." which in Latin means, "the people rule." The symbol is part of the seal of the state of Arkansas, but it belonged to the *Gazette* before Arkansas became a state. Page one carried the banner headline, "It's over! *Gazette* closes." The four-column color photograph shows a cheering *Democrat* newsroom with a grinning Hussman addressing his employees. The editorial in the bottom right corner of the front page carried a headline: "*Democrat-Gazette* born, offers best of both papers." There were page 1 sidebars headlined "News saddens even *Gazette*'s critics" and "Allin, Allbright join staff," inside stories titled "Publisher Hussman described as man of principle," "*Democrat* employees greet rival's demise with mixed emotions," "Starr's words imbued battle with personality," "War's outcome surprises some in journalism field," "No union complaints expected," "ESD to aid former *Gazette* employees in job orientation sessions," "Faubus feelings mixed over *Gazette* closure," "Steady progress key, general manager says," "Subscription overlap likely to cause confusion," and finally, on page 13A, "*Gazette* employees shed tears over the end of an era."[164] Hussman and the *Democrat* were no gracious winners, spending most of their newsprint gloating over their victory instead of focusing on the toll left by the closing of the state's oldest business, which deserved far better coverage than it received.

Brantley said the coverage of the previous day's events continued to embody "that sort of classless outlook."

> My six-year-old son said, "Dad, how can they be so mean?"[165] . . . If a [six]-year-old can understand it, anybody could understand what a mean-spirited newspaper that was that won the war.[166] . . . Certainly there was reason for them to be jubilant. They had survived

Gates weathers storm in Senate committee, wins 11-4 backing
— Page 3A

City officials kick off LR Red Ribbon drive to combat drug abuse
— Pulaski Page

Church doors open, Texas governor visits as Killeen mourns 22
— Page 4A

Arkansas Democrat Gazette

ARKANSAS' NEWSPAPER LITTLE ROCK, OCT. 19, 1991 100 PAGES 10 SECTIONS 35¢

SATURDAY

In the news

Gov. Mario Cuomo of New York, who now is considering running for the Democratic presidential nomination, said that he would resign from his third term as governor if he declares his candidacy for the 1992 race.

Rep. Dave McCurdy, D-Okla., who was considering a presidential race, said in Oklahoma City he would not run, citing his family and the shortage of time to raise campaign money.

The Rev. Jim Rentz, co-pastor of the Family Worship Center of Jimmy Swaggart, and Wayne Austin, a vice president at Jimmy Swaggart Bible College, resigned in Baton Rouge, La., but would not say if their leaving was related to the evangelist refusing this week to quit preaching following a second scandal with an alleged prostitute.

Gov. William Donald Schaefer of Maryland tightened the state's belt further by signing a bill that will cut $80 million from the current state budget of $11.6 billion, a measure that allows cuts in education, saying, "Today is not an easy time for any of us."

Anthony Jones, 18, was arrested in Baltimore and ...

It's over! *Gazette* closes

The Best of Both
Arkansas Democrat Gazette

WAR ENDS — Surrounded by a cheering crowd of employees, Publisher Walter E. Hussman Jr. announces he has paid $68 million for all the assets of the *Arkansas Gazette* and renamed his newspaper the *Arkansas Democrat-Gazette*.

$68 million buys assets, paper's name

BY ANDREW MOREAU
Democrat Business Writer

Little Rock's bitter 12-year-old newspaper war ended Friday when *Arkansas Gazette* owner Gannett Co. Inc. formally surrendered.

Arkansas Democrat publisher Walter E. Hussman Jr. announced he paid $68 million to buy the assets of the competing *Gazette*, which published its last issue Friday. Hussman's newspaper will become known as the *Arkansas Democrat-Gazette* beginning today.

"We are eternally united," Hussman said at a news conference Friday afternoon in announcing the arrangement.

Little Rock Newspaper Inc., owned by the Hussman family, will take control of the *Gazette*'s downtown office building and its east Little Rock printing plant and presses.

The agreement was signed July 3, forwarded to the U.S. Department of Justice for approval Aug. 1 and received final approval Friday after *Gazette* employees failed to find investors to help them buy the paper. Dozens of media organizations were approached about buying the *Gazette* but none showed any interest ...

News saddens even *Gazette*'s critics

The first edition of the Arkansas Democrat-Gazette, *October 19, 1991. Courtesy of Donna Lampkin Stephens*

sometimes tough decisions to win the newspaper war, but we were seven hundred people out of work. There was no coverage of us, to speak of, or our future or the industrial impact of the closure of a major manufacturing facility, which is what it was. They didn't give us the kind of coverage they'd have given a toilet plant that shut down in Arkadelphia.[167]

"The Best of Both" became Hussman's slogan, to the chagrin of many, particularly *Gazette* employees. Like many others, Dumas said he was horribly depressed, especially by that refrain.

Of course, I had a kind of jaundiced view of that. I thought maybe I'd be part of the best, but clearly I wasn't, and in fact all that went over to the *Democrat* were Richard Allin and Charlie Allbright, and they had contracts. So until their contracts ran out, they were at the *Democrat-Gazette*. That's about all there was. Everybody else was fired, everybody in the editorial department, everybody in the

> news department, photographers, editors, writers, everyone was fired except those two. We were encouraged to apply, and a number of them did and were not hired. The assumption was we would not be hired over there. We were all pretty depressed about it, and I guess at the moment, probably most of us wouldn't have been caught dead in the *Democrat* newsroom. That's how we felt that day, and I'm sure had the reverse happened, they would've felt that way over there at the *Democrat.*[168]

Brantley contended that "The Best of Both" was, in fact, a lie.

> They added nothing of the best of the *Gazette*. They added the In the News column, and they eventually would hire x-number of people to work there, but in terms of the key elements that made the *Gazette* the *Gazette*, whether it be columnists or key reporters or news features or any of those sorts of things—they picked up some comics that we had—it wasn't going to be. They had no intention of it being.[169]

The Arkansas Razorbacks were to play Texas at Little Rock's War Memorial Stadium on Saturday, October 19. UA officials honored the *Gazette* writers' press credentials, and most went. Orville Henry, the face of the *Gazette* for so long who had bailed out to the *Democrat* two years prior, met one young *Gazette* sportswriter in the press box with a hug and told her, "I am so sorry."[170] Bailey called the whole day "strange." "I didn't want them to think we'd quit the field," he said. "Afterward, I didn't have anything to do, so Harry King at that time was still with the AP, and I went down with him afterward to the Arkansas dressing room and helped him collect a few quotes."[171] Moore remembered a radio station inviting the *Gazette* staffers on for the post-game show. The host mentioned high school football, and Moore referred to a score from the previous night's game. "He said, no, that wasn't the score, and he gave me another score," Moore said. "I said, 'Well, that was the score I got in my morning paper.' I left it at that."[172] In the days following, Arkansas Razorback coach Jack Crowe presented autographed game balls from Arkansas's upset win over the Longhorns to the Fayetteville-based *Gazette* sportswriters.[173]

At a local park later on October 19, where *Gazette* employees had gathered for more grieving, reporter Hal Wofford told KARK the "new" paper was really just the *Arkansas Democrat* with the *Gazette* logo on it. "It's a mockery of what the *Gazette* stood for," she said. "I see, even on the front page, headline mistakes. It's heartbreaking."[174] Much of the heartbreak concerned the what-might-have-beens. McCord, for one, said he thought, perhaps naïvely, that Gannett could have won the battle with Hussman.

> If we'd just got some other people in there, if they had realized . . . Of course, I don't know anything about the advertising part of it, but if they had turned a real journalist from Arkansas who was running the thing, I thought there might be a chance that there would still be an *Arkansas Gazette* in Arkansas, I did, right up to the day, and that was pretty stupid, I guess. I guess I wanted it to be that way.[175]

In the Monday, October 21, edition of *USA Today*, Gannett announced the sale at the top of page 2B:

> Arkansas rival buys, then closes '*Gazette*'
>
> Gannett Co. sold the 172-year-old *Arkansas Gazette* Friday to the archrival *Arkansas Democrat* for $69 million. The *Democrat* immediately closed the *Gazette* and published Saturday under a new name, the *Arkansas Democrat-Gazette*. The sale of the *Gazette*, the oldest newspaper west of the Mississippi River, was approved Friday by the U.S. Justice Department. Antitrust laws required the approval.[176]

Although the closure was covered extensively nationwide, including multiple days of stories by the *New York Times*, those four sentences marked the extent of Gannett's coverage of the company's five-year experiment in Little Rock—and ironically even included the wrong sale price.

The explanation did not wash with Hussman, who told KARK Gannett's version was not an accurate portrayal of what happened. "Gannett closed the *Gazette* and then we bought the assets, and as I showed you this letter they gave to their employees, they pretty much acknowledged that," he said, adding that the *Washington Post* reported Gannett's version of events as well. "I imagine they may not have done it by commission but maybe just made an error in reporting."[177] But having paid $68 million—$8 million more than Gannett had paid for the *Gazette* in 1986, Hussman is disingenuous in his contention. A savvy businessman—which Hussman is—would not have paid that much more five years later just to take the building and the name. He closed the *Arkansas Gazette*, but when the Gannett Corporation surrendered in Arkansas's newspaper war, it had delivered the fatal blow. Hussman simply put the Old Gray Lady out of her misery.

Al Neuharth, who had been chairman of the Gannett Corporation in 1986 when it bought the paper from the Pattersons, said he never felt the purchase was a mistake. But he reiterated that after his retirement from the position on April 1, 1989, he had no involvement in any decisions—including the sale to Hussman—at the Gannett Company. When prodded, he refused to engage in hypothetical questions about whether the *Gazette* would have survived had he not retired.[178] While admitting that he had opinions about the way the *Gazette*'s death was handled, he would not share them "[b]ecause I do not share any thoughts publicly with anything that has happened at Gannett since my retirement."[179]

Gazette people, though, had no such reservations. John Reed, who had left the paper the previous year, said he never thought Gannett had the stomach for Arkansas's newspaper war. "From the moment they bought the paper, it was an idiotic business decision," he said. "It was a boondoggle from the start. It was like Vietnam for Gannett."[180] Wayne Jordan said the outside company "had no vision at all when it came to Arkansas." "They were condescending," he said. "They thought we were hillbilly hicks."[181] Allbright said of all the people he met from Gannett, from Neuharth on down, he would have welcomed only three into his home. "I didn't—I still don't—know what they were," he said. "There was nothing to them." He criticized the "deep pockets" theme: "What the hell does that mean? What about the newspaper? . . . They had a lot of wine and melon ball retreats, and they started calling the *Arkansas Gazette* 'the product'—the *Arkansas Gazette* is not 'the product.'"[182] Obviously, Gannett never understood that. After the announcement of the closure, a *Democrat* reporter asked Joe Mosby, the *Gazette*'s longtime outdoors writer, why the paper closed. Mosby told him, "Because Gannett never knew the meaning of the two words at the top of the front page: *Arkansas* and *Gazette*."[183]

Fifteen years after the newspaper closed, Roy Reed, John Reed's father and the former *Gazette* reporter who had remained close to the paper even though by 1991 he had been gone from it for nearly thirty years, summarized the feelings of many who loved the *Arkansas Gazette*:

> Can I just talk a little about Gannett? And I have no problem with offending anybody living or dead at that newspaper company, because I think they are trash. I knew a little about them, enough to beware. Well, I didn't know enough about Gannett.
>
> They made every wrong move that a company could make, starting with their attitude, which seemed to be, those hicks in Little Rock don't know how to run a newspaper, we'll go down there and show them how it's done. And boy, did they, did they show us how it was done.
>
> If there was an absurd contest to gain new subscribers, they would come up with it. If there was a new, bad way to write a feature story, they knew how to do it. If there was any possible way to

degrade the value of the front page of a serious newspaper, Gannett knew how to do it. The pictures that they could choose to put above the fold of the front page just cried out, "This is no longer a serious newspaper; you can turn the pages."

Fluff was substituted for content at every level of the paper, and the people they brought in from the Gannett chain were, by and large, inept, incompetent—I mean, they knew how to put out a Gannett paper; they knew very well how to put out a Gannett paper, but they did not know how to put out a serious newspaper, and they never understood that the *Arkansas Gazette* was, first of all, a serious newspaper, and had been since 1819. They had no sense of the history of the paper or of the place, knew nothing about Arkansas, and had no understanding of the resentment that they immediately caused among the readers of the paper, who understood full well what was happening to their beloved *Arkansas Gazette*. They never understood, up until the last day when they finally said, "Okay, Walter, you can have it; what'll you give us to sell out?"

And Walter Hussman—you know, I was on the other side in that. I was pulling for the *Gazette* during the whole newspaper war, but he won it, he won it, and it's not Walter Hussman that I still hold responsible for the way the *Gazette* died. It was that gang of thieves from the Gannett Company, who never understood, never wanted to understand—never will understand—what they did to that newspaper and to this state.[184]

CHAPTER NINE

Lessons Learned

WHILE THE GANNETT CORPORATION murdered the *Arkansas Gazette*, it had at least two accomplices. One was a local family ownership that failed to respond properly or quickly enough to the threat of ruthless competition that included predatory business practices (even if they did not meet the strict legal standard of such; unquestionably, they undercut the *Gazette* in terms that hurt it financially) as well as the abandonment of journalistic principles. The other was a brilliant, single-minded competitor who was willing to use such unconventional tactics to win, spending millions of dollars of his inherited family fortune in his obsessive attempt to retaliate for the Pattersons' perceived slights and to do whatever he had to ensure his company's survival.

Arkansas's newspaper war had ultimately come down to ownership. The 1978–1991 war featured three ownership models—the Pattersons' engaged local single-family ownership of the *Gazette* (until 1986); Hussman's local family privately held chain ownership of the *Democrat* (1974–1991); and Gannett's distant publicly held corporate ownership of the *Gazette* (1986–1991). Such a matrix had three possible outcomes: A Patterson family win and Hussman chain loss, in which the ownership's commitment to quality journalism and to be the voice of progressivism in Arkansas likely would have continued by now into the fourth generation, although the economic pressures of the newspaper industry and the arrival of the Internet would certainly have made things difficult for the family-owned *Gazette*; a Gannett win and Hussman loss, which would have resulted by now in a much-diminished *Arkansas Gazette* that would likely not be recognizable today by J. N. Heiskell; or a Hussman win and Gannett loss. Although the state failed to get the preferred outcome—a Patterson family win—it also was spared the worst, which would have been a Gannett win. While the *Arkansas Democrat-Gazette* retains little if any of what made the *Arkansas Gazette* one of the country's most honored newspapers, it is without a doubt far better than what would have been left had Gannett and not the Arkansan Hussman been the survivor of the state's newspaper war.

Independent local ownership has several strengths. While any newspaper has to support itself, good local owners are not wedded to the profit margin but instead are committed to quality journalism and are willing to pay for it. Good local owners are responsible for guiding their newspapers—as J. N. Heiskell had been the conscience of his *Arkansas Gazette*—and are also willing to take unpopular stands, no matter the consequences. The *Arkansas Gazette* under the Heiskell-Patterson local family ownership lived up to all these ideals. Too often, those standards are lost in corporate journalism today. Distant chain ownership is marked by two glaring weaknesses—it is absolutely focused on the bottom line, obsessed with profit margin—too often instead of and at the expense of quality journalism—and it, too often, has no feel for the community it is attempting to serve. Gannett's Arkansas experience was a textbook example of those weaknesses. Too often, the newspaper industry today is marked by these blemishes. Chains are generally not concerned with good government and good politicians for the communities they serve; instead, they are concerned with profits—and always wanting more. Indeed, if Gannett had won Arkansas's newspaper war, it would have drastically cut back on the proportion of news to advertising in an attempt to maximize profits and recoup its millions of dollars of losses. Perhaps that is the ultimate difference between family and corporate ownership. Roy Reed recalled a story of J. N. Heiskell hiring a business manager and telling him that he himself was a newspaperman—not a businessman. "'I'm in this because I want to put out the best newspaper in the state of Arkansas, and your job is simply to make enough money to put out the kind of newspaper that I want to put out,'" he recalled Heiskell saying. Reed said Heiskell "would have been ashamed" of a profit margin of 20 percent.[1] For Gannett, that is not enough.

Since the post–World War II years, the newspaper industry has generally not reacted well to competition, whether it was facing the arrival of television, the Internet, or any other aggressive opponent. The *Gazette* under the Pattersons exhibited this flaw when faced with Hussman's reinvigorated *Arkansas Democrat*. Instead of reacting aggressively, as Walter Hussman had done when faced with the failure of his newspaper, the Pattersons pulled back when they should have taken a cue from Hussman—after all, what did they have to lose? While they were right not to stoop to Hussman's level of compromising journalistic principles, surely the Pattersons could have found some way to engage in the battle instead of simply pretending the competition didn't exist. Bill Shelton, in fact, had hit on what should have been the winning strategy—matching the *Democrat* in quantity and trumping it in quality. If the Pattersons had engaged and still lost, at least the Old Gray Lady would have gone out fighting. The *Gazette* under the Gannett Corporation also failed to react correctly to the competition when it took its place opposite Hussman in Arkansas's newspaper war. The corporate owner was never able to shift gears once it put its strategy into place, even when faced with its failure.

So how did the better newspaper ultimately lose Arkansas's newspaper war? Simply, Hussman was willing to pour money from the profits of his private chain's other WEHCO properties into the *Democrat*—to the detriment of those other entities. Gannett, the public corporation, was not.

Both of those ownership models contrasted with that of the Heiskell-Patterson *Gazette*. Led by the proprietorship of the Heiskell family from 1902, the *Arkansas Gazette* had operated under the philosophy that a newspaper was more of an institution than a business, that it had obligations—sometimes difficult ones—to its readers and community. The Heiskells believed in—and supported—quality journalism and the *Gazette* as moral authority and were committed to the ideals of progressivism, reinvesting their profits into the newspaper. Under the seventy-year editorship of J. N. Heiskell, the *Gazette* never failed to live up to those obligations, even when they elicited criticism, anger, and boycotts during the Little Rock Central crisis. Simply, the *Gazette* was the conscience of the state. Under Heiskell, the newspaper would stick to its philosophy, completely overcome the censure, and rise to the most dominant position of its history by the time the old man died in 1972, when it boasted circulation advantages of more than 33,000 daily and 38,000 Sunday over its afternoon rival, the *Arkansas Democrat*.[2] For a few years following Heiskell's death, his heirs, the Patterson family, would continue his legacy of moral authority, fairness, community spirit, and commitment to quality journalism and progressivism, even as the *Democrat* changed ownership to the WEHCO chain. By the time the Hussmans had fully engaged in what would become Arkansas's newspaper war, the *Gazette* had built circulation leads of 71,997 daily and 51,100 on Sunday.[3] When Walter Hussman Jr. declared war after feeling snubbed by them, the Pattersons failed to react aggressively, instead pulling back and sitting on profits while their ferocious competitor went for broke, risking everything, engaging in marauding business practices, and compromising journalistic principles. In the war with the Pattersons, Hussman had the comparative deep pockets, although some members of his family apparently put great pressure on him to sell the *Democrat* to the *Gazette* in the early days of their ownership. Had Hugh Patterson cooperated, corporate ownership would likely never have come to the Old Gray Lady, Arkansas's newspaper war would have been over quickly, and the *Democrat* would now be a distant memory. Instead, after the tide turned and Hugh Patterson's options ran out, he was forced to look for a buyer. He had put his faith in the *Gazette*'s superior quality. But contrary to one of the newspaper's final marketing tags, quality did not make the difference, and the Pattersons sold the *Gazette* in 1986 to the Gannett Corporation, the nation's largest newspaper chain.

And that is when the fatal illness struck the Old Gray Lady.

The giant corporation shifted the *Gazette*'s focus from editor-driven to market-driven, reversing the Heiskell/Patterson philosophy of giving readers what they needed to be engaged citizens rather than what they wanted to do in their leisure time. In many ways, the distant chain trivialized the *Gazette*'s mission, which had been solid since 1902, and the resulting warring philosophies within the staff led to a major schism between the established *Gazette* reporters and editors and the Gannett imports, most of whom came in brash and presumptuous despite their lack of knowledge of and appreciation for the history and culture of the *Gazette* and Arkansas. The perception of outsiders coming in to change the state's oldest institution did not go over well among readers or Arkansans in general, but despite some hiccups, including the puzzling examples of front-page story placement, the *Gazette* retained its quality until the end, winning the general excellence award in the Arkansas Press Association's Better Newspaper Contest once it began entering the APA contests in 1988. Again, though, quality wasn't enough.

Instead, financial reasons made the difference in Arkansas's newspaper war. As the head of a privately held company, Hussman had only himself to answer to, and he never flinched while spending $42 million in his battle with the Pattersons and millions more against Gannett. Gannett ultimately lost $108 million during its five years in Little Rock; Hussman said his losses were far less but still in the tens of millions. Again, he had only himself to pacify; Gannett had to answer to nervous stockholders, most of whom had no tie to, nor knowledge of, Arkansas or the *Gazette*. For Hussman, the Arkansan, the battle had been personal since at least 1978. For Gannett, the *Arkansas Gazette* was simply a business proposition—and a distant one at that.

It is no surprise that Gannett blinked first.

Gannett's capitulation in Arkansas's newspaper war was the shot through the heart of the Old Gray Lady, which was on life support when Hussman then pulled the plug on October 18, 1991. Walter Hussman closed the *Arkansas Gazette*, but Gannett had killed it.

In a 1960 speech at the Lovejoy Convocation at Colby College, Ralph McGill, the editor of the *Atlanta Constitution*, told the audience that when a newspaper was sold or died, those left behind should examine how much of the dying came from inside rather than outside: "What sort of management and direction did the deceased have? Did the paper try to live?"[4] Those fifty-five-year-old questions are relevant in examining what happened to the

Arkansas Gazette. Gannett's ownership, particularly in the late days of the newspaper war, was ridiculous, as Carrick Patterson said. While Gannett's status as a public company finally required some fiscal responsibility, Patterson spread the blame liberally for the death of his birthright.

> The Gannett Company and the people who were there at that time should hang their heads in shame for what they did. Now, okay, maybe the Patterson family should hang its heads in shame, too, for selling to Gannett in the first place. It seemed like a good idea at the time; we had really great promises at the time. It led to the *Gazette*'s death. And if I was responsible, if my father was responsible, we're sorry. We made the best judgment we could at the time. It didn't work out at all.[5]

Fifteen years after the death of the paper, he had to compose himself when talking about it. "Gannett turned out to be fools," Patterson said. "They turned out to bring [in] people who were not competent to do the job, and they kept throwing even worse people, as it seemed. It became more and more bizarre."[6]

The roots of the death of the *Arkansas Gazette* go back to six mistakes made by Hugh Patterson. First was his decision to turn down Hussman's offer—three times—of a joint operating agreement. With the perspective of history, it is easy to point to that as a fatal mistake, but Patterson was right in his belief that the afternoon *Democrat* would have only dragged down the dominant morning paper. By that point, people did not want an afternoon paper, no matter how good it was, so Patterson's choice to turn down Hussman was right from a financial point of view. Had he made a different decision, however, the *Gazette* would probably still be here, although such a move surely would have created a whole new set of arguments and problems over business practices and other things. After the agreement expired, Patterson presumably could have declined to renew it, which would have eventually resulted in the collapse of the *Democrat*—again assuring the *Gazette*'s survival. Other Patterson mistakes included his underestimation of Hussman's persistence and willingness to lose money in the fight; hubris; the filing of the antitrust lawsuit instead of making the decision to pour those resources into the newspaper itself; his choice of attorney; and, ultimately, settling on Gannett as a buyer. In hindsight, the choice of Gannett is easy to criticize, but, as with the decisions to turn down Hussman's JOA offer and to file the lawsuit, there were extenuating circumstances that seemed at the time to validate Hugh Patterson's decision. It is a certainty, though, that Hussman could not have prevailed without those six Patterson choices, all of which turned out to be wrong.

After the sale, Hussman was savvy enough to understand that as a publicly held corporation, Gannett could not continue the costs of competition forever. On the contrary, Hussman just had to hold on long enough for the giant corporation to give up.

And Gannett would help him. During its five years of ownership of the *Arkansas Gazette*, Gannett made even more mistakes than the Patterson family had, starting first with its attitude. The vast majority of Gannett imports never understood the particular mystique of the *Gazette* and its relationship with the state and its readers. Instead, Gannett thought its new property represented a traditional market; therefore, it implemented the strategies that had seemed to work with *USA Today* and other papers to make it brighter, more colorful, flashier, with more features and less news about government and public affairs. And when nothing worked, the company was too stubborn and arrogant to change course. Even more than Patterson, Gannett underestimated Hussman's stubbornness and his willingness to lose money for the possibility of succeeding in the long run. While it is impossible to say what might have happened had Al Neuharth not decided to retire, Gannett errors in Little Rock included the choices for almost every upper management position hired from outside the *Gazette*—even while Neuharth was in charge. Most of those managers fell prey to the wildness of John Robert Starr, and he delighted in playing them like a fiddle. When they failed, they moved on to Gannett positions elsewhere, but each one left a chink in the *Gazette*'s armor that lasted for the duration of Arkansas's newspaper war.

At the *Democrat*, Meredith Oakley said the revolving door of Gannett management helped the competition.

> There was no stability there, and they'd bring in these cocky little guys who would talk big and then spend all their time going to lunch or going to dinner and enjoying the perks of editorship and not doing any of the work, and in six months they'd be gone. A staff, especially a seasoned, staid, comfortable staff that's not turning over an awful lot, resents that. It's got to be a pretty rough place to work when you don't have much respect for the bosses, especially because you don't need to—they won't be there much longer.[7]

With the sale, every move the *Gazette* would make would be scrutinized under a microscope. Indeed, the Old Gray Lady faced a no-win situation: When she ran color photos, she was selling out to the corporate mother; if she did not, she was hopelessly old-fashioned and outdated. The *Arkansas Democrat*, however, was, as Max Brantley remembered, in the wonderful position of having it both ways.[8] Undoubtedly, there was a double standard in the way the two newspapers were evaluated by readers and observers of Arkansas's newspaper war. Even Walter Hussman, who had for years allowed John Robert Starr to bad-mouth the *Gazette* for its news judgment, ethics, and professionalism, would lament the changes Gannett brought to the Old Gray Lady. If he had truly admired the *Gazette* all along, why had he piled on?

Some would argue that the *Gazette*'s death could be traced to its finest hour. A significant number of Arkansans believed—even through at least the 1980s—that the Old Gray Lady was too liberal and still trying to push its agenda on the state. Although the *Gazette* had recovered the circulation lead and gained international prestige, there remained for a generation some latent resentment for the editorial stand from 1957, and once the *Democrat* became a viable alternative—both for readers and advertisers—under Hussman, the mighty *Gazette* became vulnerable. While there were those who were always going to hate the *Gazette* and others who honestly disagreed with it but respected it for having a consistent point of view, most people who were going to buy the *Democrat* because they hated the *Gazette* probably were already buying the *Democrat*. But the *Gazette*'s opposition to the Vietnam War and later to President Richard Nixon during those polarizing times following 1957 gave its opponents more to resent and Hussman more of an opening.

WEHCO was a chain, albeit a private one, and with his vast personal wealth, Hussman was not a typical family owner. But how could Hussman, who cannot really be compared to David, have taken down the Goliath of newspaper companies? It is impossible to imagine until the long-distance corporate ownership angle is examined closely. Simply put, the Arkansas market was vastly more important to Hussman than it was to Gannett. "It would've been one of Gannett's ten largest newspapers," Hussman said. "It is our largest newspaper."[9] Ultimately, *Democrat* employees—including Hussman—knew that their jobs were on the line during Arkansas's newspaper war. With Gannett, it was different. After trying and failing at the *Gazette*, Gannett managers moved on to other places within the company. The rest of the *Gazette* employees were out of luck and left to fend for themselves.

Although Hussman played the local owner card in his battle with Gannett, he, too, represented a chain, and he used chain tactics to win Arkansas's newspaper war, syphoning the profits from his other holdings to finance his battle with the *Gazette*. Although his business tactics were the major reason for his triumph, he also proved to be an astute student of psychology, the lessons of which assisted him in his battle with Gannett. He knew Gannett would try to demoralize him with its purchase of the Old Gray Lady; he also correctly intuited that when the corporation failed to see long-term results in Arkansas's newspaper war, it would not hesitate to give up—even at the risk of killing the oldest newspaper west of the Mississippi.

Indeed, as the oldest business enterprise in Arkansas, the *Gazette*, through its example and influence, had helped shape the state's character. So what has been the result of the death of the *Arkansas Gazette* on Arkansas? To answer that, one has to compare Arkansas up to 1991 and since then. The Old Gray Lady was a strong voice for enlightened social policy, integration, equal justice, and other such progressive ideals, and its editorial influence was enormous as it argued for "all of the unpopular, un-Southern things over the years," as James. O. Powell, the retired editorial page editor, remembered.[10] Although there were clearly other factors that could also be responsible, there is unanimity among liberal Arkansas politicians that during the last half of the twentieth century, the *Gazette* had more to do with the molding of public philosophy, the government of the state, its political institutions, and the emergence of leading political figures, both at the state and national level, including President Bill Clinton, than any other entity. This unanimity of opinion is important. Powell recalled state senator Ben Allen, who served from 1966 to 1991, suggesting that the *Gazette*'s role during that time had fashioned the course of Arkansas's history. Powell agreed:

> During those twenty-five years that I was on the editorial page, there was only a handful of what I regard as good newspapers in the South. Others were arguing the same old lines that the South had always argued. When you count the good newspapers, there was Little Rock and for a while there was the *Nashville Tennessean*, and the *Atlanta Constitution* before Ralph McGill died. Down in Florida there was the *St. Petersburg Times*, consistently one of the best in the South. In North Carolina, there were the *Raleigh News & Observer* and the *Charlotte Observer*, good newspapers. But most of the big newspapers in the South were pretty bad in the years I was on the *Gazette*. Memphis, Jackson, New Orleans, Birmingham, Mobile, and Richmond—all spoke for the bourbon South.[11]

Thanks in large part to the *Gazette*'s strong editorial voice under J. N. Heiskell, in the first half of the twentieth century, Arkansas elected several progressive politicians to office, including Senator J. William Fulbright, Congressman Wilbur Mills, Governor Sid McMath, and even Orval Faubus in his early years as governor. The 1957 crisis changed his political philosophy, but once Faubus chose not to run for reelection in 1966 and Winthrop Rockefeller, a Republican, was elected governor, Arkansas began an almost uninterrupted string of progressive governors that lasted beyond the death of the *Gazette*. Although a Republican, Rockefeller was supported by the *Gazette* largely to sweep out the vestiges of the Faubus era. The Democrat Dale Bumpers was elected in 1970; after he was elected to the U.S. Senate, David Pryor was elected to replace Bumpers in the governor's office in 1974. Pryor joined Bumpers in the Senate four years later; the two became one of the most powerful state delegations in the nation's capital, as Bumpers served four terms and Pryor three. Their retirements came after the *Gazette* closed. Following Pryor in the governor's office was Bill Clinton, who was elected in 1978. He served two years before being beaten by the Republican Frank White, but Clinton returned to the governor's office two years later and stayed there from 1983 to 1992, when he was elected the forty-second president of the United States—ironically, the year after the *Gazette* closed. Clinton announced his run for president just weeks before the death of the newspaper, and his campaign ultimately was headquartered in the *Gazette* building—its first use after the death of the Old Gray Lady. Powell and others maintained that the development of all those progressive figures was very much associated with the dominance of the *Arkansas Gazette* as the leading public institution in the state.

> I have heard Dale Bumpers present this argument. He simply said if it hadn't been for the *Gazette*, Arkansas would've been just like all those other southern states, talking about Mississippi and Alabama and Louisiana and others, if the *Gazette* hadn't been the leading figure in the politics in the state in the last fifty years, and I really believe that. And whither now, I don't really know. Except for the great aberration of Winthrop Rockefeller, usually the Republican Party has just not been very good, especially in the South. I think that the state would not have fared nearly as well as it has if the *Gazette* hadn't been there, and we'll see what happens now.[12]

Powell recalled Bumpers confiding to him during the depths of the newspaper war that if the *Gazette* fell, Arkansas would go the way of Mississippi and Alabama.[13] Hugh Patterson remembered Fulbright crediting the "longtime enlightening influence of the *Arkansas Gazette*" for his thirty-two-year career in Congress, during which he served as chair of the Senate Foreign Relations Committee from 1959 to 1975.[14] Bumpers agreed that particularly from the time the Heiskell family bought the paper in 1902, Arkansas was one of the most progressive states in the South. He, among others, credited the *Gazette* for swaying the voting habits of a basically conservative population. "A lot of people voted the way the *Gazette* told them to even though in their hearts they didn't feel very comfortable with it," he said. "That's how strongly that paper influenced people."[15]

Max Brantley agreed that Clinton, among others, was the product of a state that was made possible by the *Gazette*. "Bill Clinton, Dale Bumpers, David Pryor, Sid McMath—progressive people with huge personalities and great skills—certainly won on their own merits, but I like to think, and David Pryor is among those who've said it, that some of it was possible because there was a statewide paper that was delivered to every crossroads in Arkansas that said some of these things these progressives are saying are right—it's good to raise taxes for schools, and it's right to treat people of a different color equally," Brantley said. "It provided some cover for some things that wouldn't necessarily have been easy for politicians to say, and I think you'll find all of them agree that the *Gazette* was important in their rise to power."[16]

One of the roles the *Gazette* under Heiskell-Patterson family ownership always took seriously was that of agenda setter, to bring to the reader's attention the news he or she needed to become a more knowledgeable voter and participant in the democracy. Now that the *Gazette* is gone, Arkansans are not as well informed and are thus less able to make good decisions on governing themselves.

It is particularly ironic that the *Gazette* did not live to cover Clinton's election and administration. In its absence, the local source for the national media about Clinton became the *Arkansas Democrat-Gazette*. For years, Hussman's *Democrat* had been Clinton's nemesis. The *Gazette*, while not always friendly to him, had generally supported him and would have provided the other side of the story to the national media for context. Powell went so far as to call the *Gazette*'s death just as Clinton was ascending to the national stage "the consummate irony." "It was the most progressive newspaper in the South," he said. "Clinton in a sense was the child of all the traditions the *Gazette* had had so much to do with, and then he's elected as the *Gazette* is going out of business."[17] Senator David Pryor, among others, asserted that had the *Gazette* been around, it could have changed the outcome of the Whitewater investigation, which dogged Clinton throughout two terms and ultimately led to his impeachment. "I think the *Gazette* could have painted Whitewater for what it was, which was a ridiculous political witch hunt from the very beginning," he said.[18] Powell agreed. "I don't think Whitewater was anything more than sort of a two-bit scandal, if that," he said. "The *Gazette*, of course, would have opposed that."[19] Dumas explained that the *Gazette* would have had a better picture of Whitewater and would have presented it more honestly than the *Democrat-Gazette* did. "The national media relied a lot on that, as they always do on these local issues when they come up," he said. "I doubt he would've ever been impeached had the *Gazette* survived and been a voice here."[20] The *Democrat-Gazette* was not favorably inclined to Clinton and his presidential bid, and that led to an erosion of support for him throughout the state in some of the smaller weeklies and dailies. It was the opposite of what had happened during the Central High crisis, when as the mother ship the *Gazette* had led the way for the state's smaller papers to speak out for desegregation. Such a progressive editorial voice in such a basically conservative state would almost certainly not have been possible under corporate ownership. It would have been too risky for a distant chain to go against the tide of public opinion. Someone would have been offended, which could have threatened the hefty profit margin. The Heiskells and Pattersons didn't worry about such things.

In 2006, although the *Gazette* had been gone for fifteen years, Bumpers said he thought Arkansas was still the most progressive state in the South.

> We have gone in the right direction, in my opinion. Tennessee, Alabama, Mississippi, Georgia have gone in the wrong direction. I think Arkansas has been served so well, and I think it is sort of a shining light in the South. We may not be the blue state that some states are, but I know that we've been a lot bluer than most southern states, and I think it's all because of the *Arkansas Gazette*.[21]

However, in the eight years since that interview, Arkansas has gone the way of the other southern states. All four of the state's congressmen are now Republicans, aas are both of its senators and all seven constitutional officers. President Barack Obama received just 39 percent of the state's vote in the 2008 presidential election, the lowest percentage in the country. The Arkansas legislature, which had been heavily Democratic since Reconstruction—the final southern state with a Democratic majority[22]—went Republican in the 2012 elections and punctuated those results with even more resounding wins in 2014. Powell, who died in 2010, was not surprised by the trend and traced its roots to the death of the Old Gray Lady. "The *Democrat-Gazette* has the wildest, most radical Republican commentary in the South, and Arkansas politics is shot to hell," he said.[23]

> The newspaper's voice now is entirely different from what it was. That's why it's a pity, really, that the *Gazette*'s name is hung onto it, because many people, of course, won't ever know anything about what the *Gazette* was like, and it was founded in 1819. The ads say the *Democrat-Gazette* has been an institution for almost two hundred years, and actually, [the paper today is] the *Democrat*, is what it is. The newspaper is just not the way it was and never will be, and I'm sure Walter Hussman would not want it to be like it was because

> of the great difference in the orientation politically. In the news on government and all the issues that we handle, its views are often so different from what they were under the *Gazette*'s owning family and with the people who were writing centrally for the *Gazette* in its time of dominance.[24]

While political scientists may debate such a notion, perhaps more than anything else, the death of the *Gazette* has been the agent of change for Arkansas politics. Since its death, the state's public officials are noticeably more conservative, matching the tone of debate in the state and the South. It is no coincidence that these trends have occurred since the death of the *Gazette*. Particularly from 1902 to 1991, the *Gazette* had cultivated a climate of opinion that produced running debate among Arkansans. It made people think, and its absence has left a void of progressive thinking, which would have been a loss even before the current era of conservative talk radio and Fox News that seems to have hastened the trend toward conservatism. Those developments have made the lack of progressive thinking more obvious and even more damaging. The death of the *Arkansas Gazette* has been a loss culturally, as well, as the people of the state measure their sense of who they are and their dignity.

Simply put, Arkansas is poorer for the death of its Old Gray Lady.

What set the *Gazette* apart were its principles, which were shared by most of its employees. As Max Brantley said, "The *Gazette* stood for the notion that Arkansas could be better."

> You didn't have to take the popular course. You could take the hard course and you could prevail. I don't think it pandered to the lowest common denominator. I don't think it had a chip on its shoulder about the rest of the world. It recognized every day that there was a bigger, broader world that Arkansas ought to know about, and I think if anything, that philosophy, the suspicion and small-mindedness that I see that exists in the *Democrat*, made me sad, because it's easy to cater to that kind of reader. It's easy to be against things and to be for the status quo, and I thought that Arkansas would pay some price for that becoming the dominant voice rather than a voice that was willing to take a risk and run contrary to what the herd was thinking in Arkansas.[25]

Brantley, Powell, and the rest are right.

Although *Gazette* veterans still mourn the loss of its progressive editorial voice, most agree that Hussman's newspaper today is far better than what would have been left had Gannett won the newspaper war, particularly in its news hole and news coverage. It did not take long after his victory, though, for Hussman to start to make some money-saving cuts—home delivery to some rural places was eliminated almost immediately, and advertising and subscription rates increased. In recent years, there have been significant staff layoffs and furloughs. But certainly, Gannett's cuts would have been broader and deeper. Still, many believe that Hussman's newspaper is a poor replacement for the old *Gazette*. Senator David Pryor said in 2006 he thought the *Democrat-Gazette* was still seeking its soul. Brantley finds it ironic that, although the *Democrat-Gazette* has adopted the *Gazette*'s history as its own, the recently retired executive editor of the newspaper held a view of the Little Rock Central crisis "which they now claim as their own that is contrary with virtually every historian out there," Brantley said.

> His wife wrote an article in *American Heritage* magazine in which they described the school crisis as Dwight Eisenhower's forced integration of Central High School. That is such a misstatement of the historical record as to be almost laughable. But it gives you an idea where they're coming from, and so there's a certain irony that that's currently the prevailing philosophy. But he'll turn to dust, too, and that will pass on. He'll be just another footnote along with the rest of us.[26]

Nearly twenty-four years after the death of the *Arkansas Gazette*, it is clear that its closing has ramifications for an industry in turmoil today. While the newspaper industry itself has changed immeasurably since 1991, many of the mistakes that led to the death of the Old Gray Lady are still being made every day as family ownership has dwindled and long-distance chains now control most of the country's newspaper circulation. In 2000, 77 percent of all dailies were chain-owned, up from the 70 percent when Gannett bought the *Arkansas Gazette* in 1986. Locally owned newspapers numbered 444 in 2005 (30.7 percent), down from 469 (32.4 percent) in 2002. Since 1910, the number of dailies owned by chains has increased steadily. In 2000, there were 346 independently owned newspapers, down from 1,889 in 1920. Conversely, 1,134 were owned by chains in 2000, up from 153 in 1920. The average number of dailies per chain was also up significantly, at 9.5 per chain in 2000, up from 4.9 in 1920.[27]

The mistakes that killed the *Arkansas Gazette* are reflected in corporate journalism today, and with the industry in such current turmoil, those mistakes are magnified. The chief mistake is the continued bottom-line emphasis on profits, which then leads to a number of other errors. Corporations have unrealistic profit expectations. Gannett, particularly, was spoiled by its eighteen-year string of ever-increasing quarterly profits from 1967 to 1985, which included profit margins of 30 to 50 percent at some of its properties.[28] Such numbers are impossible to maintain, and certainly so in a time of recession. The ongoing emphasis on profit margin leads ownership to cut back in order to hold onto those profits instead of to continually invest in the news product. Good journalism is expensive, and when the investment in it is cut for the sake of protecting profits, it is impossible not to have a corresponding decrease in quality—which then leads to the circle of more losses because readers are not willing to continue to pay for something that is deemed to be losing its quality, particularly in competitive media markets. While competitive daily newspaper markets are now almost nonexistent, with only twenty American cities featuring competing dailies in 2000 and the number even smaller today after, for example, second newspapers closing in Seattle, Denver, and San Francisco in 2009,[29] today's newspapers face an array of competing voices thanks to the Internet. If quality is not maintained, readers will look elsewhere, although, as with the *Arkansas Gazette*, quality alone will not ensure survival. Distant chain ownership must also be engaged in and committed to the community it serves. A failure to do so makes it far more difficult to succeed in today's competitive media market.

For years, newspapers have too often failed to respond to their competition. It is a continuation of the trend that goes back to the early days following World War II, and the Pattersons made the same mistake with the *Arkansas Gazette* when Walter Hussman declared war in the 1970s. Gannett tried to respond when it entered Arkansas's newspaper war, but it erred in its methods. It is crucial for newspapers today to respond aggressively but thoughtfully, to listen to their readers, and to offer what their online and television competition cannot—in-depth analysis by veteran journalists who can be counted on to explain things better than a fifteen-year-old pontificating on his blog. In the cacophony of today's media environment, sober, serious journalism stands out. This is what newspapers should offer. Instead, too often they have fallen prey to Gannett's model of a market-driven news philosophy. Yes, thorough government and public affairs coverage is sometimes dull and often is complicated, but it remains absolutely necessary to a democracy. Yes, people often prefer to read celebrity gossip and comics, but newspapers must, as J. N. Heiskell preached in 1935, find the right balance of giving readers what they need to know with what they want to know. Under Heiskell, the *Arkansas Gazette* was editor driven. Corporate journalism today is too market driven. Indeed, people do often prefer eating dessert to vegetables, but which choice leads to a healthy individual? Newspapers must be firm in their focus, although there should certainly be some room for the dessert of market-drive content. The Heiskells and Pattersons consistently gave their readers a serious, sober product. Gannett changed that to some degree. Today's corporate owners are more committed to their profit margin than they are to their product. By focusing on dessert, they are able to spend less money in their attempts to maintain those gaudy profit margins. After all, meat and potatoes cost more than cookies.

But product—not profit—must be a newspaper's focus. If the market-driven emphasis were working so well, the newspaper industry would not be in the pickle it is today.

In Ralph McGill's 1960 speech at the Lovejoy Convocation at Colby College, he reiterated that newspapers must never forget they serve "man and his Western civilization and the moral ethics of it."[30] In his 1935 address to the Southern Newspaper Publishers Association, J. N. Heiskell argued that the newspaper was the "final safeguard of those rights that are declared in the constitution," and that, as inscribed in the Hall of Inscriptions in the *Chicago Tribune* building, "The newspaper is an institution developed by civilization to print the news of the day, to foster commerce and industry, to inform and lead public opinion, and to furnish that check upon government which no constitution has ever been able to."[31]

Nearly a century later, corporate journalism has made it difficult for newspapers to live up to such lofty expectations. When James O. Powell wrote Heiskell's obituary in 1972, he recalled writing about the Heiskell heirs' plans to maintain the paper's great traditions. "That was all I thought about at that time, not knowing that twenty years later the *Gazette* would collapse, would go out of business," he said. "No one would ever have anticipated that."[32] When economic realities forced its family owners to sell to a corporation, the *Arkansas Gazette* first lost its soul and ultimately its life. But looking back, it should not have been a surprise. Under chain ownership, too often outside corporate hacks—instead of journalists—are brought in to the publisher and editor positions, with the predictable dismal results. Indeed, corporate ownership changes everything about a newspaper—the look, the mentality, even the heart.

Bob Lancaster summarized the situation by saying that only a couple of facts ever mattered in Arkansas's newspaper war.

> [Y]ou had, on the one hand, a publisher who was willing to spend any amount of money, to destroy any of his holdings and his own bank account, and go out and beg on the street if he needed to in order to destroy the other paper. And on the other side, you had a newspaper company that had no sense of its own publication's

> history. It was not willing to lose money forever just to be able to stay alive. And when you have that kind of ferocity on one side and that kind of indifference on the other side, then it's obvious who's going to win. . . . You got a berserker on one side and a bottom-line wuss on the other. Who's going to win?[33]

Looking back, it is not difficult to understand how Hussman won and Gannett lost Arkansas's newspaper war. But it does not make the death of the Old Gray Lady any easier to take.

Notes

Chapter 1. Introduction

1. Newspaper Association of America, Facts About Newspapers 2000, http://www.naa.org/info/facts00/index.html.
2. Ibid.
3. Newspaper Association of America, http://www.naa.org/Trends-and-Numbers/Circulation/Newspaper-Circulation-Volume.aspx.
4. Davies, *The History of American Journalism.*
5. Noam, *Media Ownership and Concentration in America,* 139.
6. Carrick Patterson, interview by author; Hugh B. Patterson, oral history interview by Roy Reed.
7. Carrick Patterson, interview by author.
8. Hussman, interview by author.
9. Roy Reed, interview by author, 2006.
10. Lancaster, interview by author.
11. Davies, *The History of American Journalism.*
12. McPherson, *The History of American Journalism.*
13. Ibid.
14. Roberts, *Leaving Readers Behind,* 2.
15. Ibid., 80.
16. Ibid., 157.
17. Ibid., 161.
18. Roberts, *Breach of Faith.*
19. Bagdikian, *The New Media Monopoly.*
20. Mathis, interview by author.

Chapter 2. 1902–1946: Early Heiskell Family Ownership

1. *National Observer,* "'Mr. J. N.' and a Legend at the *Gazette.*"
2. Lewis, "Arkansas—History of a State, and Its Newspaper."
3. Fletcher, "100 Honor J. N. Heiskell for 50 Years as Editor."
4. Heiskell Personal Papers, Eliza N. Heiskell, "Recollections of an Old Woman," 29, Series I, Subseries II, Box 2, File 10, University of Arkansas at Little Rock Archives and Special Collections.
5. Thompson, "Gentleman Editor," 15; Heiskell Personal Papers, Eliza N. Heiskell, 29.
6. Thompson, "Gentleman Editor," 16; Allsopp, *History of the Arkansas Press,* 331–32.
7. Dougan, *Community Diaries,* 149.
8. Lewis, "Arkansas—History of a State, and Its Newspaper."
9. Heiskell Personal Papers, J. N. Heiskell, unpublished autobiographical sketch, November 2, 1964, Series I, Subseries I, Box 1, File 3, University of Arkansas at Little Rock Archives and Special Collections.

10. Street, *James Street's South*, 247.
11. Heiskell Personal Papers, J.N. Heiskell, unpublished autobiographical sketch.
12. *Arkansas Gazette*, July 1, 1902.
13. Lewis, "*Gazette*, Editor Mark Milestone."
14. Ibid.
15. Heiskell Personal Papers, J. N. Heiskell, unpublished autobiographical sketch.
16. Ibid.
17. Ibid.
18. Ibid.
19. Thompson, "Gentleman Editor," 3.
20. Heiskell Personal Papers, J. N. Heiskell, *The Jolly Fellowship*, I, 2, February 1883, unpublished newspaper, Series I, Subseries I, Box 2, File 1, University of Arkansas at Little Rock Archives and Special Collections.
21. Heiskell Personal Papers, J. N. Heiskell, unpublished autobiographical sketch.
22. Lewis, "Arkansas—History of a State, and Its Newspaper."
23. Street, *James Street's South*, 248.
24. *Encyclopedia of Arkansas History & Culture*, "Fred Allsopp."
25. *Arkansas Gazette*, "J. N. Heiskell Dies at 100."
26. Street, *James Street's South*, 248.
27. Dougan, interview by Kevin Clark.
28. *Arkansas Gazette*, November 6, 1906.
29. *Arkansas Gazette*, June 16, 1909.
30. Lewis, "Arkansas—History of a State, and Its Newspaper."
31. Ibid.
32. *Arkansas Gazette*, "J. N. Heiskell Dies at 100."
33. Lewis, "Arkansas—History of a State, and Its Newspaper."
34. *Arkansas Gazette* Papers, *Arkansas Gazette: A History* (Little Rock, 1980), 12, University of Arkansas at Little Rock Archives and Special Collections.
35. Street, *James Street's South*, 250.
36. Lewis, "Arkansas—History of a State, and Its Newspaper."
37. Ibid.
38. Roy Reed, "Arkansas Paper is 150, its Editor 97."
39. Lewis, "Arkansas—History of a State, and Its Newspaper."
40. Dougan, interview by Clark.
41. *Arkansas News Archive*, Old State House Museum of Arkansas History, "Colorful samples from Jeff Davis's speeches."
42. *Encyclopedia of Arkansas History & Culture, "Arkansas Gazette."*
43. Thompson, "Gentleman Editor," 20.
44. Ibid., 23.
45. *Arkansas Gazette*, October 16, 1906.
46. *National Observer*, "'Mr. J. N.' and a Legend at the *Gazette*."
47. *Encyclopedia of Arkansas History & Culture*, "Jeff Davis."
48. Heiskell Personal Papers, *Kansas City Star*, January 16, 1913, Series I, Subseries I, Box 9, File 2, University of Arkansas at Little Rock Archives and Special Collections.
49. *Arkansas Gazette*, "A Senator's Impassioned Plea."

50. Heiskell Personal Papers, *Newark Journal*, Series I, Subseries I, Box 9, File 2, University of Arkansas at Little Rock Archives and Special Collections.
51. *Arkansas Gazette*, "J. N. Heiskell Dies at 100."
52. *Arkansas Gazette*, December 11, 1906.
53. *Arkansas Gazette*, "Library Supporter Carries Card No.1."
54. *Arkansas Gazette*, November 24, 1906.
55. *Arkansas Gazette*, "Library Supporter Carries Card No. 1."
56. *Arkansas Gazette*, March 29, 1959.
57. Thompson, "Gentleman Editor," 60.
58. Ashmore, *Hearts and Minds*, 152.
59. Thompson, "Gentleman Editor," 113–30.
60. Ibid., 137–39.
61. Ibid., 139–40.
62. Ibid., 148.
63. *Arkansas Gazette*, April 27, 1918.
64. *Arkansas Gazette*, December 5, 1919.
65. Dumas, interview by author, 2006.
66. *Arkansas Gazette*, September 30, 1902.
67. Thompson, "Gentleman Editor," 181.
68. Ibid., 183.
69. *Arkansas Gazette*, June 25, 1904.
70. Thompson, "Gentleman Editor," 187.
71. Ibid., 189.
72. Ibid., 197.
73. Thompson, "Gentleman Editor," 203.
74. Ibid.
75. Heiskell Personal Papers, Joe Stroud, "J. N. Heiskell: A Giant of Journalism," *Detroit Free Press*, January 1, 1973, Series I, Subseries I, Box 8, File 7, University of Arkansas at Little Rock Archives and Special Collections.
76. Street, *James Street's South*, 240.
77. Ibid., 241.
78. Heiskell Personal Papers, "He Filled Years His Years to the Brim," *Nashville Tennessean*, undated, Series I, Subseries I, Box 8, File 6, University of Arkansas at Little Rock Archives and Special Collections.
79. Street, *James Street's South*, 251.
80. Ibid., 252.
81. Heiskell Personal Papers, "*Gazette* still at usually busy hour in tribute to 'the boss,'" *Arkansas Gazette*, April 1, 1931, Series I, Subseries II, Box 6, File 1, University of Arkansas at Little Rock Archives and Special Collections.
82. Heiskell Personal Papers, "A Tribute," *Arkansas Gazette*, April 1, 1931, Series I, Subseries II, Box 6, File 1, University of Arkansas at Little Rock Archives and Special Collections.
83. Heiskell Personal Papers, "Mourns Passing of Loyal Friend," *Arkansas Gazette*, April 1, 1931, Series I, Subseries II, Box 6, File 1, University of Arkansas at Little Rock Archives and Special Collections.
84. Ibid.

85. Heiskell Personal Papers, "Mourn Death of Editor," *Kansas City Star*, April 1, 1931, Series I, Subseries II, Box 6, File 1, University of Arkansas at Little Rock Archives and Special Collections.
86. Heiskell Personal Papers, *Memphis Commercial Appeal*, April 2, 1931, Series I, Subseries II, Box 6, File 1, University of Arkansas at Little Rock Archives and Special Collections.
87. Heiskell Personal Papers, *Baxter Bulletin*, April 10, 1931, Series I, Subseries II, Box 6, File 1, University of Arkansas at Little Rock Archives and Special Collections.
88. Heiskell Personal Papers, "Fred Heiskell," *Arkansas Publisher*, Series I, Subseries II, Box 6, File 1, University of Arkansas at Little Rock Archives and Special Collections.
89. Lewis, "Arkansas—History of a State, and Its Newspaper."
90. Ibid.
91. Heiskell Personal Papers, Report of J.N. Heiskell, Chairman of Committee on Editorial Affairs, to Southern Newspaper Publishers Association Annual Meeting at Asheville, N.C., May 1935, Series III, Box 2, File 3, University of Arkansas at Little Rock Archives and Special Collections.
92. Ibid.
93. Ibid.
94. Ibid.
95. Noam, *Media Ownership and Concentration in America*, 139.
96. Dougan, *Community Diaries*, 206.
97. Dougan, interview by Clark.
98. *Arkansas Gazette*, "J. N. Heiskell Dies at 100"; Rutherford, "*Arkansas Gazette* Editor J.N. Heiskell: Heart and Mind."
99. *Arkansas Gazette*, "Lt.Carrick W. Heiskell, Pilot, War Casualty," December 4, 1943.
100. Heiskell Personal Papers, Lt. Carrick W. Heiskell to his family, Christmas 1942 [apparent date], Series I, Subseries II, Box 7, File 11, University of Arkansas at Little Rock Archives and Special Collections.
101. Heiskell Personal Papers, J. N. Heiskell to Effie, June 27, 1943, Series I, Subseries II, Box 3, File 1, University of Arkansas at Little Rock Archives and Special Collections.
102. Heiskell Personal Papers, Carrick W. Heiskell to J. N. Heiskell, undated, Series I, Subseries II, Box 7, File 13, University of Arkansas at Little Rock Archives and Special Collections.
103. Ibid.
104. Heiskell Personal Papers, Carrick W. Heiskell to Mother and Dad, November 21, 1943, Series I, Subseries II, Box 7, File 12, University of Arkansas at Little Rock Archives and Special Collections.
105. *Arkansas Gazette*, "Lt. Carrick W. Heiskell, Pilot, War Casualty."
106. Ibid.
107. Heiskell Personal Papers, "Many Regret Death of Lt. Heiskell," *Arkansas Gazette*, December 4, 1943, Series I, Subseries II, Box 7, File 15, University of Arkansas at Little Rock Archives and Special Collections.
108. Heiskell Personal Papers, J. N. Heiskell to Bob, January 3, 1944, Series I,

Subseries II, Box 3, File 1, University of Arkansas at Little Rock Archives and Special Collections.

109. Heiskell Personal Papers, J. N. Heiskell to Heiskell, January 3, 1944, Series I, Subseries II, Box 3, File 1, University of Arkansas at Little Rock Archives and Special Collections.
110. Heiskell Personal Papers, J. N. Heiskell to Grace, December 3, 1944, Series I, Subseries II, Box 3, File 1, University of Arkansas at Little Rock Archives and Special Collections.
111. Heiskell Personal Papers, J. N. Heiskell to Bertha, May 13, 1955, Series I, Subseries II, Box 7, File 17, University of Arkansas at Little Rock Archives and Special Collections.
112. Dougan, interview by Clark.
113. Dougan, *Community Diaries*, 255.
114. Lewis, "Arkansas—History of a State, and Its Newspaper."
115. *Arkansas Gazette*, "Fred. W. Allsopp Left Message of Farewell."

Chapter 3. 1947–1959: A New Triumvirate Takes Control: J. N. Heiskell, Hugh B. Patterson, and Harry S. Ashmore Face the Crisis at Central High

1. Ben F. Johnson, *Arkansas in Modern America*.
2. Dumas, "Sid McMath: An Arkansan for All Seasons."
3. *Arkansas Gazette* Papers, J. N. Heiskell remarks, Freedom Award dinner program, Box 1, File 28, University of Arkansas at Little Rock Archives and Special Collections.
4. Rutherford, "*Arkansas Gazette* Editor J. N. Hesikell," 82.
5. Ibid., 56.
6. Carrick Patterson, interview by author.
7. Ashmore, *Civil Rights and Wrongs*, 64.
8. Dougan, *Community Diaries*, 271.
9. *Time*, "For Leadership."
10. Ibid.
11. Rutherford, "*Arkansas Gazette* Editor J. N. Heiskell," 58–59.
12. Roberts and Klibanoff, *The Race Beat*, 50.
13. *Encyclopedia of Arkansas History & Culture*, "Harry Scott Ashmore."
14. Ashmore, *Hearts and Minds*, 203.
15. *Arkansas Gazette* Papers, "Newspaper Principles and Profits," address by Hugh B. Patterson to the Advertising Club of San Francisco, October 1, 1958, Box 3, File 104, University of Arkansas at Little Rock Archives and Special Collections.
16. Ashmore, *Hearts and Minds*, 120.
17. *Encyclopedia of Arkansas History & Culture*, "Hugh Baskin Patterson, Jr."
18. *Time*, "Arkansas Teetotaler."
19. *Arkansas Gazette*, November 27, 1948.
20. *Encyclopedia of Arkansas History & Culture*, "Hugh Baskin Patterson, Jr."
21. *Time*, "Arkansas Teetotaler."

22. Noam, *Media Ownership and Concentration in America*, 139.
23. Heiskell Personal Papers, J. N. Heiskell, speech to the Little Rock Rotary Club, January 1946, Series III, Box 2, File 3, University of Arkansas at Little Rock Archives and Special Collections, quoted in Rutherford, "*Arkansas Gazette* Editor J. N. Heiskell," 25–26.
24. Stover, "*Gazette* publisher celebrates 35th year in post."
25. Carrick Patterson, interview by author.
26. Rutherford, "*Arkansas Gazette* Editor J. N. Heiskell," 70.
27. Thompson, "Gentleman Editor," 106.
28. Hugh B. Patterson, oral history interview by Roy Reed, Part 2, 30–32.
29. Fletcher, "100 Honor J. N. Heiskell for 50 Years as Editor."
30. Reed, interview by author, 2006.
31. *Time*, "For Leadership."
32. *New York Times*, "Race in the News."
33. Brown, "Newspapers of Deep South Liberalize Negro Policies," 9.
34. Ashmore, *Hearts and Minds*, 149.
35. *Arkansas Gazette* Papers, "Newspaper Principles and Profits."
36. Fletcher, "100 Honor J. N. Heiskell for 50 Years as Editor."
37. Ibid.
38. Ibid.
39. Roberts and Klibanoff, *The Race Beat*, 33.
40. Woodhull and Snyder, *Defining Moments in Journalism*, 10.
41. Ibid., 9.
42. *Arkansas Publisher*, 2.
43. *Arkansas Gazette*, "J. N. Heiskell Dies at 100."
44. Ashmore, *Hearts and Minds*, 151.
45. Ashmore, "The South and the South's Problem," 135.
46. Roy Reed, interview by author, 2006.
47. Dougan, *Community Diaries*, 280.
48. Dougan, interview by Clark.
49. Roy Reed, interview by author, 2006.
50. Dougan, interview by Clark.
51. Dougan, *Community Diaries*, 280.
52. Reed, *Faubus*, 27.
53. Ibid., 7.
54. *Encyclopedia of Arkansas History & Culture*, "Orval Eugene Faubus."
55. Heiskell Personal Papers, "Wit And Courage," *St. Louis Post-Dispatch*, January 6, 1973, Series I, Subseries I, Box 8, File 6, University of Arkansas at Little Rock Archives and Special Collections.
56. Heiskell Personal Papers, "Apes and Atheism in Arkansas," J. N. Heiskell, *Liberty Magazine*, February 23, 1929, Series III, Box 6, File 9, University of Arkansas at Little Rock Archives and Special Collections.
57. Justice Jim Johnson, interview by author.
58. Ibid.
59. *Congressional Record*, June 5, 2006.
60. Hugh Patterson oral history interview by Reed.
61. Roy Reed, "Hugh Patterson Jr., 91; publisher worked to end segregation."

62. Rutherford, "*Arkansas Gazette* Editor J. N. Heiskell," 78.
63. Roberts and Klibanoff, *The Race Beat*, 151.
64. Roy Reed, interview by author, 2006.
65. *Arkansas Gazette* editorial, "The Crisis Mr. Faubus Made."
66. *Arkansas Gazette* editorial, "Reflections in a Hurricane's Eye."
67. Ashmore, "One Editor's Response To a National Crisis."
68. Roy Reed, interview by author, 2006.
69. Allbright, interview by author.
70. Roy Reed, interview by author, 2006.
71. Foreman, interview by author.
72. *Congressional Record*, June 5, 2006.
73. Dhonau, interview by author, 2006.
74. Heiskell Personal Papers, Christmas card from Higbee, 1958, Series I, Subseries I, Box 5, File 10, University of Arkansas at Little Rock Archives and Special Collections.
75. Ashmore, "Mr. J. N. at 91," 13.
76. *Arkansas Gazette* Papers, "Public Enemy No. 1—in Little Rock," *St. Louis Post-Dispatch*, Box 2, File 64, University of Arkansas at Little Rock Archives and Special Collections.
77. Ashmore, *An Epitaph for Dixie*, 162.
78. Rutherford, "*Arkansas Gazette* Editor J. N. Heiskell," 85.
79. Roy Reed, oral history interview by Baker, Part 3, 32; Roy Reed, interview by author, 2006.
80. Heiskell Personal Papers, Patrick Owens, "A Man and His Newspaper," *Newsday*, January 2, 1973, Series I, Subseries I, Box 8, File 7, University of Arkansas at Little Rock Archives and Special Collections.
81. Powell, interview by author.
82. *Arkansas Gazette* Papers, Bruce Catton, "Journalism on Crusade," *Saturday Review*, July 26, 1958, Box 2, File 64, University of Arkansas at Little Rock Archives and Special Collections.
83. Reed, *Faubus*, 169.
84. Heiskell Personal Papers, J. N. Heiskell letter, October 6, 1957, Series I, Subseries II, Box 3, File 1, University of Arkansas at Little Rock Archives and Special Collections.
85. Heiskell Personal Papers, "Integration Solution Unlikely, Says Editor," *Knoxville Journal*, January 22, 1959, Series I, Subseries I, Box 10, File 2, University of Arkansas at Little Rock Archives and Special Collections.
86. Ashmore, "An Epitaph for the Old Lady."
87. *Arkansas Gazette* Papers, David Bluthenthal to Hugh Patterson, December 11, 1957, Box 3, File 105, University of Arkansas at Little Rock Archives and Special Collections.
88. *Arkansas Gazette*, "An Editorial: Is Revolution the Answer?" December 13, 1957, 1; Bluthenthal to Patterson; Erwin, "3 Pulitzer Prizes Awarded for the Little Rock Story."
89. *Arkansas Gazette*, "An Editorial: Is Revolution the Answer?" December 13, 1957, 1.
90. Ibid.

91. Ibid.
92. *Arkansas Gazette* Papers, J. R. Work to Hugh B. Patterson, February 5, 1958, Box 3, File 101, University of Arkansas at Little Rock Archives and Special Collections.
93. *Arkansas Gazette* Papers, Hugh B. Patterson to J. R. Work, February 6, 1958, Box 3, File 101, University of Arkansas at Little Rock Archives and Special Collections.
94. *Time*, "For Leadership"; *Arkansas Gazette* Papers, "Newspaper Principles and Profits."
95. *Arkansas Gazette* Papers, "Newspaper Principles and Profits."
96. *Editor & Publisher*, "*Arkansas Gazette's* Reed to lead ICMA," 10.
97. Roberts and Klibanoff, *The Race Beat;* Powell, interview by author.
98. Heiskell Personal Papers, Peter Kihss, "Arkansas Daily Gets 2 Pulitzer Awards," *New York Times*, May 6, 1958, Series I, Subseries I, Box 10, File 1, University of Arkansas at Little Rock Archives and Special Collections.
99. Heiskell Personal Papers, "Heiskell Gets Columbia's New Award," *Editor & Publisher*, May 31, 1958, 12, Series I, Subseries I, Box 10, File 1, University of Arkansas at Little Rock Archives and Special Collections.
100. Heiskell Personal Papers, "'We Have Suffered,' But *Gazette* Is Not Sorry," *Memphis Press-Scimitar*, May 7, 1958, Series I, Subseries I, Box 10, File 1, University of Arkansas at Little Rock Archives and Special Collections.
101. Roy Reed, oral history interview by Baker, Part 3, 32.
102. *Arkansas Gazette*, "J. N. Heiskell Dies at 100."
103. Rutherford, "*Arkansas Gazette* Editor J. N. Heiskell," 73.
104. Ibid., 76.
105. Roy Reed, oral history interview by Baker, Part 3, 32.
106. Heiskell Personal Papers, "'We Have Suffered,' But *Gazette* Is Not Sorry."
107. Ashmore, oral history interview with Reed, 33.
108. *Arkansas Gazette* Papers, "Editor Tells Of Trouble At Little Rock," November 12, 1957, Box 3, File 105, University of Arkansas at Little Rock Archives and Special Collections.
109. Heiskell Personal Papers, J. N. Heiskell to Effie, September 22, 1957, Series II, Box 4, File 7, University of Arkansas at Little Rock Archives and Special Collections.
110. *Arkansas Gazette* Papers, *Arkansas Gazette*, pamphlet celebrating the Pulitzers and Columbia award, Box 1, File 30, University of Arkansas at Little Rock Archives and Special Collections.
111. Erwin, "3 Pulitzer Prizes Awarded For the Little Rock Story."
112. *Arkansas Gazette* Papers, *Arkansas Gazette*, pamphlet celebrating the Pulitzers and Columbia award.
113. *Newsweek*, "At 85, a Big Moment," 64.
114. Heiskell Personal Papers, Alexander F. Jones, "A Journalistic Beacon," *Syracuse Herald-Journal*, May 7, 1958, Series I, Subseries III, Box 1, File 1, University of Arkansas at Little Rock Archives and Special Collections.
115. Rutherford, "*Arkansas Gazette* Editor J. N. Heiskell," 6, recounted by Maurice T. Moore, chairman of board of trustees, speech to Columbia School of

Journalism award ceremony, New York, May 29, 1958; *Newsweek*, "At 85, a Big Moment," 64.

116. *Arkansas Democrat*, July 13, 1958.
117. Ibid.
118. Heiskell Personal Papers, J. N. Heiskell to Edward W. Barrett, June 3, 1958, Series II, Box 4, File 8, University of Arkansas at Little Rock Archives and Special Collections.
119. Heiskell Personal Papers, news release, Columbia University, texts of presentation at luncheon for presentation of the first Columbia Journalism Award, May 29, 1958, Series I, Subseries I, Box 10, File 2, University of Arkansas at Little Rock Archives and Special Collections.
120. *Arkansas Gazette* Papers, Recognition Award, Box 3, File 100, University of Arkansas at Little Rock Archives and Special Collections.
121. *Arkansas Gazette* Papers, Box 1, File 28, University of Arkansas at Little Rock Archives and Special Collections.
122. Heiskell Personal Papers, "'We Have Suffered,' But *Gazette* Is Not Sorry"; J. N. Heiskell remarks at Syracuse, March 9, 1958, Series III, Box 1, File 11, University of Arkansas at Little Rock Archives and Special Collections.
123. *Arkansas Gazette* Papers, Heiskell remarks, Freedom Award dinner program, Box 1, File 28.
124. *Arkansas Gazette*, "Large and Applauding Crowd Honors *Gazette* and Editors," 1.
125. Heiskell Personal Papers, Adolphine Terry to L.S.F., October 16, 1957, J. N. Heiskell Scrapbook, 1957–58, Series I, Subseries I, Box 10, File 1, University of Arkansas at Little Rock Archives and Special Collections.
126. *Arkansas Gazette* Papers, Virginius Dabney to J. N. Heiskell and Harry S. Ashmore, June 5, 1958; Harry S. Ashmore to Virginius Dabney, June 19, 1958; J. N. Heiskell to R. L. McGrath, May 21, 1958, Box 1, File 30, University of Arkansas at Little Rock Archives and Special Collections.
127. *Arkansas Gazette* Papers, Box 1, File 30, University of Arkansas at Little Rock Archives and Special Collections.
128. *Arkansas Gazette* Papers, Catton, "Journalism on Crusade."
129. *Arkansas Gazette* Papers, "As Another Paper Sees Us," *Arkansas Gazette*, Box 1, File 30, University of Arkansas at Little Rock Archives and Special Collections.
130. Ashmore, "Mr. J. N. at 91," 13.
131. Senator David Pryor, interview by author.
132. Rutherford, "*Arkansas Gazette* Editor J. N. Heiskell," 76.
133. Ibid., 79.
134. Ibid., 81.
135. Shipler, "The Desegregation Drama"; Roberts and Klibanoff, "The Embrace of Principled Stands," 88–89.
136. *Time*, "For Leadership."
137. Ashmore, "Mr. J. N. at 91."
138. *Arkansas Gazette*, "Ashmore Leaves *Gazette* Position."
139. Heiskell Personal Papers, J. N. Heiskell, September 20, 1959, J. N. Heiskell Scrapbook, 1958–60, Series I, Subseries I, Box 10, File 2, University of Arkansas at Little Rock Archives and Special Collections.

140. Heiskell Personal Papers, J. N. Heiskell Scrapbook, 1958–60, Series I, Subseries I, Box 10, File 2, University of Arkansas at Little Rock Archives and Special Collections.
141. Powell, interview by author.
142. Reed, *Faubus*, 274.

Chapter 4. 1960–1970: The Aftermath of Central High

1. Powell, interview by author.
2. Heiskell Personal Papers, J. N. Heiskell, "The Newspaper: Keeper of the Community Conscience," address at the John Peter Zenger Award ceremony, University of Arizona Press, Series III, Box 1, File 12, University of Arkansas at Little Rock Archives and Special Collections.
3. Arkansas Press Association, *1960 Arkansas Newspaper Directory Ratebook.*
4. Heiskell Personal Papers, J. N. Heiskell to Grace Heiskell, February 6 and February 14, 1960, Series I, Subseries I, Box 3, File 2, University of Arkansas at Little Rock Archives and Special Collections.
5. Heiskell Personal Papers, J. N. Heiskell, April 17, 1960, Series I, Subseries I, Box 10, File 2, University of Arkansas at Little Rock Archives and Special Collections.
6. Ibid.
7. *Arkansas Gazette*, "Among Ourselves."
8. Dumas, interview by author, 2006.
9. Arkansas Press Association, *1961 Arkansas Newspaper Directory Ratebook.*
10. Arkansas Press Association, *1962 Arkansas Newspaper Directory Ratebook.*
11. Arkansas Press Association, *1965 Arkansas Newspaper Directory Ratebook.*
12. Arkansas Press Association, *1970 Arkansas Newspaper Directory Ratebook.*
13. *Arkansas Gazette*, "*Gazette* Ranks 21st in Poll of Top Dailies."
14. Dougan, interview by Clark.
15. Powell, interview by author.
16. Dumas, interview by author, 2006.
17. Ibid.
18. Ibid.
19. Roy Reed, interview by author, 2006.
20. Heiskell Personal Papers, Owens, "A Man and His Newspaper."
21. Dumas, interview by author, 2006.
22. Lewis, "Arkansas—History of a State, and Its Newspaper."
23. Ibid.
24. Lewis, interview by author.
25. Lewis, "Arkansas—History of a State, and Its Newspaper."
26. Henry, oral history interview by Bailey, 2–3.
27. Harris, "*Gazette* Personalities Gave Paper a Vivid Character."
28. Ibid.
29. Henry, oral history interview by Bailey, 5.
30. Harris, "*Gazette* Personalities Gave Paper a Vivid Character."
31. Dumas, interview by author, 2006.

32. Dougan, interview by Clark.
33. McConnell, interview by author.
34. Bailey, interview by author.
35. Lewis, interview by author.
36. *Arkansas Gazette* Papers, Box 1, File 28, University of Arkansas at Little Rock Archives and Special Collections.
37. Lewis, "Arkansas—History of a State, and Its Newspaper."
38. *Arkansas Gazette*, Editorial, November 23, 1963.
39. *Arkansas Gazette*, November 23, 1963.
40. Jordan, interview by author.
41. Heiskell Personal Papers, Owens, "A Man and His Newspaper."
42. Dumas, interview by author, 2006.
43. Ibid.
44. *Arkansas Gazette* Papers, President Lyndon Johnson to Hugh B. Patterson, September 29, 1964, Box 6, File 1, University of Arkansas at Little Rock Archives and Special Collections.
45. Jordan, interview by author.
46. Powell, interview by author.
47. Ibid.
48. Heiskell Personal Papers, J. N. Heiskell, "The Newspaper: Keeper of the Community Conscience," address at the John Peter Zenger Award ceremony.
49. Ibid.
50. Heiskell Personal Papers, Ralph McGill to J. N. Heiskell, December 24, 1964, Series III, Box 1, File 5, University of Arkansas at Little Rock Archives and Special Collections.
51. Heiskell Personal Papers, James Russell Wiggins to J. N. Heiskell, December 7, 1964, Series III, Box 1, File 6, University of Arkansas at Little Rock Archives and Special Collections.
52. Heiskell Personal Papers, Clark R. Mollenhoff to J. N. Heiskell, December 15, 1964, Series III, Box 1, File 5, University of Arkansas at Little Rock Archives and Special Collections.
53. Heiskell Personal Papers, Evelyn D. Law to J. N. Heiskell, December 12, 1964, Series III, Box 1, File 5, University of Arkansas at Little Rock Archives and Special Collections.
54. *Arkansas Gazette*, "*Gazette* Designated As a Historic Site."
55. Ibid.
56. Ibid.
57. *Arkansas Gazette* Papers, W. R. Stephens to Hugh B. Patterson, June 30, 1967, Box 6, File 1, University of Arkansas at Little Rock Archives and Special Collections.
58. *Arkansas Gazette* Papers, Hugh B. Patterson to W. R. Stephens, July 3, 1967, Box 6, File 1, University of Arkansas at Little Rock Archives and Special Collections.
59. Roy Reed, interview by author, 2006.
60. Dhonau, interview by author, 2006.
61. Carrick Patterson, interview by author.
62. Ibid.

63. *Arkansas Gazette*, "Margaret Ross's History Records Our Early Years."
64. Hugh B. Patterson, oral history interview by Reed, Part 3, 33.
65. Ben Johnson, *Arkansas in Modern America.*
66. *Arkansas Gazette*, Editorial, October 16, 1966.
67. Roy Reed, *Looking Back at the* Arkansas Gazette, 4.
68. Justice Jim Johnson, interview by author.
69. *Arkansas Gazette*, Editorial, October 16, 1966.
70. *Encyclopedia of Arkansas History & Culture*, "Winthrop Rockefeller."
71. *Arkansas Gazette*, Editorial, November 10, 1966.
72. Bumpers, interview by author.
73. Powell, oral history interview by Dumas, 21.
74. Bumpers, interview by author.
75. Pryor, interview by author.
76. Bumpers, interview by author.
77. Powell, interview by author.
78. Ibid.
79. Powell, oral history interview by Dumas, 22–23.
80. *Arkansas News Archive*, "First black reporter on white Arkansas newspaper."
81. Moore, interview by author.
82. Ibid.
83. Ibid.
84. Ben Johnson, *Arkansas in Modern America 1930–1999.*
85. Roy Reed, interview by author, 2006.
86. Lewis, "Arkansas—History of a State, and Its Newspaper."
87. Lewis, interview by author.

Chapter 5. 1970–1974: Mr. Heiskell's Death and the Transition of Ownership to the Patterson Family

1. Foreman, interview by author.
2. Bailey, interview by author.
3. Foreman, interview by author.
4. Ibid.
5. *Arkansas Gazette* Papers, Margaret Ross to Dr. Belle Boone Beard, February 22, 1973, Box 1, File 43, University of Arkansas at Little Rock Archives and Special Collections.
6. Heiskell Personal Papers, "He Filled His Years to the Brim," *Nashville Tennessean*, undated, Series I, Subseries I, Box 8, File 6, University of Arkansas at Little Rock Archives and Special Collections.
7. Ross, "Wit, Wisdom His Trademarks."
8. Carrick Patterson, interview by author.
9. Roy Reed, interview by author, 2006.
10. Douglas, oral history interview by Reed, Part 2, 3.
11. Ibid., 4.
12. Carrick Patterson, interview by author.
13. Lewis, "*Gazette*, Editor Mark Milestone."

14. Carey, "On Being a Centenarian."
15. Ross, "Wit, Wisdom His Trademarks."
16. Ibid.
17. Ibid.
18. *Arkansas Gazette*, "J. N. Heiskell Dies at 100."
19. *Arkansas Gazette* Papers, Ross to Beard, February 22, 1973.
20. Dougan, interview by Clark.
21. Powell, interview by author.
22. Ibid.
23. Lewis, interview by author.
24. Powell, interview by author.
25. Arkansas Press Association, *1972 Arkansas Newspaper Directory Ratebook.*
26. Powell, interview by author.
27. Heiskell Personal Papers, *Arkansas Gazette* memo from Hugh B. Patterson to all department heads, October 16, 1972, Series I, Subseries I, Box 4, File 1, University of Arkansas at Little Rock Archives and Special Collections; "Editor of *Arkansas Gazette* to mark his 100th birthday," *Daily Enterprise*, October 30, 1972, Series I, Subseries I, Box 7, University of Arkansas at Little Rock Archives and Special Collections; Carey, "On Being a Centenarian."
28. Henry, oral history interview by Bailey, 17.
29. Powell, interview by author.
30. *Arkansas Gazette* Papers, Ross to Beard, February 22, 1973.
31. Carey, "On Being a Centenarian."
32. *Arkansas Gazette*, "J. N. Heiskell Dies at 100."
33. Heiskell Personal Papers, "Arkansas Editor, 100, Dies After Colorful Career," *Dallas Morning News*, December 29, 1972, Series I, Subseries I, Box 8, File 6, University of Arkansas at Little Rock Archives and Special Collections.
34. Powell, interview by author.
35. Hussman, oral history interview by Reed, 33.
36. Ibid.
37. *Arkansas Gazette*, December 29, 1972.
38. *Arkansas Gazette*, "300 Attend Funeral For J. N. Heiskell."
39. *Arkansas Gazette*, "Officials, Fellow Newsmen Join in Praising Editor."
40. Heiskell Personal Papers, Series I, Subseries I, Box 8, Files 6 and 7, University of Arkansas at Little Rock Archives and Special Collections.
41. Heiskell Personal Papers, *Arkansas Democrat*, "His title was editor," December 31, 1972, Series I, Subseries I, Box 8, Files 6 and 7, University of Arkansas at Little Rock Archives and Special Collections.
42. Heiskell Personal Papers, *North Little Rock Times*, January 4, 1973, Series I, Subseries I, Box 8, Files 6 and 7, University of Arkansas at Little Rock Archives and Special Collections.
43. Heiskell Personal Papers, Owens, "A Man and His Newspaper."
44. Roy Reed, interview by author, 2006.
45. Heiskell Personal Papers, W. R. Stephens to Hugh Patterson, January 2, 1973, Series I, Subseries I, Box 8, File 3, University of Arkansas at Little Rock Archives and Special Collections.
46. Heiskell Personal Papers, David W. Mullins, telegram to Mr. and Mrs. Hugh

Patterson, December 29, 1972, Series I, Subseries I, Box 8, File 3, University of Arkansas at Little Rock Archives and Special Collections.

47. Heiskell Personal Papers, Harmon L. Remmel to Hugh B. Patterson, January 5, 1973, Series I, Subseries I, Box 8, File 3, University of Arkansas at Little Rock Archives and Special Collections.
48. Heiskell Personal Papers, *Congressional Record*—Senate, January 18, 1973, Series I, Subseries I, Box 8, File 3, University of Arkansas at Little Rock Archives and Special Collections.
49. Lewis, interview by author.
50. *Arkansas Gazette*, "J. N. Heiskell Dies at 100."
51. Fletcher, "100 Honor J. N. Heiskell for 50 Years as Editor."
52. Heiskell Personal Papers, Hugh B. Patterson Jr. to Rodrigo Madrigal Nieto, January 30, 1973, Series I, Subseries I, Box 8, File 3, University of Arkansas at Little Rock Archives and Special Collections.
53. *Arkansas Gazette*, "J. N. Heiskell Dies at 100."
54. Hugh B.Patterson, oral history interview by Reed, Part 3, 25.
55. Carrick Patterson, interview by author.
56. Ibid.
57. Ibid.
58. Douglas, oral history interview by Reed, Part 2B, 16.
59. Carrick Patterson, interview by author.
60. Ibid.
61. Ibid.
62. Brantley, interview by author.
63. Lancaster, oral history interview by McCord, 7.
64. *Arkansas Gazette* Papers, W. R. Stephens to Hugh Patterson, December 4, 1973, Box 6, File 1, University of Arkansas at Little Rock Archives and Special Collections.
65. *Arkansas Gazette* Papers, Hugh Patterson to W. R. Stephens, December 11, 1973, Box 6, File 1, University of Arkansas at Little Rock Archives and Special Collections.
66. Bailey, interview by author.
67. Douglas, oral history interview by Reed, Part 1, 15–18.
68. Ibid., Part 1, 47–49.
69. Brantley, interview by author.
70. Bailey, interview by author.
71. Powell, interview by author.
72. *Arkansas Gazette*, "J. N. Heiskell Dies at 100."

Chapter 6. 1974–1986: A Change Atop the *Arkansas Democrat*, the Ensuing Newspaper War, Antitrust Lawsuit, and Sale to Gannett

1. Arkansas Press Association, *1974 Arkansas Newspaper Directory Ratebook.*
2. *Arkansas Democrat-Gazette*, "History of the *Arkansas Democrat-Gazette.*"
3. *Arkansas Democrat*, "Palmer Papers buy the *Democrat.*"
4. Hussman, oral history interview by Reed, 7.

5. Ibid.
6. Ibid.
7. Dougan, interview by Clark.
8. Hussman, oral history interview by Reed, 17.
9. Ibid., 23.
10. Ibid., 17.
11. Hussman, interview by author.
12. Hussman, oral history interview by Reed, 18–20.
13. Ibid., 23.
14. Brantley, oral history interview by Dumas, 15.
15. Brantley, interview by author.
16. Hussman, oral history interview by Reed, 24.
17. *Arkansas Gazette* Papers, *Arkansas Gazette*, "*Arkansas Democrat* Sale to Palmer Authorized for $3.7 Million Price," n.d., University of Arkansas at Little Rock Archives and Special Collections.
18. Hussman, oral history interview by Reed, 25.
19. Ibid., 26.
20. Brantley, interview by author.
21. Hussman, interview by author.
22. Ibid.
23. Hussman, oral history interview by Reed, 26.
24. Ibid., 27.
25. Ibid., 29.
26. Ibid., 27.
27. Ibid., 31.
28. Ibid.
29. Ibid.
30. Ibid., 32.
31. Ibid.
32. Sandlin, "25th Anniversary of Pivotal Decision."
33. Hussman, interview by author.
34. Hussman, oral history interview by Reed, 32.
35. Ibid.
36. Ibid., 33.
37. Ibid., 33–34.
38. Ibid., 34.
39. Ibid.
40. Hussman, interview by author.
41. Hussman, oral history interview by Reed, 35.
42. Hugh B.Patterson, oral history interview by Reed, Part 3, 9.
43. Carrick Patterson, interview by author.
44. McCord, oral history interview by McConnell, 6.
45. Hussman, oral history interview by Reed, 35.
46. Hussman, interview by author.
47. Ibid.
48. Carrick Patterson, oral history interview by Reed, 45.
49. Carrick Patterson, interview by author.

50. Hussman, oral history interview by Reed, 37–40.
51. Ibid., 42.
52. Ibid.
53. Ibid.
54. Ibid., 43.
55. *Arkansas Gazette*, "J. N. Heiskell Dies at 100."
56. Hussman, interview by author.
57. Hussman, oral history interview by Reed, 44.
58. McCord, interview by author.
59. Hussman, oral history interview by Reed, 45.
60. McCord, oral history interview by McConnell, 2.
61. Hussman, oral history interview by Reed, 45.
62. McCord, interview by author.
63. Hussman, interview by author.
64. Hussman, oral history interview by Reed, 45–46.
65. Ibid., 46–47.
66. Oakley, interview by author.
67. Carrick Patterson, interview by author.
68. Ibid.
69. Ibid.
70. Brantley, oral history interview by Dumas, 25.
71. Brantley, interview by author.
72. Ibid.
73. Arkansas Press Association, *1979 Arkansas Newspaper Directory Ratebook*.
74. Brantley, oral history interview by Dumas, 15.
75. Ibid., 33.
76. Mathis, interview by author.
77. Ibid.
78. Oakley, interview by author.
79. Bailey, oral history interview by McConnell, 29.
80. Bailey, interview by author.
81. Henry, oral history interview by Bailey, 27.
82. Ibid., 29.
83. Bailey, oral history interview by McConnell, 17.
84. Moore, interview by author.
85. Oakley, interview by author.
86. Bailey, interview by author.
87. Carrick Patterson, interview by author.
88. Dougan, interview by Clark.
89. Lancaster, oral history interview by McCord, 4.
90. Lancaster, interview by author.
91. Lancaster, e-mail to author.
92. Lewis, interview by author.
93. McConnell, interview by author.
94. Brantley, interview by author.
95. Hussman, oral history interview by Reed, 48.

96. *Arkansas Times*, "Arkansas' Newspaper War: Listen, You, I'm Bob Starr of the *Democrat* and I am Declaring War on the *Gazette*!"
97. Brantley, interview by author.
98. Hussman, oral history interview by Reed, 48.
99. Hussman, interview by author.
100. Hussman, oral history interview by Reed, 49.
101. Hussman, interview by author.
102. Oakley, interview by author.
103. Hussman, oral history interview by Reed, 49.
104. Ibid., 50.
105. Hussman, interview by author.
106. Brantley, interview by author.
107. Hussman, interview by author.
108. Lancaster, oral history interview by McCord, 14.
109. Bailey, interview by author.
110. Dhonau, interview by author, 2006.
111. Hussman, interview by author.
112. Ibid.
113. Hussman, oral history interview by Reed, 51.
114. Hussman, interview by author.
115. Dougan, interview by Clark.
116. Dumas, interview by author, 2006.
117. Ibid.
118. Sandlin, "25th Anniversary of Pivotal Decision."
119. Hussman, oral history interview by Reed, 53.
120. Allen, oral history interview by Douglas, 8.
121. Bailey, interview by author.
122. Pryor, interview by author.
123. Brantley, interview by author.
124. Ibid.
125. Carrick Patterson, oral history interview by Reed, 46.
126. Dumas, oral history interview by Reed, Part 3, 51.
127. Brantley, oral history interview by Dumas, 27–28.
128. Lewis, interview by author.
129. Brantley, oral history interview by Dumas, 29.
130. Roy Reed, oral history interview by Baker, Part 4, 2.
131. Dumas, interview by author.
132. Hussman, oral history interview by Reed, 55.
133. Ibid.
134. Ibid., 56.
135. Hussman Jr., interview by author.
136. Ibid.
137. Ibid.
138. Hussman, oral history interview by Reed, 51.
139. Ibid., 57.
140. Ibid.

141. Ibid., 57–58.
142. Hussman, interview by author.
143. Ibid.
144. Roy Reed, interview by author, 2006.
145. Brantley, oral history interview by Dumas, 22.
146. Ibid.
147. Brantley, interview by author.
148. McCord, oral history interview by McConnell, 4.
149. Ibid., 4–5.
150. Hussman, oral history interview by Reed, 58.
151. Ibid., 58–59.
152. Ibid., 59.
153. Ibid.
154. Hussman, oral history interview by Reed, 60.
155. Hussman, interview by author.
156. Dumas, interview by author.
157. Collins, Lee, and Buhayar, "Buffett says newspaper bet fueled by Arkansas model."
158. Hussman, interview by author.
159. Hussman, oral history interview by Reed, 63.
160. Hussman, interview by author.
161. Hussman, oral history interview by Reed, 63.
162. Ibid., 63–64.
163. Shelton, oral history interview by Dumas, 43.
164. Bailey, interview by author.
165. Carrick Patterson, interview by author.
166. Carrick Patterson, oral history interview by Reed, 47.
167. Wells, *Arkansas Gazette,* March 4, 1986.
168. Wells, *Arkansas Gazette,* April 15, 1986.
169. Simmons, "Publisher contemplated sale in Arkansas newspaper war."
170. *Washington Post,* "Newspaper Wins in Court."
171. Brantley, interview by author.
172. *New York Times*, "Jury Holds Little Rock Paper's Tactics Legal."
173. Jones, "Arkansas Papers Battle over More than Money."
174. *Arkansas Gazette*, March 9, 1986.
175. *Arkansas Gazette*, March 20, 1986.
176. Hussman, interview by author.
177. Ibid.
178. Powell, interview by author.
179. Oakley, interview by author.
180. *Arkansas Gazette*, October 31, 1985.
181. Sandlin, "25th Anniversary of Pivotal Decision."
182. Wells, *Arkansas Gazette*, March 11, 1986.
183. Hussman, oral history interview by Reed, 65.
184. Carrick Patterson, interview by author.
185. Dumas, interview by author.
186. Hussman, oral history interview by Reed, 65.

187. Hussman, interview by author.
188. Oakley, interview by author.
189. Hussman, oral history interview by Reed, 65.
190. Ibid., 66.
191. Ibid., 67.
192. Ibid.
193. Ibid.
194. Ibid., 68.
195. Brantley, oral history interview by Dumas, 30.
196. Brantley, interview by author.
197. Dumas, interview by author.
198. Brantley, interview by author.
199. Brantley, oral history interview by Dumas, 31.
200. Brantley, interview by author.
201. Dumas, oral history interview by Reed, 52.
202. Dhonau, interview by author, 2006.
203. Hussman, oral history interview by Reed, 69.
204. Ibid., 70.
205. Hussman, interview by author.
206. Douglas, oral history interview by Reed, Part 3, 20.
207. Powell, interview by author.
208. Mathis, interview by author.
209. Hussman, interview by author.
210. Hussman, oral history interview by Reed, 70–71.
211. Ibid., 72–73.
212. Ibid., 73.
213. Ibid.
214. Hussman, interview by author.
215. McCord, interview by author.
216. Foreman, interview by author.
217. Bailey, interview by author.
218. Wells, *Arkansas Gazette*, April 15, 1986.
219. Hussman, oral history interview by Reed, 75.
220. Carrick Patterson, oral history interview by Reed, 48.
221. Hussman, interview by author.
222. Carrick Patterson, interview by author.
223. Ibid.
224. Powell, interview by author.
225. Carrick Patterson, oral history interview by Reed, 49.
226. Hugh B.Patterson, oral history interview by Reed, Part 2, 41.
227. Ibid., Part 3, 17.
228. Ibid., Part 2, 43.
229. Carrick Patterson, interview by author.
230. Hugh B.Patterson, oral history interview by Reed, Part 2, 40.
231. Ibid., Part 2, 41.
232. Brantley, interview by author.
233. Carrick Patterson, oral history interview by Reed, 51.

234. Neuharth, oral history interview by Farris, 4.
235. Carrick Patterson, interview by author.
236. Ibid.
237. Hugh B. Patterson, oral history interview by Reed, Part 3, 17.
238. Carrick Patterson, oral history interview by Reed, 51.
239. Ibid.
240. Ibid.
241. Carrick Patterson, interview by author.
242. Brantley, interview by author.
243. Hussman, oral history interview by Reed, 75–76.
244. C. S. Heinbockel, "Publisher of *Democrat* 'not afraid.'"
245. Hussman, oral history interview by Reed, 76.
246. Ibid.
247. Stover and Scudder, "*Gazette* sold to Gannett Co."
248. Neuharth, oral history interview by Farris, 7–8.
249. Brantley, interview by author.
250. Brantley, oral history interview by Dumas, 34–35.
251. Neuharth, remarks at press conference.
252. Stover and Scudder, "*Gazette* sold to Gannett Co."
253. McCord, oral history interview by McConnell, 9.
254. Dumas, oral history interview by Reed, Part 3, 53.
255. Dhonau, oral history interview by Dumas, 54.
256. Bailey, interview by author.
257. Moore, interview by author.
258. Brummett, oral history interview by Dumas, 48–49.
259. Dumas, interview by author.
260. Dumas, oral history interview by Reed, Part 3, 54.
261. Dumas, interview by author.
262. Hanchette, oral history interview by Farris, 3.
263. Foreman, interview by author.
264. Powell, interview by author.
265. Dhonau, interview by author, 2006.
266. Dhonau, oral history interview by Dumas, 54–55.
267. Dhonau, interview by author, 2006.
268. Bailey, interview by author.
269. Powell, oral history interview by Dumas, 30.
270. McCord, oral history interview by McConnell, 9.
271. Hussman, oral history interview by Reed, 77.
272. Ibid.
273. Ibid., 78.
274. Ibid.
275. Ibid., 79.
276. Carrick Patterson, interview by author.
277. Ibid.
278. Brantley, interview by author.
279. Carrick Patterson, interview by author.

Chapter 7. 1986–1990: Gannett Ownership

1. Noam, *Media Ownership and Concentration in America*, 139.
2. *Arkansas Gazette*, "93 dailies published by Gannett."
3. Stover and Scudder, "*Gazette* sold to Gannett Co."
4. McCord, *The Chain Gang*, 123–24.
5. Bagdikian, *The New Media Monopoly*, 185.
6. Ibid.
7. *Arkansas Democrat-Gazette*, "History of the *Arkansas Democrat-Gazette*."
8. Heinbockel, "Publisher of *Democrat* 'not afraid.'"
9. Dumas, interview by author.
10. Neuharth, oral history interview by Farris, 10.
11. Hussman, interview by author.
12. Ibid.
13. Oakley, interview by author.
14. Hussman, interview by author.
15. Ibid.
16. Borden, interview by author.
17. Ibid.
18. Ellwood, interview by author.
19. Neuharth, oral history interview by Farris, 5.
20. Ibid.
21. Ibid., 5–6.
22. Dhonau, interview by author, 2010.
23. Borden, interview by author.
24. Jordan, interview by author.
25. Mathis, interview by author.
26. Matlack, "Recent Gannett acquisitions offer clues to effect of sale on *Gazette*."
27. Mathis, interview by author.
28. Neuharth, oral history interview by Farris, 4.
29. John Reed, oral history interview by Garrison, 16.
30. Dumas, interview by author.
31. Bailey, interview by author.
32. Hussman, interview by author.
33. Ibid.
34. Bailey, interview by author.
35. Hussman, interview by author.
36. Dhonau, interview by author, 2010.
37. Dhonau, interview by author, 2006.
38. Ellwood, interview by author.
39. Neuharth, oral history interview by Farris, 2.
40. Carrick Patterson, oral history interview by Reed, 53.
41. Hugh Patterson, oral history interview by Reed, Part 2, 41–42.
42. Ibid., Part 3, 27.
43. Neuharth, oral history interview by Farris, 3.
44. Hussman, interview by author.
45. Ibid.

46. *Arkansas Gazette*, "Format changes will be up to the editor."
47. Ibid.
48. Hussman, oral history interview by Reed, 85–86.
49. Ibid., 88.
50. Mathis, interview by author.
51. Ibid.
52. Hussman, oral history interview by Reed, 88.
53. Arkansas Press Association Better Newspaper News-Editorial Contest results, 1988–1991.
54. Carrick Patterson, interview by author.
55. Carrick Patterson, oral history interview by Reed, 53.
56. Bailey, interview by author, 2010.
57. Borden, interview by author.
58. Carrick Patterson, interview by author.
59. Carrick Patterson, oral history interview by Reed, 55.
60. Carrick Patterson, interview by author.
61. Ibid.
62. McCord, interview by author.
63. Ibid.
64. John Reed, oral history interview by Garrison, 17–18.
65. Carrick Patterson, oral history interview by Reed, 56.
66. Ibid., 56–57.
67. Borden, interview by author.
68. Carrick Patterson, interview by author.
69. Ibid.
70. Stover, "Speculation about changes likely until purchase of *Gazette* is final."
71. Ibid.
72. Patterson, interview by author.
73. Ibid.
74. Ibid.
75. *Houston Chronicle*, "Editor quits at Fort Worth paper."
76. Brantley, interview by author.
77. Dumas, interview by author.
78. Brantley, interview by author.
79. Dumas, interview by author.
80. John Reed, interview by author.
81. Jordan, oral history interview by Dumas, 48.
82. Dumas, interview by author.
83. Brantley, interview by author.
84. Bailey, interview by author.
85. Lewis, interview by author.
86. Ibid.
87. Dhonau, interview by author, 2006.
88. Bailey, interview by author.
89. Brantley, interview by author.
90. Dumas, interview by author, 2010.
91. Ibid.

92. Roy Reed, interview by author, 2010.
93. Dumas, interview by author, 2006.
94. Powell, interview by author.
95. Roy Reed, interview by author, 2010.
96. Douglas, oral history interview by Reed, 40.
97. Ibid., 41.
98. Ellwood, interview by author.
99. Brantley, interview by author.
100. Ibid.
101. Layton and Walton, "Continuation of Missing The Story at the Statehouse."
102. Ibid.
103. Ibid.
104. Farris, oral history interview by Troop, 41–42.
105. Ibid., 43.
106. Layton and Walton, "Continuation of Missing The Story at the Statehouse."
107. Dumas, interview by author, 2006.
108. Brantley, interview by author.
109. Dumas, interview by author, 2006.
110. Hussman, oral history interview by Reed, 89.
111. Oakley, interview by author.
112. Ibid.
113. Dumas, interview by author, 2006.
114. Foreman, interview by author.
115. Ibid.
116. Pryor, interview by author.
117. Ibid.
118. Lewis, interview by author.
119. Ibid.
120. Ibid.
121. John Reed, oral history interview by Garrison, 18–19.
122. Oakley, interview by author.
123. Moore, interview by author.
124. Borden, interview by author.
125. Mathis, interview by author.
126. McCord, interview by author.
127. John Reed, interview by author.
128. Hussman, interview by author.
129. Hussman, oral history interview by Reed, 89.
130. Ibid., 90.
131. Ibid., 85.
132. Hussman, interview by author.
133. Hussman, oral history interview by Reed, 80–81.
134. Ibid., 91.
135. Ibid., 92.
136. Bailey, interview by author.
137. Dumas, interview by author, 2006.
138. Ibid.

139. Ibid.
140. Dhonau, interview by author, 2012.
141. Dumas, interview by author, 2006.
142. Hanchette, oral history interview by Farris, 5.
143. Ibid., 5–6.
144. Ibid., 10.
145. Ellwood, interview by author.
146. Hanchette, oral history interview by Farris, 13–14.
147. Mathis, interview by author.
148. Ibid.
149. Hanchette, oral history interview by Farris, 16.
150. Ibid., 17.
151. Ibid., 21.
152. Mathis, interview by author.
153. Ibid.
154. *Encyclopedia of Arkansas History & Culture,* "Arkansas Democrat-Gazette."
155. Carrick Patterson, interview by author.
156. Hussman, interview by author.
157. Ibid.
158. Dumas, interview by author, 2006.
159. Brantley, interview by author.
160. Ibid.
161. Ibid.
162. Ibid.
163. Hussman, interview by author.
164. Ibid.
165. Ibid.
166. Ibid.
167. Ibid.
168. Hanchette, oral history interview by Farris, 31.
169. Ibid., 32.
170. McCord, interview by author.
171. Dumas, interview by author, 2006.
172. John Reed, interview by author.
173. Carrick Patterson, interview by author.
174. Dumas, interview by author, 2006.
175. Allen, oral history interview by Douglas, 8.
176. Ibid., 9.
177. Brantley, interview by author.
178. Ibid.
179. Dumas, interview by author, 2006.
180. Henry, oral history interview by Bailey, 41.
181. Ibid., 42–43.
182. Ibid., 44.
183. Ibid., 48.
184. Hussman, interview by author.
185. Dumas, interview by author, 2006.

186. Ibid.
187. Hussman, interview by author.
188. Henry, oral history interview by Bailey, 47.
189. Borden, interview by author.
190. Ibid.
191. Hussman, oral history interview by Reed, 109–10.
192. Bailey, interview by author.
193. Moore, interview by author.
194. Ibid.
195. Brantley, interview by author.
196. Roy Reed, interview by author, 2010.
197. Dumas, interview by author, 2006.
198. Brantley, interview by author.
199. King, interview by author, 2010.
200. Borden, interview by author.
201. Moore, interview by author.
202. Prescott, interview by author.
203. John Reed, interview by author.
204. Bailey, interview by author.
205. Borden, interview by author.
206. Ellwood, interview by author.
207. *New York Times*, "Gannett Names New Managers."
208. *PR Newswire*, "Gannett names editor of *Arkansas Gazette* at Little Rock."
209. Carrick Patterson, oral history interview by Reed, 59.
210. Hanchette, oral history interview by Farris, 10.
211. Ibid., 25.
212. Farris, oral history interview by Troop, 24–33.
213. Dumas, interview by author, 2010.
214. Dumas, interview by author, 2006.
215. Hanchette, oral history interview by Farris, 28.
216. Moore, interview by author.
217. Hussman, interview by author.
218. Hussman, oral history interview by Reed, 93.
219. Hussman, interview by author.
220. Hanchette, oral history interview by Farris, 47.
221. Ibid., 31.
222. Brummett, oral history interview by Dumas, 49–50.
223. Ibid., 51–52.
224. Ibid., 52–53.
225. Ibid., 54.
226. Ibid., 55.
227. Brantley, interview by author.
228. Bagdikian, *The New Media Monopoly*, 189.
229. Ibid., 199.
230. Stover, "Speculation about changes likely until purchase of *Gazette* is final."
231. Stover and Scudder, "*Gazette* sold to Gannett Co."
232. Mathis, interview by author.

233. Ibid.
234. Carrick Patterson, interview by author.

Chapter 8. 1991: The Death of the Newspaper

1. *Arkansas Gazette*, "93 dailies published by Gannett."
2. *Arkansas Business*, "Will Gannett give up the *Gazette*?"
3. Jones, "Total war almost over for Arkansas papers."
4. *Arkansas Business*, "Will Gannett give up the *Gazette*?"
5. Brantley, interview by author.
6. *Arkansas Business*, "Will Gannett give up the *Gazette*?"
7. Hussman, oral history interview by Reed, 85.
8. Dumas, interview by author, 2006.
9. Dumas, oral history interview by Reed, Part 3, 64.
10. Ibid.
11. Dumas, interview by author, 2010.
12. Ibid.
13. Dumas, oral history interview by Reed, Part 3, 62–63.
14. Dhonau, oral history interview by Dumas, 72–73.
15. Dhonau, interview by author, 2006.
16. Dhonau, interview by author, 2010.
17. Ibid.
18. Dumas, oral history interview by Reed, Part 3, 69.
19. Ibid., Part 3, 62–63.
20. Ibid., Part 3, 67.
21. Lancaster, interview by author.
22. Hussman, oral history interview by Reed, 94.
23. Hussman, interview by author.
24. Carrie Rengers, "Who is Moe Hickey?"
25. Hugh Patterson, oral history interview by Reed, Part 3, 18.
26. McCord, oral history interview by McConnell, 14.
27. Ibid., 15.
28. Ellwood, interview by author.
29. Rengers, "Who is Moe Hickey?"
30. Ellwood, interview by author.
31. Mathis, interview by author.
32. Rengers, "Who is Moe Hickey?"
33. Ibid.
34. Dhonau, interview by author, 2006.
35. Dhonau, interview by author, 2010.
36. Ellwood, interview by author.
37. Dhonau, interview by author, 2012.
38. Dhonau, oral history interview by Dumas, 75.
39. Dhonau, interview by author, 2012.
40. Dhonau, oral history interview by Dumas, 73.
41. Ibid.

42. Dumas, oral history interview by Reed, Part 3, 68.
43. Hanchette, oral history interview by Farris, 21.
44. Moore, interview by author.
45. McCord, oral history interview by McConnell, 16.
46. McCord, interview by author.
47. McCord, oral history interview by McConnell, 17.
48. McCord, interview by author.
49. Ibid.
50. Bailey, interview by author.
51. Hussman, interview by author.
52. Hussman, oral history interview by Reed, 96.
53. Ibid., 97–98.
54. Hussman, interview by author.
55. McCord, interview by author.
56. Ellwood, interview by author.
57. Ibid.
58. Dumas, interview by author, 2006.
59. Mathis, interview by author.
60. Ibid.
61. Dumas, interview by author, 2006.
62. *Arkansas Democrat-Gazette*, October 19, 1991, 9A.
63. Ibid.
64. Brantley, interview by author.
65. Arkansas Press Association Better Newspaper News-Editorial Contest, general excellence winners, a history of dailies.
66. Brantley, oral history interview by Dumas, 63.
67. Brantley, interview by author.
68. Dumas, interview by author, 2006.
69. Hussman, interview by author.
70. Reed, interview by author, 2006.
71. Lancaster, interview by author.
72. Brantley, interview by author.
73. Moore, interview by author.
74. Ibid.
75. Brantley, interview by author.
76. Pryor, interview by author.
77. Dumas, interview by author, 2006.
78. Brantley, interview by author.
79. Dumas, interview by author, 2006.
80. Farris, oral history interview by Troop, 52.
81. Brantley, oral history interview by Dumas, 65.
82. Brantley, interview by author.
83. Mathis, interview by author.
84. Ibid.
85. Ibid.
86. Dumas, interview by author, 2006.
87. KARK footage, Fall 1991.

88. Ibid.
89. Brantley, interview by author.
90. KARK footage, Fall 1991.
91. Ibid.
92. Ibid.
93. Mathis, interview by author.
94. Brantley, interview by author.
95. McCord, interview by author.
96. Roy Reed, interview by author, 2006.
97. KARK footage, Fall 1991.
98. Brantley, "Support made it all worth it."
99. Dumas, interview by author, 2006.
100. Brantley, interview by author.
101. Ibid.
102. Ibid.
103. Dumas, interview by author, 2006.
104. Brantley, interview by author.
105. Smith, "*Gazette* employee buyout fails."
106. KARK footage, Fall 1991.
107. Brantley, interview by author.
108. Mathis, interview by author.
109. *Arkansas Gazette*, "Goodbye and Thank You."
110. Dhonau, interview by author, 2010.
111. Ibid.
112. McCord, interview by author.
113. Dhonau, interview by author, 2006.
114. Dhonau, interview by author, 2012.
115. *Arkansas Gazette*, October 18, 1991.
116. Brantley, interview by author.
117. Ibid.
118. Moore, interview by author.
119. Dhonau, interview by author, 2006.
120. Dumas, interview by author, 2006.
121. Bailey, interview by author.
122. Brantley, interview by author.
123. Ibid.
124. Lancaster, interview by author.
125. Home video from the *Gazette* building.
126. Mathis, interview by author.
127. McCord, interview by author.
128. Ibid.
129. Hussman, oral history interview by Reed, 98–99.
130. Mathis, interview by author.
131. Ibid.
132. Brantley, interview by author.
133. Dhonau, interview by author, 2006.
134. Dumas, interview by author, 2006.

135. Mathis, interview by author.
136. Ibid.
137. Ibid.
138. Jordan, oral history interview by Dumas, 49.
139. Ibid., 51.
140. Dumas, oral history interview by Reed, Part 3, 79–80.
141. Brantley, interview by author.
142. Allbright, oral history interview by Haddigan, 14, 23.
143. McCord, interview by author.
144. Pryor, interview by author.
145. Lancaster, interview by author.
146. Ibid.
147. Ibid.
148. Oakley, interview by author.
149. Lancaster, interview by author.
150. Hussman, interview by author.
151. Hussman, oral history interview by Reed, 101.
152. Ibid., 101–2.
153. KARK News, October 18, 1991.
154. KARK footage, October 18, 1991.
155. Ibid.
156. Ibid.
157. Brantley, interview by author.
158. Lewis, interview by author.
159. Carrick Patterson, interview by author.
160. Roy Reed, interview by author, 2010.
161. Carrick Patterson, interview by author.
162. Hussman, oral history interview by Reed, 97.
163. Hussman, interview by author.
164. *Arkansas Democrat-Gazette*, October 19, 1991.
165. Brantley, interview by author.
166. Brantley, oral history interview by Dumas, 70.
167. Brantley, interview by author.
168. Dumas, interview by author, 2006.
169. Brantley, interview by author.
170. Author's personal knowledge.
171. Bailey, interview by author.
172. Moore, interview by author.
173. Author's personal knowledge.
174. KARK News, October 19, 1991.
175. McCord, interview by author.
176. *USA Today*, "Arkansas rival buys, then closes '*Gazette*.'"
177. KARK footage, Fall 1991.
178. Neuharth, oral history interview by Farris, 2–3.
179. Ibid., 7.
180. John Reed, interview by author.
181. Jordan, oral history interview by Dumas, 54.

182. Allbright, oral history interview by Haddigan, 24.
183. Mosby, oral history interview by Garrison, 33.
184. Roy Reed, interview by author, 2006.

Chapter 9. Lessons Learned

1. Roy Reed, interview by author, 2006.
2. Arkansas Press Association, *1972 Arkansas Newspaper Directory Ratebook.*
3. Arkansas Press Association, *1979 Arkansas Newspaper Directory Ratebook.*
4. Heiskell Personal Papers, Ralph McGill speech at 1960 Lovejoy Convocation at Colby College, Waterville, Maine, November 10, 1960, Series I, Subseries III, Box 1, File 8, University of Arkansas at Little Rock Archives and Special Collections.
5. Carrick Patterson, interview by author.
6. Ibid.
7. Oakley, interview by author.
8. Brantley, interview by author.
9. Hussman, interview by author.
10. Powell, oral history interview by Dumas, 25.
11. Ibid., 25–26.
12. Powell, interview by author.
13. Powell, oral history interview by Dumas, 26.
14. Hugh B.Patterson, oral history interview by Reed, Part 3, 30.
15. Bumpers, interview by author.
16. Brantley, interview by author.
17. Powell, interview by author.
18. Pryor, interview by author.
19. Powell, interview by author.
20. Dumas, interview by author, 2006.
21. Bumpers, interview by author.
22. Sarah D. Wire, "Democrats rally behind Beebe."
23. Powell, oral history interview by Dumas, 26.
24. Powell, interview by author.
25. Brantley, interview by author.
26. Ibid.
27. Noam, *Media Ownership and Concentration in America*, 139.
28. Bagdikian, *The New Media Monopoly*, 185.
29. Noam, *Media Ownership and Concentration in America*, 139.
30. Heiskell Personal Papers, McGill speech at 1960 Lovejoy Convocation at Colby College.
31. Heiskell Personal Papers, Report of J. N. Heiskell, Chairman of Committee on Editorial Affairs, to Southern Newspaper Publishers Association Annual Meeting at Asheville, N.C.
32. Powell, interview by author.
33. Lancaster, oral history interview by McCord, 11–12.

Bibliography

Allbright, Charles. Interview by author. Videotape. Little Rock, Ark. September 4, 2006.

———. Oral history interview by Michael Haddigan. *Arkansas Gazette* Project. University of Arkansas Pryor Center for Oral and Visual History. http://pryorcenter.uark.edu/projects/arkansasgazette/CAllbright.pdf (accessed June 1, 2005).

Allen, Nate. Oral history interview by Bob Douglas. *Arkansas Gazette* Project. University of Arkansas Pryor Center for Oral and Visual History. http://pryorcenter.uark.edu/projects/arkansasgazette/NAllen.pdf (accessed May 30, 2006).

Allsopp, Fred W. *History of the Arkansas Press for a Hundred Years and More*. Little Rock: Parke-Harper, 1922.

Arkansas Business. "Will Gannett give up the *Gazette*?" September 16, 1991.

Arkansas Democrat. July 13, 1958.

———. "Palmer Papers buy the *Democrat*." March 4, 1974.

Arkansas Democrat-Gazette. October 19, 1991.

———. "History of the *Arkansas Democrat-Gazette*," http://www.arkansasonline.com/tools/newspaperhistorymain/.

Arkansas Gazette. July 1, 1902.

———. September 30, 1902.

———. June 25, 1904.

———. October 16, 1906.

———. November 6, 1906.

———. November 24, 1906.

———. December 11, 1906.

———. June 16, 1909.

———. April 27, 1918.

———. December 5, 1919.

———. November 27, 1948.

———. March 29, 1959.

———. Editorial. November 23, 1963.

———. Editorial. October 16, 1966.

———. Editorial. November 10, 1966.

———. December 29, 1972.

———. October 31, 1985, http://www.lexisnexis.com (accessed November 8, 2011).

———. March 9, 1986, http://www.lexisnexis.com (accessed November 8, 2011).

———. March 20, 1986, http://www.lexisnexis.com (accessed November 8, 2011).

———. October 18, 1991.

———. "93 dailies published by Gannett." October 31, 1986.

———. "300 Attend Funeral For J. N. Heiskell, Editor of *Gazette*." December 31, 1972.

———. "A Senator's Impassioned Plea." November 2, 1972.

———. "Among Ourselves." June 19, 1960.

———. "An Editorial: Is Revolution the Answer?" December 13, 1957.

———. "Ashmore Leaves *Gazette* Position." September 22, 1959.

———. "Format changes will be up to the editor." October 31, 1986.

———. "Fred. W. Allsopp Left Message of Farewell." April 11, 1946.

———. "*Gazette* Designated As a Historic Site; 24th Paper Honored." September 16, 1966.

———. "*Gazette* Ranks 21st in Poll of Top Dailies." April 11, 1960.

———. "Goodbye and Thank You." October 18, 1991.

———. "J. N. Heiskell Dies at 100; Led Paper As Editor 70 Years." December 29, 1972.

———. "Large and Applauding Crowd Honors *Gazette* and Editors." June 4, 1958.

———. "Library Supporter Carries Card No. 1." *Gazette* Staff Tribute to J. N. Heiskell. November 2, 1972.

———. "Lt. Carrick W. Heiskell, Pilot, War Casualty." December 4, 1943.

———. "Officials, Fellow Newsmen Join in Praising Editor." December 29, 1972.

———. "Margaret Ross's History Records Our Early Years." November 16, 1969.

———. "Police Reporter Dies; Long Career Brought Honors." December 29, 1972.

———. "Reflections in a Hurricane's Eye." September 9, 1957.

———. "The Crisis Mr. Faubus Made." September 4, 1957.

Arkansas Gazette Papers, University of Arkansas at Little Rock Archives and Special Collections.

Arkansas News Archive. Old State House Museum of Arkansas History, "Colorful samples from Jeff Davis's speeches." http://www.oldstatehouse.com/collections/classroom/arkansas_news.aspx?issue=24&page=4&detail=274.

———. "First black reporter on white Arkansas newspaper." http://www.oldstatehouse.com/collections/classroom/arkansas_news.aspx?issue=20&page=7&detail=228.

Arkansas Press Association. *1960 Arkansas Newspaper Directory Ratebook*.

———. *1961 Arkansas Newspaper Directory Ratebook*.

———. *1962 Arkansas Newspaper Directory Ratebook*.

———. *1965 Arkansas Newspaper Directory Ratebook*.

———. *1970 Arkansas Newspaper Directory Ratebook*.

———. *1972 Arkansas Newspaper Directory Ratebook*.

———. *1974 Arkansas Newspaper Directory Ratebook*.

———. *1979 Arkansas Newspaper Directory Ratebook*.

———. Better Newspaper News-Editorial Contest. General excellence winners, a history of dailies.

———. Better Newspaper News-Editorial Contest results, 1988–1991. *Arkansas Publisher*, XVII. August 1947.

Arkansas Times. "Arkansas' Newspaper War: Listen, You, I'm Bob Starr of the *Democrat* and I am Declaring War on the *Gazette*!" May 1979.

Ashmore, Harry S. *An Epitaph for Dixie*. New York: W. W. Norton & Company, 1957, 1958.

———. "An Epitaph for the Old Lady." *Arkansas Business*, November 25, 1991.

———. *Civil Rights and Wrongs: A Memoir of Race and Politics, 1944–1996*. Columbia: University of South Carolina Press, 1997.

———. *Hearts and Minds: A Personal Chronicle of Race in America*. Cabin John, MD: Seven Locks Press, 1988.
———. "Mr. J. N. at 91." *American Society of Newspaper Editors Bulletin*, December 1963.
———. "One Editor's Response to a National Crisis." *Arkansas Gazette*, November 2, 1972.
———. Oral history interview by Roy Reed. *Arkansas Gazette* Project. University of Arkansas Pryor Center for Oral and Visual History. http://libinfo.uark.edu/specialcollections/ACOVH/default.asp#Gazette (accessed April 22, 2005).
———. "The South and the South's Problem." *Arkansas Gazette*, February 5, 1948, reprinted in *Nieman Reports* 53/54, 4/1 (1999/2000).
Author's personal knowledge.
Bagdikian, Ben H. *The New Media Monopoly*. Boston: Beacon Press, 2004.
Bailey, Jim. Interview by author. Videotape. Little Rock, Ark. August 17, 2006.
———. Oral history interview by Jerry McConnell. *Arkansas Gazette* Project. University of Arkansas Pryor Center for Oral and Visual History. http://pryorcenter.uark.edu/projects/arkansasgazette/JBailey.pdf (accessed July 19, 2006).
Borden, Paul. Interview by author. E-mail. January 18, 2012.
Brantley, Max. Interview by author. Videotape. Little Rock, Ark. April 17, 2006.
———. Oral history interview by Ernest Dumas. *Arkansas Gazette* Project. University of Arkansas Pryor Center for Oral and Visual History. http://pryorcenter.uark.edu/projects/arkansasgazette/MBrantley.pdf (accessed July 12, 2005).
———. "Support made it all worth it." *Arkansas Gazette*, October 17, 1991.
Brown, Robert W. "Newspapers of Deep South Liberalize Negro Policies." *Editor & Publisher*, December 13, 1952.
Brummett, John. Oral history interview by Ernest Dumas. *Arkansas Gazette* Project. University of Arkansas Pryor Center for Oral and Visual History. http://pryorcenter.uark.edu/projects/arkansasgazette/JBrummett.pdf (accessed February 12, 2012).
Bumpers, Senator Dale. Interview by author. Videotape. Washington, D.C. July 28, 2006.
Carey, Robert. "On Being a Centenarian: An Autumn Visit with John Netherland Heiskell." *The Quill*, February 1973.
Collins, Margaret, Edmund Lee, and Noah Buhayar. "Buffet Says Newspaper Bet Fueled by Arkansas Model." Bloomberg News, March 2, 2013, http://www.bloomberg.com/news/2013-03-02/buffett-says-newspaper-bet-fueled-by-arkansas-model.html.
Congressional Record. S5427. June 5, 2006.
Davies, David R. *The History of American Journalism: The Postwar Decline of American Newspapers, 1945–1965*. Westport, CT: Praeger, 2006.
———, ed. *The Press and Race: Mississippi Journalists Confront the Movement*. Jackson: University Press of Mississippi, 2001.
Dhonau, Jerry. Interview by author. Videotape. Conway, Ark. March 20, 2006.
———. Interview by author. Videotape. Conway, Ark. April 27, 2010.

———. Interview by author. E-mail. February 25, 2012.
———. Oral history interview by Ernest Dumas. *Arkansas Gazette* Project. University of Arkansas Pryor Center for Oral and Visual History. http://pryorcenter.uark.edu/projects/arkansasgazette/dhonau.pdf (accessed October 11, 2005).
Dougan, Michael B. *Community Diaries: Arkansas Newspapering, 1819–2002.* Little Rock: August House, 2003.
———. Interview by Kevin Clark. Videotape. Conway, Ark. September 15, 2005.
Douglas, Bob. Oral history interview by Roy Reed (four parts). *Arkansas Gazette* Project. University of Arkansas Pryor Center for Oral and Visual History. http://pryorcenter.uark.edu/projects/arkansasgazette/BDouglas1997part1.pdf; http://pryorcenter.uark.edu/projects/arkansasgazette/BDouglas1997part2.pdf; http://pryorcenter.uark.edu/projects/arkansasgazette/BDouglas1997part3.pdf; http://pryorcenter.uark.edu/projects/arkansasgazette/BDouglas2000.pdf.
Dumas, Ernest. Interview by author. Videotape. Little Rock, Ark. February 2, 2006.
———. Interview by author. Videotape. Conway, Ark. April 13, 2010.
———. Oral history interview by Roy Reed (four parts). *Arkansas Gazette* Project. University of Arkansas Pryor Center for Oral and Visual History. http://pryorcenter.uark.edu/projects/arkansasgazette/EDumas1.pdf; http://pryorcenter.uark.edu/projects/arkansasgazette/EDumas2.pdf; http://pryorcenter.uark.edu/projects/arkansasgazette/EDumas3.pdf; http://pryorcenter.uark.edu/projects/arkansasgazette/EDumas4.pdf (accessed November 6, 2005).
———. "Sid McMath: An Arkansan for All Seasons." Special supplement from McMath Woods P.A., Attorneys at Law. *Arkansas Times*, June 13, 2012.
Editor & Publisher. "*Arkansas Gazette*'s Reed to lead ICMA." July 8, 1967.
Ellwood, Susie Miles. Interview by author. Videotape. Little Rock, Ark. September 4, 2006.
Encyclopedia of Arkansas History & Culture, s.v. "*Arkansas Democrat-Gazette*" (by Rex Nelson), http://www.encyclopediaofarkansas.net/encyclopedia/entry-detail.aspx?search=1&entryID=2343 (accessed August 3, 2012).
———, s.v. "*Arkansas Gazette*" (by Donna Lampkin Stephens), http://www.encyclopediaofarkansas.net/encyclopedia/entry-detail.aspx?entryID=2344 (accessed June 9, 2012).
———, s.v. "Fred Allsopp" (by C. Dennis Schick), http://www.encyclopediaofarkansas.net/encyclopedia/entry-detail.aspx?search=1&entryID=2481 (accessed April 2, 2011).
———, s.v. "Harry Scott Ashmore" (by Nathania Sawyer), http://www.encyclopediaofarkansas.net/encyclopedia/entry- detail.aspx?entryID=1579 (accessed February 23, 2008).
———, s.v. "Hugh Baskin Patterson, Jr." (by Donna Lampkin Stephens), http://www.encyclopediaofarkansas.net/encyclopedia/entry-detail.aspx?entryID=4227 (accessed October 11, 2009).
———, s.v. "Jeff Davis" (by Raymond O. Arsenault), http://www.encyclopediaofarkansas.net/encyclopedia/entry- detail.aspx?entryID=98 (accessed June 9, 2012).
———, s.v. "Orval Eugene Faubus" (by Roy Reed), http://www.encyclopediaofarkansas.net/encyclopedia/entry- detail.aspx?entryID=102 (accessed June 15, 2012).

———, s.v. "Winthrop Rockefeller" (by Tom W. Dillard), http://www.encyclopediaofarkansas.net/encyclopedia/entry- detail.aspx?search=1&entryID=122 (accessed July 14, 2011).

Erwin, Ray. "3 Pulitzer Prizes Awarded for the Little Rock Story." *Editor & Publisher*, May 10, 1958.

Farris, Anne. Oral history interview by Don Troop. *Arkansas Gazette* Project. University of Arkansas Pryor Center for Oral and Visual History. http://pryorcenter.uark.edu/projects/arkansasgazette/AFarris.pdf (accessed January 18, 2012).

Fletcher, John L. "100 Honor J. N. Heiskell for 50 Years as Editor." *Arkansas Gazette*, June 28, 1952.

Foreman, Gene. Interview by author. Videotape. Little Rock, Ark. July 13, 2006.

Graham, Hugh Davis. *Crisis in Print: Desegregation and the Press in Tennessee.* Nashville: Vanderbilt University Press, 1967.

Hanchette, John. Oral history interview by Anne Farris. *Arkansas Gazette* Project. University of Arkansas Pryor Center for Oral and Visual History. http://pryorcenter.uark.edu/projects/arkansasgazette/JHanchette.pdf (accessed March 15, 2012).

Harris, Sam G. "*Gazette* Personalities Gave Paper a Vivid Character." *Arkansas Gazette*, November 16, 1969.

Heinbockel, C. S. "Publisher of *Democrat* 'not afraid.'" *Arkansas Gazette*, October 31, 1986.

Heiskell Personal Papers. University of Arkansas at Little Rock Archives and Special Collections.

Henry, Orville. Oral history interview by Jim Bailey. *Arkansas Gazette* Project. University of Arkansas Pryor Center for Oral and Visual History. http://pryorcenter.uark.edu/projects/arkansasgazette/OHenry.pdf (accessed April 19, 2005).

Home video from the *Gazette* building. October 18, 1991.

Houston Chronicle. "Editor quits at Fort Worth paper." September 3, 1987, http://www.chron.com/CDA/archives/archive.mpl/1987_486258/editor-quits-at-fort-worth-paper.html (accessed November 3, 2011).

Hussman, Walter. Interview by author. Videotape. Little Rock, Ark. October 24, 2005.

———. Oral history interview by Roy Reed. *Arkansas Democrat* Project. University of Arkansas Pryor Center for Oral and Visual History. http://pryorcenter.uark.edu/projects/arkansasdemocrat/WHussmanDemocrat.pdf (accessed June 10, 2005).

Johnson, Ben F., III. *Arkansas in Modern America 1930–1999.* Fayetteville: University of Arkansas Press, 2000.

Johnson, Jim. Interview by author. Videotape. Conway, Ark. September 19, 2006.

Jones, Alex. "Arkansas Papers Battle over More than Money." *New York Times*, March 23, 1986, http://www.lexisnexis.com (accessed November 8, 2011).

———. "Total war almost over for Arkansas papers." *New York Times*, October 14, 1991, http://www.lexisnexis.com (accessed November 8, 2011).

Jordan, Wayne. Interview by author. Videotape. Conway, Ark. April 8, 2010.

———. Oral history interview by Ernest Dumas. *Arkansas Gazette* Project.

University of Arkansas Pryor Center for Oral and Visual History, http://pryorcenter.uark.edu/projects/arkansasgazette/WJordan.pdf (accessed March 21, 2010).

KARK News, October 18, 1991.

———. October 19, 1991.

———. Footage. Fall 1991.

King, Harry. Interview by author. Telephone. April 1, 2010.

Lancaster, Bob. E-mail to author. July 9, 2006. *Arkansas Times*, April 21, 2000.

———. Interview by author. Videotape. Sheridan, Ark. July 6, 2006.

———. Oral history interview by Bob McCord. *Arkansas Gazette* Project. University of Arkansas Pryor Center for Oral and Visual History. http://pryorcenter.uark.edu/projects/arkansasgazette/BLancaster.pdf (accessed May 20, 2006).

Layton, Charles, and Mary Walton. "Continuation of Missing The Story at the Statehouse." *American Journalism Review*, July/August 1998, http://www.ajr.org/Article.asp?id=3280 (accessed October 18, 2011).

Leidholdt, Alexander S. *Standing Before the Shouting Mob: Lenoir Chambers and Virginia's Massive Resistance to Public-School Integration.* Tuscaloosa: University of Alabama Press, 1997.

Lewis, Bill. "Arkansas—History of a State, and Its Newspaper." *Arkansas Gazette*, November 16, 1969.

———. "*Gazette*, Editor Mark Milestone." *Gazette* Staff Tribute to J. N. Heiskell. *Arkansas Gazette*, November 2, 1972.

———. Interview by author. Videotape. Little Rock, Ark. July 13, 2006.

Mathis, Deborah. Interview by author. Videotape. Washington, D.C. July 29, 2006.

Matlack, Carol. "Recent Gannett acquisitions offer clues to effect of sale on *Gazette*." *Arkansas Gazette*, October 31, 1986.

McAuliffe, Kevin Michael. *The Great American Newspaper: The Rise and Fall of the Village Voice*. New York: Scribner's, 1978.

McConnell, Jerry. Interview by author. Videotape. Little Rock, Ark. May 5, 2006.

McCord, Bob. Interview by author. Videotape. Conway, Ark. June 6, 2006.

———. Oral history interview by Jerry McConnell. *Arkansas Gazette* Project. University of Arkansas Pryor Center for Oral and Visual History, http://pryorcenter.uark.edu/projects/arkansasgazette/RMcCord.pdf (accessed April 22, 2006).

McCord, Richard. *The Chain Gang: One Newspaper versus the Gannett Empire*. Columbia: University of Missouri Press, 1996.

McPherson, James Brian. *The History of American Journalism: Journalism at the End of the American Century, 1965–Present*. Westport, CT: Praeger, 2006.

Moore, Wadie. Interview by author. Videotape. North Little Rock, Ark. July 18, 2006.

Mosby, Joe. Oral history interview by Jerol Garrison. *Arkansas Gazette* Project. University of Arkansas Pryor Center for Oral and Visual History. http://pryorcenter.uark.edu/projects/arkansasgazette/JMosby.pdf (accessed August 28, 2012).

National Observer. "'Mr. J. N.' and a Legend at the *Gazette*." September 28, 1964.

New York Times. "Gannett Names New Managers." August 16, 1989. http://www.nytimes.com/1989/08/16/business/

the-media-business-gannett-names-new-managers.html (accessed January 21, 2012).
———. "Jury Holds Little Rock Paper's Tactics Legal." March 27, 1986, http://www.lexisnexis.com (accessed November 12, 2011).
———. "Race in the News." August 11, 1946.
Newspaper Association of America. Facts About Newspapers 2000, http://www.naa.org/info/facts00/index.html.
———. http://www.naa.org/Trends-and-Numbers/Circulation/Newspaper-Circulation-Volume.aspx.
Newsweek. "At 85, a Big Moment." May 19, 1958.
Neuharth, Al. Oral history interview by Anne Farris. *Arkansas Gazette* Project. University of Arkansas Pryor Center for Oral and Visual History, http://pryorcenter.uark.edu/projects/arkansasgazette/ANeuharth.pdf (accessed March 3, 2012).
———. Remarks at press conference. KARK News. October 31, 1986.
Noam, Eli. *Media Ownership and Concentration in America.* Oxford: Oxford University Press, 2009.
Oakley, Meredith. Interview by author. Videotape. Little Rock, Ark. July 5, 2006.
Patterson, Carrick. Interview by author. Videotape. Conway, Ark. September 8, 2006.
———. Oral history interview by Roy Reed. *Arkansas Gazette* Project. University of Arkansas Pryor Center for Oral and Visual History. http://pryorcenter.uark.edu/projects/arkansasgazette/CPatterson.pdf (accessed July 17, 2005).
Patterson, Hugh B. Oral history interview by Roy Reed (three parts). *Arkansas Gazette* Project. University of Arkansas Pryor Center for Oral and Visual History. http://pryorcenter.uark.edu/projects/arkansasgazette/HPatterson1.pdf; http://pryorcenter.uark.edu/projects/arkansasgazette/HPatterson2.pdf; http://pryorcenter.uark.edu/projects/arkansasgazette/HPatterson3.pdf (accessed April 22, 2005).
Powell, James O. Interview by author. Videotape. Cammack Village, Ark. June 22, 2006.
———. Oral history interview by Ernest Dumas. *Arkansas Gazette* Project. University of Arkansas Pryor Center for Oral and Visual History. http://pryorcenter.uark.edu/projects/arkansasgazette/JPowell.pdf (accessed April 2, 2006).
PR Newswire. "Gannett names editor of *Arkansas Gazette* at Little Rock." March 6, 1990. www.highbeam.com/doc/1G1–8207974.html (accessed January 4, 2012).
Prescott, Gene. Interview by author. Videotape. Conway, Ark. February 23, 2006.
Pryor, David. Interview by author. Videotape. Little Rock, Ark. July 12, 2006.
Reed, John. Interview by author. Videotape. Conway, Ark. April 6, 2010.
———. Oral history interview by Jerol Garrison. *Arkansas Gazette* Project. University of Arkansas Pryor Center for Oral and Visual History. http://pryorcenter.uark.edu/projects/arkansasgazette/JReed.pdf (accessed March 11, 2010).
Reed, Roy. "Arkansas Paper is 150, its Editor 97; Both Thriving." *New York Times,* November 21, 1969.

———. *Faubus: The Life and Times of an American Prodigal.* Fayetteville: University of Arkansas Press, 1997.

———. "Hugh Patterson Jr., 91; publisher worked to end segregation." *New York Times* News Service, June 4, 2006.

———. Interview by author. Videotape. Hogeye, Ark. August 11, 2006.

———. Interview by author. Videotape. Conway, Ark. April 22, 2010.

———. *Looking Back at the Arkansas Gazette: An Oral History.* Fayetteville: University of Arkansas Press, 2009.

———. Oral history interview by Harri Baker (seven parts). *Arkansas Gazette* Project. University of Arkansas Pryor Center for Oral and Visual History. http://pryorcenter.uark.edu/projects/arkansasgazette/RoyReed3.pdf; http://pryorcenter.uark.edu/projects/arkansasgazette/RoyReed4.pdf; http://pryorcenter.uark.edu/projects/arkansasgazette/RoyReed5.pdf; http://pryorcenter.uark.edu/projects/arkansasgazette/RoyReed6.pdf; http://pryorcenter.uark.edu/projects/arkansasgazette/RoyReed7.pdf; http://pryorcenter.uark.edu/projects/arkansasgazette/RoyReed8.pdf; http://pryorcenter.uark.edu/projects/arkansasgazette/RoyReed9.pdf. (accessed April 22, 2005).

Rengers, Carrie. "Who is Moe Hickey?" *Arkansas Business*, June 17, 1991.

Roberts, Gene. *Breach of Faith: A Crisis of Coverage in the Age of Corporate Newspapering.* Fayetteville: University of Arkansas Press, 2002.

———. *Leaving Readers Behind: The Age of Corporate Newspapering.* Fayetteville: University of Arkansas Press, 2001.

Roberts, Gene, and Hank Klibanoff. *The Race Beat: The Press, the Civil Rights Struggle, and the Awakening of a Nation.* New York: Vintage Books, 2006.

———. "The Embrace of Principled Stands." *Nieman Reports* 60, no. 2 (Summer 2006): 88–89.

Ross, Margaret. *Arkansas Gazette: The Early Years, 1819–1866.* Little Rock: *Arkansas Gazette* Foundation, 1969.

———. "Wit, Wisdom His Trademarks." *Arkansas Gazette*, November 2, 1972.

Rutherford, William K., Jr. "*Arkansas Gazette* Editor J. N. Heiskell: Heart and Mind." M.A. thesis, University of Arkansas at Little Rock, 1987.

Sandlin, Jake. "25th Anniversary of Pivotal Decision: Trial turned page in newspaper war." *Arkansas Democrat-Gazette*, March 27, 2011.

Shelton, Bill. Oral history interview by Ernest Dumas. *Arkansas Gazette* Project. University of Arkansas Pryor Center for Oral and Visual History. http://pryorcenter.uark.edu/projects/arkansasgazette/BShelton.pdf (accessed August 3, 2011).

Shipler, David K. "The Desegregation Drama." *Columbia Journalism Review* 45, no. 4 (November/December 2006): 91–95.

Simmons, Bill. "Publisher contemplated sale in Arkansas newspaper war." Associated Press, March 19, 1986, http://www.apnewsarchive.com/1986/Publisher-Contemplated-Sale-in-Arkansas-Newspaper-War/id-9d5f024e427a854ec61398e3a38d0311 (accessed November 8, 2011).

Sloan, Wm. David. *American Journalism History: An Annotated Bibliography.* Westport, CT: Greenwood Press, 1989.

Sloan, Wm. David, and Laird B. Anderson. *Pulitzer Prize Editorials: America's Best Writing, 1917–2003.* Ames: Iowa State University Press, 1994.

Smith, David. "*Gazette* employee buyout fails." *Arkansas Gazette,* October 18, 1991.
Stover, Bob. "*Gazette* publisher celebrates 35th year in post." *Arkansas Gazette,* November 18, 1983.
———. "Speculation about changes likely until purchase of *Gazette* is final." *Arkansas Gazette,* November 1, 1986.
Stover, Bob, and James Scudder. "*Gazette* sold to Gannett Co." *Arkansas Gazette,* October 31, 1986.
Street, James Jr., ed. *James Street's South.* Garden City, NY: Doubleday & Company, 1955.
Swayne, Elizabeth Eames. "The Last Families: A Study of Metropolitan Newspaper Ownership, 1950–1967." Ph.D. diss., Northwestern University, 1969.
Teel, Leonard Ray. *Ralph Emerson McGill: Voice of the Southern Conscience.* Knoxville: University of Tennessee Press, 2001.
———. *The History of American Journalism: The Public Press, 1900–1945.* Westport, CT: Praeger, 2006.
Thompson, John A. "Gentleman Editor: Mr. Heiskell of the *Gazette.*" M.A. thesis, University of Arkansas at Little Rock, 1983.
Time. "Arkansas Teetotaler." December 6, 1948, http://www.time.com/time/magazine/article/0,9171,853592,00.html (accessed June 3, 2007).
———. "For Leadership." May 19, 1958, www.time.com/time/printout/0,8816,864366,00.html (accessed June 3, 2007).
USA Today. "Arkansas rival buys, then closes '*Gazette.*'" October 21, 1991.
Washington Post. "Newspaper Wins in Court." March 27, 1986, http://www.lexisnexis.com (accessed November 12, 2011).
Wells, George. *Arkansas Gazette.* March 4, 1986, http://www.lexisnexis.com (accessed November 12, 2011).
———. *Arkansas Gazette.* March 11, 1986, http://www.lexisnexis.com (accessed November 12, 2011).
———. *Arkansas Gazette.* April 15, 1986, http://www.lexisnexis.com (accessed November 12, 2011).
Williamson, Samuel T. *Imprint of a Publisher: The Story of Frank Gannett and His Newspapers.* New York: McBride, 1948.
Wire, Sarah D. "Democrats Rally behind Beebe." *Arkansas Democrat-Gazette,* August 19, 2012.
Woodhull, Nancy J., and Robert W. Snyder, eds. *Defining Moments in Journalism.* New Brunswick, NJ: Transaction Publishers, 1998.

Index

B

D

E

F

G

H

I

J

K

P

Q

R

T

U

V

W